"This book's vignettes of grassroots initi⟨a⟩ sustainable and scalable alternatives to the c⟨⟩ and marketisation of early childhood educat⟨⟩ childhood education activists and observers ⟨⟩ counter-hegemonic narrative, these exampl⟨e⟩ nents should energize those seeking to effect ⟨⟩

Eva Lloyd, *Director at The International Centre for the Study of the Mixed Economy of Childcare and visiting Professor at the University College London*

"This book deftly reveals and challenges the encroachment of neoliberalism upon early childhood education. For several decades, in many parts of the world, neoliberalism has infused early childhood education policy. And policy in turn, has (attempted to) permeate how we construct ourselves as educators, academics and researchers, how we position children and families, and the aspirations we seek from early childhood education itself. Nevertheless, this is an optimistic book, reminding us that neoliberalism is not, nor ever has been, an inevitable political condition. There are many points of resistance. Throughout the world, early childhood educators, researchers and providers envisage their work differently, countering the narrative that positions early childhood education as a commodity, parents as consumers, and children as human capital. This book shares vignettes of these acts of resistance, reminding us of our own agency, our capacities to be catalysts for change. Our resistances operate on many levels and are apparent in many different ways: in our conversations, the values we reinforce or question, our interactions and intentions, the way we research. Ultimately, as this book asserts, we must advocate for the right of all children to an early childhood education that recognises them as citizens in the here and now."

Frances Press, *Professor of Early Childhood and Education Policy, Manchester Metropolitan University*

THE DECOMMODIFICATION OF EARLY CHILDHOOD EDUCATION AND CARE

The Decommodification of Early Childhood Education and Care: Resisting Neoliberalism explores how processes of marketisation and privatisation of ECEC have impacted understandings of children, childcare, parents, and the workforce, providing concrete examples of resistance to commodification from diverse contexts.

Through processes of marketisation and privatisation, neoliberal discourses have turned ECEC into a commodity whereby economic principles of competition and choice have replaced the purpose of education. *The Decommodification of Early Childhood Education and Care: Resisting Neoliberalism* offers new and alternative understandings of policy and practice. Written with co-authors from diverse countries, case studies vividly portray resistance to children as human capital, to the "consumentality" of parents, and to the alienation of the early childhood workforce. Ending with messages of hope, the authors discuss the demise of neoliberalism and offer new ways forward.

As an international book with global messages contributing to theory, policy, and practice regarding alternatives to a neoliberal and commodified vision of ECEC, this book offers inspiration for policy makers and practitioners to develop local resistance solutions. It will also be of interest to post-graduate students, researchers, educators, and pre-service educators with an interest in critical pedagogy, ECEC policy, and ECEC practice.

Michel Vandenbroeck is an Associate Professor in Family Pedagogy at Ghent University, Belgium.

Joanne Lehrer is an Associate Professor in the Department of Education at the Université du Quebec en Outaouais, Canada.

Linda Mitchell is a Professor in the Division of Education at the University of Waikato, New Zealand.

Contesting Early Childhood
Series Editors: Liselott Mariett Olsson and Michel Vandenbroeck

This ground-breaking series questions the current dominant discourses surrounding early childhood, and offers instead alternative narratives of an area that is now made up of a multitude of perspectives and debates.

The series examines the possibilities and risks arising from the accelerated development of early childhood services and policies, and illustrates how it has become increasingly steeped in regulation and control. Insightfully, this collection of books shows how early childhood services can in fact contribute to ethical and democratic practices. The authors explore new ideas taken from alternative working practices in both the western and developing world, and from other academic disciplines such as developmental psychology. Current theories and best practice are placed in relation to the major processes of political, social, economic, cultural and technological change occurring in the world today.

In Dialogue with Reggio Emilia
Listening, Researching and Learning, Second Edition
Carlina Rinaldi

Rethinking Environmental Education in a Climate Change Era
Weather Learning in Early Childhood
Tonya Rooney and Mindy Blaise

Slow Knowledge and the Unhurried Child
Time for Slow Pedagogies in Early Childhood Education
Alison Clark

The Decommodification of Early Childhood Education and Care
Resisting Neoliberalism
Michel Vandenbroeck, Joanne Lehrer and Linda Mitchell

For more information about this series, please visit: www.routledge.com/Contesting-Early-Childhood/book-series/SE0623

THE DECOMMODIFICATION OF EARLY CHILDHOOD EDUCATION AND CARE

Resisting Neoliberalism

Edited by Michel Vandenbroeck, Joanne Lehrer, and Linda Mitchell

LONDON AND NEW YORK

Cover image credit: Ariella Galita

First published 2023
by Routledge
4 Park Square, Milton Park, Abingdon, Oxon, OX14 4RN

and by Routledge
605 Third Avenue, New York, NY 10158

Routledge is an imprint of the Taylor & Francis Group, an informa business

© 2023 selection and editorial matter, Michel Vandenbroeck, Joanne Lehrer, and Linda Mitchell; individual chapters, the contributors

The right of Michel Vandenbroeck, Joanne Lehrer, and Linda Mitchell to be identified as the authors of the editorial material, and of the authors for their individual chapters, has been asserted in accordance with sections 77 and 78 of the Copyright, Designs and Patents Act 1988.

All rights reserved. No part of this book may be reprinted or reproduced or utilised in any form or by any electronic, mechanical, or other means, now known or hereafter invented, including photocopying and recording, or in any information storage or retrieval system, without permission in writing from the publishers.

Trademark notice: Product or corporate names may be trademarks or registered trademarks, and are used only for identification and explanation without intent to infringe.

British Library Cataloguing-in-Publication Data
A catalogue record for this book is available from the British Library

ISBN: 978-1-032-11029-5 (hbk)
ISBN: 978-1-032-11030-1 (pbk)
ISBN: 978-1-003-21810-4 (ebk)

DOI: 10.4324/9781003218104

Typeset in Bembo
by KnowledgeWorks Global Ltd.

CONTENTS

Contributor Biographies   *viii*

Introduction: From the Politically Impossible to
the Politically Inevitable   1
Peter Moss

1   On Commodification and Decommodification   15
Michel Vandenbroeck, Joanne Lehrer, and Linda Mitchell

2   Resisting Children as Human Capital   28
*Joanne Lehrer, Brooke Richardson, Michel Vandenbroeck,
and Linda Mitchell*

3   Resisting the Consumentality of Parents   81
Michel Vandenbroeck, Joanne Lehrer, and Linda Mitchell

4   Resisting the Alienation of the Workforce   147
Linda Mitchell, Michel Vandenbroeck, and Joanne Lehrer

5   Conclusions   214
Michel Vandenbroeck, Joanne Lehrer, and Linda Mitchell

References   *223*
Index   *254*

CONTRIBUTOR BIOGRAPHIES

Vina Adriany is an Associate Professor at the Department of Early Childhood Education and a Head for Centre of Gender and Childhood Studies, Universitas Pendidikan Indonesia. Her research focuses on the issues of gender and social justice in early childhood education, the construction of children and childhood in marginal communities, as well as the impact of neoliberalism in ECE. Her research mostly adopts theories that include feminist poststructuralism and postcolonialism. She is currently an editorial board member Policy Futures in Education, SAGE; International Journal of Early Years Education, Routledge; Global Childhood Studies, SAGE; and Children and Society, Willey. She was a guest editor for Policy Futures in Education for "Neoliberal policies and practices of early childhood education in Asia". She was also a guest editor for Journal of Pedagogy for "Decolonialisation of Early Childhood Education". She is currently editing a special issue of "Indonesian Perspectives of Early Childhood Education" for Policy Futures in Education Journal.

Sonja Arndt is a Senior Lecturer in the Melbourne Graduate School of Education at the University of Melbourne and Leader of the Global Childhoods Seminar Series. Her studies of teachers' cultural identity formation and intercultural relationships led to her work in the New Zealand Aid Programme, UNICEF Indonesia, and the Indonesian Ministry of Education and Culture, where she worked on the design and implementation of an ECE teacher mentoring programme in Kupang, Indonesia.

Maarit Alasuutari is a Professor of Early Childhood Education and PI of the multidisciplinary research profiling action "Social Sustainability for Children and Families" at the University of Jyväskylä, Finland. Her recent research topics include early childhood policies and services, parent-teacher relationship, children's position and voice in ECEC, and documentation in ECEC. Professor Alasuutari has published widely nationally and internationally.

Royne K. Berget is Industry leader for non-profit kindergardens in Virke. He was educated as a kindergarden teacher at Høgskolen in Finnmark in 1997, and since then has taken continuing education in leadership – Løft metoden. He has 23 years of experience as a Kindergarden teacher, of which 18 years was as leader of Smedhusåsen barnehage SA (until December 2020). Royne has been active in special interest representation and lobbying for the kindergarden-sector through different organisations and resource groups for several years. He has also written lots of chronicles, has held lectures about challenges in the kindergarden-sector throughout Norway, and has contributed with chapters/vignettes in several textbooks.

Marie-Laure Cadart is a medical doctor and an anthropologist. She worked for many years in preventive health care before engaging in professional development and research. She committed herself in the resistance against the commodification of early childhood and was one of the initiators of the collective « Pas de 0 de conduite pour les enfants de 3 ans ». She is a member of the board of the National Union of preventive health physicians and an honorary member of the board of ACEPP (the association of parent-led early childhood centres).

Donella Cobb is a Senior Lecturer in the School of Education at the University of Waikato and Co-Director of the Centre for Global Studies in Education. Donella's research explores the political economy of education, education policy, and teacher development. From 2018 to 2020, Donella worked as an advisor for the New Zealand Aid Programme, UNICEF Indonesia, and the Indonesian Ministry of Education and Culture to implement an ECE teacher mentoring programme in Kupang, Indonesia.

Nicole Cummings-Morgan is a Registered Early Childhood Educator (RECE), and Ontario Certified Teacher (OCT), a children's book author and the Executive Director of W1derus Educational Workshops, a not-for-profit organisation. Nicole is the team lead for the Community of Black ECES, which is a community of practice with the Association of Early Childhood Educators of Ontario (AECEO). Her goal, professionally and personally, is to support children, families, and individuals be the best they could be. She is particularly interested in helping those within her Black community.

Lisa Johnston is a Registered Early Childhood Educator, PhD Student in the Faculty of Education at York University, professor, and childcare activist. Her research addresses the lives of early childhood educators at the intersection of pedagogy and policy, disrupting neoliberal and developmental temporalities that shape ECEs and their work and seeking to create possibilities for ECEs to have time to think. Lisa also leads an activist community affiliated with the Association of Early Childhood Educators Ontario (AECEO) that builds the political capacities of Early Years Professionals and strengthens our collective voice in the fight for Professional Pay and Decent Work.

Raella Kahuroa, PhD, is a Researcher at the University of Waikato, Hamilton, New Zealand. Her research interests include critical pedagogy, democracy in education, and place-based education. Her doctoral thesis focused on unpacking critical pedagogy teaching and learning interactions in an early childhood setting. Recent research has included exploring working theories of Covid-19 with young children, exploring belonging with refugee and immigrant children, and walking and storying the land with young children.

Olivera Kamenarac, PhD, is a Senior Lecturer at the University of Waikato, New Zealand. Her main research interests include philosophy in/of education, educational policies, educational subjects and subjectivity, identity, and wellbeing politics. Her doctoral research examined the effects of shifting discourses in New Zealand's early childhood policies and practices on teachers' work and identities over the last two decades. Olivera's most recent research explores possibilities for transforming educational spaces, places, subjects, and subjectivity through feminist posthumanist lenses.

Kirsti Karila is an Emerita Professor of Early Childhood Education and Care at Tampere University, Finland. Professor Karila has held an active position in developing the ECEC system in Finland. Her research areas include professionalism, institutional cultures, and policies in ECEC. Professor Karila has recently studied the municipal-level ECEC policies, parents' choices, and children's early childhood education trajectories in the CHILDCARE Consortium Finnish Childcare Policies: In/equality in Focus, funded by the Strategic Research Council (Academy of Finland). Now, she investigates the inclusive transitions from ECEC to primary education in the European InTrans project.

Joanne Lehrer is an Associate Professor of Preschool Education in the Department of Educational Sciences at the University of Quebec in Outaouais. Her research interests focus on early childhood education and care contexts and the intersections between individual experiences and societal discourses in the pursuit of social justice. She has explored relationships with families, educational transitions, professional identities, children's experiences, and the history of ECEC and preschool education in Quebec. She is a member of the quality of early childhood educational contexts research team and of the Sketching narratives of movement towards comprehensive and competent early childhood educational systems across Canada project. She participates in local and regional early childhood consultation tables and associations and has co-edited the following books: *Relationships with Families in Early Childhood*

Education and Care: Beyond Instrumentalization in International Contexts of Diversity and Social Inequality (with Fay Hadley, Katrien Van Laere, and Elizabeth Rouse); *La recherche en éducation à la petite enfance: Origines, méthodes et applications* [Research in Early Childhood Education: Origins, Methods and Applications] (with Nathalie Bigras, Annie Charron, and Isabelle Laurin); and *L' éducation préscolaire au Québec: Fondements théoriques et pédagogiques* [Preschool Education in Quebec: Theoretical and Pedagogical Foundations].

Stig G Lund works at the Danish Union of Early Childhood and Youth Educators – BUPL – in Copenhagen as a special adviser. He has a pedagogue education and has completed further studies at the Danish School of Education. He has worked as a pedagogue and head of a kindergarten, and was an elected member of the National Board of BUPL. Since 1982, he has worked at BUPL on educational and professional issues within early childhood education and care. On behalf of BUPL and the European Trade Union Committee on Education – ETUCE – he was member of the European Commission's working group on ECEC from 2012 to 2014 and 2018 to 2020.

Hoana McMillan (Ngai Te Rangi, Ngāti Porou, Ngāti Kahungunu) is a lecturer in initial teacher education at the University of Waikato. Her research interests include Māori education, indigenous education, kōhanga reo, Māori assessment practices, educational leadership, and Māori communities.

Linda Mitchell is a Professor of Early Childhood Education at the University of Waikato, New Zealand, and currently Leverhulme Visiting Professor at Manchester Metropolitan University, working with MMU staff on the project, Theorising democracy in education. She was a leading official and advocate in the early childhood teachers' unions in New Zealand for 15 years during the 1980s and 1990s. She has subsequently spent many years researching early childhood education policy and practice, and critiquing the marketisation and privatisation of early childhood education. She has also researched with early childhood teachers in New Zealand to explore transformational pedagogical approaches based on principles of social justice and support for young children to develop as proactive, informed citizens of a bicultural Aotearoa New Zealand. Her most recent publications include Democratic Practices and Policies in Early Childhood Education and Care. An Aotearoa New Zealand case study, and a range of articles and book chapters from her research, Refugee and immigrant families in early childhood education: Constructing pathways to belonging. Her current research is a two-year TLRI-funded project, Renewing participatory democracy: Walking with young children to story and read the land.

Peter Moss is an Emeritus Professor of Early Childhood Provision at UCL Institute of Education, University College London. His work covers a wide range of areas including early childhood education and care, and the relationship between early childhood and compulsory education; the relationship between employment, care and gender; and democracy in education. Much of his work has been cross-national, and he has led a European Commission network on childcare and an international network on parental leave. His books include Loris Malaguzzi and the Schools of Reggio Emilia: A selection of his writings and speeches, 1945–1993 (edited with colleagues from Reggio Emilia); Transforming Early Childhood in England: Towards a democratic education (edited with Claire Cameron); and Neoliberalism and Early Childhood Education: Markets, imaginaries and governance (with Guy Roberts-Holmes).

Tullia Musatti is an Associate Senior Researcher at Institute of Cognitive Sciences and Technologies, National Research Council of Italy. She conducts research on children's cognitive processes in early years, peer sociality in early childhood education and care centres, and parents' perspectives on young children's care and education. She is the author of several books and articles.

Esther Oduolowu is a full Professor of Early Childhood Care and Education in the Department of Early Childhood and Educational Foundations, University of Ibadan, Nigeria. She has over 25 years teaching and research experience at the university. Her research interests focus on early learning, stakeholders' capacity development, and child rights advocacy. She was adjunct Professor to the University of Victoria, Canada, and a visiting scholar at the Kennesaw State University, Kennesaw Georgia, United States of America. She has published widely in learned journals nationally and internationally. She belongs to professional bodies, like CEI and OMEP.

Alana Powell is a RECE and the Executive Director at the Association of Early Childhood Educators. She completed her MA in Early Childhood Studies from Toronto Metropolitan (formerly Ryerson) University. Her research critically explores care discourses in early childhood and seeks to reposition care and care work as central in politics, practice, and advocacy. Her work builds the collective power and voice of ECEs, children, families, and communities so they can influence policy change that benefits us all.

Brooke Richardson is an Adjunct Faculty in the Department of Sociology at Brock University (Canada) and President of the Association of Early Childhood Educators of Ontario. Brooke has published and presented nationally and internationally on topics related to social policy and Canadian children/families. Her current research, embedded in feminist ethics of care and political theory, examines the increasing privatisation of the childcare sector, COVID-19 childcare policy responses, gendered conceptualisations of the early childhood educator, and the position of care in child protection.

Pablo Rupin is a sociologist (Universidad Católica de Chile), Master in Public Policy Management (Universidad de Chile), and holds a PhD in education (Université Sorbonne Paris Nord - ex Paris 13), with a thesis on parent participation in community ECEC in Chile. Currently, he is assistant professor at the O'Higgins University in Chile. His research concerns families and children's socialisation. He also worked with JUNJI, the formal agency for public preschool in Chile.

Kylie Smith is a professor of early childhood at the University of Melbourne's Melbourne Graduate School of Education. Kylie's research draws on participatory methodologies and critical theories to explore and develop praxis that supports social justice pedagogies in the everyday classroom.

Dwi Purwestri Sri Suwarningsih, MEd, is currently a PhD candidate at Te Kura Toi Tangata School of Education at the University of Waikato, New Zealand. Her doctoral research focuses on the mentoring relationship for ECE teachers' professional development in Kupang, Indonesia. She earned her Bachelor's degree in Psychology from Wangsa Manggala University, Indonesia, and Post Graduate Diploma in Education and an MEd from Victoria University of Wellington, New Zealand. She has 20+ years of experience working with local and international NGOs as well as in one of the United Nations Agencies in Indonesia, and her work is focusing on children's development and teachers' professional development.

Michel Vandenbroeck is an Associate Professor in Family Pedagogy and head of the Department of Social Work and Social pedagogy of Ghent University in Belgium. His research focuses on early childhood education and care, family policies, and parent support programs, with a particular interest for processes of in- and exclusion in contexts of diversities. He is president of the board of VBJK, the Centre for Innovation in Early Childhood and serves as a member of the advisory board of "Opgroeien," the governmental agency competent for early childhood education and parent support in Flanders. Together with Liselott Olsson, he is the coordinating editor of the Contesting Early Childhood series, in which he recently published "Revisiting Paulo Freire's Pedagogy of the Oppressed" (2000) and "Constructions of Neuroscience in Early Childhood Education" (2017). For his work on the relations between pedagogy, policy, and practice in early childhood care and education, he received an honorary PhD from Tampere University and from the University of Uppsala.

Marcy Whitebook founded the Center for the Study of Child Care Employment (CSCCE) at the University of California, Berkeley, in 1999, leading the organisation for two decades, and now serving as CSCCE Director Emerita. Her writings have contributed to the national and international discourse about how poor compensation and working conditions, and racialised wage policies that undermine effective teaching, risk the personal and familial well-being of the workforce, and contribute to inequitable services for children and families. A former infant, toddler, and preschool teacher, Marcy has been a lifelong activist for a more just early care and education system.

Gail Yuen is an Associate Professor in the Department of Education Policy and Leadership at The Education University of Hong Kong. Gail focuses on policy and advocacy for young children, as well as teacher education. The market approach to early childhood education, especially in the context of Hong Kong, is her main theme of work. Gail has recently moved onto researching kindergarten space, trying to heighten policy attention on spatial injustice experienced by the sector and explore alternatives and education experimentations with teachers in daily practice.

INTRODUCTION

From the politically impossible to the politically inevitable

Peter Moss

In 2021, "Neoliberalism and Early Childhood Education: Markets, Imaginaries and Governance" was published in the *Contesting Early Childhood* series, authored by Guy Roberts-Holmes and myself. In his foreword to the book, Professor Stephen Ball, a leading scholar of neoliberalism in education, made a strong and striking claim:

> Neoliberalism now configures great swathes of our daily lives and structures our experience of the world – how we understand the way the world works, how we understand ourselves and others, and how we relate to ourselves and others...We are produced by it.
>
> *(Ball, 2021, p. xv)*

In the book, Guy and I set out how neoliberalism configures one facet of our lives: early childhood education,[1] and the participation in it of young children, parents and workers. We argued that neoliberalism was a powerful force, dominant for several decades, but that despite its power and being deeply problematic, it was also "eminently resistible and eventually replaceable" – and that, indeed, now was a necessary and opportune time to be building resistance and plotting its replacement.

This current book is a perfect sequel to our earlier book. It is full of concrete examples, drawn from many parts of the world, that demonstrate how neoliberalism can be challenged, here and now, and pointing to some of the sustainable alternatives that may replace neoliberalism's fetishism of commodification, privatisation and marketisation. But before readers move on to this rich material, it may be useful to recap some of the main ideas from the earlier book and our argument that resistance and alternatives to neoliberalism and its prescriptions are urgently needed and entirely feasible.

What are we talking about?

The world has been living through an era of neoliberal hegemony, since neoliberalism made the global big time in the 1980s. The result is that, as Stephen Ball says, neoliberalism now reaches far and wide, and goes deep into all aspects of our lives. Take the material aspects of daily existence. Whether it's schools or bus services competing for custom, or the privatisation of public utilities and the sub-contracting of public services to businesses, or the marginalisation of trade unions and the vaunting of a "flexible" labour market, or the turning over of care for older people or residential care for children to private providers, neoliberalism has become the normal backdrop to life in many places, to the extent that it now seems natural and self-evident. How else, we may ask, could things be?

Yet despite its enormous influence on all aspects of our lives, many people today can neither name nor describe neoliberalism. As philosopher of economic thought, Philip Mirowski, observes, "even at this late hour, the world is still full of people who believe that neoliberalism doesn't really exist," so that it might be said that neoliberalism hides itself in full view, "almost to the point of passing as the 'ideology of no ideology'" (Mirowski, 2013, p. 28). And this invisibility, as openDemocracy co-founder Anthony Barnett puts it, "contributes to its influence and success – just try to oppose something that you cannot name" (Barnett, 2020) Even if the existence of the subject is broached, people may struggle to see the relevance of neoliberalism to their lives, including to their education and employment. Cristina Vintimilla has included neoliberalism in the early childhood courses she has taught at a Canadian university, and notes how it has provoked either "a tense, awkward moment of silence" or became "a source of contestation."

> A colleague asked me once, 'Why should one teach neoliberalism in an early childhood degree?" My students have asked: "Why should we bother studying this?"; "Why should we bother with neoliberalism when we have to learn how to teach children?"
>
> *(Vintimilla, 2014, p. 79)*

So what is neoliberalism? It has been described variously as a "thought collective" and a "theory of everything" (Mirowski, 2013), as a "set of ideas that offer a coherent view about how society should be ordered" (Tronto, 2017) and as an "intellectual and political movement" (Monbiot, 2016). It is in fact all of these things, but at heart it can be seen as a story that lays claim to tell the world how human life works and what needs to be done to bring about an ideal future, truly a totalising grand narrative.

At the heart of neoliberalism is the "economisation" of everything, described by American political theorist Wendy Brown (2016) as "the conversion of non-economic domains, activities and subjects into economic ones extend[ing] market metrics and practices to every dimension of human life; political, cultural, personal, vocational, educational." Everything becomes economic, even human relationships, all reducible to economic valuation, calculation and transactions. Central to these transactions is the creation of markets where sellers and buyers can be brought together to trade anything and everything, and where neoliberalism's prime values of competition, individual choice and calculation can work their supposed magic. The whole point of neo-liberalism, writes political scientist Susan George (1999), "is that the market mechanism should be allowed to direct the fate of human beings. The economy should dictate its rules to society, not the other way around"; this doctrine, she adds, is leading us towards the "demolition of society."

Through the process of economisation, neoliberalism turns everything into a marketable or tradable private commodity – the process of commodification. It also "thoroughly revises what it means to be a human person" (Mirowski, 2013), calling forth a very particular image of the individual. This ideal neoliberal subject is an economic being – *homo economicus*, self-interested and competitive, independent and self-reliant, an informed consumer constantly calculating for every aspect of life what is in her or his best interests and with "every kind of human activity [reconfigured] in terms of rational self-investment and entrepreneurship." She or he must be constantly ready for whatever new twist or turn takes place in the economy and employment, infinitely flexible and responsive to the changing needs of the market, an entrepreneur of the self: as Stephen Ball puts it, "malleable rather than committed, flexible rather than principled – essentially depthless."

These ideas are not new. But they have become increasingly influential across the world since the 1980s, spreading out from the neoliberal movement's epicentres in the UK and USA. Margaret Thatcher and Ronald Reagan were the movement's political standard bearers, but they were preceded and backed by a dense network of influencers – individuals, think tanks, university departments and international organisations, the "thought collective" that had been working on a programme for neoliberalism and its implementation from the 1950s onwards, and thus were ready when the economic crises of the 1970s turned neoliberalism from the politically impossible to the politically inevitable. Not only inevitable but unarguable. Neoliberals themselves have taken the view that, in the words of Margaret Thatcher, "there is no alternative" to neoliberalism itself: neoliberalism is, from this perspective, the end of history. As Susan George (1999) comments, neo-liberalism seems

> as if it were the natural and normal condition of humankind. No matter how many disasters of all kinds the neo-liberal system has visibly created… no matter how many losers and outcasts it may create, it is still made to seem inevitable, like an act of God, the only possible economic and social order available to us.

And if there are no alternatives to neoliberalism, no legitimate or necessary arguments to be had about ends, then there is no need for politics. Political questions, with no one right answer but only alternative and often conflicting answers, the essence of democratic politics, are replaced by technical questions, to which there is only one right answer, an answer about means not ends that can be decided by economic and other technical experts, then left to management to ensure performance, without any semblance of democratic input or of meaningful choices. Societies, thus, become increasingly depoliticised, with contestation about ends (what do we value? what matters? what do we want?) replaced by technical assessments of means (what works? what return on this investment?), active citizens re-cast as calculating consumers.

The neoliberal movement draws on other, related ideas. "Human capital" theory, first articulated in the 1950s, has become immensely influential today referring to the knowledge, information, ideas, skills and health of individuals, all the capacities needed for economic success. Gary Becker, a neoliberal economist and early proponent of human capital theory, claimed that "this is the 'age of human capital' …The economic successes of individuals, and also of whole economies, depend on how extensively and effectively people invest in themselves" (Becker, 2002). Another example of "economisation," the human being reduced to a unit of capital, "human capital" complements the neoliberal image of *homo economicus,* that essentially economic and entrepreneurial subject.

"Public choice" theory has undermined trust in public institutions and public service by claiming people "are primarily driven by venal self-interest…[wanting] to control others and take away their resources" and viewing "government as an unfortunate necessity that needed to be constrained at all costs" (Parramore, 2018). While "new public management" has imported the methods of private business into the domain of public services, including greater competition and an insistence on explicit standards and measures of performance in the interests of output control. Thus from all sides, the idea of public services provided by a public sector for the public good has come under attack, opening the way for their selling off or replacement by private providers and their reconceptualisation as marketable commodities offering private benefits to customers.

Neoliberalism and early childhood education

Compulsory and higher education have been well-served by studies of neoliberalism. They have detailed how neoliberalism has circulated in these sectors of education since the 1980s via what has been called the Global Education Reform Movement (GERM), which "has increasingly become adopted as an educational reform orthodoxy within many education systems throughout the world" (Sahlberg, 2012). The main symptoms of GERM have been the spread into schools of market logic, business management models and test-based accountability, the standardisation of education with the specification of performance standards for pupils, schools and countries and a narrowing of curriculums to focus on core subjects of literacy, numeracy and science. Less attention, however, has been paid to early childhood education, though some warnings have been sounded, with Margaret Sims (2017) arguing that neoliberalism has had "a devastating impact on the early childhood sector with its focus on standardisation, push-down curriculum and its positioning of children as investments for future economic productivity."

In "Neoliberalism and Early Childhood Education: Markets, Imaginaries and Governance," Guy Roberts-Holmes and myself have looked further into neoliberalism's impact on early childhood provision, pedagogy and policies. Our attention has been mainly focused on countries in the Anglosphere, where neoliberalism originated and has been most deeply felt, so I welcome the wider geographical spread of the current book. England, indeed, gets top billing in the earlier book because in so many ways, it has been at the forefront of the neoliberal project for early childhood, and all other, education, acting as what Stephen Ball (2017) has called a "social laboratory of experimentation and reform."

"Neoliberalism and Early Childhood Education" starts its analysis with markets and marketisation, since, as already noted, markets are at the heart of neoliberalism (including GERM, neoliberalism's educational manifestation). We write that markets

> are where neoliberalism's virtues – commodification, competition, calculation, choice – are enacted and honed…In neoliberalism's world-view, introducing and expanding markets is the answer to every social, economic and political problem – including the provision and improvement of early childhood education and care. "Market logic" pervades this sector as much as other sectors of education.
> (Roberts-Holmes & Moss, 2021, p. 62)

Early childhood education has been marketised in many countries, and this is often linked to privatisation – though public provision can also be put on the market, being then required to compete for "customers" with other public as well as burgeoning private services. Private services can be provided by a variety of non-profit bodies (e.g. charities, co-operatives, other social enterprises) as well as by for-profit businesses. Mostly such businesses are small-scale, owning just one or two services, but there are also and increasingly larger businesses and corporations operating across several countries and often backed by private equity or other investors, as this report from October 2021 exemplifies:

> [The company] Busy Bees has bought the New Zealand-based Provincial Education group, which operates 75 settings, providing more than 5,500 places across the North and South Islands. The acquisition of Provincial Education, the third largest early childcare education provider in New Zealand, from majority shareholder Waterman Private Capital, Ascentro Capital and its founders, is expected to complete at the end of this month (October). As part of the deal, Provincial Education's management team will continue in their roles. Busy Bees Childcare has also taken over the Think Childcare Group of 71 sites and more than 7,100 places in Australia.

> Together the deals mean the nursery group will operate 222 settings across Australia and New Zealand. This is in addition to 417 sites in Europe, 127 in North America and 83 in Asia
>
> *(Morton, 2021)*

Overall, there is a trend of larger players buying up smaller operators in a process of market consolidation. For example, a recent study of private "childcare" in England concludes that

> the shape of the market for the private-for profit childcare company sector is one of company growth and consolidation, through acquisitions and mergers. This is evidenced by the top 25 companies (ranked by number of settings) showing a significant increase in the last five years in the number of places ... [T]his 'growth' is caused by mergers and acquisitions, without the creation of new places
>
> *(Simon et al., 2022, p. 32).*

The same study also records another market trend: the spread into this sector of financialisation, described as "a process involving the increasing role of financial motives, the financial markets, financial actors and financial institutions in the operation of the domestic and international economies." The researchers into private "childcare" in England found, when focusing on medium to large companies, "clear patterns of acquisitions and mergers and indebtedness... We also identified that a considerable amount of money is being extracted for debt repayment." As well as being heavily indebted, these companies often have "very complex financial structures involving foreign investors and shareholders. They have necessarily adopted a shareholder model of corporate governance."

A recent example of financialisation involves early childhood centres being the subject of corporate behaviour that treats them as property assets that can be used to generate finance for new acquisitions. The English nursery chain called Just Childcare, founded in 2004 and which had grown by 2021 to own 64 nurseries, was bought in that year by Partou, a Dutch nursery group, itself part of a larger entity, Kids Foundation, which has more than 900 settings across Northern Europe, mainly in the Netherlands. Kids Foundation is in turn itself owned by private equity company Onex Partners and investment company Waterland. The purchase of Just Childcare by Partou was funded by a "sale-and-leaseback" deal, involving the sale of the freeholds of 23 of Just Childcare's nurseries to LXi REIT, a real estate investment trust based in London, which then leased the nurseries back to Partou. The magazine that ran this story continues that

> Cairneagle Associates [an 'international strategy consultancy specialising in education, media, and technology'] told *Nursery World* that the benefit of sale-and-leaseback for nursery groups is that it releases capital to invest in expansion and it can also dilute ingoing multiple [sic].

> In terms of financing expansion, nursery groups have four options – existing cash, debt (bank or other), equity investment such as private equity, or taking it out of the property through sale and leaseback, which is experiencing a bit of a resurgence… [Sale-and-leasebacks are] a really important mechanism for investors to reduce the upfront payment for businesses, and if the rent yield is good (which it often is), it will also dilute the multiple paid for the business. This might be after buying the business. By releasing capital, you could go and buy another X nurseries, which you could not have done otherwise. A lot of this is about the perceived best use of capital…The market is extremely hot at the moment, and the opening up of sale leaseback options is likely to further stimulate the marketplace of buyers (for those investors and strategics that prefer leaseholds), which is also good for sellers.
>
> *(Gaunt, 2021)*

Here, gathered up in this story, is neoliberalism incarnate. Apart from rampant financialisation, the profit motive and consolidation of ownership, we can see how the commodification and marketisation of early childhood education operating at two levels: a market of consumers (parents) seeking to buy "nursery" services (though these consumers, let alone children, clearly play no part in this example of financial wheeler dealing); and, as is the case here, a market of businesses seeking to buy other businesses, looking for ways to raise finance for expansion – and often, too, calling on the services of companies that act as brokers. Here, for example, is one such company that advices on buying and selling nursery businesses ("an effective strategic partner for business buyers and sellers…[with] decades of experience and unrivalled insight in our chosen sectors: hotels, pubs, restaurants, childcare, healthcare, convenience retail, leisure and medical"). For this brokerage company, reporting on a webinar titled "What does Covid-19 mean for the childcare market?" the future looked bright, the pandemic notwithstanding:

> Despite being in uncertain times, we are still seeing wide ranging investor interest spanning from private equity, through to first-time buyers, trade operations, alongside global and indeed domestic financial institutions, all of whom are attracted to the [nursery] sector due to the strong underpinning demographic drivers, demand and supply factors and indeed the opportunity to consolidate in what is a very fragmented market.
>
> *(Christie and Co., 2020).*

As this current book and the earlier book by Guy Roberts-Holmes and myself make clear, marketisation and privatisation have happened widely in early childhood education – yet governments have been so thoroughly captured by the story of neoliberalism that they have made little attempt to research how marketisation and privatisation work and with what consequences, or indeed to compare them with alternative ways of organising early childhood services. However, such evidence as does exist suggests that markets in these services do not work well as markets. Economist Gillian Paull sums up the situation thus: "Childcare is not a typical good or service. Its inherent nature contains a number of characteristics which create problems in the functioning of the market and means that the market outcomes may not meet parents' preferences at minimum cost" (Paull, 2012).

But the problem goes beyond market malfunctioning and whether or not these malfunctions might be rectified by this or that measure to make the market work better. It is the very principal that is deeply problematic to some: as the editors of this book note, "scholars [have] begun to not only document that childcare *does not* function as a market, and that childcare *cannot* function as market, but also that childcare *should not* function as a market and that parents *should not* be considered rational consumers." This is critically important. The marketisation and associated privatisation of early childhood services are based on the assumption that they are simply private businesses, which are tradeable commodities themselves (being bought and sold) as well as selling commodities ("childcare" and "learning") to individual parent-consumers. But many would contest that assumption, arguing that these services should be viewed as public goods and collective benefits, and inscribed with values of democracy, solidarity, cooperation, inclusion and equality, values that are inimical to marketisation and privatisation. For based as they are on competition and individual choice, and with extensive private ownership, privatised and marketised services generate inequality and division and are commodities devoid of democratic accountability.

Turning from markets to the imaginaries of neoliberalism, we describe in our book how neoliberalism has created a distinct set of economised and instrumental images in early childhood education. The young child is an empty vessel to be filled with competencies, a not yet ready adult starting out on a constant process of readyfication whose end point is to eventually become *homo economicus,* a good investment for the creation of future human capital. The parent is a customer and consumer, an achieved *homo economicus* seeking out "childcare" in the market, but also a stock of acquired human capital that must not go to waste. "Childcare" services are businesses selling a commodity of care to employed (and usually higher income) parents and also a factory or processing plant producing predefined outcomes, the development targets or learning goals laid down by government. While the early childhood worker is a businesswoman, honing the skills needed to survive and succeed in a competitive marketplace, and also a technician, able to apply effective human technologies to achieve predefined outcomes.

Images are immensely important and effective; they help govern policy, practice and identity, the very sense of who we and others are. As we write in our book, these images

> are normative, representing the identity or subjectivity that neoliberal beliefs ascribe to people, but also to institutions; according to these beliefs, this is who people and what institutions, such as early childhood centres, should be. But they are also productive, in that neoliberalism seeks to

produce or create people and institutions in its own image – a process that Foucault terms subjectification, the formation or production of subjectivity through power relations, dominant discourses and regimes of truth.

(Roberts-Holmes & Moss, 2021, p. 91)

Neoliberalism's images of early childhood education are both constructed and expressed through the stories we tell and the language we use. I have written elsewhere about what I take to be the dominant neoliberal story or narrative told today about early childhood education, in particular in the Anglophone world, what I term "the story of quality and high returns":

> It is a story of control and calculation, technology and measurement that, in a nutshell, goes like this. Find, invest in and apply the correct human technologies – aka 'quality' - during early childhood and you will get high returns on investment including improved education, employment and earnings and reduced social problems. A simple equation beckons and beguiles: 'early intervention' + 'quality' = increased 'human capital' + national success (or at least survival) in a cut-throat global economy. Invest early and invest smartly and we will all live happily ever after in a world of more of the same – only more so.
>
> *(Moss, 2014, p. 3)*

This is not the time or place to go into why I find the story naïve and reductionist, troubling and unsatisfying (to find out more, go to Moss, 2013, Chapter 4). I would note here the centrality of language in the stories we tell, and draw attention to the particular vocabulary that is so prominent in the "story of quality and high returns" and so central to neoliberalism's capture of early childhood education. It is a distinctive language: technical, managerial, economistic. It is the language of "outcomes" and "quality," "testing" and "assessment," "interventions" and "programmes," "evidence-based" and "best practice," "investment" and "human capital," "preparation" and "readiness," "markets and marketing."

Finally, in our book Guy Roberts-Holmes and I turn to neoliberalism and governance in early childhood education, governance being the way in which organisations and systems are governed or controlled. In his foreword to our book, Stephen Ball (2021) gives an indication of the range of means neoliberalism deploys to this task:

> The metier and modalities of neoliberalism, both its modus operandi and modus vivendi, are visibility, accountability, transparency, measurement, calculation, comparison, evaluation, ratings, ranking, indicators, metrics and indices. These now infuse, inform and construct large parts of our social life, and the life of the early years classroom, of the nursery and parenting, producing particular forms of our relation to ourselves and to others.
>
> *(p. xvi)*

What we can see here is the importation of New Public Management into early childhood education (as it has been into other sectors of education and beyond); indeed, New Public Management has been described as the neoliberal way of governance (Vabø, 2009, p. 2). All those "modalities" listed by Stephen Ball add up to introducing standards (for the performance of children and services) and their constant assessment through measurement, making such ratings visible and enabling comparisons that in turn supposedly enable more informed judgements by consumers and greater control by managers.

New Pubic Management's principles, with their drive to control and improve performance, have led to an ever tighter governing of children, workers and services. They have ridden roughshod over complexity, diversity and creativity, and disdained the values of uncertainty and unexpectedness, of wonder and surprise. They have led instead to the adoption and maintenance of what the Italian educator Loris Malaguzzi called "prophetic pedagogy," which

> knows everything beforehand: it knows everything that will happen. It knows everything and it has no uncertainty, it is absolutely imperturbable, it contemplates everything and prophesies everything and sees everything; sees everything to the point that it is capable of giving recipes for the parts of an action, minute by minute, hour by hour, objective by objective, five minutes by five minutes. This is a coarse and cowardly thing, which is humiliating to teachers' ingenuity and a complete and visible humiliation of children's ingenuity and potential.
> *(cited in Cagliari et al., 2016, p. 422)*

Prophetic pedagogy has gone hand in glove with what Malaguzzi, equally contemptuously, called "Anglo-Saxon testology," with its "rush to categorise… where it is enough to do some tests on an individual and immediately the individual has been defined and measured in some way…which is nothing but a ridiculous simplification of knowledge, and a robbing of meaning from individual histories" (ibid., pp. 331, 378). No uncertainty, humiliation, simplification, robbing meaning – this is just one part of a long charge sheet against neoliberalism, a charge sheet that calls for resistance and makes replacement very urgent.

Resisting and replacing neoliberalism

> We view neoliberalism as deeply problematic, eminently resistible and eventually replaceable…we think neoliberalism has little or no future and turn to alternatives; for if the neoliberal mantra has been "there are no alternatives," ours is that "there are alternatives."
> *(Roberts-Holmes & Moss, 2021, p. 4)*

Guy Roberts-Holmes and I take neoliberalism very seriously and have no illusions about its cultural hegemony, manifest in its strong hold on the collective psyche, not least that of policy makers who accept no alternative. Neither do we have any doubt that this neoliberal hegemony has had disastrous consequences. To name but a few: its deeply unappealing vision of people and society, with its cynical image of the self-interested and calculating subject; its reductionist belief that the market should determine the fate of human beings; its economisation of every nook and cranny of life and its disdain for the "public"; and its depoliticisation of society, leaving a pervasive sense of powerlessness in the face of the mantra that there is no alternative. Furthermore, neoliberalism has left a trail of destruction in its wake, including increasing inequality and insecurity, democracy and solidarity undermined, and welfare states seriously reduced in their capacity to protect; not to mention accelerated environmental degradation fuelled by a voracious desire for consumption and growth, which turns out to be both profoundly damaging and totally unsustainable.

Political scientist Sheri Berman sums up the situation:

> Over recent years, the negative consequences of neoliberal capitalism have become impossible to ignore. It contributed to such traumatic events as the 2008 financial crisis as well as such destructive long-term trends as rising inequality, lower growth, increasing monopsony [a market with only one buyer] and growing social and geographic divides. Moreover, its impact has not been limited to the economic sphere: these events and trends have negatively influenced western societies and democracies as well.
>
> *(Berman, 2019)*

Some economists share this bleak assessment. Nobel prize-winning economist Joseph Stiglitz (2019) bluntly concludes that:

> The credibility of neoliberalism's faith in unfettered markets as the surest road to shared prosperity is on life-support these days. And well it should be. The simultaneous waning of confidence in neoliberalism and in democracy is no coincidence or mere correlation. Neoliberalism has undermined democracy …[A]fter 40 years, the numbers are in: growth has slowed and the fruits of that growth went overwhelmingly to a very few at the top. As wages stagnated and the stock market soared, income and wealth flowed up, rather than trickling down…If the 2008 financial crisis failed to make us realise that unfettered markets don't work, the climate crisis certainly should: neoliberalism will literally bring an end to our civilisation'.

His words are echoed by another economist, Kate Raworth (2017):

> The market, promised the neoliberals script, is the road to freedom, and who could be against that? But putting blind faith in markets – while ignoring the living world. Society, and the runaway power of banks – has

taken us to the brink of ecological, social and financial collapse. It is time for the neoliberal show to leave the stage: a very different story is emerging.

(p. 70)

As both these economists suggest, not only has neoliberalism almost brought the house down, it hasn't delivered even in its own terms: its blind faith in markets hasn't worked out as expected, epitomised by the 2008 financial crisis, and leading yet another economist to conclude that "[what we were told by the neoliberal economists] was at best only partially true and at worst plain wrong…the 'truths' pedalled by free-market ideologues are based on lazy assumptions and blinkered visions" (Chang, 2011). Given this track record, it is unsurprising that when the Covid pandemic came along, few if any voices called out to leave it all to the market: solutions were sought in the public sphere, through public health, public employment measures and public finance.

The mess we find ourselves in as a result of a generation of neoliberalism and the prescriptions of its zealots is depressing and shocking. But Guy Roberts-Holmes and I are also hopeful in our book, arguing that neoliberalism has now entered into crisis, becoming a "zombie" ideology. Unable to contribute to the resolution of the crises we are living through or to offer us hope for a better, healthier and more sustainable future, neoliberalism lurches onwards, continuing to wreak havoc and waiting to be finished off if only we have the imagination, creativity and determination to put something better in its place.

In this weakened state, neoliberalism is eminently resistible. We suggest in our book some forms that such resistance can take, with an emphasis on critical thinking: for example, questioning assumptions and assertions, putting a "stutter" in dominant discourses; adopting what Stephen Ball (2016) calls a politics of refusal, in which through acts of "voluntary inservitude, of reflective indocility," we can withhold our consent to the subjectivity that neoliberalism seeks from us and work "to define ourselves according to our own judgments"; working with minor politics, those "minor engagements in the everyday" that manifest in local activism; and through words and stories, adopting a different vocabulary, and listening to and telling different stories about early childhood education.

The present book provides an important addition to our earlier discussion, with stories of actual resistance by educators and parents, drawn from a range of countries. Each one is a reminder that, as Foucault contends, "where there is power, there is resistance" (Foucault, 1978, p. 95). Put another way, if there was to be no resistance, the relationship would no longer be one of power but simply of slavery – and we have not been reduced to that relationship, certainly not in education. Developing this theme, Stephen Ball adds that "[l]ike power itself, resistance is manifold and operates at a multiplicity of points in different forms, in many small acts and passing moments" (Ball, 2013, p. 32).

Resistance to the neoliberal status quo is essential. But we can and must go further than resistance. For neoliberalism, in its zombie form, is ripe for replacement; it has run out of road, and like all hegemonic regimes has now entered into a spiral of terminal decline. As historian Adam Tooze has written, in an article titled "Has Covid ended the neoliberal era?"

> seeing 2020 as a comprehensive crisis of the neoliberal era – with regard to its environmental, social, economic and political underpinnings – helps us find our historical bearings. Seen in those terms, the coronavirus crisis marks the end of an arc whose origin is to be found in the 70s.
>
> *(Tooze, 2021)*

In this situation, of neoliberalism itself in crisis in the midst of a host of other converging crises, we can usefully turn to the advice given 60 years ago by economist Milton Friedman, one of neoliberalism's godfathers, when he and other neoliberals were working to overturn the post-war hegemonic Keynesian regime.

> Only a crisis – actual or perceived – produces real change. When that crisis occurs the actions that are taken depend on the ideas that are lying around. That, I believe, is our basic function: to develop alternatives to existing policies, to keep them alive and available until the politically impossible becomes politically inevitable inevitable.
>
> *(Friedman, 1962/1982, p. ix)*

The crisis, or rather crises, are now upon us, they are occurring. The challenge today, therefore, is to work on alternative ideas and alternative policies, only this time to overturn and replace neoliberalism, a prospect which seems to be moving from the status of "politically impossible" to that of "politically inevitable." And to do so in an inclusive and democratic way, enabling widespread participation by citizens.

In my view (and I readily acknowledge other views exist), this process of building alternative ideas and policies means working to develop a public system of early childhood education, fully integrated and based on democratic and solidaristic values and on an ethics of care and an ethics of an encounter (see Dahlberg & Moss, 2005 for a fuller discussion of these relational ethics). It means working on and declaring new images of the child, the parent, the worker and the early childhood centre, images based on citizenship and rights, protagonism and potentiality. It means working on forms of social governance, which starts from analysing and refining the meaning and application of key concepts such as "public" and "democratic accountability." It means working on and propagating new rationales for early childhood education, rationales that are no longer dependent on naïve economic claims of the "story of quality and high returns" variety. And, of course, it means working on the meaning of "education," for example revisiting the German concept of *Bildung* discussed in this book, and also on what pedagogy will best enable that education (for a fuller discussion of this sketchy outline, see Moss & Cameron, 2020).

This building work does not need to take place in isolation or to start from scratch. It can draw on rich, existing resources. It can and should be in dialogue with others in different fields who share a common agenda: for example, if the sort of system touched on above requires a process of de-privatisation and de-marketisation of early childhood education, in other words the de-commodification of early childhood education, we should not only be sharing ideas and experience with others in our field, but going beyond to exchange with others who are seeking to de-privatise and de-marketise other services and utilities (see, for example, the Public Futures website – publicfutures.org – with its International Database of De-privatised Public Services[2]). But nearer to home, it can and should be drawing on the ideas and experience of those who are already contesting and resisting neoliberalism in early childhood education, whether it be by researching, writing, networking – or through providing innovative alternatives to existing policies and services.

Which is the right place to hand over from the author of one book contesting and resisting neoliberalism to the authors of another, to tell their alternative stories of challenge and resistance to the commodification of early childhood education and care.

Notes

1 I choose the term "early childhood education," rather than "early childhood education and care" because I consider education to be the main (though not the only) purpose of early childhood services and that care, understood as an ethic, should be an integral and essential part of all education (and other public) services; as the editors of this volume write, "we feel that there is an urgent need to centre care in ECE spaces." So, this means every service inscribed with care, and not separate "childcare services for working parents," a term and concept that has lent itself to the commodification of services; as the editors of this volume again write, "[c]reating spaces where children are physically safe is theoretically more congruent with the marketisation/commodification of childcare than the idea of ensuring that children have rich, meaningful, and caring pedagogical experiences."
2 "Services like water, energy, healthcare and education build the foundation for healthy, just and sustainable communities. All over the world, citizens, public authorities and labour unions have been mobilising to bring these vital services and infrastructures back into public hands. Putting social needs and community wealth ahead of financial profit, diverse forms of public organisation are emerging to provide public services in sustainable, democratic and affordable ways. This is an open and interactive space for creating and exchanging knowledge on Public Futures."

1
ON COMMODIFICATION AND DECOMMODIFICATION

Michel Vandenbroeck, Joanne Lehrer, and Linda Mitchell

An explanation of terms and background

A variety of terms are used to describe the early childhood care and education (ECEC) and the childhood practitioner, and these vary across countries. We commonly refer to ECEC as an umbrella term for all provisions that address the care and the education of children before compulsory school age. When speaking about the practitioners, we use terms that are common in each country context, and are used by country authors. These are early childhood educator (for instance in Canada), teacher or worker or educator (in the US), childcare pedagogue (in Denmark), teacher or kaiako (in New Zealand). These terms are used interchangeably. The term "assistant" is used in some countries for staff in ECEC who do not hold an ECEC qualification. For general discussion, we use the term "practitioner" or "worker."

In many countries, especially in the affluent world, institutional child care was first introduced in the late 19th and early 20th centuries as a form of charity. Consequently, child care was in the hands of charitable upper class organisations, either philanthropies organised by factory owners during the first industrial revolution, faith-based organisations, or charitable organisations for colonial urban poor. In many cases, child care remained a "necessary evil" for a female labour force living in most precarious conditions (Vandenbroeck, 2006). In the 1960s and even more so in the 1970s, feminist movements successfully fought for child care in order to support women's participation in the paid workforce, arguing for ECEC as a high quality and publicly funded provision for all, rather than a private charity. Since then, the organisation of the care and the education of young children has been constructed through various differing narratives, as diverging policies have been put in place. In Sweden, for instance, ECEC from birth to compulsory school age became one integrated – mostly public – provision and an entitlement for every child and family. Sweden was the first country to consider child care a right for all children and thus as a responsibility of the State. In many other countries, a split remained between child care for the youngest children (usually under age 3) and preschool for older children (often from 3 to compulsory school age) and much of the provision remained organised by private and community-based organisations for many decades. Private organisations may be for profit (e.g. in the UK and the US), while community-based and faith-based provisions usually are not for profit. The extent to which ECEC is considered a public service for families (and thus a responsibility of public authorities and publicly funded) or a more private commodity (and thus a parental responsibility and funded through charities or private funding) has historically always been related to more general conceptions of the welfare state. In more liberal welfare states, ECEC has traditionally been more of a private than a public responsibility, while social-democratic conceptions have a longer tradition of ECEC as a public responsibility. Communist and socialist countries also conceptualised child care as a State responsibility, and have a long history of public ECEC. Conservative or corporatist welfare states have adopted a somewhat in-between policy, with large proportions of ECEC run by private non-profit organisations that are to some – varying – extent funded with public means (Esping-Andersen, 2009). In all cases, the traditional patriarchal concept of the family with a male breadwinner and a female caregiver has become obsolete and ECEC is seen as both a means to ensure women's access to the paid labour market and as necessary for children's optimal development, indeed as a human right. However, the debate with regards to the extent to which child care should be an individual familial responsibility, and therefore a private commodity, or an essential universal provision, and therefore a public good, remains salient, especially in relation to policy in countries without a universal public ECEC system. Neoliberal ECEC policies have also influenced the way that ECEC is conceptualised and carried out.

Over the past 20 years, ECEC has been commodified and privatised at an unprecedented pace. Remarkably, this has been the case across both liberal and social democratic welfare states, and in countries with differing ECEC models, be it in diverging and often hybrid ways. Globally, the market is increasingly believed to be a more efficient provider of ECEC than governments, despite a growing body of evidence to the contrary. Depending on a country's historical, cultural, political, and geographical situation, the impact of neoliberalism on ECEC may be different. Yet privatisation, marketisation, commodification or corporatisation seem to be concepts that describe changes in the ECEC field over the last two decades in every continent.

The concepts of privatisation, marketisation, commodification, and corporatisation are interrelated, but need to be disentangled. By *privatisation*, we mean the process by which early childhood education and care provision is increasingly organised by private providers, with less public provision, or regulation by public authorities (be it local, regional or national authorities). Privatised ECEC may be managed by for-profit providers (small businesses as well as large corporate organisations), faith-based NGOs or other non-profit organisations. When the process of privatisation also includes a growing share of ECEC in the hands of for-profit providers, this is labelled as *marketisation*: the process by which an increasing number of childcare or early education spaces is organised as for-profit businesses, be they independent ECEC centres or large multinational childcare chains. As Farris and Marchetti (2017, p. 114) note, "The process of marketization of care can be regarded as the intensification of dynamics that had been set in motion by care commodification: both spring from the neoliberal reconfiguration of the role of the state as one that ensures the functioning of markets, and the transformation of citizens into consumers individually responsible for their care needs."

The argument for the process of marketisation is the expectation that the market will create better incentives for providers to offer parents more choice, competitive pricing and good quality. It is expected that competition will lead to a better balance between service supply and demand, to better value for money and that parents will choose services that are good quality. In many countries, the (partial or total) shift from supply-side funding to demand-side funding is one of the main measures that governments take to privatise or marketise ECEC. *Supply-side funding* provides financial assistance to ECEC services meeting regulated requirements, e.g. for staffing and operation, or direct provision of ECEC. *Demand-side funding* provides financial assistance directly to service users (e.g. vouchers, tax credits or fee subsidies), who then pay the service (Cleveland & Krashinsky, 2002).

Marketisation, in addition, may take the specific form of *corporatisation*, when major multinational corporate businesses take over large parts of the childcare market, often by acquiring pre-existing smaller businesses or private services (Farris & Marchetti, 2017; Gallagher, 2018). Corporatisation may be regarded as a consolidation of privatisation and marketisation (Press & Woodrow, 2005). In that case, the shareholders may be international corporate financial or private equity groups, with particular managerial and economic approaches. For these corporate businesses to invest in child care, they expect to make a profit. The profit may come from varying sources, including restrictions of the operating costs, real estate assets, and buying and selling ECEC provision.

By *commodification*, we mean a broader trend, including the processes of privatisation and marketisation as well as other ways in which education in general and ECEC in particular are turned into a commodity. This means that education is framed in economic terminologies (supply and demand, cost-benefits, return on investment); that providers are supposed to deliver a service that is transparent and competitive; that children are framed as passive users of that service; and that parents are framed as consumers, who need to make the right choices for their children. The idea of education as a commodity is antagonistic with the concept of education as a public good (Moss, 2009) and with the concept of care (Richardson, 2021). Commodification affects not only financial and managerial aspects of ECEC but also the way that services are organised for children, focusing on activities that are considered productive for their future economic contribution to society, and rigid time management that satisfies parents, as consumers, and reassures them that their investments are accounted for. This productivity imperative leads to a loss of sense in practice or to a sense-less standardisation (Valentim, 2016). Commodification is one of the salient ways by which the economy penetrates all other domains in the context of neoliberalism (Roberts-Holmes & Moss, 2021). According to Lamont and Pierson (2019), commodification involves the transformation of resources that were once provided as public goods into ones available only as purchasable commodities. In a context of rising economic inequality, commodification can play a significant role in spreading inequality to other domains. According to Richardson (2021, p. 6), "Care is commodified in a way that serves the interests of already privileged individuals/groups/companies while systematically excluding others from sociopolitical life." By gradually magnifying the implications of these income disparities for life chances and well-being, commodification processes can greatly intensify the long-term implications of purely economic inequality.

Commodification can take very different forms and is not limited to the privatisation or marketisation of ECEC. One example is the Finnish *kotihoidontuki* (Child Home Care Allowance) that can be used by parents who decide not to send their children to ECEC. Despite rendering (often mothers') care work at home visible, in practice, the Child Home Care Allowance paradoxically individualises parental responsibility for maintaining a balance between family life and employment. It reinforces the idea that attaining that difficult balance between one's role as a parent, as a citizen, as an individual with dreams and needs, as a partner, and as a career person is a strictly private matter. However, decisions in this vein run along socio-economic lines and the Child Home Care Allowance has contributed to enhancing the educational gap as well as gender and other inequalities in the labour market (Terävä, Kuukka, & Alasuutari, 2018). Another example of commodification is the growth of market-driven preschool programmes, often elaborated in the US and other affluent Western countries and increasingly being franchised in the global South. These programmes are not only an expression of the commodification of pedagogy, but also export a particular developmentalist image of the active, liberal, and rational child and of what ECEC is (Adriany, 2017), rendering race-, class- and gender-based privilege invisible (Smith, Tesar & Myers, 2017). It can be argued that the commodification of early childhood education and care also functions as a form of governance that produces a particular childhood as an investment (that needs to be made profitable by the right parental decisions), with particular values (of individual happiness and success) that need to be invested in (Vintimilla, 2014). In that vein, pedagogical approaches, or programmes, such as "Montessori" or "Reggio," have become a label and a marketing instrument to promote one's "business" (Newberry, 2010), rather than a search for democratic education and a basis for experimentation.

The *glocal* practice of commodification

Commodification can be identified in multiple global contexts. For example, in 2000, the Australian Child Care Benefit introduced a demand-side subsidy to parents that flowed directly to the centre attended by their child, and in so doing, supported the introduction of larger for-profit providers, often taking over smaller childcare businesses (Sumsion, 2013). California's welfare reform program of 1997 also reinforced a voucher system, allowing more poor families to access child care, yet directing public money to license-exempt providers, with less stringent quality standards than the childcare services that were funded directly by the California Department of Education. A study conducted in 2006 on the consequences of this policy revealed lower qualifications and higher staff turnover in the voucher programs, compared to the programs that were funded directly (Whitebook, Kipnis, & Bellm, 2007). In Quebec, since 2003, new legislation has facilitated private child care through subsidising private ECEC services and a tax relief for parents using unsubsidised private care arrangements was established in 2008 (CRRU, 2021). These policies wished to compensate for the lack of available places in the public *Centres de la petite enfance*. Studies in 2003 and 2014 revealed that the quality of private for-profit services and the working conditions in those contexts are lower than in the public and cooperative services (Bellemare, 2019; ISQ, 2004; ISQ, 2015). In the Netherlands, from 2005, the Dutch Childcare Act profoundly reorganised child care. Funding shifted from supply-side funding through the local authorities to demand-side funding through employers and tax reductions, resulting in a substantial increase in market approaches and the advent of corporate business (Akgunduz & Plantenga, 2014). Between 2003 and 2010, the share of non-profit providers in the Netherlands diminished from 60% to 30% and has continued to decrease ever since. It has been documented that both staff satisfaction and process quality are lowest in the corporate childcare sector and highest in value-driven non-profit organisations (Van der Werf, Slot, Kenis & Leseman, 2020). It has also been documented that the inclusion of children living in more vulnerable situations and respect for diversity are more problematic in Dutch corporate child care compared to not-for-profit provision (Romijn, 2021). Facing the many difficulties and abuse related to the demand-side funding, the Dutch government that took office in 2021 expressed its ambition to return at least in part to supply-side funding. In Hong Kong, the chief executive of the Hong Kong Government announced the introduction of a voucher system in 2006, leading to increased market participation in early childhood settings (Yuen, 2013). The same year, the British Child Care Act made local authorities the "last resort" in organising child care in the UK, to be turned to only when private providers do not deliver (Penn, 2013). In Finland, since the enforcement of the *Act on Service Vouchers in Social Welfare and Health* (569/2009) in 2009, many municipalities have begun to provide ECEC vouchers for families to pay for private child care. As a result, the private ECEC sector has expanded significantly, especially during the past decade, and now accounts for 17% of all ECEC provision (Ruutiainen, Alasuutari, & Karila, 2019).

Commodification has also had an impact in countries that were believed to be immune to privatisation, such as France. In her well-documented 2013 book on childcare markets, Eva Lloyd (2012) described France as a country with 60 years of state-funded and state-provided ECEC and therefore resistant to the trend of commodification. One year later, Lloyd and Penn (2014) reaffirmed that the French system illustrates how direct public funding and stringent regulation may counter the childcare market's potentially negative aspects. However, between 2013 and 2017, 25% (2013) to half (2017) of the growth in childcare places is due to "micro-crèches," which are almost all private initiatives. In 2016, 58% of all newly created childcare spaces in France were in private for-profit organisations, financed through demand-side funding (called *Complément de libre choix du mode de garde, or CMG de la Paje*) rather than traditional supply-side funding (called *Prestation de Service Unique*) (Haut Conseil de la famille, de l'enfance et de l'âge, 2018). By 2021, two French private for-profit providers (People&Baby and Babilou) respectively owned 550 and 700 childcare centres and had highly influenced the governmental decisions to loosen the adult-child ratios (https://pasdebebesalaconsigne.com).

A decade ago, privatisation, marketisation and commodification of child care were typical in countries that were traditionally described as liberal welfare states, in particular in English-speaking countries such as Australia, Canada, the US, the UK, and New Zealand (Bettio & Plantenga, 2004; Gallagher, 2018; Lloyd & Penn, 2012) and countries with demand-side funding were the exception, rather than the rule in Europe (Lloyd & Penn, 2014). The examples above, among many others, show that today elements of privatisation and commodification of ECEC seem to be everywhere. The European Union strived to liberalise and privatise "Services of General Interest," so as to promote competition in the internal markets, arguing that these services are of "economic interest," and that privatisation and liberalisation will benefit "the consumer" through increased "choice." While the Child Guarantee programme of the European Commission urges its Member States to invest in ECEC between until 2030, it does not limit privatisation of the sector in any way. However, NGOs representing people living in poverty and social exclusion question who really benefits from the commodification of care services (Ünver & Nicaise, 2018). While social services of general interest (including ECEC) are explicitly exempt from regulation to promote competition (European Commission, 2012), public authorities in Europe increasingly rely on private partners for the provision of services and these services are considered to fall under the European rules of the internal market and competition more and more frequently.

One could rightly argue that commodification is a *glocal* issue: it impacts ECEC worldwide, but it does so in local ways, depending on localised histories, cultures and politics. As a result, commodification needs to be studied in glocal ways, through analysing both global tendencies and their local shapes, forms, and consequences. In several countries, in times of austerity (Lloyd & Penn, 2014), commodification has been accompanied by deregulation and lowering quality standards. To give but some examples: in France, Flanders, and California, expected staff qualifications have been lowered for private provision. In Flanders and the UK, adult-child ratios have been increased and limitations on group sizes are now more fluid in Flanders in order to enhance efficiency in the presence of restricted budgets and to make it easier for private providers to make a profit. In other countries (i.e. the Netherlands), initial quality problems have, on the contrary, led to increased state funding and stricter regulations. Nevertheless, working conditions in Dutch private for-profit centres remain worse than in value-driven NGOs (Van der Werf, 2020).

While commodification may have diverse consequences in different regions, its political rationales and legitimations are remarkably similar worldwide. It is assumed that children are the private responsibility of their parents, that parents are consumers, and that markets meet consumers' needs (Mitchell, 2012). The rationale is that the market will create better incentives for providers to offer consumers more choice and competitive pricing, leading to an acceptable level of quality and consumer satisfaction for a reasonable price. Consumers are expected to select the service that offers the best price/quality ratio, allowing the sector to adapt more quickly to changing circumstances (Plantenga, 2012). We argue that these assumptions should be understood as political ideologies, rather than as based on empirical evidence. In fact, economists as early as the 1990s have empirically demonstrated that childcare is a quite imperfect market, that parents do not behave as consumers, and that private childcare markets do not evolve towards an optimal price/quality ratio, whatever that may mean (Blau, 1991). Over the last few decades, scholars have repeatedly shown that the assumptions of rational parental choice, higher quality, or better adaptation of supply and demand are flawed and that very often commodification has resulted in lower wages and staff qualifications, changing images of children with a stronger focus on schoolification, precarious overall quality, and increased inequalities (e.g. Mocan, 2007; Moss, 2009; Sosinsky, Lord & Zigler, 2007). In the presence of a growing body of robust empirical evidence demonstrating that the assumptions underlying the childcare market are false, the continuing belief in commodification by policy makers cannot be understood other than as an ideological choice that must be debated and confronted with alternative visions for competent childcare systems.

Considering commodification as a glocal issue also means closely monitoring and analysing its impact in various parts of the world. Some countries (e.g. US, Australia, and Hong Kong) have a long tradition of liberal policies, marked by decentralisation and a plea for reduced state involvement, considering child care as the private responsibility of parents. These countries share a history of private provision. In contrast, other countries (e.g. Sweden, Denmark, Norway, and France) have a social democratic tradition in which education – including ECEC – is historically considered as a public good and where commodification is a rather recent phenomenon. Some countries (e.g. The Netherlands, Canada outside of Québec) have a tradition of one-and-a-half-earner-households, where women traditionally stayed at home or worked part time. These countries have historically only invested in child care in a very limited capacity. Yet, confronted with the demographic and social changes after the golden 1960s and 1970s, there was a need to invest in child care during periods of budgetary restrictions and therefore they turned to the market and private capital to compensate for the lack of public childcare spaces (Bettio & Plantenga, 2004).

There are many other local differences. While in some countries the shift to demand-side funding was accompanied by deregulation (e.g. France), other countries have maintained or increased central regulations on structural quality criteria (e.g. the Netherlands). To further complicate matters, in some countries, such as Brazil, a dichotomised vision of childcare commodification has emerged, where crèches are dedicated to nutrition, care, and hygiene for the children of the working class, and kindergartens are dedicated to physical, social and affective development through play, movement, and self-expression for middle-class children (Valentim, 2016). As a result, the childcare landscape is diverse and in many countries, it forms a hybrid or patchwork landscape where NGOs, public, and diverse forms of private provision co-exist (Whitty, Lysack, Lirette, Lehrer, & Hewes, 2020). Any critical analysis of the impact of commodification as well as of ways to resist its effects will need to take this diversity of contexts into account, rather than attempt to present ECEC in universal or dichotomous terms.

The concept of cultural hegemony

The neoliberal imaginary, as Roberts-Holmes and Moss (2020) labels it, is not an ideology that is purely forced upon us. The child as a future productive citizen, the practitioner as a technician, the parent as a consumer, all these images related to commodification are not just the result of some imaginary power that functions in purely coercive ways. The concepts discussed in this book are rather to be considered as co-constructed by parents, practitioners, researchers and policy makers. The concept of *cultural hegemony*, as developed by the Italian philosopher Antonio Gramsci, might help to understand the issue, as the work of Gramsci continues to be a source of inspiration for critical pedagogy (Manojan, 2019). Gramsci described cultural hegemony as the more or less "spontaneous" consent given by great masses of the population to a general direction imposed on social life by the dominant group. This consent is historically caused by the prestige – and consequent confidence – which the dominant group enjoys because of its position and function (Lears, 1985). It does not mean that ideas and worldviews are forcefully imposed. The essence of the cultural hegemony is not manipulation but legitimation. The keys to success are ideological and economic: a cultural hegemony needs a worldview that appeals to a wide range of groups within the society, and the dominant groups must be able to claim with at least some plausibility that their particular interests are those of society at large (Lears, 1985). That is exactly what the language of choice does, it is a notion that appeals to many, even when it serves the interests of some more than of others and may function as a way to perpetuate inequalities. That is why, according to Gramsci, subordinate groups may participate in maintaining a symbolic universe, even if it serves to legitimate their domination. In other words, they can share a kind of half-conscious complicity in their own victimisation. A salient example is provided by Morabito and colleagues (2016) in their study on the conceptions that parents have about equal opportunities and the role of ECEC in Mauritius. Mauritius has a long history of inequality, where social class runs along ethnic lines, shaped by French and English colonisation and immigration from Asian countries. The Creole ethnic group is descendant from slaves and remains the most marginalised group, affected by negative stereotypes. The Indo-Mauritians are descendants of indentured labourers and have moved from poverty to middle-class status. The small Chinese community is mostly self-employed as shopkeepers. The descendants of white colonial rulers are a small minority, yet constitute an economic élite. The Mauritian educational system is highly competitive and tends to polarise learning outcomes. Inequalities in school achievements are strongly related to families' socio-economic and ethnic status. Yet, when parents are interviewed about (un)equal opportunities in early childhood education, they use the language of choice and meritocracy to discuss their aspirations for their children, as if there were no structural barriers to those choices. Participants from the lower socio-economic groups were very well aware of the existence of discrimination based on ethnicity, but still individualised disadvantage as a personal parental responsibility, stating that they failed as role models for their children. While the educational system reproduces social inequalities in Mauritius, both high SES parents and low SES Creole parents adhered to the discourse on education as a social lift. In sum, they were not unaware of structural barriers, but they still individualised unequal opportunities and considered the lack of opportunities for their child(ren) as their personal responsibility. The point that Gramsci wishes to make is not fatalism. There are indeed other examples, where parents have taken the lead to contest mainstream discourses, such as kōhanga reo, Pacific ECEC centres and the playcentres in New Zealand, based on parents' aspirations and understanding of inequalities in a post-colonial context. The point Grasmci makes is that hegemonic culture depends not on the brainwashing of "the masses" but on the tendency of public discourse to make some forms of experience readily available to consciousness while ignoring or suppressing others (Lears, 1985).

> Everyone has a number of "conceptions of the world," which often tend to be in contradiction with one another and therefore form an incoherent whole. Many of these conceptions are imposed and absorbed passively from outside, or from the past, and are accepted and lived uncritically. In this case they constitute what Gramsci calls "common sense" (or, in another

context, "folklore"). Many elements in popular common sense contribute to people's subordination by making situations of inequality and oppression appear to them as natural and unchangeable … It is contradictory—it contains elements of truth as well as elements of misrepresentation—and it is upon these contradictions that leverage must be obtained in a "struggle of political hegemonies."

(Forgacs, 2000, p. 421)

Gramsci realised that every language contains the elements of a conception of the world and that is particularly the case for the language of choice that is inherent to the commodification of ECEC. The available vocabulary helps mark the boundaries of permissible discourse, discourages the clarification of social alternatives, and makes it difficult for the dispossessed to locate the source of their unease, let alone remedy it (Lears, 1985, pp. 569–570). The words, ideas, values, and experiences of dominant groups are validated in public discourse; those of subordinate groups are not, though they may continue to thrive beyond the boundaries of the dominant opinion. This is in line with what Bourdieu and Passeron (1970) labelled as *institutional violence* when they analysed how the educational system reproduces the social order: the ways in which some experiences, values, and meaning-making are presented as self-evident and valid for all (i.e. what knowledge is scholarly knowledge, what behaviours are acceptable for a student, how parents need to relate to teachers). Bourdieu and Passeron stressed that subordinate groups may accept these norms and values as their own, interiorise them and – by doing so – interiorise their own oppression. Core to this internalised oppression or cultural hegemony is the individualisation of educational responsibilities, that is contingent upon the figure of the entrepreneurial self and consumer choice.

As Press and Woodrow (2005) argue, the commodification of child care reinscribes democracy as consumer choice and erodes the concept of child care as a public good and collective responsibility. This process masks the need to ask critical questions about the fundamental values ECEC should embrace, prioritises business principles of profitability and efficiency, and replaces the image of children as active and competent citizens to objects of social policy and consumer services. It also replaces the image of parents from citizens to consumers, and of educators as professionals with agency engaged in relational practice to employees fulfilling requirements to "make children's learning and/or development visible to others (parents, funders, governments, etc.) in a way consistent with the neoliberal ideals of efficiency and accountability" (Richardson, 2021, p. 8). In many countries, the global Covid-19 pandemic has led to an acknowledgement of social and educational services, including ECEC, as essential services, and to the creation of free, public, 24-hour childcare for other essential workers seemingly overnight (Bezanson, Bevan, & Lysack, 2020). More time and research is needed to understand how the pandemic impacts commodification or decommodification of ECEC in the post-pandemic era. A fine-grained examination of the micro and macro politics involved in the commodification of children's day-to-day realities in ECEC contexts will shed light on the problems and processes inherent in this disturbing trend. However, it is equally important to insist on the fact that commodification of ECEC is not inevitable, and that our purpose for illuminating it is also to better equip ourselves and others to resist it. Therefore, it is equally important to share examples of resistance to the commodification of ECEC.

Resistance and counter-hegemonies

The main focus of this book is not so much the commodification of ECEC but rather the necessary resistance against this cultural hegemony. It is the search for alternatives, for diverse forms of decommodification or counter-hegemonies, in the terminology of Gramsci.

Our use of the term *decommodification* is broad in that we include the various movements of resistance that refuse the neoliberal claim that there is no alternative to commodification. It is the process of change, often from the bottom up, sometimes driven by progressive policy makers, invigorated by grass-root organisations, by alliances among parents, or between parents and professionals, by scholars who embrace democracy, by individual practitioners, by researchers who document and study alternatives, by various advocates and organisations who make it clear that there are other stories to be told and by political actors who refuse the one-size-fits-all approach to ECEC and develop ways to revive the public responsibility for the care and the education of young children. It is these voices that are central in this book.

The book presents three mains sections that document the impact of commodification on three distinct but interrelated protagonists: children, parents and professionals. The first section explores how commodification leads to an understanding of children as tied to a market economy, positioning them as passive vessels, learning subjects, as at-risk and as risky, and finally as human capital. These understandings of children are tied to historic understandings of who and what child care is for. We trace the development of child care for "vulnerable" and "troubled" children and mothers; as an instrument of cultural assimilation; as gardens for the romantic blossoming of middle- and upper-class children; and as economic investments for nation states. The recent focus on child care as an economic investment has led to technologies of surveillance and control, standardised assessment and quality measurement, as well as daily video surveillance, commercialised and globalised curricula. Case studies provide examples of resistance at multiple levels, from individual children resisting conformity at an Australian daycare centre, over examples from Norway, Nigeria and Indonesia, to Maori kōhanga reo as a culturally affirming community alternative to for-profit childcare, and the use of Islamic religious discourse to counter a neoliberal colonial view of child care in Indonesia. These examples challenge what some have come to understand as the foundation and justification of ECEC, providing inspiration and hope that ECEC can be a reciprocal, responsive, and valuable process of meaning-making and relationships.

A second section investigates the impact of commodification on parents. It critically examines what it means when parents are reconfigured as consumers. It first argues that the empirical evidence does not concur that parents can act as critical consumers as there is hardly any relation between parental preferences and appreciations and what experts would label as "quality." It then continues to argue why parents also should not be viewed as consumers. Based on concrete examples from Flanders, Finland and Hong Kong, we argue that the concepts of parental choice and commodification increase structural inequalities and at the same time tend to blame the victims for these inequalities. More importantly, the section shows that alternative stories are possible. The interesting concept of social governance in Italian ECEC is explained in its historical and actual context. The case of Hong Kong shows that civil action and advocacy can turn the tide and move early childhood education away from a market towards a more public policy, where finances shift back from demand-side to supply-side-funding. The study of community-based early childhood centres in Chile shows that values of solidarity and cooperation can entail very different conceptions of child care, be they public or private. France has a long tradition of a sustainable network of parent-led childcare initiatives that also functions as an important social actor critically involved in advocacy when it comes to family policies.

The third section looks at what commodification and decommodification may mean for the workforce. It argues that images of the ECEC workforce are entangled with dominant constructions of the purposes of ECEC and the ways in which ECEC is organised, funded and provided. It shows that historical divides between notions of care and education have perpetuated splits in the composition of the workforce and in pay, employment conditions and qualification requirements that favour educators working in settings deemed to offer "education." It then analyses international data about pay and employment conditions of ECEC educators, arguing that further factors contributing to differentials and inequities are ownership (public, community not-for-profit, and private for-profit), levels and delivery of government funding, regulations and bargaining arrangements. A main argument is that commodification and privatisation compete with and override democratic goals that are in the best interests of ECEC participants and locally constructed aspirations for a "good" education. Educators are alienated by commodification to become what Peter Moss (2006) has termed "technicians," producers of predetermined outcomes that attract economic returns, within systems of over-prescribed curriculum, assessment and accountabilities. What is valued lies at the heart of resistance, illustrated in stories from Ontario, US, Aotearoa New Zealand, and Denmark. Within all the acts of resistance, educators played a leading role, as people in daily contact with children and families and who understood the complexity and demands of their work. The case of Ontario shows the value of a professional association of educators to enable social linking and individual empowerment, critical analysis of oppressive structures and practices, and organised action for transformative change. In the US, where privatisation and marketisation are at an extreme, it was educators acting collectively in the Worthy Wage Campaign who engendered public discussion and awareness of "quality" ECEC, and educator pay and working conditions, and measures needed to improve these. Cases in Aotearoa New Zealand and Denmark illustrate the power of educators working through their unions and in alliances with others – parents, researchers, community organisations – to advocate for equitable pay and employment conditions, and through considered research and analysis, to promote the role of the state in ECEC provision and educator employment negotiations. Individual acts of resistance were also discussed in this section, illustrating the barriers and affordances of organisational systems at a local level.

Each of these sections considers both the global and the local. Each contains a theoretical introduction on the global aspects of how commodification affects (and is affected by) respectively children, parents and the workforce, illustrated by empirical studies, conducted in different parts of the world. These sections were fuelled by experts from these regions in close collaboration with the editors of the book. In addition, each section illustrates alternative stories of challenge and resistance to the commodification of ECEC, illustrated by concrete examples of how governments, unions, or grassroot organisations in different continents have created alternative realities. While these examples are embedded in specific local contexts, they may serve as inspiration to reimagine and reinscribe ECEC as a public good.

Together, the alternatives show the many possible faces of counter-hegemonies. Gramsci explained that what is usually considered as common sense is far from being consensual and that in the internal inconsistencies of the dominant discourse lay the possibilities to develop counter-hegemonies. In Chapter 4, we theorise the necessity and feasibility for these counter-hegemonies to arise, be they in the form of individual micro-resistances or in a collective urge for alternatives.

A final discussion analyses broader issues of impacts on local communities and societies at large, including issues of inclusion, social cohesion, democracy and equity. It explores what can happen when the importance of a collective whole is reinvigorated with a focus on rights and democratic participation through collective action.

2
RESISTING CHILDREN AS HUMAN CAPITAL

Joanne Lehrer, Brooke Richardson,
Michel Vandenbroeck, and Linda Mitchell

With the collaboration of:

Vina Adriany, Royne K. Berget, Hoana McMillan,
Esther Oduolowu, and Kylie Smith

Introduction

The commodification of early childhood education and care (ECEC) impacts children's daily experiences in a number of ways. First, it leads to conceptualisations of children and childhood that are tied to the idea of a market economy and positions children as future human capital. The human capital discourse, or the idea that children's value is commensurate with their future economic outputs to society, has become increasingly pronounced over the past 30 years. Neoliberal values driving commodification (hyperindividualism and market logic) have and continue to position children and the adults who care for them as technocratic mechanisms for furthering economic growth. These images of children as human capital lead to discourses that rationalise ECEC as a commodity. Commodifying care (and education) also brings with it the very real possibility that children, and their subjective experiences, are overtly ignored, becoming an afterthought rather than central to childcare policy and practice. Yet, there are a number of ways that children, educators, and parents practically resist these conceptualisations and act to decommodify ECEC on a daily basis. This chapter explores the impacts of commodification on our images of children and childcare, and explores alternative theoretical conceptions of ECEC that have been articulated in Australia, Aotearoa/New Zealand, Indonesia, Nigeria, and Norway.

Part I: dominant conceptualisations of children and childcare in increasingly commodified contexts

Conceptions of children and childhood

The sociology of childhood posits that childhood is continually "constructed and reconstructed both for children and by children" (Prout & James, 2015, p. 7).

Childhood is a social institution, and the way we understand what it means to be a child is culturally situated and specific, as much as it is based on universal biological facts (Prout & James, 2015). Recent theorizing of children and childhood has problematized a number of different images used to situate children within a commodified market approach to ECEC: the child as passive object (Roberts-Holmes & Moss, 2021); the child as learning subject (Adriany, 2018); the child in need of saving (Bloch, Holmlund, Moqvist, & Popkewitz, 2003; Newberry, 2017); the child as risk to society (Newberry, 2017); and the child as future tool to improve the nation's economy (Langford et al., 2017; Lightfoot-Rueda, 2018). This section will consider each of these images, before presenting an example of how Australian children conform to and resist the moulding of their identities in relation to these images, performing as political actors in strategic ways. While the Australian case presents children as plural, recognizing individuality and diversity, the images of children within human capital discourse presents the child as singular, normative, static, and universal. Below we elaborate on these conceptualisations of children and childhood that underscore the dominant human capital discourse that has come to commodify children and childhood.

The child as passive vessel

Roberts-Holmes and Moss (2021) explain that when childcare is conceived as a business transaction between parents (consumers) and caregivers (providers of a commodity), children are positioned as the passive objects of these transactions. They are a thing "to be cared for, to be acted upon, to be a source of future human capital and profit, and whose interests are secondary to those of the parent-consumer and the business-provider" (p. 111). This conceptualisation also positions the passive child as the recipient of services intended to produce predetermined outcomes, leading to a level playing field, each child prepared for school and for later economic success in a standardised and uniform way. For these passive children to achieve the outcomes that have been determined for them, they must be regulated, governed, made to conform, and to learn and develop in a specific way.

The child as learning subject

The child as learning subject has been explored by Adriany (2018) and Newberry (2017) as "active, liberal and rational" (Adriany, 2018, p. 94) and as an "empowered, self-directed learner" (Newberry, 2017, p. 77). In this conceptualisation, childhood is universal and "normal" children all follow the same developmental path (Burman, 2008; Cannella & Viruru, 2005). This image of the child pathologises both children in the global South, who are seen as less developed than children in the Global North (Adriany, 2018; Penn, 2011), and children in the Global North who are members of marginalised communities (Heydon & Iannacci, 2008). The child as learning subject actively pursues their education "under the watchful eyes of experts" (Newberry, 2017, p. 78). This surveillance requires interventions, including "developmentally appropriate" practice and play-based learning to transform children into empowered learners. According to Newberry (2017), "play and play-based education are precursors to commodity consumption" (p. 78). The learning child is an independent individual, making choices and bettering him or herself in preparation for adult life in a neoliberal society.

The child in need of saving

The image of the empowered learning child can be contrasted with the traumatised child (Newberry, 2017) or the disadvantaged child in need of saving (Bloch, Holmlund, Moqvist, & Popkewitz, 2003). Programmes designed to provide means to identify and deal with trauma, developmental delays, or other deficiencies position children as in need of saving from potential negative outcomes related to the sociodemographic contexts of their families and communities (i.e. Heberle & Carter, 2020; Taylor et al., 2020; Zeraatkar et al., 2020) or from trauma related to war, natural disasters, poverty, and abuse (Newberry, 2017). Terms and phrases such as "early intervention," "critical periods," and "the years before five last the rest of their lives" support a moral panic and time-sensitive imperative to intervention, with children as innocent victims of adult incompetence. Early childhood educators are shaped by this conception as they come to understand their role as "optimizing children," to save them from their parents (who are assumed to be incapable of ensuring the attachment necessary for optimal brain development) and to justify often invasive and disrespectful interventions (Gillies, Edwards, & Horsley, 2017).

The child as risk to society

Children, typically from low-income backgrounds, are not only positioned as "at-risk," they are also positioned as a source of risk to society. Authors such as Bernazzani, Côté, and Tremblay (2001), Piquero, Farrington, Welsh, Tremblay, and Jennings (2009), and Teymoori et al. (2018) blame "poor parenting skills," as well as parents' age, level of formal education, family structure, and income for disruptive behaviours in early childhood that are theorised to lead to delinquent and criminal behaviours in adolescence, such as "violent crime, school maladjustment and school failure, alcohol and drug abuse, and social maladjustment" (Teymoori et al., 2018, p. 2). To protect society from these dangerous children, they need to be enclosed in various institutions, "from juvenile courts to social service agencies" (Newberry, 2017, p. 82). In this model, risk is conceptualised as a result of individual choice (Newberry, 2017). Therefore, if only parents made better choices, the child would be able to contribute to society instead of threatening it.

The child as future tool to improve the nation's economy

This conceptualisation values children as an economic investment. As Vandenbroeck (2020) describes, the Heckmanization of ECEC refers to "the reduction of meaning of early childhood education to its econometric dimensions" (p. 188).

According to Roberts-Holmes and Moss (2021), "Once we begin to [...] value them in terms of the return they represent on investment, then we risk losing sight of their intrinsic value, their rich and varied potential, their humanity" (p. 111–112). This investment logic is directly tied to the commodification of childcare, as it is not viewed as a public good, like universal public elementary (primary) education, but as belonging to the private sphere (Langford et al., 2017). This image of the child as an investment in the future leaves no space for children's subjectivity in the here and now – only a projection of what they can or *should* be, as defined in economic terms.

These various problematic conceptualizations of children dominate ECEC policy, media, and public discourse. Yet, they co-exist alongside images of competent, agentic, capable child-citizens often presented in curriculum frameworks and within the field of Child Studies. In fact, it is not uncommon for a human capital discourse to be used at a public policy level to justify ECEC funding while other public policy documents – particularly those related to curriculum and the daily practice of ECEs – embrace the agent, capable, knowledgeable child. Daily interactions in childcare centres are not immune to these discourses, they shape how educators and parents view ECEC and distort and narrow possibilities for children. Perhaps what is least considered amidst the widely accepted language of human capital in relation to young children are the consequences for the children themselves. The various conceptualizations described above strip children of their agency and power to position and define themselves. Children's relational experiences in the here-and-now are either absent or given tokenistic representation at a public policy level. Not surprisingly, this has immediate, negative consequences for children in ECEC settings (Langford & Richardson, 2020). The following case illustrates an alternative vision, exploring how Australian children conform to and resist the moulding of their identities during a game of cards in the book corner.

Resisting neoliberal belongings, beings, becomings in Australian early childhood classrooms

Kylie Smith

Developmental ideologies and neoliberal education policies shape how children are seen, listened to, assessed, and reported on, in and out of the early childhood classroom. In Australia, young children are positioned as commodities of the state that require quality early childhood education to ensure that they are productive future national and global citizens who will contribute to the economy and growth of the nation (Moss, 2014; Smith, Tesar, & Myers, 2016). When children sit outside white Western developmental norms, interventions are planned and clinical discourses are "administered" to ensure children reach their "full" potential through the achievement of developmental milestones. In Australia, the preschool period has been a site for neoliberal education policies since 2007 with Price Waterhouse Coopers and The Front Project's (2019) reporting on the "returns" for "smart" investment from a business model:

> Australia's current federal, state, and territory early childhood education policy supports all children to attend an early childhood program in the year before school. The analysis found this policy provides a significant return on investment (ROI) of 1:2. The evidence indicates for every dollar invested now, Australia receives $2 back over a child's life. This is a higher return than many infrastructure projects that are essential to support a growing population and sustain a competitive Australia.
>
> *(p. 3)*

One of the ways the government has invested in the early years was the development of the first national early childhood framework. *Belonging, Being and Becoming: The Early Years Learning Framework for Australia* (EYLF) (Department of Education, Employment and Workplace Relations (DEEWR), 2009). The EYLF identifies learning outcomes that frame the development of curriculum, assessment, and reporting which is monitored through the National Quality Framework and asks educators to support the development of children's strong sense of identity as one of the learning outcomes.

But what does belonging and identity mean in an Australian context? Entanglements of identity, belonging, being, becoming, voice, and agency are twisted within white developmental discourses that shape and squeeze children into assimilation and performances of conforming to be the good subject, the successful and competent child and future adult. This vignette will explore ways that children conform to and resist the moulding of identities and subjects, and perform as political actors in strategic ways. To recognize and respect alternative ways that children perform childhood, adults must rethink the taken-for-granted truths of developmentalism and children as future citizens who are the nation's future capital to invest in. One way to begin this reconceptualizing journey is to consider what Dahlberg (2003) calls the ethics of an encounter, where children are listened *to* and *with* differently, and where adults are open to learn from children and consider how their own biases mark children as other when they deviate from the neoliberal norm.

Cheating at cards

Cheating at Cards is an encounter that occurred in a 3- to 5-year-old preschool room called Spider Room in an Australian long daycare centre. The encounter created opportunities for me to think rhizomatically, to deterritorialize developmental truths, and make visible the multiplicity of moments in the early childhood classroom that privilege and silence different children. Drawing on the text and multiple discourses make possible a re-encounter with the moment to create assemblages that rupture taken-for-granted truths about the child. This re-encounter maps different discourses and reconstitutes the subject to create "new lines of flight" for more socially just ways of understanding children and their sense of identity and belonging (Deleuze & Guattari, 1988). In the next section, I describe the encounter and use rhizoanalysis to explore ways of decommodifying the developmental child.

> One morning Isabel, Donald, Malcolm and Nell (pseudonyms) were playing a game of snap in the book corner with a standard pack of playing cards. Snap is a card game where children match pairs and collect cards to win the game. The player who wins all the cards wins the game.
>
> Donald places a card on top of the pile and then places his hand on it and says Snap!
>
> ISABEL: No Donald.
> DONALD: But look, it's the same.
> ISABEL: Donald can I tell you something?
>
> (Isabel becomes upset as Donald attempts to collect the pile of cards that he feels he has "won").
>
> ISABEL: D O N A L D arr arr arr (crying)
>
> Isabel reaches over to Donald to get the cards. The teacher Gemma enters the area and sits down next to Donald. Gemma looks at Isabel who explains what has happened.
>
> ISABEL: Donald um there were cards um there and then those there and you put that card on there so that's not the same is it?
> DONALD: Yes it is there were two mans.
> ISABEL: Well Donald look (she shows Donald the cards). Is that right? That's not right.
> GEMMA: Donald I didn't see what happened but the ten and the king are not the same ok? We only snap when you've got two of the same.
> ISABEL: No we're playing letters we're playing that ... Malcolm it's your turn.
> GEMMA: Ok Isabel explain to Donald what he has to do. If you're not playing snap then I don't know what you're doing.
> ISABEL: Oh we're playing Nell...we're matching the letters (numbers).
> GEMMA: Ok so you need another king. Now why doesn't Donald have any cards Isabel?
> ISABEL: He does!
> DONALD: I do!
> GEMMA: Ok then take your cards.
> ISABEL: Ok now it's my turn because Nell had a turn.
> DONALD: No it's my turn.
>
> Donald places a card down and snaps his hands down on the cards.

ISABEL: Donald look...a three and a seven. Donald that's not right!
GEMMA: Donald, Donald...I think what Donald's...
ISABEL: Look a three and a seven.
GEMMA: Ok what you need to do is match up the numbers ok? This is a number three and that's a number seven ok? I know this one has love hearts but there are only three love hearts this one actually has seven. Ok so what you have to try doing is look for the number that is on the top there and try and match that one for a snap.

Encounters of commodification

Mapping the discourses in operation allows me to consider the commodification of childhood. This encounter highlights how adults and children operate within discourses, consciously and unconsciously taking up different subject positions to "belong" in the classroom. How might we consider Gemma coming into the game as the expert professional to teach Isabel and particularly Donald skills and knowledge within developmental theories? She supports the development of cognitive skills – one to one correspondence (*Donald I didn't see what happened but the ten and the king are not the same ok? We only snap when you've got two of the same*); numeracy – identifying numbers (*This is a number three and that's a number seven*); and social and language skills – encouraging the children to talk with each other (*Ok Isabel explain to Donald what he has to do*). How could we deconstruct the way Isabel performs "good" child by policing Donald's developmental gaps or delays in understanding the rules of the game (*Well Donald look. Is that right? That's not right*)? How does Isabel perform the apprentice interventionalist teacher explaining the rules (*...we're matching the letters (numbers)*)? What are the politics of belonging in this moment?

Returning to the encounter

Gemma moves away from the group and the card game continues. The encounter plays out, taking unexpected twists and turns. The children continue to take turns but none of the numbers match. Isabel looks at the card she is about to place down and changes the rules of the game so that her card will match with the card on the pile.

ISABEL: Ok now can we play snap of the shapes?

Nell and Donald do not reply. Isabel places her card down and snaps. Donald tries to stop Isabel from taking the cards.

ISABEL: Cause there was...cause Donald...cause do...cause Nell.
DONALD: No, I want to show you something.

Donald tries to move Isabel's hands from on top of the cards.

ISABEL: But Donald. But Donald. But Donald (her voice becomes louder).
DONALD: No these...I want to show you something.

ISABEL: Donald we're not playing the same matching Donald we're not playing the letters game.
DONALD: I want to show you something. I want to show you something.
ISABEL: (her voice is getting louder) Donald! Donald...

Gemma walks back into the area and as she walks past. I mention to her that Isabel is cheating and that she has changed the rules.

ISABEL: But Gemma we're playing now we're playing matching.

Donald lifts Isabel's hand off the cards.

DONALD: No, that's the seven.
ISABEL: We're playing matching the shapes.
GEMMA: Ok.
ISABEL: But Donald is not listening.
GEMMA: Ok Bel it's really not fair to change the rules on Donald. I sat here and I asked you what you were playing and you explained it to Donald. Do you remember that? Just a little while ago?
ISABEL: Yeah but now we're playing a different game.
GEMMA: Ok you can't just do that Bel. Donald doesn't know that you've done that. Nell doesn't know that you've done that. And that is not how Onya and I've taught you to play snap. Ok? We match the numbers or the people. Well because Bel I'll show you. In effect if you actually do match these you've got seven of spades there and you've only got five. The only way you can match that is if you find another number seven so...which means we need to find another one of that which is a spade and I don't know if there are any.
ISABEL: But Gemma you really you really...Oh yeah we've gotta do the same as that. Thanks Gemma!
GEMMA: Do you understand that?
ISABEL: Yes.
GEMMA: Ok. Donald, do you understand that?
DONALD: Yeah.
ISABEL: Ok my turn. Ok my turn.
GEMMA: Ok now what's happened Bel is you've ended up with all the cards that were here. Probably Donald's cards and your own cards so you need to split some of those please...because Donald's only got one in his hand.

Donald walks out of the area.

ISABEL: Bye then.
GEMMA: Do you think it's fair that Donald has to move out of the game Bel?
ISABEL: Yeah.

Discourse of individualism and success

Neoliberalism promotes discourses of individualism where success sits at the site of the individual person but this is complicated when individuals have competing understandings of success. Isabel was not able to find a match to win the game and changed the rules to win. What are the implications of this for Donald who learnt the rules and followed the instructions and was able to recite the rules back to Isabel - *No that's the seven*? What does Donald have to give up to continue to play the game and belong to the group? How do children navigate belonging beside or with individualism? The EYLF recognizes the importance of belonging:

> Experiencing belonging – knowing where and with whom you belong – is integral to human existence. Children belong first to a family, a cultural group, a neighbourhood and a wider community. Belonging acknowledges children's interdependence with others and the basis of relationships in defining identities. In early childhood, and throughout life, relationships are crucial to a sense of belonging. Belonging is central to being and becoming in that it shapes who children are and who they can become.
> *(Department of Education, Employment and Workplace Relations, 2009, p. 7)*

Statements such as *relationships are crucial to a sense of belonging* fail to recognize the operations of power dynamics within the classroom and their effect on children's voice and agency as they perform and silence subject positions to belong and be included in the classroom. Neoliberal agendas colonize empowerment discourses traditionally associated with student voice, in practice through the co-option of terms such as choice and empowerment to a market agenda (Nelson & Charteris, 2021, p. 214). The way children come to be understood and assessed is deeply embedded within hegemonic, neoliberal power relations which includes those who conform and excludes others. The question becomes how do we redefine the "rules" in a way that upholds more equitable power relations and therefore a more inclusive sense of belonging. Jennifer Sumsion and Sandie Wong (2011) interrogated "belonging" within the EYLF, arguing that there is a need to bring conceptual and theoretical tools to understand or gain insight into the different dimensions of belonging. Sumsion and Wong (2011) remind us that belonging is not fixed or a binary but is relational and performative, always in motion and flux. This means there can be acts of resistance, silence, inclusion, and exclusion entangled in any given moment that shift and move across the day in the classroom.

For Donald, his teachers and I had observed and documented ways that his social and emotional development impacted his interactions with others:

> Donald has difficulty in taking turns… He often forgets the rules or limits and expectations of the room. He becomes upset when consequences to not following the rules are enforced.
> *(documented teacher observation)*

How did the discourse of the delayed child make it possible for Isabel to drive her agenda to win through engaging with rules and changing them? How did this make it possible for Gemma to initially accept that Donald wasn't following the rules? And how did Isabel utilize this? Gemma asked Donald – *Ok. Donald do you understand that?* Donald did understand the rules and even when he performed the "good" child, following the rules of a developmental agenda and monitoring others' performances, his understandings were challenged and he was reinstructed.

Neoliberalism and human capital fail to recognize the political site of the early childhood classroom. How might Gemma's comment *Ok Bel it's really not fair to change the rules on Donald. I sat here and I asked you what you were playing and you explained it to Donald. Do you remember that? Just a little while ago?* on the surface be seen as an ethical encounter with children? Gemma challenges Isabel and calls out unfairness. How does Isabel avoid engagement with equity discourses through the performance of the docile child being guided by the expert teacher – *But Gemma you really you really...Oh yeah we've gotta do the same as that. Thanks Gemma!?* While the EYLF advocates for child participation and children's voices, there is a lack of theorizing of these concepts:

> Viewing children as active participants and decision makers opens up possibilities for educators to move beyond pre-conceived expectations about what children can do and learn. This requires educators to respect and work with each child's unique qualities and abilities.
> *(Department of Education, Employment and Workplace Relations, 2009, p.10)*

Part of the Australian neoliberal policy agenda is the politics of quality through the national quality standards. Quality standards provide the illusion of a neutral value free classroom where highly qualified teachers produce quality programmes which provide equal access and opportunity for all children, irrespective of gender, class, race, ethnicity, ability, and religion. If I hadn't seen Isabel "cheating," would I have assumed that Donald was being disruptive and moved him out of the area or would I have "taught" Donald the skills he needed to play the game properly? Nelson and Charteris (2021) reminds us that:

> Neoliberalism has been implicated in intensifying social injustice. Therefore, for student voice to maintain its radical social justice intent, remaining alive to its multivalences is critical.
> *(p. 227)*

Multivalences is a concept that recognizes the diverse ways that children take up and speak or perform interpretations, meanings, and values.

Donald walks away from the game with Isabel waving him off – *Bye then.* Gemma asks *Do you think it's fair that Donald has to move out of the game Bel?* Isabel responds with *Yeah.* What does fair mean in this and other moments in the classroom? Did Donald move away from the game because he had learnt that belonging in this situation was to have the rules change and for him to be silent and lose?

Did he walk away as a powerful act to disengage Isabel's control over the event and him as part of the encounter? Did Isabel take up neoliberal discourses of fairness as individual success and in this case her winning the card game? If we think about the ways power operates in multiple ways, then in this encounter you could understand Donald as disempowered and disengaged, where he has given up trying to create space to be listened to. But in the same moment you might also recognize Donald as powerful and that walking away is an act of resistance. By walking away, Donald shuts down Isabel's control of the game and chooses to move to another space.

This case study brings forward an everyday encounter to reflect on. It shows how children operate through and across discourses in powerful ways. The commodification of childhood raises questions about how children perform multiple childhoods through discourses to achieve individual success. Policy and framework documents use words or concepts like belonging, agency, voice, and participation. Within neoliberal ideologies, this translates into developmental milestones, competition, and individualism. How do teachers get drawn into these discourses that limit our opportunities to see the multiple performances of identity and the implications for belonging and social justice? How do the many children like Donald in our classrooms give up on the possibilities of belonging or accept how they are positioned so that they can belong within the discourses imposed on them?

Part II: dominant conceptualisations of childcare – what is childcare for?

Just as it is important to critically examine how children are conceptualised and to connect these ideas to broader discourses operating in, around, and through us, it is also important to reflect on how we conceptualise the purpose of childcare itself. The tension around the purpose of childcare, or organised programmes for young children without their parents/guardians present, is evident in the myriad of terms used to refer to these programmes: early childhood education; early learning; daycare; kindergarten; preschool; day nursery; educare; infant schools; playschool; and likely many others. The most widely used term, embraced by international organisations such as the Organization for Economic Community Development (OECD) and UNICEF, is early childhood education and care or ECEC. As discussed below, each of these terms emerged at a particular time and place and thus carry different thinking about the purpose of these programmes. While the terms are by no way an indication of the values an individual programme adopts, it is a helpful discursive strategy to identify the evolving thinking about the purpose of ECEC over time and across contexts. The following section will outline dominant framings of ECEC, exploring how they have emerged historically, how they are articulated in the present, and how they interact with the commodification of ECEC. These are followed by ideas that challenge and resist, indeed seek to decommodify, ECEC.

Conceptualisation 1: custodial care of vulnerable children and "troubled" mothers/families

In North America, Australia, and Western European countries, programmes that care for children in their parent/guardian's absence have historically been referred to as "daycare" or "nursery." These terms reflect a basic, custodial care approach to caring for children whereby the main goal is keeping children physically safe in their parent's absence. The purpose of the earliest childcare-like programmes in North America and Europe in the late 19th and early 20th centuries was to provide a place to "put" children (passive objects) whose mothers were unable to care for them. Programmes were typically supported through religious or philanthropic organisations, often upper/middle class, white, religious (Christian), women, who organised and provided care to children living in poverty (Atkin, 2001; Fournier, 2018; Humblet & Vandenbroeck, 2007). To access these charitable nurseries, mothers who were alive and seemingly able bodied had to be deemed "deserving" (formally or informally) of this support (for example, being widowed or sick), making it socially acceptable to abandon her primary social function as mother.

When the first organised, childcare-like programmes emerged in Western Europe and North America, there was often overlap between "daycares" and orphanages. They were simply group care settings where parents were absent – sometimes permanently and sometimes temporarily (Friendly & Prentice, 2009). Indeed, "day nurseries" have been referred to as the "compromise of the nineteenth-century ideal of mothers nurturing children at home and institutional care in an orphanage" (Prochner, 2000, p.40). Relating back to the images of the child discussed above, the child as a passive vessel in need of saving informs the "daycare/nursery" conceptualisation of childcare programmes.

While women working outside the home did become slightly more common and socially acceptable in the pre-war years as factories expanded and industrialisation/automation took hold, children attending nurseries were still the exception. Again reflecting an image of children in need of saving, "charitable" nurseries that did exist were typically located in poor, working class communities where mothers struggled to meet their children's basic physical needs (Shdaimah & Palley, 2016).

Childcare did not secure a place in the mainstream in the West until World War II. With men needed in armies, it suddenly became not only acceptable, but desirable for middle-class women to work outside of the home. For the first time in North America, governments rather than religious and/or philanthropic organisations, took the lead in organizing and funding day nurseries for the masses (Wartime Day Nurseries Act in Canada, the Lanham Act in the United States). The average, upstanding mother was no longer shamed but celebrated for working outside the home (i.e. patriotically contributing to the war effort) and offered publicly funded "day nursery" care for her children during working hours. This shift re-positioned childcare as a programme suitable for all children, not only those in need of "saving."

Interestingly, despite the social elevation of childcare programmes during the war, ECEC was largely excluded from post-war budding welfare states in wealthy English-speaking countries. Emergency funding to wartime "day nurseries" was cut in the US and Canada in 1945, sending a clear message to mothers to go home and resume their primary societal role as wife and mother.[1] In many ways, this policy move eerily foreshadowed funding to emergency childcare programmes for "essential" workers in some jurisdictions without universal public childcare provision throughout the COVID-19 pandemic. Just as with the war, once the peak of the pandemic subsided, publicly funded emergency childcare programmes for essential workers in Canada (outside of Quebec) were closed and the centres resumed their reliance on fees paid by parents (Friendly, Forer, Vickerson, & Mohamed, 2021). In both cases, significant public funds were streamed directly to childcare centres to maintain/expand operations during the apex of the crisis and then were abruptly pulled when the immediacy of the crisis subsided. The dominant conceptualisation of childcare was one of replacing maternal care so mother's (now) essential labour outside the home could be maximised. In neither of these cases was childcare about the experiences of the children, though in both cases, it did illustrate the state's potential role in ensuring children's access to childcare programmes (i.e. less about "saving" "at-risk" children and more about a necessity for all).

Though the terms "daycare" and "nursery" were abandoned in research, policy, and academic spaces decades ago, both the words and the thinking and ideological values attached to these terms persist. Much of the childcare policy discussion in the global north, and increasingly in the global south, continues to focus on children's basic physical and psychological protection/safety while their mothers are working. What has changed is that instead of children needing "saving" from their socially delinquent mothers, it is generally expected and accepted that children will spend a significant portion of their days in non-parental care.

It is also worth noting that "daycare" and "nursery" are commonly used in the everyday language of children, families, and educators in Canada, the US, and Australia. The term "daycare" is used in English in Canada, by children, parents, educators, and the general public. In Québec, the same is true of the word "*garderie*" (nursery or keep-place, care-place), which continues to be used by educators, parents, and children attending both private "*garderies éducatives*" (educational nurseries) and *centres de la petite enfance* (not-for-profit government subsidised and regulated early childhood centres). In the UK, the word "nursery" continues to be used in more formal, institutionalised spaces. For example, the Ofsted website (regulator of childcare programmes) includes "day nursery" and "nursery school" as categories of "childcare and early education." Of course, the terms "daycare" or "nursery" do not determine how programmes define themselves, or their pedagogical approach, but it is worth reflecting on where these terms came from and if/how this language continues to influence dominant societal thinking about the purpose of ECEC today.

Creating spaces where children are physically safe is theoretically more congruent with the marketisation/commodification of childcare than the idea of ensuring that children have rich, meaningful, and caring pedagogical experiences. The "product" of childcare in a market system that offers custodial-type care sets a low bar: children being physically intact at the end of the day. If the child is not injured, does not go missing, does not become ill, and/or seems reasonably unharmed, the consumer (parent) should be satisfied. Sadly, in highly marketised systems typified by unaffordably high fees and very few childcare options, parents often hope for this lack of harm. When parents cannot access or afford formal childcare programmes that are either funded and/or regulated by the state, many children end up in commodified unregulated childcare "programmes," unknown to governments or any overseer, where providers may have no experience and/or education in caring for young children – including basic health and safety. In a 7-month period spanning 2013–2014, four young children died in such settings in one Canadian city (Marin, 2014). Through a custodial care conceptualisation of caring for children, a "product" that does not deliver can be, and has been, fatal. It becomes necessary both to resist two ideas here: 1) the idea that "good" childcare means a lack of harm and 2) that there is, and can ever be, a clear commodifiable "output" of childcare at all. When we resist the latter, it becomes impossible to think about caring for children as anything but an ongoing, messy, non-linear process.

Conceptualisation 2: Cultural assimilation and "infant schools"

It has been argued that another purpose of childcare, or "output" of commodified care, has been to assimilate children into dominant cultural practices/norms. The term "infant school" originated with some of the earliest programmes for children in Europe in the eighteenth and nineteenth centuries. "School" has an undertone of formal instruction and/or immersion in didactically teaching children how they *should* be in the world. Describing one of the first "infant schools" in France in the 1700s, Prochner (2000) notes:

> The school operated on a part-time basis as an educational experiment and a mission of the church. Children were taught basic hygiene, social manners, nature studies, and such practical skills as knitting. Oberlin [Lutheran minister who opened one of the first infant schools] hoped that some of the school culture acquired by the children would be carried back into their homes to influence their parents.
>
> *(p. 25)*

In this way, it becomes apparent that some of the earliest infant "schools" were not about caring for or educating children or their parents at all but using the opportunity to assimilate both the children and their families to specific cultural and/or religious norms. Similar arguments have been made in relation to pioneering childcare programmes in North America. For example, through an examination of the West End Creche in Toronto, Canada, Atkin (2001) convincingly argues that a key purpose of childcare in the pre-war years (1920s–1940s) was to transmit "whiteness" alongside Christian ideals.

It is worth recognizing that for many years, colonised countries (such as Canada, the US, and Australia) mandated and enforced the attendance of Indigenous children at government supported and religiously run residential schools – typified by horrendous abuse, neglect, and death (Truth & Reconciliation Commission of Canada, 2015). While residential schools are not typically considered a "childcare-like" programme, they were government-funded programmes that "cared" for thousands of children, sometimes as young as 3 years old. Certainly, cultural assimilation and/or genocide in relation to Indigenous populations was very much on the minds of leaders in relation to these programmes. The purpose of residential schools was to maintain colonial, hegemonic relations in society through positioning Indigenous children as a "risk" to society.

While residential schools no longer exist (though child welfare systems have arguably picked up where they left off), colonisation through education, specifically ECEC, continues through commodified curricula grounded in human capital discourse. Standardised curricula and "intervention" programmes aimed at children and parents are big business (Roberts-Holmes & Moss, 2021). At a local level, pre-packaged curriculum aimed at "maximizing" children's potential are developed, patented, bought, sold, and applied to children (and educators). In the context of globalisation, these curricula can be viewed as a colonizing tool when programmes from wealthy English-speaking countries (e.g. the US and Australia) are implemented through World Bank initiatives into market-driven preschool programmes and non-profit NGOs in other counties (Adriany, 2018; Kennedy, 2006; Newberry, 2010; Viruru, 2005). In addition to devaluing and erasing local cultural understandings of children and their education, the imposition of a developmental view of children and the use of assessment tools based on "universal developmental norms" leads to what Penn (2011) describes as the *othering* of children in the global south, as well as any child who doesn't neatly fit within prescriptive developmental norms in the global north. This process has led to the businessification of early education, and the commodification of childhood (Viruru, 2005).

At a public policy level, governments have also entered into ECEC curriculum development, albeit often by contracting academics to write these documents. In Canada, provincial governments have recently invested significant resources into developing curriculum framework documents that conceptually challenge developmental norms and the human capital discourse. For example, New Brunswick, British Columbia, Alberta, and Ontario have all developed curriculum documents which focus on children's relationships with each other, educators, and the environment. These documents are grounded in local contexts and cultural values (Government of British Columbia, 2019; Government of New Brunswick, 2017; Government of Ontario, 2014; Makovichuk, Hewes,

Lirette, & Thomas, 2014). The material reality in these jurisdictions however is that the pedagogical practices put forward in the documents remain elusive in a field where resources are scarce. It is very difficult to ask educators to engage critically with children when there are far too many children in a room, educators have few breaks and/or planning time and recruitment and retention rates of qualified educators is a persistent challenge. In many ways, the lofty curriculum goals outlined in these well-intentioned frameworks are deceiving, as they suggest governments understand and appreciate the importance of innovative pedagogical practice, while they simultaneously erect barriers to enabling these practices. While there may be no ill intent, it is common for those writing political messaging about ECEC to be unfamiliar with the content of curriculum documents and therefore, they do not understand the structural support needed to enact ECEC pedagogy. For example, governments in Canada have done little to address the chronically low wages and poor working conditions of educators – necessary precursors to recruiting and retaining qualified educators who can meaningfully engage with critical pedagogies (AECEO, 2017).

To what extent childcare programmes and curricula "socialize" children into the dominant culture and/or serve to perpetuate the ongoing sociopolitical order today remains an important consideration. Certainly, Kylie Smith's case in the Australian context speaks to the role that childcare programmes may play in reinforcing dominant values and norms, specifically of hyperindividualism and obedience to "rules," to the occlusion of the critical examination of power relations. And of course, the more that hegemonic, neoliberal discourses are re-enforced, the more resistant they are to change. The outcome is the ongoing marketisation/commodification of childcare and other care sectors. The following case illustrates Māori resistance to colonial education in Aotearoa/New Zealand through reliance on traditional language, cultural values, and beliefs about children as powerful and in control of their destinies. This is followed by another case, presenting the role of globalised ECEC as a neoliberal and commodifying force in Indonesia, and exploring the possibility of Islamic religious discourse as a language of resistance.

Kōhanga reo

Hoana McMillan

Kōhanga reo are transformational sites symbolizing Māori resistance to Western norms and the reclamation of tino rangatiratanga (self-determination) over their lives. They were born in response to the impact of colonization that stripped Māori of their land, language, and culture. Assimilationist policies and practices aided the development of an education system that prioritized Western knowledge and values, and later demanded instruction in the English language (Simon & Smith, 2001). This colonizing mission was further supported by inflicting physical punishment on children for speaking the Māori language (Simon & Smith, 2001; Tawhiwhirangi, 2014; Walker, 2016), and in doing so, traumatized families and disrupted the intergenerational flow of the language. The enduring influence of colonization has resulted in the deficit theorizing of Māori, Māori underachievement, and the ongoing struggle for recognition of the Māori language and culture (Bishop, Berryman, Tiakiwai, & Richardson, 2003; Jackson, 2016).

By the 1970s, a new generation of Māori emerged who had experienced firsthand what it was like to live without their language, and with that loss came a burning desire to fight for it (Moon, 2013; Arapera Royal Tangaere, 2014). The catch-phrase "kei a tātou anō te ara tika" – the answers are within us – inspired Māori to take charge of their destiny, and to look to their cultural roots for solutions (Reedy, 2013). Māori language immersion from a young age was considered the best approach to language revitalization, the kaumātua (elders) remarking, "put the child to the breast and start talking Māori to the child from that point on," and that language was to be "caught not taught" (Tawhiwhirangi, 2003, p. 100). Kōhanga reo were conceived for this purpose and materialized by harnessing the collective power of whānau (Māori social networks). Kaumātua (elders) were assigned the role of teaching te reo Māori, with parents to assume responsibility for the overall operations. Hapū (sub-tribes) and iwi (tribes) were thought of in terms of providing additional resources and support to help drive the overall success of the movement (Te Kōhanga Reo National Trust, 1995). Marae (traditional housing complex) provided the opportune setting to establish kōhanga reo as they reconnected Māori with their traditional housing, land, and Māori ways of being on the land (Tawhiwhirangi, 2003). In 1982, the first kōhanga reo was established at Pukeatua Marae, Wainuiomata and by 1985, there were close to 400 in operation (Waitangi Tribunal, 2013). Kōhanga reo had become "the most vigorous and innovative educational movement" the country had seen (Reedy, 2013, p. 45). Importantly, kōhanga reo belonged to Māori and showed that Māori could rally together to make decisions for themselves (Arapera Royal Tangaere, 1997a).

Government intervention during these early years was minimal until kōhanga reo were brought under the Ministry of Education where there were clear indications of desires to have influence over them. As part of this move, kōhanga reo were now subject to the Early Childhood Regulatory Framework which focused on the administration, curriculum, and the health and wellbeing of children based on Western perspectives (Arapera Royal Tangaere, 2012; Education Review Office, 1997). The development of a bicultural early childhood curriculum *Te Whāriki* (Ministry of Education, 1996) provided the opportunity to reaffirm kōhanga reo objectives. However, government policies continued to place strain on the relationship with kōhanga reo. For example, lower funding rates forced many whānau and kaiako to leave the movement (Arapera Royal Tangaere, 2012). Government reports also tarnished the kōhanga reo reputation through classifications of it as a low-quality provider (Waitangi Tribunal, 2013). Kōhanga reo pushed back by lodging an urgent claim with the Waitangi Tribunal[2] citing ongoing prejudice by the government to undermine the objectives of kōhanga reo. The outcome of the Tribunal hearing ruled in favour of kōhanga reo and made recommendations for better policy alignment and support.

Despite the challenges endured by the kōhanga reo movement, it has remained committed to providing quality Māori immersion opportunities for children and families. The philosophy of kōhanga reo remains focused on Māori language and culture, strengthening the mana (prestige) of Māori, and encouraging tino rangatiratanga (self-determination) over their lives (Mitchell, Royal Tangaere, Mara & Wylie, 2006). These fundamental beliefs are firmly entrenched in the four pou (posts) or cornerstones of the movement which are: the Māori language and culture; family involvement in decision-making and management; accountability to the children, each other, and to the movement; and the well-being of children and their families. At a national level, Te Kōhanga Reo National Trust has developed support systems for those involved in the day-to-day running of kōhanga reo including courses that aid Māori language development and resources to guide curriculum delivery (Te Kohanga Reo National Trust, n.d).

Te whāriki a te kōhanga reo

In 2017, a review of the early childhood curriculum resulted in a separate curriculum for kōhanga reo entitled *Te Whāriki a te Kōhanga Reo* (Ministry of Education, 2017). This shift acknowledged the right of kōhanga reo to approach learning and development differently from their early childhood counterparts. For the movement, it was also an opportunity to once again reassert their tino rangatiratanga over kōhanga reo.

A key focus of *Te Whāriki a te Kōhanga Reo* is the "mana" of children. Reedy (2013) describes mana as "the enabling and empowering tool that supports children to control their destiny" (p. 47). Within kōhanga reo, the mana of each child is fostered through five cultural settings: Mana Atua (The power of the Gods); Mana Whenua (The power and status of the Land); Mana Tangata (The power and status of People); Mana Reo (The power and status of the Language); and Mana Aotūroa (The power and status of the Environment) (Te Kōhanga Reo National Trust, 2020). As children experience these cultural settings, they are observed in relation to four dimensions of development namely: Tinana (physicality), Wairua (spirituality), Hinengaro (cognition), and Whatumanawa (emotion). This vision of children is a powerful alternative to the conceptualisations of children as empty vessels or a commodity as described above.

Te kōhanga reo ki rotokawa

Te Kōhanga Reo ki Rotokawa was established in 1984 and is located in the central North Island of New Zealand. In a visit from the Education Review Office (ERO),[3] the kōhanga reo was challenged in relation to the way in which they made learning visible through assessment and questioned in terms of what was made visible in this process. This led the kōhanga reo to develop their own approach to assessment that recognized the objectives of kōhanga reo, and the importance of mana and the holistic development of their children (McMillan, 2020).

The following excerpts are drawn from the assessment approach of the kōhanga reo known as *Ngā Kōrero Tuku Iho*. The approach involves groups of parents and teachers gathered together to wānanga (talk) about the mana of their children. Importantly, they are localized examples of Māori reclaiming their right to do things differently.

Example 1 translation of Whaea Tori (teacher) sharing her observations of Punaromia (child)

Tori: This was the last week of term one. I took the older children to the new bike track at the school. At the beginning, Waiorangi and Kikorangi were going fast around the track. They had no concerns. Punaromia stood at the beginning of the track and watched them both. After that she navigated her way carefully and slowly around the track so she wouldn't fall, and so she could familiarise herself with it. Once she did so she was able to get going. She was now familiar with the different parts of the track and how to stay safe.

This relates to Mana Aotūroa and the things she likes - to play and watch her friends… She stood and watched the children before she went. She's very observant and cautious. She likes to [work] it out first before she gives it a go and she knows her limits. By observing her environment, she feels safe to actually go, to ride her bike along the path. She was connecting with Papatūānuku (earth mother). Punaromia was making sense of her environment using her body, and emotions to guide her. Doing her own research so she could feel safe. I am so proud of her.

Example#2 Mother Hinewai sharing her observations of her daughter Punaromia

Hinewai: Last week we were in Mahia for a tangi (funeral). We don't often go to our marae. Tyler isn't really connected with his marae, and neither am I even though we're in Rotorua. But we went to our big boy's marae down in Mahia and the kids straight away felt at home and comfortable. I think it is because they are immersed in te reo [the Māori language], and there were a lot of reo speakers there and Puna was like 'kei te kōrero Māori' (they are speaking Māori). It's not her first choice of language at home. We always have to correct her, you know tell her to speak in te reo at home, but at the marae she just wanted to speak te reo all the time.

But this particular day [when] we were on our way home we stopped off at the beach and she was pointing out all these things 'kei hea taku anga' (where is my shell), using her reo. She even starting singing, cos [because] Tama-nui-te-rā (the sun) came out, kei te whiti mai a Tama-nui-te-rā (the sun is shining), singing that song that they wrote, her and Whaea Abi [one of the teachers][…] I was just really blown away by her use of reo there and actually how comfortable she felt being immersed in it, and being on the pā (fortified village) and how comfortable they were actually around the whole tangi situation.

I'll just put it up with kia mārama te reo Māori me te kōrero Māori (understanding and speaking the Māori language) and her Mana Reo because that was the biggest thing I think for her. The physical side – language is the lifeline of our culture and I think as a child you don't recognise that, well she kind of did, because she just saw all and heard all she did and immediately switched over to that. Her spirituality - every language has its own spirit, every language is precious, really instilling that. And then I think for us as parents it was important that we keep immersing her in that environment, so I don't know how that looks whether we visit our marae here or whatever just to keep her connected. She definitely showed a lot of happiness, and slightly more confident than her usual self, her usual hide behind māmā (mum), hide behind pāpā (dad). She was quite happy to talk to others who spoke te reo to her so that was really cool.

Conclusion

Kōhanga reo is a transformational movement that continues to push back against Western influences. Empowering Māori families enables them to take control of what matters most in the education of their children and determine a curriculum that will prepare them for life. For Māori, this includes the mana of the child and supporting their holistic development. Additionally, kōhanga reo is a living example of the ability to resist neoliberal influences by keeping traditional knowledge and values at the forefront of all decision-making.

Religious discourse on Indonesian early childhood education and care: A possibility of resisting or perpetuating neoliberalism?

Vina Adriany

Introduction

The ideology of neoliberalism highly influences ECEC practices in Indonesia. As Harvey (2007) defines, neoliberalism can be identified as the gradual removal of the state's responsibility from social provision. Up to the present, ECEC in Indonesia is not part of compulsory education and hence, is not free. Despite the government's rhetoric that ECEC is a form of human capital investment, the budget for it remains relatively low compared to other levels of education such as primary and higher education.

This case aims to explore the possibility for ECEC in Indonesia to resist hegemonic languages of neoliberalism. As Foucault (1978) asserts, when "there is power, there is resistance," though as he also continues, "this resistance is never in a position of exteriority in relation to power" (p. 78). Here, in this section, I would like to present resistance with all its complexity. The resistance may not be frontal and direct; nevertheless, it provides teachers, parents, children, and all educators a possibility to construct another meaning of ECEC.

A brief introduction to ECEC in Indonesia

Messiness and complexities mark the landscape of ECEC in Indonesia. The government's attention to ECEC began when they established a Directorate for Early Childhood Education under the Ministry of Education in 2001. The government was assisted by the World Bank when they were first involved in ECEC (Denboba, Hasan, & Wodon, 2015; Hasan, Hyson, & Chang, 2013). Without a doubt, the involvement of the World Bank and other international donor agencies marks the legacy of neoliberalism and of global imperialism. Through a loan provided by the World Bank, the government continues to share and delegate its responsibilities in ECEC to international donor agencies.

The World Bank's involvement in Indonesian ECEC is deemed part of the government's attempt to increase children's access and participation, especially in rural areas. However, at the same time, this also demonstrates the irony of the government's attitude towards ECEC. As mentioned before, just like in other parts of the world, ECEC is believed to be a mechanism for maximizing human capital. Drawing from Heckman's theory, it is widely promoted by the government that every cent spent on a child will bring a higher return in the future (Heckman & Masterov, 2007). Yet, the budget allocated for ECEC remains relatively low. It is estimated that the budget for ECEC is only 2.5% of the country's total funding for education (Kemendikbud, 2021). So, in other words, as mentioned above, the government continues to rely on loans from international donor agencies and share the budget with the private sectors. The human capital discourse hence is not effective in getting the resources necessary to ECEC. Rather, it becomes a means to perpetuate neoliberalism.

ECEC in Indonesia is marked by a division between the formal and non-formal ECEC centres. Formal ECEC has some government oversight because it must comply with the government's regulations and the notion of quality. For instance, a teacher in formal ECEC needs to hold at least a bachelor's degree in early childhood education or psychology. Formal ECEC also provides services for children aged four to six and must be open for at least three hours a day and be held at least five times a week. It is important to note that formal ECEC does not necessarily mean public ECEC. Most ECEC centres in Indonesia are private, with only 2% of the 202,991 ECEC centres being public kindergartens (Kemendikbud, 2020). And even in the very few public kindergartens, parents still pay fees. Again, this illuminates the impact of neoliberalism on the ECEC sector where education is treated as the responsibility of individuals and the private sector. It also demonstrates the extent to which ECEC has been commodified in the country. Non-formal ECEC is mainly established through women's unpaid labour. There is no minimum educational requirement. Anybody can become a teacher in non-formal ECEC. Many teachers in non-formal ECEC are primary school graduates (Newberry & Marpinjun, 2018). However, the absence of educational qualifications also excludes these teachers from gaining access to the government's professional development programme. Eventually, this situation will also exclude them from having access to extra salaries because teachers in formal ECEC can get additional income once they pass the in-service teachers' professional development programme.

Previous research done by Newberry (2010, 2012) and Newberry and Marpinjun (2018) also demonstrates that the development of non-formal ECEC is done mainly by mobilizing housewives in villages. Like in other parts of the world, ECEC in Indonesia is often seen as an extension of motherhood. The fact that the government uses motherhood as a tool for ECEC expansion might illuminate the perpetuation of state gender ideology that continues to place women in domestic and caring spaces. At the same time, people's voluntarism to enact ECEC centres is also often rooted in religious teaching. Many people believe that educating young children is part of their religious duties. The intersection between gender and religious discourse in Indonesian ECEC often contributes to teachers' poor wages and working conditions. Teachers are made to believe that their low salary is justified because teaching and caring for young children is both their maternal and religious obligation (Newberry & Marpinjun, 2018). Women's volunteerism in ECEC is an example of how power travels through discourse and not through coercive measures. These women are participating in and celebrating the discourse.

The money from the World Bank is mainly used to develop non-formal ECEC for poor people in villages. However, the financial assistance cannot be used to pay either the teachers' salaries or the children's tuition fees. Most of the fund is spent on teacher training or parenting programmes. Therein lies ideas that ECEC teachers, especially those in the non-formal ECEC sector, are less competent because they do not have university degrees. Parents in the villages are also treated as having poor parenting skills, and hence as in need of training to have their parenting corrected. Therefore, while the loan from the World Bank might improve children's access and participation in ECEC and expand the number of ECEC centres in the country, it does not automatically resolve inequities between formal and non-formal ECEC. To complicate matters, most non-formal ECCE is situated in rural areas. Hence, the inequalities between ECEC centres also reflect inequalities between rural and urban areas.

Neoliberalism and developmentalism

As political and economic discourses, neoliberalism often travels through another discourse. As Foucault (1980) argues:

> Power must be analyzed as something which circulates, or rather as something which only functions in the form of a chain...Power is employed and exercised through a net-like organization. And not only do individuals

circulate between its threads, they are always in the position of simultaneously undergoing and exercising this power.

(p. 98)

In Indonesian ECEC, one dominant discourse that often perpetuates the legacy of neoliberalism is developmentalism. Here, it is defined as a branch of psychology, namely child development theory. This theory is based on an understanding that young children will undergo several stages of development. These phases occur universally irrespective of the children's sociocultural context. Postdevelopmentalist scholars have criticised this theory. Postdevelopmentalism is an umbrella term that aims to challenge the pervasiveness and question the universalist claims of developmentalism (Edwards, Blaise, & Hammer, 2009). Post-developmentalism includes feminist poststructuralist, queer theories, posthumanism, postcolonialism, Confucianism, and so forth.

In Indonesia, developmentalism is very powerful. It is circulated in the government's documents and policies, teachers' training curriculum at the university level, and the kindergarten curriculum. To govern ECEC in the country, the government set up two regulations. Both regulate how the curriculum and practices of ECEC are carried out (The Ministry of Education and Culture Republic of Indonesia, 2014a, 2014b). In these regulations, it is stated that the purpose of ECEC is to cater to young children's needs with developmentally appropriate practices. Children's development is divided into five spheres. They are physical, language, social-emotional, cognitive, and religious. Each of the developmental spheres are broken down into several indicators. A critical analysis of the child development indicators yields how these indicators are often built upon the norms and values of middle-class children in the Global North (Penn, 2002). Therefore, the indicators may be insensitive towards the lives and experiences of children in the Global South, such as Indonesia (Adriany & Newberry, 2021). However, these indicators of children's development continue to be the basis for teachers' assessments of kindergarten children. Children will be separated into two main categories: not yet developing or developmentally on track. The assessment regime in Indonesian ECEC is compelling as the data is needed as part of the government's report to global initiatives such as the Sustainable Development Goals. In 2021, through the Centre for Statistics Indonesia, the Indonesian government has initiated the Children Development Index, an assessment tool to measure children's level of development to indicate how many Indonesian children are developmentally on track. The instrument is influenced by international children's assessment such as Early Development Instrument. Instead of spending more of the ECEC budget that can be on making ECEC accessible for every child, the government allocates funds to developing universal assessments tools and standards for children's development. As Formen (2017) argues, in a neoliberal state, the government shifts its responsibilities from providing access to social provision to developing more standards. The government's roles and surveillance are not weakened, but they are distributed.

The discourse of developmentalism also promotes neoliberal subjects. Central to developmentalism is child-centred pedagogy. Within this pedagogy, young children are constructed as active beings who can build their knowledge. In this sense, young children within child-centred pedagogy are constructed as free and rational beings. Child-centredness also strongly emphasises individualism. In this sense, the values of child-centred ideologies are in line with neoliberal values (Burman, 2008; Newberry, 2010; Walkerdine, 1998).

This is precisely one of the issues within the implementation of child-centred pedagogy. Child-centred pedagogy emphasises a child as an individual, and hence, it obscures children's social, historical, and cultural context. A child's level of development is seen as predominantly determined by individual factors such as nutrition and brain size. More prominent social factors such as poverty and the country's inequalities are not taken into consideration. While child-centred pedagogy is supposed to be a progressive pedagogy, its adoption in Indonesia is often classed because it is adopted by expensive, franchised, or international kindergartens. Without any doubt that the notion of child-centredness has contributed to ongoing commodification of ECEC (Newberry, 2010). In Indonesia, child-centred pedagogy also acts as a tool for continuing colonisation. In 2005, for example, the Indonesian government purchased the license to implement Beyond Circle and Centre Time (BCCT), a pedagogical approach from Florida, United States of America. The permit was only valid until 2010. The fact that the government has to buy a license in order to be able to implement BCCT in ECEC centres in the country signifies the legacy of colonialization. Both the implementation and termination of BCCT were done as top-down policies from the government to all ECEC centres in the country (Adriany, 2019).

Religious discourse: a possibility for resistance or a vehicle for continuing neoliberalism?

The ECEC curriculum in Indonesia divides children's development is into five spheres, namely physical, language, social-emotional, cognitive, and religious. The dominant theories of child development do not normally include the religious sphere. The inclusion of religious or spiritual development can also be found in other regions of the world.

Despite the fact that Indonesia is a democratic country, religion plays very important roles in people's everyday life. The first principle of *Pancasila* (Indonesia's state philosophy) is to believe in one God. At the moment, the government recognises six major religions in the country: Islam, Roman Catholicism, Protestantism, Hinduism, Buddhism, and Confucianism. In reality, there are actually many more religions in Indonesia. Many Indigenous groups adopt Indigenous belief such as "*sunda wiwitan, kepercayaan, and kejawen.*" However, since Islam is the most observed religion in the country, the religious developmental sphere is often associated with Islamic values. This is obviously problematic since, as mentioned before, Indonesia is a country with many different religious traditions.

In this case, I would argue that the inclusion of the religious developmental sphere might yield the possibility for ECEC in Indonesia to resist the dominant language of neoliberalism. As explained before, ECEC in Indonesia is characterised by its focus on assessment. Almost all aspects of children's development have to be measured. When a child reaches their final year of kindergarten, before entering primary school, they will be subjected to a school readiness test and evaluated on whether or not they are ready for primary education. All the children's developmental spheres are broken down into details and measurable indicators that can be assessed quantitatively. The religious sphere becomes the only one that is not elaborated into particular indicators. Being an academic in ECEC, I often have first-hand experience seeing how the religious sphere of children's development is questioned by people from international donor agencies because they see the religious sphere as something that cannot be measured. Educators and policymakers in Indonesia often defend the inclusion of the religious domain before the international donor agencies. The inclusion of the religious sphere might therefore be seen as a form of resistance because, as I mentioned before within neoliberalism, ECEC is seen as a form of investment. ECEC has been reduced to a vehicle to attain a country's economic development and hence, education is perceived as nothing but economic activities. The inclusion of religious aspects offers a possibility for teachers, parents, and children to emphasise children's spirituality and go beyond an economic meaning of education (Kuusisto, 2022). The religious sphere in ECEC in Indonesia appears to serve as a hybrid space. As a country with a long history of colonialisation, Indonesia is characterised by its postcolonial conditions, especially since ECEC in the country too often acts to perpetuate the legacy of neoliberalism and neocolonialism. As Bhabha (1994) asserts, there will exist a hybrid space in the postcolonial society, a place where local and colonial cultures interact and negotiate with one another. This hybrid space is a grey area going beyond the binary of the coloniser and colonised (Bhambra, 2014). As Day (2016) explains, religion often becomes an imaginary space for people to resist the hegemonic language of neoliberalism. To borrow a phrase from Bloom (2013), resistance could "offer individuals an opportunity to secure themselves as a 'subject'" (p. 228). An economic being is substituted by a new subject, a religious being.

However, religion is like a double-edged knife. Despite the fact that religion might become a tool to resist colonialism and neoliberalism, it still operates under neoliberal ideology that sees ECEC as a commodity. During fieldwork that I did in 2019 in a religious kindergarten, I was struck by how on one hand the kindergarten tried to complement the BCCT approach to ECEC with religious values. However, this kindergarten is one of the most expensive ECEC centres in the city. Part of the reason it is so pricey is that they have to purchase the exclusive license to adopt BCCT in their curriculum. Hence, while the practice might yield an act of negotiation, it illuminates the convenient marriage between neoliberalism and religion. As Aksoy and Eren Deniz (2018) argue, in a country where religion plays an important role, it is often used as a vehicle to sustain neoliberalism. However, because the kindergarten is highly expensive, they obviously will still exclude children who are coming from low-class economic backgrounds. ECEC remains a personal choice that depends on one's financial capital.

At the same time, as Karl Marx's famous quote, "religion is an opium of the people" asserts, religion is often used to preserve the status quo (Rinaldo, 2013). As explained before, in the case of ECEC, religion is often used to justify teachers' low salaries. Again, while religion might offer the possibility to provide an alternative to neoliberalism, particularly with its critique against rationality and measurement, it also can become a vehicle that continues to promote neoliberalism.

Conclusion

This case aims to present the possibility to see the emergence of religious discourse within Indonesian ECCE as a possibility to contest the pervasiveness of neoliberalism. With the country's emphasis on measuring young children, recognizing religion as part of children's development offers teachers, parents, and policymakers a space to go beyond the quantification of the young children and their development. However, Foucault reminds us that each discourse has multiple meanings and those meanings are often in contradiction with one another. While religious discourse might serve as a form of resistance, it might also perpetuate commodification of ECEC or even become a form of political identity in problematic ways. Hence, there is a need to carefully conceptualise the roles of religion within the ECEC context in Indonesia. However, this case might demonstrate day-to-day resistance to neoliberalism taken up by people in countries in the Global South such as Indonesia. This possibility to resist neoliberalism is not perfect, in fact, it is messy and complex, but nevertheless it allows teachers and educators to reimagine another meaning of children and education that goes beyond economic discourse.

Conceptualisation 3: Kindergarten or "children's garden"

Before "daycare" and "nursery" programmes were organised to replace maternal care and/or assimilate children as described above, programmes existed for young children with an entirely different purpose: a romantic place for young children to learn and grow. Unlike "daycare," which was mainly focused on "troubled" (read *working*) mothers or "infant schools" that sought to assimilate children into dominant norms, kindergartens centred the child as a learning subject, as discussed above. Kindergarten programmes opened to the idea of conceptualizing children as budding, full-of potential humans rather than a messy bundle of physical needs in need of a mother or mother-substitute's protection. Pedagogy, or the method or practice of teaching, was theorised, studied, and practiced in these spaces. Pioneering theorists such as Jean Jacques Rousseau, Freidrich Froebel, Maria Montessori, Rudolf Steiner, Loris Malaguzzi, and John

Dewey thought deeply about what children could/should learn and how. These theorists, themselves highly respected members of society, had the space and resources to creatively experiment with children's learning.

While infant schools and daycares sought to fix or prevent possible harms to children, or the deviancy of children themselves, the idea of kindergarten lent itself to romantic images of children: kind, sweet, curious, and altruistic. While not explicit, there is an underlying image of a prototypically pure and innocent child who will learn and grow under the "right" conditions.

These romanticised pedagogical spaces existed at the same time as the orphanage-like "nurseries," "daycares," and/or religious-based infant schools (and residential schools in Canada and the United States). They truly could not have had more different purposes. One was for the poor, destitute, and "savage," and the other for the curious, innocent, privileged child who deserved to thrive. One was a last resort associated with the socially deviant mother ("daycare"), while the other an indication of a "good family with high standing in society" ("kindergarten"). One was about passing time during the day and the other about making every moment meaningful. In contrast to the Islamic case explored previously, in the case of Christian religious-based infant schools and/or residential schools, the purpose was destroying the child's spirit, while kindergarten was about the child discovering, playing, and growing (Humblet & Vandenbroeck, 2007).

These privileged, romanticised ideas of learning and growing in kindergarten spaces continue to pervade professional and marketing discourse around ECEC today. It is increasingly common to see childcare programmes being "branded" to conjure up images of a romanticised learning environment to sell "services." For example, Montessori is often considered to be a desirable "brand" of ECEC in North America as it is equated with a unique, superior pedagogical experience that strengthens a child's creativity and independence (typically at a higher cost to parents). That there is little to no oversight or standards around what the Montessori approach *is* and/or who qualifies as a "Montessori" provider is rarely brought up by parents or professionals. The perceived prestige of "Montessori" on its own may be enough for parents to believe their child is receiving the richest learning experience. Similarly, the "Reggio-Emilia approach" is also marketed and used as justification for private ECEC charging exhorbitant parent fees.

More concerning, "big box" childcare programmes (large-scale, corporately-run, multi-site locations) are increasingly developing and selling their own brands of childcare, and therefore a superior childhood. For example, one large corporate provider in Canada claims their centres offer a "superior environment that fosters a lifelong love of learning in each and every child" (BrightPath, 2022). Many of these mass childcare providers go as far as to develop their own curriculum packages (i.e. "Alphamania" and "Muchkinetics"), thereby branding their numeracy/literacy learning activities and using these programmes as a selling feature for consumers/parents (discussed further in the human capital conceptualisation below as well as in Chapter 3 of this book on parents as consumers). It has been established elsewhere that these same corporate childcare centres are also *more* likely to violate government health and safety requirements and pay their staff some of the lowest wages in the sector (Richardson, 2017; 2021). In any case, it becomes clear that highly commodified, mass childcare programmes have become apt at presenting/selling their programmes in a romanticised light (often through professionally designed and maintained websites) while what occurs in the programme may look and feel very different for children, educators, and families (Robert-Holmes & Moss, 2021).

Similarly, commodification of ECEC in Asian countries such as China, Malaysia, and Singapore prioritizes the business success of corporate childcare, ignoring children's needs, interests, desires, and agencies, unless these are useful for marketing purposes, such as to "motivate children with a playground inspired by a popular online game" (Lim, 2017, p. 25). According to Lim (2017), "the needs of children can become overshadowed by the need for institutions to focus on being competitive in a free market, being attractive to consumers, and becoming financially profitable" (p. 21). Childcare programmes are considered businesses above all else, created to meet adult needs. ECEC is increasingly branded as "elite and international" (Koh & Ziqi, 2021, p. 1) and imported curricula, such as "Montessori, SmartReader, COSMOTOTS" (Mustafa et al., 2014, p. 117), are adopted to attract parents/consumers. In these contexts, gaps between the rich and the poor are exacerbated, as high-income parents queue to enrol their children in "elite" branded corporate childcare that teach English as a foreign language and develop "linguistic capital, creativity and imagination (through play-based learning) and intercultural capital" (Koh & Ziqi, 2021, p. 9). These programmes are inaccessible to low-income families. Governments justify their lack of investment in a public system by stating that the private, corporate sector fosters diversity, experimentation, and innovation (Lim, 2017). Not surprisingly, the elite international kindergarten industry in Asia is growing and expanding, worth over 60 billion USD in China alone (Koh & Ziqi, 2021). There is also a "commercial shadow industry" (Lim, 2017, p. 23) of academically oriented enrichment programmes offering phonics and math instruction during evenings and weekends to kindergarten children (ages three and up) in Asia (who attend elite play-based programmes during the weekdays) as well as in North America (Orcos et al., 2019).

As has been illustrated above, commodifying the care/education of children through branding programmes and/or curriculum is typically little more than a marketing strategy. Exacerbating the problem, those childcare programmes that do genuinely engage with a particularly pedagogical approach in a meaningful way, particularly when these are for-profit centres, are likely to be lost amidst the shuffle. Centres with a strong pedagogical compass, who think critically about how children are conceptualized, are more likely to invest in invisible aspects of the programme like planning time for educators, ensuring there are more qualified staff, and ensure that staff experience decent wages. These are two aspects of childcare programmes that are foundational to rich, meaningful learning/care experiences for children, yet well-intentioned consumers (parents) do not often think/ask about. The description of the programme on the professionally designed website may be their only source of information. As parents/consumers make childcare decisions in a market context of overall scarcity, the intersection of commodification and romanticized understandings of children and childhood is not about the children or about the actual care and education experience. Successfully branded programmes are likely investing in the branding process itself rather than in the complex process of caring well for children, families, and educators.

The following case documents the history of Indigenous, Islamic, and Western conceptions of childhood and childcare in Nigeria, before presenting a pan-African project that developed an Indigenous curriculum and outlining challenges to implementing it.

Recentering Indigenous philosophy of early childhood education in some African States

Esther Oduolowu

In this section, I will discuss the African Indigenous and Islamic forms of early childhood education. Thereafter, I will explain the current form of early childhood education and then the Indigenous curriculum we developed to complement the existing Western-oriented form of early childhood curriculum popularly used in our early childhood facilities/schools in Nigeria and other African countries.

Indigenous early childhood education

"*The Child is the father of the man*" (Fafunwa, 1967). This saying is the springboard on which the philosophy of Yoruba Indigenous approach of early childhood was laid. This model predates all other models of education that Indigenous people operated among various ethnic groups before a nation named "Nigeria" came to be in 1914. In this proverb, the child is highly esteemed as the future leader who will take charge of affairs in the next generation. A Kenyan proverb refers to children as the "foundation of humanity" (Lanyasunya & Lesolayia, 2001). These two proverbs, and many others in African countries, show the similarities in African philosophies about the child and his/her significant status in the society.

Early childhood education has been an integral part of the total informal education system in the Nigerian setting since the pre-colonial period. The early years of childhood are taken to be very important in the life of the child and what happens during this period is believed to matter for the child's life. The education of the child therefore forms a significant part of the total education programme in the Indigenous society. The Indigenous nurturing and education for the child begins from conception. From conception, the mother is placed under the care of the herbalists, experienced mothers in the family who provide guidance in relation to food, medicine, exercises, and daily routine until the child is born. The child is nurtured and reared in a traditional way to appreciate the cultural values and become integrated into the society through initiation, festival, ceremonies, and other rituals. In the Indigenous settings, Africans have their own system of Indigenous education which is designed to meet both the needs of the children and members of society. It does not have a planned curriculum and it is unwritten. The goals are focused on the development of the child's latent physical skills, character training, respect for elders, intellectual skills, acquisition of specific vocational training, development of sense of belonging, and appreciation and promotion of the cultural heritage of the community. The education is acquired through observation and participation. Opportunities are constantly created by the societies for children to learn by doing. The environment forms the resources to support all learning. Even though the curriculum is not formally written down, it has content, intent, and purpose. Its organisation is patterned to reflect the beliefs, customs, and experiences of the society where the child lives (Adesina, 1988).

The overall purpose of Indigenous education is multifaceted, and its goal is to produce an individual who is honest, responsible, skillful, cooperative, and conforms to the social order of the society. The child's education is the responsibility of all knowledgeable and credible members of the society (parents, extended family members, older siblings, etc...). The implementation is also the collective responsibility of the parents, family members, and community members (Are, 2007). The family members, particularly the mothers, facilitate all aspects of the child's life by interacting with the child and informally training him/her in numbering, folktales, proverbs, local games, and language usage. Moral education is very important and courtesy in the form of politeness, respect, responsible living, integrity, and hard work is greatly emphasised. All these are integrated into the child's daily routines and the livelihood of the family and community members (Nsamenang, 2004).

There are some practices that were inherent to the Indigenous education system in the pre-colonial period that would no doubt transform our current education system in the post-colonial period. Such practices include the pedagogical approach. Traditional educators are known to help children learn to think. They frequently use riddles to prompt children to think out answers. It is not enough to set good examples and tell children what to think. The critical thinking skills needed to solve daily problems as children encounter them are embedded in Yoruba proverbs. For example, one of the Yoruba proverbs says that "omo ti you je asamu, kekere lo ti ma use enu samusamu," meaning a smart child will show the evidence of critical thinking from a very early age (Oduolowu, 2011).

Helping children to take on real responsibilities is one of the great virtues of Indigenous early childhood education. Allowing children to complete chores, run errands, and take responsibility for their younger siblings, parents, and other family members is not limited to the Yorubas alone but is common among many ethnic groups in Africa. This participatory hands-on-minds-on approach enhances creativity and knowledge construction. It is a departure from the methodology that permeates early childhood education practices, particularly in our public schools. In Indigenous education, limits are set for children. In other words, there are boundaries to guide the children's play in the environment and interact with adults and others within and outside the family setting. An example of such boundaries or limits includes respect for others and taking turns.

This promotes balancing independence and control, ensuring that children have limits along with independence (Osanyin, 2012). Too much freedom leads children to feel overwhelmed. Additionally, fostering moral development and a happy family is another practice that we prioritise. In this way, every kinsman is accepted as an important family member, both close and distant relations. The traditional African family is a closely-knit family. A closely-knit family provides a strong network and support system, offers opportunities for children to learn values and traditions, and be mentored by those outside the immediate family. The mentors provided the community-based experiences that are judged to be the foundation to building children's resilience, character, and morality. This is accepted to be what is needed for the upbringing of responsible citizens.

The Islamic form of early childhood education

Prior to the adoption of the Western form of early childhood education in many societies in Africa, Islamic education existed alongside the Indigenous education system. Traditional Koranic centres were established by Islamic teachers called Mallams to care for Muslim children. Fafunwa (1974), an educationist, a University Don, and one-time Minister of Education in Nigeria who wrote extensively on indigenous education, said that "as early as a child can walk short distance from home, the child should be enrolled in Koranic centre for foundation education in Islamic knowledge." In traditional Koranic centres, children as young as three are exposed to short verses from the Koran and encouraged to read and write in Arabic (Fafunwa, 1974; Kolawole, 1989). Unlike Indigenous education, Islamic education is formal and faith-based. It is organised in the mosque or private buildings and the curriculum is mainly based on the Koran. This model of early childhood education continues to exist in core Islamic States in Nigeria. It is the only model that some Muslim children are exposed to from childhood to advanced levels. This is a deliberate attempt to jettison the common early childhood education model and pay attention to inculcating moral education and avoid the commodification of education.

The Western form of early childhood education

The Western form of early childhood education accompanied the missionaries to Africa in the middle of the 19th century. The earliest participants were those who were associated with the missionaries (Maduewesi, 1999). These nursery schools were organized in the churches by wives of missionaries for their children or by nuns for children of foreign and local dignitaries. The colonial officials got involved later by working together with the missionaries and incorporating preschools in the existing elementary schools though adding infant classes (infants I-III) (Musa, Abubakar and Danladi, 2017). The curriculum of this nursery education incorporated games, stories, arts and crafts, painting, and any activities that were thought to be suitable to children's age.

Despite this development during the colonial era, "all efforts for provision of early childhood education were confined to the non-governmental/private sector and received little or no support from the government" (Tor-Anyiin, 2008, p. 2). In addition, as other Europeans, such as colonialists and traders joined the missionaries by sending their children to the preschools, more preschools were therefore established in Government Reservation Areas (GRAs). After a few years, some African parents who had had exposure to Western education abroad started sending their children to these schools.

The expansion of Western ECEC gained momentum in Africa because of several initiatives that happened globally, regionally, sub-regionally, and nationally (Awopegba, Oduolowu, & Nsamenang, 2013). Such initiatives include Convention on the Rights of the Child, 1989, Dakar Framework for Action on Education for All (2000), Moscow Framework for Action and Cooperation-Harnessing the Wealth of Nations (2010), African Early Child Development (ECD) International Conference Series (1999, 2002, 2005, 2009, etc.). The ECD International Conference highlighted Africa's central themes and philosophies on ECD provision. These and many other conventions, conferences, and initiatives have supported campaigns in Africa about the benefits of early childhood care and education (ECCE) provision and contextualizing it to make it more relevant to African children and our societal needs. What informed this position is the fact that the African perspectives, values, and useful practices are missing from Western ECCE programmes in many African countries, including Nigeria. African children were losing their identity. For example, children's names, mode of fashion, language, food choice, and many more are influenced by other cultures. At the school level, classroom practices deviate remarkably from African Indigenous early childhood education? (Majebi and Oduolowu, 2020). For example, the method of teaching, medium of instruction, and the instructional materials used to betray the culture of the learners' immediate environment, even though the National Policy on Education in Nigeria and the existing curriculum acknowledged and recommended culturally appropriate practices. There was therefore a need to develop an Indigenous ECCE framework.

Developing an indigenous ECCE framework

It was in search of solutions to these challenges that calls were made for expanding ECCE and designing contextually relevant curriculum for African children, particularly the vulnerable and excluded. This project was prompted by the global campaign that "young children are rights holders" (related to the CRC), the inclusion of ECCE as a priority for the African Union Plan of Action for the Second Decade on Education for Africa (2006–2015), and the Association for the Development of Education in Africa's (ADEA) working group focused on ECD. The International Institute for Capacity Building in Africa (IICBA), with the support of UNICEF (Uganda), the Federal Ministry of Education (Nigeria), OMEP (World organisation for preschool education), and the International Task Force on Teachers (ITFT), provided the funding and technical support for the project. Patience O Awopegba of IICBA coordinated the project and two international well-recognized African ECD experts, Professors Bame Nsamenang (Cameroon) and myself, Esther Oduolowu (Nigeria) contributed to writing the curriculum framework. Awopegba, Nsamenang, and I co-authored the project with the support of Professor Alan Pence, the then UNESCO chair for ECD. These African scholars worked with other colleagues from the following African countries: Ethiopia Lesotho, Nigeria, South Africa, Ghana, Burkina Faso, Republic of Congo, and Uganda to develop the curriculum framework. One of the thrusts of the project is making ECCE relevant to the needs of the African child by considering what is in the best interest of the child. A strength-based approach was adopted in developing the curriculum. It incorporated the knowledge, skills, values, and timeless wisdom of early child care and education that originated in Africa and is still relevant in our globalised world. Some of the highlights of the curriculum are: the use of mother tongue as the/a mode of instruction at the early childhood stage; a participatory pedagogical approach; prioritizing Indigenous norms, values, and morals; a mode of assessment that is individually based to strengthen the strengths and improve the challenges of learners; the use of culturally/contextually relevant resources; child-to-child practice where older children/siblings help in the upbringing of the youngsters; and psychosocial surveillance, where adults within the family or community closely observe children to monitor and ensure acceptable interactions with others and encourage positive behaviours of the children. Elders/adults in the children's environment served as observers, teachers, carers, child assessors, and parents in all respects. Elders in African traditional society saw the business of bringing up children as a collective responsibility. These and many others are missing in the curriculum currently in use in many of our early childhood classrooms. For example, traditional plays, game-songs, local poems, stories, riddles accompanied with practicing good manners, norms, and values are culturally responsive Indigenous activities that are absent from the current curriculum but should be embedded in the classroom daily routines of the children. These culturally responsive activities would not only enhance children's social enculturation but would develop their curiosity, innovation, and resilience as they navigate what is yet to come.

Conceptualisation 4: childcare as a human capital and/or economic investment for nation-states

Over the last few decades, there has been and continues to be increasing awareness that a child's early experiences are foundational for psychological, social, and emotional well-being throughout the lifespan (Shonkoff and Phillips, 2001). A group of highly respected professionals (i.e. scientists, psychiatrists, psychologists, and social workers) has emerged as "experts" in child development whereby there has been a shift to the application of technical, "scientific" knowledge (for example, the ages and stages rooted in Piagetian theory) to maximise the developmental potential of children. Rather than meeting children's physical needs (daycare/nursery), assimilating children into the status quo (infant schools), or providing child-centred learning experiences (kindergarten), language has shifted to one of "education," whereby achieving predetermined developmental "milestones" is the goal.

Because of the (allegedly) strong links between developmental outcomes, academic achievement, the (future) economic productivity of children, key economists (i.e. James Heckman), and powerful international health and economic organisations such as the OECD, the World Health Organization (WHO), and the World Bank frame early childhood education as a prudent financial investment for nation-states (and individual taxpayers). For example, the WHO asserts that "enabling young children to achieve their full developmental potential [through early childhood development programmes] is a human right and an essential requisite for sustainable development" (World Health Organization, 2020). The World Bank refers to investment in early childhood education as "the smartest thing a country can do" (The World Bank, 2021), while the OECD's ECEC network defines its mission as developing "effective and efficient policies for education and learning to meet individual, social, cultural and economic objectives" (Organization for Economic Co-operation and Development, 2021).

When increasingly commodified ECEC programmes rely heavily on the human capital discourse, the process of caring *for*, *about* or *with* children, families, or educators is deprioritised (if not ignored entirely). Once the human capital is the focus, the child's subjectivity becomes invisible. As the cases from various geographical regions throughout this chapter problematise (and actively the resist), the human capital/development discourse lends itself to the objectification of children and educators, whereby educators are the mechanisms of providing universal "input" (teaching prescriptive curriculum models) and children (hopefully) meet the expected outcomes. The "success" of policies, educators, and programmes alike is measured by child "outcomes" which are then translated in Dollars/Yens/Euros (i.e. state savings on juvenile "delinquency," higher employment rates, and internationally competitive workforces). Even more dangerously, the flip side of this is that policies, programmes, and educators that do not deliver more "developed" children in the long term are vulnerable to being considered a waste of resources and/or a failure.

To some degree, all the cases included in this chapter illustrate the global salience of the human capital discourse. This can be seen in Kylie's Smith's observation where Isobel (along with her educators) reinforces developmental discourses through positioning Donald as behind or as lacking understanding. Vina Adriany's description of ECEC in Indonesia articulates how an expensive, Western, development curriculum (Beyond Circle and Centre Time) is explicitly connected to funding through the World Bank. Esther Oduolowu (Nigeria/Africa case) notes that African "perspectives, values and useful practices" are systematically occluded from the early childhood development programmes that are funded/supported through various organisations (for example, African Childhood Development International Conference Series). Finally, the

Barnehageopprøret (described in a case study below) resists a futuristic human capital framing of caring for children through rejecting the use of formal assessments for language and literacy development in kindergartens.

The intersection of the human capital discourse and commodification of ECE

The human capital conceptualisation of children and childcare is particularly problematic in increasingly commodified childcare systems. The prevailing understanding is that parents are purchasing a more "developed" child. The thinking is that, through participating in a developmentally based childcare programme (allegedly informed by child development "experts"), children will score better on standardised tests of numeracy, literacy, and even social and physical development. It goes without saying that developmentalism's extreme objectification of children leaves absolutely no space for children to imagine, define, and/or voice what is of interest or valuable to them in their experience of growing up.

Another major concern with the human capital/economic conceptualisation of childcare is ethical: it is morally troubling that a child's value is a product of what they can *do* rather than who they are. When the human capital discourse takes over childcare programmes, the programmes are positioned as a mechanism for maximizing children's current and future economic worth. As insinuated in the quote from Roberts-Holmes and Moss (2021) above, the active, complex process of caring for children becomes a static "thing" to be bought and sold in the free market. Like cars, couches, and crayons, care is purported to be a "good" whose value reflects its cost. Parents are the consumers, often spending significant funds on early childhood education "services," while children's development (and therefore further economic potential) is the outcome. The human-and-more-than-human costs of this discourse are enormous: meaningful, thoughtful, responsive, exploratory moments in a healthy, sustainable environment. At a very basic level, the market growth we have enjoyed in the last century is simply unsustainable from an environmental perspective: even if every child were to "succeed" in maximizing their human capital potential, without a fundamental shift in priorities, the child (who is likely miserably conforming to expectations) may not have an Earth to live on when they grow up.

Technology and commodification of children's development

Technologies that seemingly increase "accountability" in relation to children's development are quickly becoming a key feature of childcare programmes (not to mention a profitable venture in their own right). For example, it is increasingly common for childcare programmes to use synchronous communication apps whereby educators, supervisors, and parents are in constant communication with each other. While there is a wide scope of how these apps function, the general idea is that parents as consumers can be kept updated, moment to moment, of their children's "progress": your child is asleep, your child ate four slices of apple, your child is colouring, etc…These apps provide real-time "evidence" to consumers, ensuring they are satisfied with the "service" *they* (not their child) are receiving. Once again, the agency of both the child and educators evaporates with such technologies while educators and administrators go to extreme lengths to "prove" the worthiness of their programmes.

While not the focus of this section of the book, it is worth noting how these apps further the socially conservative idea that children are the sole responsibility of parents. There is an implicit assumption that "good" parents are constantly monitoring and interacting with these apps in some way, as others cannot be trusted with their children's well-being. It's also possible that parents may worry that educators or other parents are judging their absence from, or over-involvement in, these platforms. Again, the pre-occupation is with the parent's perception of what is happening rather than centring the child's (and educator's) experience, concerns, worries, fears, hopes, or joy. Interestingly, in publicly oriented systems, such as Denmark, the use of these technologies has been resisted by educators and some parents who note the significant time these technologies take away from direct interactions with children (Richardson, 2021).

Another phenomenon that has taken hold in highly commodified childcare contexts is video feeds, accessible online to parents. Considered a selling feature in large corporate childcare chains, programmes often live stream footage of every playroom where parents can login and view their children at any time during the day. The thinking here is that parents (consumers) can see exactly what is happening while it is happening and intervene if necessary (by contacting the centre). The message here is that educators cannot be trusted and that parents must constantly protect their children. The grave ethical implications (discussed below) of this surveillance are glossed over as children's and educators' images are accessible to parents on demand. Unless a parent is viewing the feed for hours a day, the context of what they are viewing is lost. Furthermore, the videos typically do not have audio, omitting the possibility that the voices of either the child or educator could be heard. In some Canadian provinces, live streaming of childcare "services" is a standard feature of corporate care, not yet having infiltrated community-based (not for profit) childcare.

Ethically, these technologies are deeply troubling. They are a major violation of children's privacy and agency, once again positioning children as vulnerable, helpless, and in need of saving. Children are most likely unaware that a play-by-play of their day, photos, and/or video streams are being uploaded to a live platform. Educators are similarly silenced through these technologies, as questioning the surveillance model implies they are hiding something or, at the very least, are resisting transparency. In reality, educators are very concerned about the time these technologies take away from their direct interactions with children as it requires them inputting data regularly (Richardson, 2021). Educators express concern about violating the children's privacy. While conducting interviews with educators who worked in rooms with video feeds in Toronto, Canada,

I (Brooke) heard story after story of educators taking action to protect children's privacy in rooms with cameras. For example, several educators described taking a child who had an accident to an area of the room that the camera couldn't capture. There is also the ongoing concern that children's images are available online for predatory reasons – the very mechanism of "protection" could very well be compromising a child's safety in the cyber-crime market. In any case, these technologies are not designed to meet children's needs, but rather the needs of a commodified, surveillance-based system rather than implementing a carefull approach to caring about/with/for children.

Standardised assessment of children and childcare "quality"

Standardised assessment tools, whether they are designed to evaluate the children themselves or the quality of childcare, are another example of commodification, marketisation, and corporatisation (Lloyd & Penn, 2014). When governments purchase these tools from "corporate businesses, whose primary commercial interest is getting shareholders a good return on capital invested" (Lloyd & Penn, 2014, p. 388), public investment in ECEC goes towards evaluation and accountability, instead of towards adequately funding programmes (i.e. increasing staff wages, supporting educators' professional learning, increasing the number of educators in programmes, or ensuring educators have adequate planning time).

Assessment of children

Developmentalism, and the human capital discourse, places educators in a nearly impossible position. To be considered "good" professionals, children must deliver high scores on standardised assessments. In programmes with even more narrowly defined curriculum "packages," in the form of standardised learning activities, it also compromises the autonomy of professionals in the learning process. There is no room for creativity, innovation, diversity, agency, and/or critical thinking, let alone valuing other ways of knowing/being (for example, local Indigenous knowledges). It goes without saying that prescriptive, standardised "tick-box" types of learning/child development outcomes are rarely the priority of educators interested in engaging in meaningful pedagogical experiences *with* children. Interestingly, this also creates additional tensions between parents and educators who are already in a conflicted relationship due to unacceptably high parent fees and chronically low staff wages. Parents may want to see "outcomes" when this is likely not what motivates educators. The ultimate losers are the children whose lived experiences become reduced to overly simplistic assessment scores.

In 2016, the OECD put out a call for tenders for a child assessment tool to use for the International Early Learning Study (IELS) (i.e. "baby PISA"). As noted by Pence (2016), there was "virtually no public, or early childhood field visibility or input" (p. 54). An international consortium was selected as the international contractor for the project, "consisting of the Australian Council for Educational

Research, the International Association for the Evaluation of Educational Achievement and cApStAn" (Moss & Urban, 2019, p. 208). The original call for tenders was followed by each of the three countries that agreed to participate in the pilot phase (England, Estonia, and US) soliciting contractors to administer the study (GovTribe, 2022; Moss & Urban, 2019). In both England and the US, the selected contractors are also involved in the PISA study of 15-year-olds: National Foundation of Education Research, an independent non-profit educational research provider in England, and Weststat, an employee-owned corporation that provides health, education, social policy, and transportation services in the US (Diaz-Diaz et al., 2019; Moss & Urban, 2019). The IELS has been criticised as a universalist, decontextualised, and standardised approach to assessment of children that employs technocratic tools (Carr, Mitchell, & Rameka, 2016; Moss et al., 2016; Pence, 2016; Urban, 2017; Urban & Swadener, 2016). While the standardised assessment of children, and comparison of countries, is deeply concerning, the call for tenders is what interests us in the context of exploring how ECEC is commodified (OECD, 2016). Urban and Swadener (2016) raise the concern about corporate profits as the driving force behind ECEC provision, especially in the context of scarcity and inadequate funding of ECEC. That global publishing companies create testing materials and then provide the "solutions" for the "problems" they identify, create "opportunities for further profit-making interventions" (Urban & Swadener, 2016, p. 11). Such an approach opens "public education sectors to corporate profit interests and channels scarce resources from the public sphere to private, corporate profit" (p. 11).

Along these lines, there is significant money to be made in private tutoring services and/or enrichment programmes that purport to bring children to an "acceptable" developmental level. For example, international tutoring company Kumon (established in the 1950s in Japan) now has regional offices serving all five continents, publishing and research branches as well as their own branded schools in Japan and Switzerland. Today, the company is worth almost four and half million Yen. In 2012, the Baby Kumon programme was launched for 1- and 2-year-olds (Kumon Institute of Education, 2022). And of course, these programmes are expensive and extremely time-consuming for many families already burning the candles at both ends. It is worth questioning the human cost of these neoliberal cultural norms. In many ways, we appear to be running in circles coming up with more diagnoses, categorizing more children, and designing/assigning more interventions (often only accessible to the privileged). While the child's mind is purportedly at the centre of all of this, the child's embodied, subject experience, and relations with those around him/her/they are invisible.

Assessment of "quality"

While the idea of evaluating standardised and universal ideals of childcare quality has been criticised for the past three decades (Dahlberg & Asen, 2002; Dahlberg, Moss, & Pence, 1999; Moss & Pence, 1994), governments continue to funnel public funds into quality evaluation purportedly ensuring accountability. Because of quality's inextricable entanglement with developmentalism and outcome-based thinking, the academic early childhood community has largely moved "beyond quality" (Dahlberg, Moss, & Pence, 2013; Early Childhood Pedagogies Collaboratory, 2020). That academics and researchers are increasingly challenging the very idea that "quality" is something that can be measured or that exists external to people's lived experience is an excellent example of resistance to commodification. The international *Reconceptualizing Early Childhood Education* community is an example of an international, organised group that prioritises thinking more meaningfully and deeply about what matters in ECEC. Even if this thinking is not yet disrupting the material conditions of commodified childcare programmes, that "expert" knowledge has and continues to expand beyond developmentalism inspires hope that other ways of doing ECEC are possible.

The key function developmentalism plays at the programme-level within a commodified system of ECEC is as a yardstick to measure "quality." Just as children are assessed by their scores on developmental checklists, childcare programmes are subjected to standardised assessments to determine the "quality" of their programme.[4] Governments, eager to justify the return on investment of their childcare programmes in a neoliberal context of accountability for public spending, and well-intentioned parents in market systems of ECEC, demand "high quality" ECEC. Quality assessments are now developed by university employed researchers who then profit from these tools by founding or partnering with publishing companies. Two examples of US researchers creating quality assessment tools that have been adopted by Canadian provincial governments will be presented.

The first example of the impact of a commodified quality assessment tool can be observed in Quebec (Canada). Quebec was the first region in North America to create a publicly funded childcare system in 1997. After consulting with researchers and conducting their own quality evaluations in 2003 and 2014 (ISQ, 2004, 2015), Quebec's Ministry of Family developed a quality evaluation process in 2021 (Gouvernement du Québec, 2021). Part of this assessment involves the *Classroom Assessment Scoring System* (CLASS; Pianta, LaParo & Hamre, 2008). The CLASS was developed by researchers at the University of Virginia and the University of North Carolina. Teachstone Training (the company the researchers founded to sell their assessment tool) has an estimated annual revenue over $45 million US per year (Growjo, 2022). This company sells the manual, scoring sheets, training programmes, certification and recertification approval, as well as providing an array of curricular support tools to ensure better scores on the CLASS. The Quebec government also paid for translation of these documents and training materials, as well as validation of the French versions. They then hired a private firm, ServirPlus, to carry out the assessments. Adding insult to injury, a not-for-profit organisation has partnered with Teachstone to accredit/certify/recertify trainers and evaluators for the CLASS in Quebec (CASIOPE,

2022). Teachstone Training (2022) boasts that the CLASS is currently in use "nationwide and around the globe." Quebec is but one example of the big business of quality assessment in ECEC. Public funds are being used to enrich a corporate interest, with university researchers, who likely benefited from public research funds, profiting from the sale of their products.

Another example of a commodified assessment of childcare quality, and of ECEC practitioners, is the Teaching Pyramid Observation Tool (TPOT), designed to "promote social emotional competence in infants and young children" (Brookes Publishing, 2022). This tool has been adopted by the Alberta (Canada) government as part of the ASaP project (Access, Support and Participation) and the GRIT (Getting Ready for Inclusion Today) programme (Government of Canada, 2020; GRIT, 2022). While Alberta has a less developed public ECEC system than Quebec, their early years curriculum framework is inspired by reconceptualist thinking, developed in collaboration with early childhood educators and based on critical and reflective thinking. In contrast to a deficiency-based developmental approach, Alberta's curriculum framework conceptualises children as "mighty learners and citizens" (Makovichuk et al., 2014). Despite the incompatibility of TPOT with their curriculum framework, the Alberta government invested a significant portion of their ECEC budget in quality assessment and educator mentoring using the TPOT (R.A. Malatest & Associates, Ltd., 2020). Similar to the CLASS, the authors of this tool, Mary Louise Hemmeter, Patricia Snyder, and Lise Fox, researchers at Vanderbilt University, University of Florida, and University of South Florida, have also published scientific articles about the tool's validity (i.e. Fox, Hemmeter, & Snyder, 2014; Hemmeter, Snyder & Fox, 2018; Snyder, Hemmeter, Fox, Bishop, & Miller, 2013), blurring the boundaries between economic and academic productivity and profitability. Fortunately, as Peter Moss reminds us in the introduction to this book, commodification and the human capital narrative is not the only possibility for ECEC.

Conceptualisation 5: childcare as a site of experimentation and political resistance

An example of childcare as a site of resistance can be found in the history of ECEC in communal and collective utopian political projects. In communist and socialist countries, ECEC was seen as actively contributing to a revolutionary future through the shaping of utopian citizens since the 1930s. Government-supported childcare was considered important both because it allowed mothers to work and because communal ECEC was seen as an effective way to ensure that all members of the rising generation shared official party values and viewpoints (Kirshenbaum, 2013; Piattoeva, Silova, & Millei, 2018). Similarly, collective childcare on Israeli kibbutzim (collective communities, typically farms) has existed since the 1920s, with intentions of raising future generations of Zionist socialists (Aviezer et al., 1994). Other intentional communities, including

Summerhill School in England (Readhead & DfE, 1996), viewed childcare as critical to building a better world. Regardless of the many legitimate critiques, one might have about both Soviet and Israeli society, this framing of universal collective childcare as a means for contributing to a political project is contrary to the idea of childcare as a private commodity.

Another example of the focus on pedagogy in resistance to commodification is Scandinavian ECEC. In the postwar period, Denmark, Norway, Sweden, and Finland built universally accessible childcare systems, thereby positioning childcare as a typical part of childhood for all young children. Unlike in Canada, the US, and Australia, these systems are still in place today. "Pedagogues," the educators employed in the programmes, are not primarily concerned with either education or ensuring children's physical health/safety in parents' absence. While they do both, their concern is ensuring children's well-being in the present moment as well as the formation (*dennelse/dannelse*) of democratic citizens (Richardson, 2021; Brogaard-Clausen & Ringsmose, 2017). This is similar to the German concept of *bildung* (Ødegaard & White, 2016; Thompson, 2015). *Dennelse* refers to "the child's and adult's ethical engagement in developing knowledge and competences [...] based in the values of democracy and a good life," with goal of working "towards a better and more meaningful society" (Brogaard-Clausen & Ringsmose, 2017, p. 238). Pedagogues' priority is providing meaningful relational experiences with children and their families in the context of upholding the highly valued social democratic sociopolitical order. Almost all children in these countries are enrolled in childcare by age 3 (often referred to as "kindergarten" programmes) prior to formal school entry at age 6 or 7, while the majority are enrolled in "nursery" programmes from ages 1 to 3. Even if parents do not work or study full-time, children still attend these low-cost, conveniently located, typically public not-for-profit programmes.[5]

The role of a pedagogue is distinct from a teacher (educator of older children), as academic learning is not considered appropriate for children prior to school in Nordic countries. Learning is valued, in the sense of learning how to be with other children, adults, and the natural environment. Similarly, the head of a programme is not referred to as a "supervisor" or "director" but as a "leader," as their role is not seen as hierarchically "above" pedagogues. This democratic structure is central to the overall purpose of early childhood programmes: creating a space where children, families, and staff feel cared for and can care well for others, in the programme and beyond. Children are neither romanticised nor pathologised, but simply respected and honoured as already human beings with important thoughts, feelings, interests, fears, and hopes. Like all of us, they are finding their way in a confusing, often overwhelming world (Brogaard-Clausen & Ringsmose, 2017; Richardson, 2021). Other research has explored what it means to be an early childhood professional in various international contexts (Miller, Dalli & Urban, 2012; Urban, Vandenbroeck, Van Laere, Lazzari, & Peeters, 2012).

While there is certainly an infiltration of North American ideals rooted in developmentalism in Nordic childcare, pedagogues (with the support of parents) are resisting these standardised, outcomes-based approaches to practice. The Barnehageopprøret (Kindergarten Uprising) in Norway, 2019 childcare protests in Denmark and the pressatläge in Sweden are concrete examples of parents, pedagogues, and citizens coming together to resist the standardisation of childcare programmes and curriculum. These grassroots advocacy movements have been successful in resisting legislation that would have facilitated the implementation of standardised curriculum and programme measures (for example, a heavier reliance on government oversite/regulation as we currently see in North American, highly commodified systems).

The ongoing work of the Kindergarten Uprising in Norway, the *Barnehageopprøret*, is particularly unique as the main tactic of the resistance was sharing parents' and educators' stories. Through sharing "stories" that highlighted the indefensible mismatch between developmentalism, commodification, and children's well-being, parents and educators painted a clear picture of how oppressive discourses, combined with material deficiencies, play out in children's, parents', and educators' daily lives in kindergarten programmes in Norway. The short stories, first shared through social media and then picked up by the mass media (hashtags #Indefenceable, "#Actually," and #Really), highlighted how contextually bound, responsive, caring interactions are systematically deprioritised by government policies attempting to standardise curriculum and/or reduce the number of staff in programmes. For example, one educator explained,

> I do not have enough arms nor a lap big enough to give all the children what they need. I'm in my third year as a kindergarten teacher and I'm completely exhausted. My heart bleeds for the children. They deserve so much more.
>
> *(Barnehageopprøret, 2021)*

In 2018, the *Barnehageopprøret* successfully stopped the government's plan to map and test the language skills of all 5-year-olds, while also reducing the number of staff required in programmes. Unfortunately, the government persisted and the campaign is ongoing. Today, the campaign is still concerned with both staffing and pedagogical standards, particularly in pandemic times. A public social media post from December 2021 (addressed to "Kindergarten rebels") asserts that the group will "continue to protest, write posts and support professionals on behalf of the children" (Barnehageopprøret, 2021).

Sadly, how long standardisation and "outcome"-based "learning," alongside decreased staffing resources, can be resisted in these jurisdictions is questionable. Things are moving in the "wrong" direction. For example, in Denmark, smaller pedagogy training programmes located in different areas of Denmark were amalgamated into one large institution in Copenhagen in 2018 (Richardson, 2021). The localised, training programmes that fostered relational pedagogical experiences for post-secondary students and faculty have been replaced with streamlined, impersonal mass lectures. While it may be more economically "efficient" for postsecondary institution to structure pedagogue training this way, it brings with it the same ethical and moral concerns of mass, commodified childcare provision: the experiences and needs of children/students and educator/faculty are occluded. The final case included in this chapter gives an insider perspective of the *Barnehageopprøret* from a seasoned, self-identified kindergarten "rebel."

The *Barnehageopprøret* in Norway: An insider perspective of a kindergarten rebel

Royne K. Berget[6]

Introduction

In 2013, The United Nation's Committee on the Rights of the Child expressed concern over the threat to child's play posed by increased demands for more formal educational programmes for children. There is no doubt that this concern is manifested in kindergarten (care/education programmes for children aged 0–5) and the first years of school (aged 6–8) in Norway. Over the past several decades, children's play has been sacrificed to make room for pre-defined, prescriptive educational goals mainly in fear of unsatisfactory PISA results. Little evidence suggests that this approach has been successful. If play is not taken seriously in both kindergarten and school, and kindergarten professionals, parents, and allies do not take steps to protect play, then children's well-being will suffer.

A core belief of mine, and my fellow "rebels," is that kindergartens are not factories and kindergarteners are not products. We believe the goal of kindergarten is for children to engage in positive, meaningful play and care experiences, in a responsive, relationally safe environment. Unlike a factory model that produces children who acquiesce to standard ideals, kindergarten should be a place where children are seen, heard, and actively participate in shaping their learning environment.

This case explores my experiences as a leader of the *Barnehageopprøret* (Kindergarten Rebellion or Uprising) in Norway – a movement that began in late 2015 and continues to this day. I have been a part of this movement since the beginning and remain in the action group today. Beginning as a small Facebook group primarily of educators expressing concern about the standardisation of kindergartens in Norway, the *Barnehageopprøret* has now gained national and international attention as a group that has effectively resisted neoliberal kindergarten policy measures. But of course, the struggle is ongoing. There is still much work to be done.

Since 2000, the following observations can be made about kindergartens in Norway:

- Downward pressure in regard to staffing levels
- A shift away from play to formal didactic learning

- The implementation of formal educational tools and programmes to assess children and/or map children's development
- Less pedagogical freedom for educators
- A culture of silence where educators are afraid to speak out about their concerns
- An increasing presence of private, commercial childcare actors/players developing local kindergarten programmes
- Commercial actors (motivated by profits) exerting significant and increasing influence on kindergarten policy and politics
- Lack of parent voice in programmes (parent surveys are commonly misused to create an artificially good picture of the reality in the kindergarten)
- A shift towards a financing system that creates and reinforces social inequality

As mentioned above, in the last 15 years, commercial actors have gradually grown larger and more powerful in Norway. They have and continue to gain influence over policy makers, and therefore, the direction of the kindergarten sector, including the pedagogical methods of educators. With their own lobbyists employed to influence politicians, these commercial actors manage to advance their views and interests, which often conflict with the professional values of practitioners.

In the autumn of 2016, the Ministry of Education held public consultations where unions (representing the kindergarten workforce), municipalities, and kindergarten owners were asked for input to develop a new Kindergarten framework. On November 11, 2016, the representative of the Ministry of Education and Research stated the following:

> In the law on kindergartens, the owner is legally responsible for the quality and content. There is therefore a need to ensure that the owners can use the systems and methods that they believe are important to ensure this. But a smart owner will of course seek advice from their staff. Companies with a significant level of ownership in the sector have joint procurement of systems and programmes that they currently have the full right to use. Therefore, the freedom of method has been deliberately taken out in the consultation proposal.

Clearly the voices of educators were ignored. The new framework emphasised school-like tools and methods that prescriptively outlined what educators ("employees") taught and how. I, and many of my colleagues, were and are concerned that we could very quickly end up with a kindergarten sector that was controlled by a handful of large commercial players fundamentally motivated by profits rather than the well-being of people – particularly children. Our fear, which remains ongoing, is that commodification will reduce educators to puppets simply applying methods that may be meaningless to their/our professional practices. Kindergarten owners are not experts in early learning. They are experts in maximizing profit margins, but because they have acquired power and influence, their "methods" are implemented. It is not easy for anyone – parents, educators, or children – to speak against a powerful owner making money from their own educational programmes. Educators were quickly becoming technicians applying the methods their employers demanded. We were worried (and rightly so) that professional autonomy, spontaneity, and job satisfaction would disappear and the children become an injured third party.

Becoming and being a kindergarten rebel

In November 2016, I reached a breaking point. I was so frustrated with how standardisation and application of externally imposed "methods" was exploiting children and educators that my health began to suffer. Since 2012, the kindergarten programmes I worked in were on the list of the worst municipalities in the country when it came to staffing levels coupled with low subsidies. Low subsidies often led to the need to compensate with larger groups of children in kindergarten. I felt I was at war with the management of the municipality's administration to secure necessary funding for adequate staffing levels and group sizes that were conducive to a positive pedagogical experience for children.

Yet, most politicians and the management in the municipality deliberately misrepresented these problems. In the media, they claimed that there was no cause for concern over a drive towards what was being called, "efficiency." A top manager in the administration even stated in a meeting that *"children benefit from being a little scared."* In this way, government officials were aware that staffing levels and group sizes were leading to frightening situation for children, but attempted to position this as necessary and even "beneficial."

The same politician who claimed children *"benefit from being scared"* also stopped employees from providing Psychological Pedagogical Services (PPT) and special educational assistance in kindergartens (this time because we protested against efficiency). The atmosphere in our kindergarten programme and the sector overall was not good, to say the least. In parallel with these public statements discrediting children's experiences, there was increasing pressure on educators to produce children who were more developmentally advanced. Play, childhood, and a child's right to actively participate in programmes was on the decline, whilst more standardized and controlled pedagogical systems and methods were increasing. The focus shifted towards more imposed pre-packaged curriculum programme and tools, all the while mapping and measuring this formalised learning. Educators' professional autonomy and children's well-being were at stake.

Getting frustrated and feeling somewhat hopeless that online articles and emails to politicians weren't getting us anywhere, a small group of educators created a closed Facebook group which we called "The kindergarten of the future – best for the children." We invited kindergarten people (educators, administrators, and allies) from all over the country to give their opinions about what was best for the children. Among other things, I wrote this in the description of the group:

> Let's start a kindergarten revolution, where those who work in kindergarten, we who are actually the experts, set the agenda for the sector. Together we are stronger.

This Facebook group brought together many people who previously did not know each other. Through ongoing discussions and sharing information, it quickly became apparent that many people cared about the pressing issues in kindergarten in Norway and we quickly began to build a community. I am not saying that it was this group that started the *Barnehageopprøret*, but it is true that several of the people included in this group later took on leadership roles in the movement. It was also around this time that the language of *opprør*, meaning rebellion, emerged. We actively referred to ourselves, and continue to refer to our movement as the *Barnehageopprøret*, which quite literally translates to "kindergarten rebellion." And of course, we – the people of the movement – are the rebels bringing rebellion to life.

We kept our online conversations going for several months, letting our thoughts, ideas, and concerns simmer. When the government presented its report to parliament on March 19, 2016, the *Barnehageopprøret* caught fire!

The government report, loosely translated to "Better Content in Kindergartens," was to lay the foundation for a new framework plan for what Norwegian kindergartens should be. Among other things, the government wanted a standard of language skills that children had to meet. They also wanted a description of how kindergarten better prepares children for formal school. This was the event that triggered professionals to act, as there was a widespread consensus among educators that such an approach to early learning would be devastating for children and to the idea of childhood.

For me personally, being a part of the group ignited a fighting spirit. I was no longer just thinking about my kindergarten and municipality, but the whole kindergarten sector. We had to believe that it was possible to influence the elected representatives in parliament so that all children and employees would have an almost equal and better time in kindergarten.

The kindergarten teacher Eivor Evenrud from Oslo, who was a publicly profiled voice in the debates about the kindergarten sector, took the initiative to organise a meeting in response to the report. Since more than 200 people expressed their interest in this meeting, we borrowed an auditorium at the then Oslo and Akershus University College. On April 20, 2016, more than a hundred people flocked through the doors.

In the auditorium, kindergarten teachers, parents, researchers, and professors were gathered, with one thing in common: we were angry, sad, and upset with the direction the government was trying to take kindergarten. Yet, there was a renewed sense of hope as we could see and feel that there was will and passion to resist these externally imposed measures. As frustrated and tired as I was, I felt hope and rejuvenation. I felt inspired by all those who got up, spoke, as it provided a much-needed boost after years of feeling defeated. I had never encountered this fighting spirit before. It was in this coming together in Oslo that the *Barnehageopprøret* really took off.

One of the first things we did was create an "action group" – a group who would turn our worries and concerns into concrete actions that we could take. An immediate opportunity we had at the time was that the government report on "Better content in kindergardens" was to be heard in Parliament a month later. While there was not much time, the *Barnehageopprøret* was growing quickly and being noticed. Media pressure increased in the coming weeks. When the report was due to be heard in parliament, we had organised a protest where hundreds of kindergarten teachers stood in line outside the entrance to parliament. I was proud to be among them. The employees in parliament were taken by surprise. There were close to a hundred protestors who did not come in, simply because there was no room.

In this case, our efforts made a difference. The implementation of language standards and school-readiness outcomes of children were voted down. The rebels could celebrate! A new framework plan for kindergartens was drafted and adopted and this time it did not include the standardised language assessments.

It was as if someone had turned on a light. Finally, the kindergarten teachers dared to speak out. We were being heard. And we would not stop there.

Several of the passionately engaged members in the action group gathered for a new meeting just before Christmas in 2017. A new battle was upon us. The government had proposed a new staffing norm which was now out for consultation. We were concerned because there was no requirement for this new norm (itself not concerning) to apply throughout the opening hours of kindergartens. It thus looked good on paper (and would sound good in political announcements) but could be harmful for children. If this legislation passed, there would be long periods of the day when employees had to be responsible for far *more* children than the staffing norm stipulates. If a staffing norm were to make a difference, it would have to apply throughout the entirety of the kindergarten's opening hours. We, the rebels, turned our energy towards resisting these new norms. Now we had to carve out a strategy before it was too late.

In Sweden, there had already been an uprising about low staffing levels among kindergarten employees. They had received attention on social media through the hashtag #pressatläge (pressured situation). The question was whether we could achieve something similar in Norway. If so, what should we call it? It had to be something that was not used in other contexts. And it had to be eye-catching and evoke emotion.

In January, the action group decided on the hashtag #indefensible. We all agreed that the actions of the government in relation to kindergarten were simply impossible to defend. Now there was one thing left to do. The employees in the kindergartens had to dare to share their troubling stories from kindergarten life.

The government's proposal for a new staffing norm led to increasing engagement in the Facebook group. Within a few days, thousands of new members joined the group.

It is not easy to talk negativity about life in kindergarten. We knew we would get criticism from within the sector because publicly sharing negative stories about kindergartens upset educators and administrators who were doing the best they could. But we felt we had to talk about what is not right to make things better. While there was some resistance to the *Barnehageopprøret* from within the sector, solidarity with the movement increased as our motivations (exposing what was not okay and demanding better experiences for children) became clearer. More voices came on the scene with sharper and more precise language than before. On February 15, 2018, the action group issued an invitation to kindergarten employees to share their stories with the hashtag #indefensible. On our Facebook page we stated:

> "Everyone is encouraged to share their kindergarten story. We need to shed light on these issues!"

Within a couple of days over a hundred #indefensible stories came in. They were about children who needed a diaper change but had to wait; crying children whom educators could not comfort due to other demands; educators feeling forced to tell white lies to parents to blunt the reality of how difficult things sometimes were; and substitute teachers who had not been paid by centre owners. The posts kept coming. Over 350 came in in two months – more than five new stories every single day.

Through the #indefensible campaign, we had an agreement with Dagsavisen – a local online newspaper. In partnership with them, we published the stories and then shared them on Facebook. Between February and May 2018, #indefensible stories were the most read and shared debate posts at Dagsavisen.

Enlightened by the *Barnehageopprøret* and the stories from educators, Caroline Marita Omberg, mother of two, established the Facebook-group "Parents' Uprising" (*Foreldreopprøret*). Since that groups' inception (April 2018), our two groups have collaborated closely.

The key issue bringing together the parent and educator kindergarten uprising movements were concerns about staffing levels. However, building a parent movement was compounded by the fact that few parents know the reality of the staffing situation in kindergartens. Parents are only there a few minutes every day to drop off and pick up their kids. Most kindergarten educators and administrators have been too good at pretending that everything is fine and only conveying sunny stories of life in kindergarten (the "white lies" referred to above). The #indefensive stories being published and shared caught the attention of parents. With parents and educators allied in their concerns, the hope was that all kindergarten rebels, educators, and parents alike could get the attention of the politicians in parliament.

And we did. Outside parliament on May 9, 2018, the *Barnehageopprøret* handed over several hundred #indefensible stories to The Minister of Education, and other politicians. In addition, the *Foreldreopprøret* (parent uprising) had collected over 26,000 signatures that were handed over.

At this event, one rebel made an appeal to those in power on behalf of the *Barnehageopprøret*. She put into words everything that is demanded and expected of kindergarten educators. She stated:

> Among other things, we (educators) are supposed to:
>
> - prevent bullying and mental health problems;
> - detect and deal with abuse and neglect;
> - ensure social equalisation, integration, and good language skills;
> - facilitate good self-esteem;
> - create an environment for play, joy of life, and social development;
> - lay a good foundation for the rest of life;
> - see each individual child and meet their needs.

We know that good kindergartens can have a positive impact on children's development, mental health, and opportunities to do well in life. Unfortunately, kindergartens can also have a negative impact on children, if what we provide in kindergarten is poor. Low staffing and large groups of children combined with the wrong staff is a sure way to deliver poor quality. Since we know that good kindergartens provide a health benefit, we must also care for them by caring for what matters most – adequate staffing and competent employees who have the authority and autonomy to use their professional competence in their work.

Resistance in action

The *Barnehageopprøret* action group has used many different tactics to resist. Organised through a closed Facebook group, we make strategic plans, share responsibilities, support each other, provide input, ask for help or guidance, and design articles and posts or agree on status updates. All the different forms of action we have initiated have been posted, shared, and advertised on Facebook and sometimes also on Twitter.

One less contentious tactic was to implement "Red Day." This was a day where educators were encouraged to dress in red and post photos on social media to bring attention to the issues in kindergarten. This was a "harmless" and positive unifying form of action that led to great political involvement of educators. Many parents also dressed their children in red to show their support. It seemed that far more people were willing to publicly share their support for the movement public than when they had to describe their working conditions in negative ways.

As a follow-up to the #indefensible campaign of 2018, we launched the #actually and #really campaigns in September 2019. Stories with the hashtag

"#really" focused on what is *really* happening in kindergartens while those with the hashtag #actually painted a picture of what staffing levels are *actually* necessary for positive learning experiences. Again, we received an overwhelming response.

Another effective, more contentious tactic was focusing on the perspectives of children. In connection with Kindergarten Day on March 12, 2018 (a union-led event that highlights the important work of educators around a particular theme), we launched the #Iwonder campaign. Instead of centring the voices of educators, we turned it around to focus on children who we observed to be worried, anxious, and insecure due to the inadequacy of staffing levels. We posted generalised concerns that we believed children felt. For example:

"I wonder if anyone sees that I'm sad today?"

"I wonder if anyone will take care of me?"

"I wonder if I'll get help going to the bathroom"?

This campaign was a huge success, with lots of sharing and attention given to the insufficient staffing norm. While the union were not pleased with this tactic as it seemed to undermine the day they organised to celebrate educators, it was incredibly effective at getting the attention of citizens. In a meeting with the unions, I (as a representative of the *Barnehageopprøret*) apologised and promised to not use this day as a springboard for further action in the future.

In summary…

In summary, resistance works. While our campaigns have been, and continue to be, an enormous amount of work, the successes we have achieved are worth it. We successfully rejected the government's initial framework that pushed language standards and the overall academic push-down of formal didactic teaching/learning to kindergartens. We managed to take out the most problematic aspects of the staffing norm while also upholding a degree of pedagogical autonomy for educators (though it is far from good enough). Perhaps most importantly, educators came together, with parents, and found their voices. Children's needs and experiences were centred and appeared to matter to a broad public. In just under 2 years, the kindergarten teacher became a political player to be reckoned with.

The *Barnehageopprøret* is quite unique in its unification of educators and parents. As educators, we can be accused of whining and blackmailing for our own gain. Being allied so strongly with parents made these accusations almost impossible to uphold. Clearly, parents' and educators' primary concerns were with the children.

Another success of the movement is that we've been noticed in an international community. For example, in October 2019, Kari Eide (a former kindergarten educator) presented the story of the kindergarten uprising at the

Reconceptualising Early Childhood Education conference, in New Mexico, USA. I am very excited to share my narrative in this book chapter. Who would have thought that a small group of kindergarten educators from Norway would achieve everything we have achieved when we started the uprising 6 years ago?

I'm not sure if we would have managed this to the same degree, and at least not as effectively, without social media as a tool. We became visible to many and the grassroots and the decision makers have become closer as a result of the engagement on social media.

In the national election in September 2021, the first outspoken kindergarten rebel was voted in as a representative in parliament, Hege Bae Nyholt, from Rødt. She is now chair of the Education and Research Committee. The battle for better staffing is not over, and there is now new blood in the action group, committed rebels ready to speak on behalf of the children. The pandemic has only highlighted how insufficient the staffing norm actually is, and how important it is that the kindergarten uprising continues to fight for kindergarten rights and better staffing in the country's kindergartens.

In February 2022, a new campaign, like the previous ones, was released on Facebook, called #sayit. Again, the focus was on encouraging kindergarten people to anonymously say the things they may be too afraid to say to their employers or leaders.

At the same time, a positive campaign with the term kindergarten 2030 was introduced, with reels and pictures shared on Instagram. This campaign shows that things are much better (in an imaginary 2030), because politicians and the public finally took responsibility for ensuring children, educator, and parents have positive experiences in kindergarten. While the work can be exhausting, our victories are well worth the effort. Our children, and those who care about and for them, truly deserve better.

Concluding thoughts

This section explored the various discourses used to position childcare as a commodity. We are particularly troubled by the deep entrenchment of children as future human capital in a market economy and ECEC as a technology to ensure that children will continue to be moulded into economically productive future adults. The cases from Australia, Aotearoa/New Zealand, Indonesia, Nigeria, and Norway provide concrete examples of alternatives and of resistance to this dominant neoliberal story. In both Australia and Aotearoa/New Zealand, children are understood as agentic actors in the present moment. While Vina Adriany presents the Indonesian context and reflects on the possibilities of Islamic religious discourse to counter a globalised neoliberal vision of childcare as a commodity, Hoana McMillan presents a success story that requires continual struggle to ensure its survival, of a Māori national and community initiative to reimagine ECEC as upholding and promoting Māori cultural values that position children as powerful and in control of their destinies. Esther Oduolowu's case on valuing Indigenous African ECEC theories and practices is another setting where decolonisation and decommodification go hand in hand. The *Barnehageopprøret* is an example of the inextricably connected, embodied needs of children, educators, parents, and allies organizing themselves to ensure their needs are met. These examples challenge what some have come to understand as the foundation and justification of ECEC. They provide inspiration and hope that educators, families, and communities can listen to young children, and reimagine what childcare can be, neither a commodity nor a service, but a space for democratic community building, well-being in the here and now, fun, laughter, joy, and love, unique and responsive to local contexts and cultures.

This entire section begs the question of offering an alternative. How can things be different? What other ways of caring for children might we wish to see? While there are a plethora of different options, we propose that a care(full) pedagogy that centres the needs of the humans and more-than-humans involved in the care process is a starting point. Inspired by the work of Rachel Langford (2019), Joan Tronto (2013), Jean Keller and Eva Feder Kittay (2017), and other feminist ethics of care theorists, we feel that there is an urgent need to centre care in ECE spaces. Care is defined as "the every-thing that we do to maintain, continue, and repair our "world" so that we can live in it as well as possible" (Tronto, 1993, p. 103). Amidst the ongoing violence of neoliberalism and commodification, repair is what is so urgently needed. Through an ethics of care lens, good care is fundamentally rooted in the lived experiences of caregivers and care receivers, two roles that are not mutually exclusive but always overlapping and intersecting. We wonder how paying attention to the phases of care, caring *about* (noticing need), caring *for* (taking responsibility for care), care *giving* (act of meeting need), care *receiving* (active response of care-receiver), and caring *with* (listening to others and acting in a politically informed way) (Tronto, 2013) could act to interrupt the ongoing commodification of childcare in an increasingly unsustainable world.

We recognise this model, in and of itself, is not perfect. Indeed, feminist ethics of care has been criticised on many fronts, not least of which is its lack of an intersectional analysis. However, we argue that if the final stage of care, caring *with* others (including the more-than-human world), is genuinely respected, we can get off the path to destruction we are currently on and begin to repair ourselves, each other, and the places and spaces in which we live.

In accordance with a feminist ethics of care (Langford & Richardson, 2020; Langford, Powell, & Bezanson, 2020), we posit that reconceptualizing ECEC as a reciprocal, responsive, and valuable process includes making meaning through relations and accepting that ECEC is a complex, time-intensive process that simply does not fit within a neoliberal framework of commodification. Good care cannot be made more "efficient" through applying technologies: it can only be done with effort, reflection, humility, and an openness to the other.

Notes

1 In some cases, childcare programmes that had been funded through emergency wartime measures remained operational, but alternative funding streams were sourced. For example, in Ontario, Canada, the City of Toronto (often in collaboration with private organizations or partners) stepped in to ensure programmes did not close their doors. Nevertheless, the end of WWII marked the end of direct federal funding to childcare programmes in Canada.
2 A non-government organization tasked with addressing Māori grievances.
3 The New Zealand government's external agency that evaluates the services of educational providers.
4 Throughout this section, "quality" is consistently put in quotation marks as we, the authors, would argue that quality can be thought about in a variety of different ways based on one's understanding of the value and purpose of childcare.
5 There is a darker side to these optional ECEC programmes, as immigrant children have been required to attend at least 25 hours a week if they live in neighborhoods with a high proportion of immigrants. When participation is mandated for marginalized groups in this way, the programmes reflect a concerning assimilation agenda (Barry & Sorenson, 2018).
6 Translation from Norwegian to English by Phillip Anthony Sampson, Child and youth worker in Smedhusåsen kindergarden SA.

Some parts of the text in this chapter are inspired or taken from the report; #uforsvarlig: Historien om et barnehageoppprør - «#inDefensible: The story of a kindergarten uprising », by Jørgen Jelstad. Published on Utdanningsnytt.no, 28.05.2018.

3
RESISTING THE CONSUMENTALITY OF PARENTS

Michel Vandenbroeck, Joanne Lehrer, and Linda Mitchell

With the collaboration of:

Maarit Alasuutari, Marie-Laure Cadart, Kirsti Karila, Tullia Musatti, Pablo Rupin, and Gail Yuen

Consumentality, a cultural hegemony

When education becomes a commodity, parents are increasingly viewed as consumers. This is most noticeable in contexts of marketisation and privatisation of early childhood education and care (ECEC). Parents as customers are expected to critically compare the ECEC at offer, and to consider quality, price, and practicalities (e.g. distance or opening hours). Adam Smith's ideology regarding the invisible hand of the market forms the basis for the assumption that parents are consumers who engage in rational decision-making to select childcare. If parents act as rational consumers, eventually, the market is expected to adapt by creating an offer that will respond to demand; by increasing the quality of this offer to attract clients in a competitive environment; and by eventually offering a sound balance between price and quality. That is what the argument (or theory) states would happen if the market were perfect, but empirical studies demonstrate otherwise. An early wave of critical studies argued that ECEC does not function as a perfect market and never will, due to information asymmetry among other reasons, since the necessary conditions are not and can never be ensured. Parents cannot have information for instance on the meaningful interactions between adults and children and among the children. A typical study in this vein was conducted by James Walker (1991). The study is based on concepts developed by economists, such as the concept of the perfect market and its efficiency. In this context, efficiency means: "the ability to produce the most goods and services for the resources available" (Walker, 1991, p. 51). The study documents why childcare is not "efficient" and therefore not a perfect market. It argues that understanding market operations (or, equivalently, assessing market efficiency) should precede normative policy analysis and design and that therefore government intervention is necessary. However, the study does not challenge the idea

DOI: 10.4324/9781003218104-4

that childcare *should* be marketised and that policies *should* try to create childcare markets. Nor does it challenge the idea that childcare is reduced to an instrument for labour market policies, that is policies that allow mothers to enter the labour force. What they do criticise is information asymmetry. Walker (1991, p. 53) for instance shows that "information on prices in the childcare market is scarce" and that – in the absence of government regulations – "the child care industry has been forced to compromise the quality of care it currently offers." Despite their critical stance, this first wave of critics continued to adopt a narrow economic perspective of ECEC and seemed to utterly regret the "malfunctioning" of ECEC in such economic terms (e.g. Walker, 1991, Mocan, 2007). Another typical example of this economic perspective is a study by Naci Mocan. He compared the assessment of quality by parents with what he labels as "the actual quality." The results of his study, he argued, "demonstrate the existence of information asymmetry and adverse selection in the market, which provide an explanation for low average quality in U.S. child care market" (Mocan, 1997, p. 743).

If parents were only better informed, the argument goes, the childcare market would become more efficient and welfare costs would be reduced (Walker, 1991). It is remarkable that studies from an entirely different standpoint, namely in the field of developmental psychology, follow the same reasoning. As a typical example, Debby Cryer and Margaret Burchinal (1997) report about how "parents as childcare consumers" assess quality and they compared these assessments with quality ratings by trained experts, to find out that parents rated the quality significantly higher than experts did. That obviously does not come as a surprise as parents cannot rate the process quality of the service that takes place when they are absent. As Cryer and Burchinal (1997, p. 35) noted: "When parents and observers rated the quality of aspects of care that were easy to monitor, differences in parent/observer quality scores were smaller than when they rated aspects that were more difficult to monitor." The authors gave several different interpretations of their findings (e.g. parents assume that what is most important for their child will be present; parents compare with their home situation; etc.). Cryer and Burchinal's final conclusion was that "(…) the specifics of the dimensions of high quality may need to be taught to parents before they can assume the role of effective advocates for high quality care that will help to optimise their children's development" and thus that "Further study is needed before policy makers can feel secure in relying on parents as well-informed consumers or effective monitors of early childhood programs" (Cryer & Burchinal, 1997, pp. 55–56).

Three things are striking in this vein of research. First, the alignment between economists and developmental psychologists on the assumption that childcare *is* or at least *should be* a market (albeit an imperfect one) and that parents can or should be viewed as consumers. Second, the individualisation of parental responsibility about quality and the concurrent withdrawal of public responsibility; and third, the lack of reflection on what constitutes quality. It is indeed remarkable that economists and developmental psychologists both accept the idea of parents as consumers of commodified childcare without questioning it. It could be assumed that reasoning in terms of the market is what economists do (however, certainly not all economists think that way), but it is illustrative of the dominance of economic thinking that permeates all other aspects of life, that this conceptualisation is shared by scholars in psychology. While they both agree that ECEC does not function as a market, they also both agree that this is deplorable, as if they are unable to come up with another meaning for ECEC. They do not seem to be able to come up with another conceptualisation of the relationship between public and private responsibilities over a common good.

The parent as a consumer is, by all means, an individual. It is he (but more often she) who is assumed responsible for the right childcare choice. According to Walker (1991), that parent should be educated to be ready to take on this responsibility. Cryer and Burchinal (1997) argue that there is not much one can do, as this parental deficit is inherent in their position as outsiders. Of course, some scholars disagree. Shlay and colleagues (2005), for instance, did similar research with low-income African American mothers. They found that parental definitions of quality mirrored professional standards, as the parents desired childcare characteristics that were consistent with how child development experts define and evaluate childcare quality. Their conclusion was: "The study findings do not suggest that low-income families do not want to pay for quality care. On the contrary, parents believe that quality has economic value, and they are willing to pay more for it. They may not, however, be able to pay the full cost for quality care" (Shlay, Tran, Weinraub, & Harmon, 2005, p. 414). Scholars who frame parents as being in deficit (such as Walker) as well as those in defence of parents (such as Shlay et al.) both view childcare in economic terms as a commodity and think in terms of value for money. Both share the view of the ideal parent as a critical consumer. They also see the parent as (at least partly) responsible for the quality of childcare, as explicitly stated in Cryer and Burchinal's (1997) study. If only the parent was better informed, Mocan (1997) argued, she would be better equipped to *monitor* quality and to obtain or choose childcare that was a better value for its price. In other words, for Mocan and many other scholars in the field, not only is the parent responsible for the quality of childcare, but also for the failure of the market. Only two options remain for this vein of research in order to reach the common goal of the "perfect market" (and there is little doubt that this is the common-sense idea of what is to be aimed for): either the parent (for Mocan among others) has to be improved or we need a quest for more competition so that critical choice becomes more feasible (for Shlay et al. among others).

Finally, a third remark is to be noted regarding the concept of quality. In all the examples mentioned here, what exactly quality *is* is not questioned or explored in the study. Quality is a truth, something objective out there, that can be studied and that, above all, can be measured and expressed as a number. Parental judgements can therefore be compared to expert judgements, as if there is no disagreement among experts on what are the more important dimensions of quality and as if these expert judgements are above all suspicion or debate. For instance, when parents rate quality higher than experts do (as most studies show), then it seems obvious for the researchers to look for reasons why parents fail in their judgements, or why they "overrate" quality. Of course, scholars also may respect that parents attach value to aspects that are overlooked by experts (such as valuing ethnic and cultural diversity, in Shlay et al., 2005 study), but then, that is seldom included in their definition of "quality." Rather, it is labelled as "values," apparently a somewhat lower status judgement, because "values" are considered less objective than the concept of "quality."

In all cases, the language of choice is the dominant language in the field. Parents are expected to choose childcare in the best interest of their child. They may do so in better or worse ways, but in all cases that is what parents are supposed to do. And thus, the use of childcare is believed to be the result of that choice. When a child ends up in a lower quality childcare, this means that parents should have made a better choice. The status of consumer and the language of choice reduce the parents to passives clients, whose only possibility is to change to another provider when he or she is not "satisfied." That is of course an entirely different (and quite shallow) conception of democratic participation as it denies parents the possibility of a dialogue on the meaning of ECEC while reducing parental opinions to client *satisfaction*.

The concept of parent satisfaction has remained a central topic in research about childcare and it has been too easily assumed that satisfaction is related to childcare quality. When all or most parents are satisfied, then all is well, isn't it? A typical example of the language of parents as consumers is found in a report of a study on childcare needs, commissioned by the Flemish government (Vanpée, Sannen, & Hedebouw, 2000). It examined "parental choice," assuming that what parents do (that is: where they enrol their child) is the result of a rational choice, based on their preferences. Then they assessed client satisfaction and noted that parents were highly satisfied, whether they used well-regulated and well-funded public childcare or made use of private, poorly funded provision where staff had no professional qualifications and rather poor working conditions. The report concluded: "the general satisfaction shows that all parents in general find what they were looking for and that the different childcare systems have similar quality, despite strengths and weaknesses that may be present in each system." Subsequently, the report was used to legitimise the poorly funded and poorly regulated childcare sector. It is a salient example of how the language of parents as consumers, and of choice and satisfaction, legitimates the withdrawal of public responsibility. The alleged connection between choice, satisfaction, and quality has also in other parts of the world been used as a legitimation of inequalities and of the status quo (see Gingras, Audet, & Nanhou, 2011 for a similar example in Québec).

If all parents are satisfied, all is well in the best of possible worlds, isn't it? No, it is not. The fact is that parental satisfaction has little to do with quality. Neither with quality, as traditionally expressed by experts, nor with how parents conceive of quality or of what ECEC means to them. A case in point is another and more recent study in Flanders, collecting satisfaction rates of 2,650 parents from 380 infant and toddler childcare settings. The settings were also evaluated by childcare experts with mainstream observational instruments to assess process quality (i.e. CLASS Infant and CLASS Toddler). Quality, in this study, thus focused on meaningful interactions between the adults and the children with two main dimensions: emotional support (including sensitivity and responsivity to the children's needs, closeness, and confidence) and educational support (including for instance language support, extension of the child's experience, and quality of feedback). Just as in most studies, results revealed that satisfaction showed very little variation, as most parents were quite satisfied with all provisions, despite important quality differences, as measured by the instruments. One can indeed ask what else to expect. Would it not be very difficult to be unsatisfied as a parent with the quality of the childcare used, when the dominant discourse assumes that the use of a specific form of childcare is the result of one's individual choice (and thus the individual's responsibility)? Second, the researchers found that the slight variations in satisfaction were only very moderately explained by variations in childcare quality, nor by characteristics of parents or of services (Janssen, Spruyt, & Vandenbroeck, 2021). According to Meyers and Jordan (2006), what parents mean by "quality" and "satisfaction" may very well reflect their accommodation to the competing demands of earning and care giving responsibilities. According to Janssen et al. (2021), satisfaction reflects the accommodation to the constraints of limited choice, related to availability and affordability and according to De Swaan (1972) "satisfaction" merely expresses how well one finds to have acted as a parent, which, in this case, may be a reflection of how one has interiorised the individual responsibility and the language of choice. Whatever the assumptions made, there is a consensus that satisfaction is not a quality criterion and one can wonder what it exactly is that is expressed by the concept and what it means that is used in the narratives on quality.

The assumption that parents are consumers and that childcare functions like a market assumes that the consumer chooses the product that is most adapted to his or her needs, preferences, and values. However, in a majority of countries, there is a substantial shortage of places, especially for the youngest children. Therefore, "choice" is a disputable concept, as some parents have far more choice than others. In most EU countries, for instance, there is a geographical inequality, meaning that higher income families have more choice than their lower income counterparts (Vandenbroeck, 2019). As Erica Burman (1997) stated, the language of choice may very well serve to mask structural forms of inequality. The case of Finland is an interesting example of what the language of choice provokes and how it may contribute to inequality, as the research of Maarit Alasuutari and Kirsti Karila shows in the following case study.

The language of choice: The case of Finland

Maarit Alasuutari and Kirsti Karila

Finland's ECEC includes centre-based services and family daycare, but the latter is quite rare nowadays. In 2019, only about six percent of children attending

ECEC were enrolled in public family daycare (THL, 2020). Finnish ECEC is based on the principle of educare, in other words, it is an integrated service that provides both care and education for children aged 0–6 years. In Finland, the language of parental choice focuses on two "choices." The first "choice" is made when the parental leave period ends, and the child is 9–10 months old. Then, parents can opt either for a cash-for-care benefit or public/publicly subsidised ECEC services. The benefit is called child home care allowance (*kotihoidon tuki*) and it is paid until the child turns three. As the name of the benefit suggests, it is typically linked with the choice of home care, although it can also be used to buy informal care services. If the parents opt for ECEC services, they may be faced with the second "choice" and need to decide whether they want to enrol their child in private or public ECEC provision. While both these "choices" are commonly seen as giving parents the possibility of deciding what is best for their child and their family (Hiilamo & Kangas, 2009; Ruutiainen, Alasuutari, & Karila, 2020), parents' possibilities of "choosing" are not equal. Historically, the two "choices" also differ considerably.

Child home care allowance

The child home care allowance was established in some Finnish municipalities in the 1960s as a state experiment, and became a statutory benefit nationwide in 1984. The enforcement of the child home care allowance was a result of a compromise between the Social Democrats, the Centre Party, and the National Coalition Party. For the Centre Party, the benefit meant a compensation for the rural families who did not need or have access to public daycare – as ECEC services were called at the time. The Coalition Party again saw home care allowance as a means to support private care solutions. The other part of the compromise, and what the Social Democrats got, was the statutory entitlement to daycare for all children under 3 years of age, which came into force in 1990. In 1996, the entitlement to a place in ECEC with an income-related parental fee was expanded to include all children under school age (Anttonen, 1994; 1999; Repo, 2010). Still today, the legislation denies the entitlement to ECEC for those children for whom the parent is paid a home care allowance. Thus, the Finnish policies include an either-or positioning of home care and ECEC.

Since the 1980s, Finnish society has changed significantly and the child home care allowance has lost its original importance as equalising state support for rural families. However, throughout the decades, the child home care allowance has become a central issue in Finnish debates on childcare policy (Hiilamo & Kangas, 2009; Rantalaiho, 2010; Salmi, 2006) and still has strong support in national policy, although children's participation in ECEC is increasingly encouraged. The child home care allowance consists of a care allowance, which is not affected by the family's income, and a care supplement that depends on the size and gross income of the family. In 2021, the care allowance amounted to €343 per month for one child under 3 years of age, while the maximum amount of the care supplement was about €184 per month. The child home care allowance can also be paid for the older siblings of the child under 3 years. In 2019, families were paid about €103 per month for each additional child under 3 years of age and €66 per month for each child over 3 years of age but under school age, if the children were not enrolled in ECEC (Kela, 2021).

Besides being on the national political agenda, the child home care allowance is also important in municipal policies and many municipalities pay a local supplement on top of the nationally regulated benefit. Depending on its amount, the municipal supplement seems to have an impact on parents' decisions (Räsänen, Österbacka, Valaste, & Haataja, 2019), and it is considered a means to control the demand for ECEC services (Lahtinen & Svartsjö, 2020).

Nowadays, almost all parents – predominantly mothers – receive a home care allowance at least for a few months after the parental leave period and many until the child is about 2 years of age (Räsänen, Österbacka, Valaste, Haataja, 2019). Based on its popularity, the child home care allowance seems to have become an option for all families in Finland. However, due to the municipal supplements, the option is not the same everywhere in the country; there is an issue of regional inequality. In terms of family income, how profitable it is to them to opt for the home care allowance depends on where the family lives. Furthermore, since the home care allowance was established, it attracts parents and families differently. Mothers from lower socioeconomic groups without a permanent employment more often opt for home care allowances and care for their children at home for longer periods of time than mothers from more affluent families (Närvi, 2014; Räsänen, Österbacka, Valaste, Haataja, 2019). For these mothers, the home care allowance might provide a better and more "honourable" income than an unemployment compensation does. The allowance might also be more profitable for the family than a dual-salary and paying for ECEC services.

The child home care allowance and the interlinked either-or positioning of home care and ECEC may also have consequences for the siblings of the under 3-year-old if they do not attend ECEC (Kela, 2021). Municipal supplements to the home care allowance may demand the home care of all the under-school-age children in the family (Närvi, Salmi, & Lammi-Taskula, 2020). Thus, the benefit includes an incentive – or may even require parents to – exclude 3–5-year-old children from attending ECEC.

Overall, the child home care allowance is much debated in Finland from sociopolitical, gender, and economic viewpoints. The argumentation underlines the negative impact of the allowance on women's careers, income, and future pensions. Moreover, the need to increase labour market participation, and through it, national prosperity, is emphasised. At the same time, the child home care allowance and its local supplements can be considered a family-friendly policy. The allowance has strong support among parents of young children, although many consider the municipal supplement system unequal. Many parents want to spend time with their young child(ren) and therefore opt for home care and the home care allowance (Sulkanen et al., 2020). The flip side of the coin is that the norm of home care of a young child is strong in Finland – at least partly due to the home care allowance. Thus, it may not be easy for parents to "choose" differently and enrol a young child in ECEC. Parents/mothers who enrol their 1-year-old in ECEC seem to struggle with a moral dilemma regarding whether ECEC can be considered best for their child and if they can be considered good enough parents if they do not care for their child at home (Terävä, Kuukka, & Alasuutari, 2018).

Public or private?

While the "choice" regarding home care and ECEC dates back to the 20th century, the other "choice" – between public and private ECEC – has entered Finnish ECEC discourse during the 2010s as a result of demand-based subsidies paid in particular by municipalities to support local private ECEC provision. Traditionally, Finnish ECEC has been predominantly public. A minor share of ECEC has also been provided by small, local for-profit entrepreneurs and non-profit agents that have been publicly subsidised through a daycare allowance available since the late 1990s. In 2000, of all children attending ECEC in Finland, 3.9 percent were enrolled in private services (Säkkinen & Kuoppala, 2017). Since the enforcement of the Act on Service Vouchers in Social Welfare and Health, AoSV (569/2009) in 2009, many municipalities have begun to provide ECEC vouchers for families. Moreover, municipalities may pay a local supplement. As a result, the private ECEC sector has expanded. In 2019, 18 percent of all children attending ECEC were enrolled in private ECEC (Säkkinen & Kuoppala, 2020). At the same time, private providers have changed in character as large national and multinational for-profit companies have begun to provide ECEC services in many municipalities and bought out small providers. However, this process has mainly taken place in cities and more densely populated areas and the share of private provision can exceed 40 percent in some larger municipalities. These developments differentiate ECEC provision from the provision of primary and secondary education, which is almost exclusively a public responsibility and protected from profit interests (Tuori, 2021).

As the geographical variation in the location of private ECEC provision suggests, parents in less populated areas do not usually have a "choice" between private and public ECEC, since these areas do not interest market-based for-profit ECEC providers or the municipality does not support their use. When private services are available, the fees they charge families depend on the local subsidy system, as well as on family size and income. If the subsidy is only partly income-based or a lump sum, the ECEC fee of low-income families will be a larger proportion of the household budget compared to what more affluent families pay (Ruutiainen, Alasuutari, & Karila, 2020). Furthermore, regardless of the form of the subsidy, private ECEC fees often seem to be somewhat higher than fees in public ECEC (Ruutiainen, Alasuutari, & Karila, 2020), although both have to follow the same regulations and quality standards. Research on the selectivity of the private ECEC clientele is still scarce in Finland. However, recent examinations suggest that "choosing" private services is linked to higher parent education and income (Ruutiainen, Räikkönen, & Alasuutari, 2021; Ruutiainen, Räikkönen, Alasuutari & Karila, in press).

Although private ECEC is presented as a "choice" for parents (Ruutainen, Alasuutari, & Karila, 2020), many parents seem to be unsure or have doubts about it. Two recent surveys addressed to parents of 1-year-old (Hietamäki et al., 2017) and 4-year-old children (Sulkanen et al., 2020) included five similar items studying the respondents' attitudes about private ECEC services. Based on the parents' responses, many of them do not quite know what to think about the increase in private ECEC provision. For example, over 50 percent of the parents of 4-year-olds responded "neither disagree nor agree" to several of the five items (Sulkanen et al., 2020, pp. 68–69). Most often parents expressed their opinion about the statement. "Municipalities should invest more in municipal ECEC provision than in subsidizing private services." Over 53 percent of the parents with a 4-year-old child agreed with this statement (Sulkanen et al., 2020, p. 68). Thus, it seems that many parents resist the marketisation of ECEC in Finland but also that many adhere to the privatisation. Both surveys also demonstrated an interesting difference among parents. In small municipalities, where there often are no private services, parents agreed more often with the statement "Private ECEC services should be more readily available" than parents in larger municipalities and cities, where the services are typically available. The parents in large municipalities and cities expressed more doubt about the quality of private ECEC (Hietamäki et al., 2017; Sulkanen et al., 2020). These findings suggest that public ECEC has strong support and trust among Finnish parents.

The Covid-19 pandemic and the lockdown in Spring 2020 have shown the vulnerability of market-based ECEC. Due to financial problems, some large multinational for-profit companies have shut down some of their ECEC provision in 2021. In one night, the "choice" of private ECEC may have become a nightmare for parents. Since municipalities in Finland are responsible for organising ECEC for all children living in their area, the shutting down of private services immediately became an issue for municipal ECEC provision. Municipalities were obligated to deal with the acute demand for services in these situations. Thus far such vulnerability of private ECEC services has not been topicalised in public discussion, nor has it been studied in Finland.

Political choice

Although the language of choice is inevitably part of Finnish childcare policy discourse, there seem to be some governmental tendencies that tackle the issues inherent in the two key "choices" presented above. While the Government's programme (Programme of Prime Minister Sanna Marin's Government, 2019) states that the child home care allowance system will not be changed, the government's decisions to lower ECEC fees can be seen as a means to decrease the benefit's incentive to home care, at least regarding the siblings of the child whom the benefit is paid for. Thus, the governmental decisions can be seen as aiming at lessening the "either home care or ECEC" tension in Finland. Increasing the participation in ECEC also motivated the national experiment of 20 hours per week free of charge ECEC for 5-year-olds for the period 2018–2021 (Siippainen et al., 2019). The same government also addressed for-profit ECEC and ordered a report on legal possibilities to restrict profit making in private ECEC (see also the example of Sweden in the section on Resisting the Alienation of the Workforce). According to the report, restrictions could perhaps be possible regarding pre-primary education, which is provided for 6-year-old children mostly in ECEC centres, but considering ECEC as a whole, restrictions to profit making might contradict the right to business and industry enforced in the Finnish constitution (Tuori, 2021). Thus, it seems that ECEC is rather conceived as a business than as education and that the language of "choice" regarding private and public ECEC services can still flourish unless pressure concerning investing in public ECEC services becomes stronger and attracts the attention of policymakers.

Choice and individual responsibility: a dispositive

Only recently have scholars begun to not only document that childcare *does not* function as a market, and that childcare *cannot* function as market, but also that childcare *should not* function as a market and that parents *should not* be considered rational consumers. Cleveland (2008) for instance claimed that childcare is of public interest. It is at the crossroads of employment policies, equal opportunity policies, gender policies, as well as educational policies and thus a matter of public interest that goes far beyond the accumulation of private needs and wants. That makes it a matter of public interest and thus of democratic negotiation, not of the sum of individual satisfactions. When parents rate quality, Cleveland (2008) states, they may not be rating the same thing as the external quality evaluation tools that are used, and their preferences might reflect diverse values. An Australian study, for instance, found that parents also identified societal issues beyond regulations as important quality indicators, including engagement with the local community and staff job satisfaction (Fenech, 2012).

Consumantality and the language of choice in early childhood care and education did not appear alone. They are part of a broader *dispositive*. For Michel Foucault (1994/2001), the term dispositive means a heterogeneous assemblage including discourses, institutions, architectural features, regulations and legislations, administrative measures, scientific narratives, philosophical propositions, morale, philanthropy, in sum, things that are said and things that remain silenced. What constitutes the dispositive, according to Foucault, is the relation between these apparently unrelated elements. At a certain moment in history, such a dispositive seems to respond to an urgency and it has a strategic function of domination, privileging particular power relations. The commodification of childcare, the legislative shift from supply-side funding to demand-side funding (through vouchers or tax reduction), the discourse of parental choice and satisfaction, together with the rise of a parent support industry, and a scientific discourse on the importance of the early years, materialised among others in the increasing popularity of neurosciences may – in this case – be considered as a real dispositive in the Foucauldian sense. That is not to say that all these different elements have been conceived together with the explicit or implicit aim to dominate. But they originate in a same (here: neoliberal) historical spirit and they create a specific social order, or at least have the societal *function* of maintaining a specific inequitable social order.

The term *parenting* emerged around the same time in English language policy documents, as the term *parentalité* did in French documents (Martin, 2015) and *opvoedingsondersteuning* (parenting support) in Dutch and Flemish policy documents. This new language is illustrative of how parenting support became a political issue in many European countries and beyond (Daly, 2015). Not only have parenting support initiatives mushroomed since the late 1990s, their nature also changed, towards parenting advice and skills training, rather than broader family support and towards greater state engagement with how parents rear their children, questioning their competence in this role (Daly, 2013). The types of interventions and services delivered to parents increasingly include information to parents containing expert knowledge on optimal child development and child-rearing; organised parenting classes and programmes aimed at training parenting skills, and group discussions where parents are expected to reflect on their own parenting behaviours; one-to-one counselling by experts, often with standardised protocols such as Triple P or Incredible Years; peer home-visiting programmes in which parents (mostly mothers) from a specific targeted group are trained to implement a home-visiting protocol to their peers in standardised programmes such as HIPPY and its many local variants; meeting groups of targeted parents who are believed to be at-risk, such as teenage parents, parents in poverty, ethnic minority fathers, single parents, etc. Parent support activities seldom take the form of civic engagement, policy advocacy, alliances of citizens that are supported to advocate for better quality ECEC, public provision, social housing, child-friendly environments, raising minimal wages, or safer traffic, despite the fact that these issues could genuinely support parents in their parenting roles. Most types of publicly funded parenting support frame the parent as an individual, focusing on the skills that need to be acquired, on critical introspection and stressing the individual responsibility of the parent (most often the mother) for the child's future. This raises questions such as why do States – across the political spectrum – think that parents need to be trained? How come childrearing in family homes has re-emerged as a social policy domain? What is precisely believed to be the social problem to which parent education is framed as the solution? When did we begin to think about skills when we think about the parent-child relationship? How come parents accept this? And why is it that this "parenting turn" has occurred in so many countries in this precise historical timeframe, a timeframe of consecutive economic crises, concurrent with the withdrawal of the State in other domains, of privatisation of public provision?

During this timeframe, governments in several countries published coercive laws in relation to parenting. A case in point is France, where after the riots in French suburbs in Autumn 2005, the Institut National de la Santé et de la Recherche Médicale (2005) analysed what they labelled as the causes of juvenile delinquency, using a developmental lens, and identifying risk factors for juvenile delinquency in early childhood. The report looked at parental education as the source of the problem and the possible solution to it. This formed the core of a political discussion in the French Senate and the Assemblée that led to proposing several legislative initiatives in the early years to prevent the risk of juvenile delinquency (Bockel, 2010). It generated uproar among early childhood professionals who allied in an association named *Pas de zéro de conduit pour les trois ans (no zero for conduct for the 3 year olds)*, gathering over 200,000 signatures in a few weeks' time. Despite the protests, legislation introduced the detection of early signs of risk (including parents who allegedly "refused" to speak the dominant language to their children), changing the legal protection of professional secrecy of social workers, and forcing certain parents of young children "at risk" to accept the supervision of a civil servant educator and eventually, the forced placement of children in internship in cases where their parents refuse the aid offered to them in parent support programmes (Collectif, 2006; Neyrand, 2006). The British Anti-Social Behaviour Orders (ASBOs) and Parental Orders are another example, framing deviant behaviour that is not strictly illegal and making coercive use of parent support programmes. Several countries lowered the compulsory school age, making early childhood education compulsory and – in so doing – decided that parents who do not send their child regularly enough to preschool are to be sanctioned. As a result, the question of why children of specific parents (i.e. parents with a migrant background) are less often present in preschool and what would be the needs of these children or their parents, or why the preschool may be less adapted to their expectations, disappeared from the public forum and what remained was deviance from the norms in which these parents did not have a say (Van Laere & Vandenbroeck, 2017).

In a previous section of this book, we commented on the conceptualisation of the child as a risk. Here, we witness its counterpart: the parent as a risk. A common feature of the parent support policies as well as of their more coercive variant is the focus on risks and the conceptualisation of parent support as risk management, supported by a "scientification" of parenting. As Knijn & Hopman (2015) argued, inspired mainly by psychological and epidemiological studies on the risks for children and young people, this has resulted in a large increase in diagnoses of deviations or potential deviations from so-called normal development. Parents as well as professionals are alarmed by each apparent sign of deviance and attempt to find solutions via a wide variety of intervention programmes, particularly those programmes defined as evidence-based. Such a focus on risks invites speculation about what can possibly go wrong and frequently, what can possibly go wrong is equated with what is likely to happen (Furedi, 2009 in Lee, 2014). The anxiety about parenting is influenced by profound sociological changes in the family, since the normative heterosexual marital household as a life-long construction has stopped being the prevailing norm. Today, legal parenthood does not necessarily coincide with educational responsibility or biological parenthood. As a result, what or who constitutes a family is not an unchangeable given, no longer subject to natural or religious laws, but a temporary cultural construct, made by humans and therefore always able to be unmade by humans. Marital roles, gender roles, and parenting roles do not necessarily coincide and are now less moulded by tradition than by personal choice (or at least they are perceived to be so). As a result, the French sociologist Gerard Neyrand (2012) argues, when the family disappears, the individual parent appears and this generates a mistrust in the parent, who is suspected not to be up to the task and up to his (yet mostly her) responsibilities. The individualisation of parenthood and its educational responsibilities ignores traditions of extended families taking responsibilities, just as it ignores ways in which ECEC, as well as other social services, can operate from a principle of empowerment to support social networks (Geens & Vandenbroeck, 2013).

Of course, this is not to be understood as something that parents passively undergo. Parents are active consumers of advice books and trainings, searching for the most appropriate ways to let their baby sleep, to toilet train their toddler, to give their children a head start with reading skills or early mathematics, to navigate through their child's adolescence, and so on. As Furedi (2001) explains, since parenting has been transformed from an intimate relationship, involving emotion and warmth as well as dreams, into a skill, involving technical expertise, the role of the expert assumes a special significance. To make matters worse, child professionals do not merely give advice. They intrude into parents' lives and undermine their confidence. Fundamental in the experts' advice is the idea that young children are highly vulnerable and that the first years in life are determinant to later development. Furedi (2001) labelled this as infant determinism. It is paired with parental determinism: the idea that what parents do will in the long term determine what children become. Even more importantly, what professionals do is help parents to help themselves (Knijn & Hopman, 2015), as the parenting turn also means a declining state responsibility regarding the contexts in which parents take up their parenting roles. It is one of the defining characteristics of the neoliberal welfare state, a welfare state that does not compensate for failures of the capitalist market but invests in future success; a welfare state with a growing focus on risk management, including the risk of future welfare costs, concerned with children's future employability. It is a welfare state where the protection against risks (of unemployment, of illness…) is considered a cost that needs to be avoided at all times, rather than a civil right. In this vein, the risk of infant and parent determinism is not only that parents would harm their children, but even more so that if parents do not do what is necessary for the optimal development of the child, they harm their future employability, the economy, and thus society. This forms the legitimation for far-reaching interventions, not of the public domain *against* the private domain, but of the state in agreement *with* parents who have interiorised their individual responsibility. The German legislation, for instance, framed it as *Aufwachsen in öffentlicher und privater Verantwortung* (growing up in public and private accountability) under the auspices of an *achtsamer Staat* (an attentive state) (Ostner & Stolberg, 2015). But, as Furedi (2001, p. 162) aptly notes:

> From the Government downwards, everybody involved in the parenting debate reiterates the need to support parents and families. Parents do need support, but not the kind that is generally on offer. Parents need access to quality childcare, and we need child-friendly communities. Most important of all, as parents we need to know that the decisions, we take about the future of our children will be supported and not undermined by the rest of society. Sadly, the term 'support' is often used as an euphemism for offering advice and training about how parents should behave. Parenting education is primarily oriented towards altering adult behaviour and providing mothers and fathers with skills that they allegedly lack. The pity is, however, that projects that aim to transform incompetent adults into skilled parents have the unintended consequence of disempowering mothers and fathers and empowering the professionals.

Ideology and hegemony

What we have labelled as *consumentality* is the reduction of parents to clients or consumers, not only in legislative texts and research, but also in the thoughts and minds of parents themselves. This consumentality can be considered as a result of a dispositive in the Foucauldian sense. Many different and heterogeneous elements coincide: scientific research (e.g. the use of neuroscience that sketches a deterministic view on the first years of life and thus stresses parental responsibilities); institutions (e.g. mushrooming parent support services that tend to individualise parental responsibilities); legislation (both coercive regulations and changing funding mechanisms, including funding parent advice services and skills training as well as shifting from supply side to demand side funding of ECEC); publications (the proliferation of parenting advice books that very often lead to making parents feel even more insecure); and especially changing conceptions of the role of the State and the very nature of the welfare state. The result of these political changes may not be what is promised and advocated for. The marketisation of childcare has increased its inequality, rather than resulting in more equal opportunities. The language of choice has not offered more choice (at least not for all). Competition in ECEC has not increased quality. Demand-side funding has not created innovation or flexible childcare, and parents have never been more doubtful, insecure, or, as Furedi (2001) noted, paranoid.

One can wonder what it means that there is a lack of evidence to support the shift towards a market in public and welfare policies in general and ECEC in particular, concurrent with an emphasis on "evidence-based policy and practice" (Beresford, 2005). It is indeed strange to notice that governments increasingly stress the need for evidence-based policies and demand that political decisions are backed by scientific research on their effectiveness and efficiency. As Roberts-Holmes and Moss (2021) noted, this is a distinguishing feature of neoliberal societies: the importance of measurements and outcomes. It may come as a surprise that in this context, the discourse on the benefits of commodification are not questioned, despite the empirical evidence that points to the opposite of what is aimed for.

It must mean that we are dealing with an ideology, a political belief that serves some interests better than others. In this case, the ideology of neoliberalism; the ideology that there is no society, only individuals; the ideology that one gets what one deserves in a meritocratic and fair society; the ideology of capitalism and of the primacy of the invisible hand of the market; the ideology of freedom and free choice; the ideology of ECEC as a means to prepare employable, productive, entrepreneurial, self-sufficient citizens; the ideology of parents as rational and responsible investors in their child's future. From a Gramscian perspective, ideologies strive to become hegemonical. In other words, they want us to believe that there is no alternative and that the interests of the privileged coincide with the interests of society as a whole. Beresford (2005) suggests that we should ask these obvious questions: what gains has commodification resulted in and for whom? What costs have there been to parents and to which parents? The ideology of childcare as a market (and thus allegedly inherently fair) has repeatedly been proven wrong. Empirical research has time and again shown that quality does not improve when childcare is privatised, that inequality increases and that parents do not act as rational consumers in a market as they are supposed to do. Why then, is this image of childcare and of parents as consumers still prevailing? The Finnish case also shows that the language of choice is not a matter that is imposed on parents by some external force, but that it is also internalised by parents. Parents are convinced that it is indeed their responsibility to make the right choices for their child(ren) and that these choices are an individual matter, despite the evidence showing that they are politically steered. The interiorisation of the idea that parents need to act as consumers is what we label as *consumentality*, in reference to Foucaults' notion of governmentality, or how our rationality and our mentality may be governed. In the concluding chapter of this book, we will elaborate on the concept of *cultural hegemony* as developed by Gramsci, as this concept may help us to understand how ideas become pervasive and accepted also by those who do not profit from these ideas. Gramsci also theorises how resistance can occur and how *counter-hegemonies* can be constructed.

Resistance and refusal

The concept of the parent as consumer and its language of choice construct a specific power relation between the parent and the ECEC provider, positioning the parent in a passive role: playing the role of the consumer or client who either accepts the provision as it is or changes to another provider. This is coherent with a specific conceptualisation of what "parent participation" means. Janssen and Vandenbroeck (2018) analysed how parent participation is conceptualised in early childhood curricula in 13 countries. They found that in those jurisdictions where ECEC is mainly conceptualised in terms of a preparation for compulsory schooling and focuses more narrowly on early learning, the participation of parents is more often described as being unidirectional (from the service to the parents) and it takes the form of advising and informing parents. When the conception of ECEC is more holistic or based on social pedagogy, the participation may be conceptualised in more democratic and bidirectional ways. In the scholarly literature, however, the former seems to prevail. Devlieghere, Li, and Vandenbroeck (2020) analysed how parent involvement is conceptualised in English language academic literature, while Li and Vandenbroeck analysed its conceptualisation in Chinese language scholarly literature. Both studies found that parent involvement is predominantly conceived as a means to an end that has not been discussed with parents. In other words, the conceptualisation of the role of parents is not discussed with parents. The commodification of ECEC constructs parents as allegedly critical consumers and assumes that this will enhance parents' voice. Not only is there a lack of evidence to back this assumption, but whether the involvement of parents in debates on education should take place on the individual level (Beresford, 2005), rather than on the community level, is also a question that requires reflection.

Gramsci posits that cultural hegemonies can be resisted and can yield counter-hegemonies. When the debate about parents as consumers is beyond facts, the issue is not only that parents *cannot* be considered as consumers. More importantly, we argue that parents *should not* be viewed as consumers. In very different parts of the world, the role of parents has been conceptualised in different ways, resisting and refusing consumentality. In what follows, we give four examples from three different continents. We start theses alternative cases in Italy. Tullia Musatti is an internationally renowned scholar for her studies on ECEC as democratic places and she describes how the Italian concept of *gestione sociale*, the social governance of early childhood education as a public good, emerged after the Second World War, but also how it evolved, in relation to changing demographic and political contexts. The Italian experience shows that other conceptualisations of parent-professional relations are possible and how these are related to a view on the societal and socialising role of ECEC in the lives of children, parents, and communities.

The second case, studied by Gail Yuen, a first-hand witness and activist scholar, analyses how a market-oriented system with demand-side funding in the capitalistic project of Hong Kong has changed, influenced by an alliance of civil society, parents, and professionals. In so doing, the case illustrates how alliances between parents and professionals can shift prevailing power relations.

The third case is analysed by Marie-Laure Cadart, a long-standing active observer and participant in a movement of childcare centres that are organised and led by parents. This case is located in France, a European country with a long history of public childcare, yet with historically few possibilities for parents to express their values (Mozère, 2000). It shows a very different image of the parent, as a collective and agentic actor, resisting the dominant meaning of early childhood education and creating innovative yet sustainable forms of parent-led childcare.

The last case, studied by Pablo Rupin, is located in Chile and looks at community-based preschools that offer a sustainable alternative to the individualisation of parental choice. Their meaning stretches way beyond ECEC or even education and deals with local development, the rights of indigenous populations, and more.

None of these cases are a model to follow as they are each deeply embedded in their specific local historical, cultural, social, and political contexts, as the authors explain. But each of them shows that alternatives are possible, feasible, and most likely sustainable. They illustrate how counter-hegemonies emerge and persist when individual voices and needs merge into collective urgencies.

Participation and parents' involvement in Italian ECEC

Tullia Musatti

In Italy, relationships with parents have a central role in defining ECEC quality and are considered a distinctive feature of Italian ECEC culture (New, Mallory, & Mantovani, 2000). This case study will briefly describe how this issue is intertwined with the history of public ECEC provision, its creation and growth, and the development of an original educational culture, in which political and ethical perspectives, pedagogical theories, and educational practices are developed and interconnected. Even the COVID-19 pandemic, which has precluded any social interaction and challenged the relationships between families and ECEC centres, has highlighted the vitality of ECEC culture and its capability to adapt to this new situation. At the present time, Italian ECEC culture is facing new challenges due to the need to extend ECEC provision in all areas of the country, the diversity of social contexts, and a complex political agenda.

The early years of ECEC in Italy and *gestione sociale*

Most ECEC services for young children that existed in Northern and Central Italy in the first half of the 19th century were directed to underprivileged and poor children, but in the years following the Second World War, the social and cultural scenario shifted. The economic and social crisis caused by the war and by the collapse of the fascist state was counterposed by a fierce request from women, which stemmed from their greater participation in the workforce during the war as well as in the Resistance struggle against fascism and the Nazi occupation. Moreover, women's success in achieving the right to vote assigned them a new role in political life. Hence, the battles for the reconstruction of schools following their destruction during the war were accompanied by a demand for educational institutions for young children. Although these institutions had a name that still evoked a vision of ECEC centres as replacing mothers' care (*scuole materne*), the struggles for a public commitment to women's and children's welfare were characterised by a strong drive for the cultural rebirth of the country after the fascist period. Two important elements characterised the struggles: a vision of early childhood education as a social palingenesis inspired by libertarian impulses and a request for new forms of citizen participation in political choices concerning collective goods.

Both these aspects are apparent in the regulation of *scuole materne* provided by many local governments administrated by left-wing parties in the following years. The term *gestione sociale* (social governance) designates the participation of both parents and representatives of the community in choices concerning the management of the schools (Malaguzzi, 1971). Despite the contradictions that emerged in the actual experience, in which the opinions and requests of parents were in contradiction with the more general perspective of the community committees (AA.VV, 1972), the stress on the involvement of the local community in educational institutions broadened the cultural horizons of Italian public ECEC from its beginning. The *gestione sociale* shaped the regulations of municipal schools but also suggested an educational approach based on a different way of relating to people and to institutions. It also put forth the idea that participation at large is a fundamental element of ECEC quality (Spaggiari, 1997). Moreover, by indicating that the final addressee of ECEC is the local community, it recognised that ECEC can play an important role in the cultural renewal of social life. Vice versa, it contributed to building a new image of young children in the community and suggested that ECEC centres should maintain constant relationships with the neighbourhood when organising activities with children.

Two successive events, related to important developments in Italian ECEC provision, gave negative or positive evidence of how the links between ECEC centres and local communities can be crucial for the further elaboration of ECEC culture. In 1968, the national government established programmes of *scuola materna*, catering to 3–6-year-old children, within state primary schools. Even though their regulation guaranteed parents' participation on school committees, during the implementation of participative procedures, the involvement of the local community became lost and a bureaucratic perspective predominated. Conversely, a few years later, when the drive for participation once again animated the struggles of women's organisations and trade unions for a national intervention to create and finance childcare services for children under 3, the *gestione sociale* was a focal point of the new national act that was finally introduced (Law 1044/1971). The fact that the construction and governance of the new centres, *nido*, were entrusted to local governments provided new impetus for the implementation of the *gestione sociale*.

Indeed, the meanings conveyed by *gestione sociale* influenced the development of the *nido* pedagogical culture, which had to be created anew in the absence of pre-existing conceptualisations suitable for infants and toddlers. For example, although the new municipal services absorbed the pre-existing structures and personnel of the *Opera Nazionale Maternità e Infanzia* (National Work for Maternity and Childhood), operating since 1923 for the social assistance of mothers and children in need, they bitterly opposed its cultural approach, which emphasised hygienic and sanitary aspects of childcare and contrasted with parents' attitudes and behaviour. It is interesting that, during this debate, the main argument concerned the participation of parents and communities, which local governments had to guarantee.

The concept of *gestione sociale* provided the services with important suggestions on how to innovate regarding relationships between professionals and parents by sharing decisions on the governance of *nido* and considering parents' participation in its daily life. The issue of participation also permeated the relationships within the group of professionals, which was composed of educators and other collaborators, inducing them to refuse a hierarchy between their different roles, and supported the group's autonomy in defining the educational project and in sharing educational and care responsibilities (Mantovani, 1976). An important indirect effect of such a participatory perspective was that the in-service training initiatives, which local governments were required to organise each year, involved the whole group of professionals (often including cleaners and cooks). This contributed to creating a shared vision of children's actual competences and potential development among all the professionals.

In the following years, Italian ECEC experienced important changes. Families' demand increased constantly. The great number of *scuole materne*, later renamed *scuole dell'infanzia (school of early childhood)*, provided by the state school system, together with municipal and private schools, mostly provided by catholic associations (which are partially funded by the state if they adhere to a national regulation including families' participation), progressively allowed an overall provision for 90% of 3–6-year old children.

Centres for infants and toddlers, provided only by municipalities and partially financed by regional governments, grew at a slower pace and were mostly in the northern and central areas, where women's employment was more common. Since the end of the 1990s, many municipalities, which could not expand their own provision because of the economic crisis in the country and the restrictions imposed by the national government on local expenditures, activated collaborations with private initiatives, mostly social cooperatives, to satisfy families' demand. These centres cater to children who cannot find a place in the municipal centres and operate in close collaboration with the municipal administration within a framework of precise rules regarding the organisation of the service (schedules and calendars, educator/child ratio, and indoor and outdoor environment), including formal procedures for parents' participation. As parents in some cities, when they address their request to local authorities, can declare their preference for a specific ECEC centre operating in their neighbourhood, private centres pay special attention to relationships with parents and generally to their own image in the neighbourhood.

The educational alliance between ECEC professionals and parents

An important role in the growth of families' demand for ECEC centres has been played by the profound change in parenting structures and attitudes that has taken place in Italy, as in many other European countries (Musatti, 2007). Mother's and father's roles towards caring and educating their child have become less distinct, while both of them were more and more sensitive and anxious about the impact of their child's first experiences on her future development and well-being. This had a two-fold effect on parents' attitudes towards ECEC provision in general and their relationships with ECEC professionals. Not only did the goal of providing their child with an educational and social experience with other children increasingly appear in parents' motivations to request a place at an ECEC centre, but more and more frequently, parents' appeal to be supported in dealing with their child's care and education emerged in daily communication between parents and professionals. Coping with such a request was gratifying for professionals as it acknowledged their expertise in child education and care but at the same time suggested new reflections on their own attitudes towards parents as well as new practices. The combination of these elements led to a new balance between professionals' and parents' reciprocal expectations and promoted important innovations in the ECEC world.

Actually, over the years, it has been possible to observe the implementation of an increasing variety of practices for establishing positive relationships with parents as well as for involving families in the life of the ECEC centres. Even the procedures designed to implement parental participation in the decisions concerning centre governance were enriched by more attention paid to interpersonal relationships.

It is important to stress that, although in some centres, a specific professional is identified for each child as a reference person, the interpersonal relationship with the child's parents is handled by all the educators responsible for a group of children and discussed in collegial meetings between them. The pedagogical coordinator, whose role is to support the quality of the professionals' work in the centres, does not intervene directly in their relationship with parents, except in cases of serious conflict.

A new view on parents' involvement also emerged in some official acts, in which, alongside indications for the participation of parents in the centre governance, new expressions have been introduced, such as "debates between parents" and "participation in the life of the child." Finally, the expression "educational alliance with families" began to appear in the reflections of professionals with increasing frequency.

In the Reggio Emilia approach, in which *participation* has always been considered as a basic component of ECEC quality, it has been stated repeatedly that it is necessary to present parents with a range of proposals to meet their different organisational or psychological and social needs. In this regard, Rinaldi (1984) suggested a keyboard on which it is possible to play different melodies according to the audience as a metaphor. Nowadays, all good-quality centres propose a variety of activities directed to promoting parents' knowledge about children's experience in the centre, or their involvement in meetings and other social activities organised by professionals (Bove, 2007).

One of the most relevant and widespread practices in ECEC for under 3s is the *inserimento* (insertion), which consists of gradual entry to the ECEC centre together with her mother or father during the first period of attendance. This practice was initially focused on the child's separation from the mother but now has been named *ambientamento* (acclimatisation) (Balduzzi, 2015) as it is designed to support the child's familiarisation with the social and material environment and includes promoting parents' participation. Thus, the practice can represent the first step in the transition from a parental attitude of abstract trust in the ECEC institution and its providers to an interpersonal relationship with the professionals who care for their child. It lays the groundwork for a mutual understanding between parents and professionals that will be deepened later through day-to-day contact.

Other practices are implemented to involve parents in their children's experience in the centres and to create continuity with their experience at home. These practices will not commit parents to proposing activities similar to those used in ECEC centres at home in order to reinforce children's learning processes. Rather, they aim to acquaint parents with children's experiences within educational services through systematic documentation procedures. In the following, I will report on some practices observed in ECEC centres in the city of Pistoia within the framework of action research projects (Musatti et al., 2016).

For many years, in all Pistoia's centres for under 3s, at the end of each week, professionals have written a report on the children's experiences and displayed it for the parents to see. Some centres compose the weekly reports in a book that parents can take home in turn, so that, at home, they can retrace the story of the experience at the centre with their child. A similar function is performed by lending objects, which are charged with special emotional and symbolic meanings shared among the group of children at the centre, to each family in turn at weekends.

For children attending the municipal *nido Il Faro*, having two stuffed birds from the ECEC, important characters of their play with peers as well as a small plush doggie named Peggy with her kennel for the children at the *nido LagoMago* are brought to the homes (Musatti, Giovannini, Mayer & Group Nido Lagomago, 2013), making them the object of further experiences shared with their parents, and this constitutes an emotional and cognitive experience. For their parents, the experience helps them to learn more about their children's activities at the ECEC and constitutes a way of keeping in touch with the imaginary world that the child is constructing. In these *nido*s, as in many other Italian centres, it is also customary to lend the parents some picture books that their child particularly loves for a few days. It would not be a wild guess to say that the path of these transitional objects from the educational centre to home, therefore moving in the opposite direction from the traditional one, corresponds to a new perspective on the complexity and importance of sociality in the cognitive and emotional development of children in their first years. Practices that promote parents' participation in the life of the centres are also widespread, proposing social events for the group of children and their parents together, such as an outdoor party, a day trip before the summer holidays, or convivial moments reserved for parents and professionals. For example, for some years, a Pistoia *nido* ran a choral group in which many parents and professionals participated.

We could say that, in these cases, the educational centre tries to open up to forms of sociality in which not only are the children given the opportunity to live all in their multiple identities as children in the family, grandchildren in the extended family, and members of the community *nido* or school at once, but also where parents and other family members can act out their parental identity in moments of extended sociality outside of the family context, both in the presence and absence of their child. A similar objective is pursued by events extended to the local community, such as when a group of centres organises meetings in the city squares where professionals narrate traditional local tales to both children and parents.

The sustained attention for interpersonal relationships with parents is also enriched by initiatives aimed at expressing interest in each parent's personal identity on the part of ECEC professionals, as well as reinforcing her feeling of belonging to the community which is slowly forming in the centre and includes both adults and children. For example, in many *nidi* e *scuole dell'infanzia*, parents intervene to narrate episodes from their childhood or habits and rituals of their culture. In a municipal *nido* in Pistoia, parents, grandparents, and professionals set up a large display case together in which they arranged an object that reminded them of their own childhood or of their culture.

The world of Italian ECEC has also been able to embrace new needs of parents in a more direct way. In our country, as in many other countries, the organisation of social life has changed greatly as a result of increasing urbanisation and nuclearisation of families, with the consequent loosening of family ties. In the specific case of parents of a young child who does not attend an ECEC centre, either because one is not available or because the child's parents made this choice, daily life spent by parents together with their only child can be found to be inadequate with respect to both the parents' and the child's need for social contacts. In many cities, where there was already a substantial provision of ECEC centres for children under the age of 3, the local government created *Centres for Children and Parents*, which children access along with a parent or other family member to play with other children and parents (Mantovani & Musatti, 1996). The analysis of the social climate and interactions activated in these centres showed the benefits in terms of reassurance, support, and empowerment that parents gain from the relationship with others who show similar psychological commitment to the experience of caring for and educating a young child (Musatti et al., 2016).

What distinguishes these centres from similar services operating in other countries (Hoshi-Watanabe, Musatti, Rayna, & Vandenbroeck, 2015) is that most of Italian services, whether public or run by private initiatives, are networked with other existing ECEC centres in the area and are operated by the same type of professionals (educators and pedagogical coordinators). This also facilitates the transition of children and parents from these centres to a mainstream service, such as a *nido*.

New challenges

The COVID-19 pandemic has had a dramatic impact on both the lives of families and the ECEC centres, which, like all schools in the country, closed from March to September 2020. During these months, children were deprived of their social and learning experiences, parents had to reorganise their family life to balance their work at home with their childcare commitments, and both children and adults experienced an intense and close relationship confined within their domestic walls. In many cities, ECEC professionals took up the challenge of keeping the relationship with children and families alive and supporting them in coping with the new situation by making use of communications at a distance via phone, video calls, and chats (Mantovani et al., 2021). These initiatives were implemented by ECEC providers and were supported by specific national guidelines (Ministero Istruzione, 2020). Through this long-distance contact, professionals offered children storytelling and book readings and proposed activities that parents could carry out with their children at home. This contact was much appreciated by families and increased how children as well as parents valued the ECEC centres for what they mean in the lives of children and in their own lives as parents (Di Giandomenico & Picchio, 2021).

The pandemic worsened the social and economic conditions of many families, especially in southern areas of Italy, and further highlighted the association between material poverty and cultural and educational disadvantages for children. The heated political debate on how to combat this situation, which has been labelled *educational poverty*, has focused on the need to ensure that every child has access to an educational centre from an early age. Indeed, expanding ECEC centres for under 3s and overcoming inequalities in their accessibility between regional areas are among the major objectives of a recent national Act (D.lgs 65/2017). Now, the European support from the Next Generation Fund has made it feasible to build a large number of ECEC centres in underprivileged areas.

The national Act has connected all centres for under 3-year-old children and *scuole dell'infanzia* into an integrated ECEC system and has outlined a complex architecture of public governance of the system, in which the reciprocal roles and responsibilities of national, regional, and local governments in planning, regulating, and financing a high quality ECEC system are specified and in which the private initiatives will be included. The overall intention is to commit the national and regional governments to a major and coherently combined investment in the creation of new centres for children under 3s and the general qualification of all ECEC provision. At the same time, the nature of locally embedded service of the educational centres for young children would be guaranteed, since the governance of the ECEC system is entrusted to local governments.

Implementing such a system in the most deprived southern regions of the country, four of which fall under the EU's convergence objectives because they have a per capita GDP below 75% of the EU average, is an important challenge. In these areas, the virtuous circle between ECEC extension, women's employment, and economic or social well-being of the local community never started and, as a result, municipal administrations have not developed knowledge, skills, and resources for governing the ECEC sector (GruppoCRC, 2021). For this reason, it appears necessary that substantial economic support from the central government be accompanied by training and informational support to regional and local governments during the planning and implementation of a more extensive and qualified ECEC provision within the framework of the national system. It is now a question of avoiding hasty and disruptive policies such as resorting to the distribution of vouchers to be spent in private ECECs, and instead developing forms of co-operation between the various public (state and municipal administrations) and private ECEC providers, guaranteeing continuity between education for under 3s and for 3–6-year-old children, and, most importantly, modifying the image of educational provision for young children in the local community.

All this means rehearsing the important message conveyed by the expression *gestione sociale* that related well-being of children and parents to cultural and social development of the local community. So, once again, participation of both families and the local community in the governance of children's education in the first 6 years of life seems to be a decisive card in the struggle for equity and inclusion.

A specific proposal of the national act moves in this direction by suggesting the aggregation in the same building or in neighbouring buildings of a variety of ECEC centres for under 3s, such as *nidos* and/or centres for children and parents, together with *scuole per l'infanzia* for 3–6-year-olds, and in connection with primary education institutions. These aggregates, labelled *Poli per l'infanzia*, will make it easier to build articulated and coherent educational provision from 0 to 6 years. Most importantly, they will provide a unified point of reference for families in the local community, allow greater continuity in the relationships between parents and educational centres, foster social contacts and relationships between families, and support parents' capability to make their own choices regarding their child's education. This proposal, like others that are under discussion in this period for older children, aims to create an intermediate place between families' everyday lives and public institutions as well as social links within the larger local community, and to promote respect for cultural diversity and social inclusion.

The *In* and *Out* of the voucher scheme: a story of resistance in Hong Kong

Gail Yuen

Introduction

The hegemony of neoliberalism, manifested exponentially in structures and everyday lives, is under increasing scrutiny for its undesirable impact that exacerbates inequality and insecurity, and undermines democracy (Roberts-Holmes & Moss, 2021). Neoliberalism has grown into "the common-sense way many of us interpret, live in, and understand the world" (Harvey, 2005, p. 3). By reducing everything to economic terms, neoliberalism turns its justifications into seemingly self-evident and objective truths, making its underlying values and assumptions invisible (Rizvi & Lingard, 2010). Tronto (2013), in discussing caring democracy, argued that markets render support to some people at the expense of others while allowing the escape of personal and collective responsibility from the adverse impact on historically marginalised groups in society. Connell (2013) troubled the neoliberal politics in commodifying education, highlighting problems of rationing resources, blurring public-private relationships and creating structural mechanisms that favour market competition to legitimise winners and losers. These consequences of neoliberalism are worrying.

As an international city which has prided itself on its commitment to the global economy, Hong Kong is subject to the inevitable influence of neoliberalism. It is believed that neoliberalism has a natural life cycle, similar to the rises and falls of dominant ideologies (e.g. communism, social democracy) in previous times (Roberts-Holmes & Moss, 2021). Hong Kong, however, has not been exposed to much of these momentous cycles, probably due to its colonial history and capitalistic trajectory. While democratisation remains limited, the city has enjoyed a free and relatively democratic way of living, with civic education first introduced to local kindergartens and schools in 1985 (Goodstadt, 1998; Morris & Sweeting, 1991; Sweeting, 2004; Wong, 2021). As such, the political, economic, social, and cultural particularities of Hong Kong are also significant to the gradual crafting of the global-local neoliberal cascade.

Hong Kong is a capitalistic project, whether it is under the past British colonial rule or current government as a Special Administrative Region (SAR) of the People's Republic of China. The British colonial government adopted a laissez faire approach to the city's development for over 150 years (Hampton, 2016). In response to rapid population and economic expansions, the post-war period from the 1970s onwards saw greater involvement of the colonial government in the provision of public goods, covering education, social welfare, health, and housing (Chan, 1997). Within education, the priority always went to primary and secondary schools and higher education institutions to meet the human capital demand (Yuen, 2008). As for early childhood education, it rested in the hands of voluntary organisations and private enterprises (Young, 1965). Voluntary organisations are non-profit bodies, often affiliated with church and charity groups; these organisations also manage many publicly funded primary and secondary schools. The early childhood market in Hong Kong continues to be predominantly run by non-profit providers. This contrasts considerably with the tremendous growth of for-profit providers of early childhood services in various parts of the world (Lloyd, 2019). Nevertheless, the non-profit nature of operation in Hong Kong cannot spare itself from the threat of neoliberalism as the SAR government assumes a more active role in promoting privatisation for early childhood education. This came as almost no surprise, on the basis that Hong Kong, having acquired international status as a financial centre, is highly susceptive to the influence of global forces (e.g. the Asian Financial Crisis in 1997 and Global Financial Crisis in 2008). Economic adversity was further aggravated by health-related crises like the outbreak of *severe acute respiratory syndrome (SARS)* in 2003. The budgetary constraints caused by a series of crises constituted a rich terrain for neoliberal rationalisation of early childhood education, and education in general, to be privatised and marketised, revealing an official scepticism towards the effectiveness of the provision of public goods in solving problems (Roberts-Holmes & Moss, 2021).

Capitalistic thinking, increasingly shaped by the neoliberal technology of control, is deeply ingrained in the economic-focused society of Hong Kong. It has become such a common language of daily life that people frequently describe their individual initiatives (e.g. taking classes, enrolling in studies) as "value-adding," just like the local Octopus card used for transportation and consumption. The long-lived competitive market environment has normalised particular subjectivities and relationships among children, parents, and teachers, not to mention the image of early childhood institutions as businesses. Neoliberalism is of course not the sole factor contributing to the normalisation of these subjectivities and relationships. The insecurity of the middle class (Lui, 2011) and longstanding Chinese cultural emphasis on education (Ng, 1984) also play a role in commodifying early childhood education as it sets off the education race. In light of serious concerns about children's well-being and prolonged issues about sustainability, quality, and equity, there have been periodic grassroot efforts organised to involve parents, teachers, and interested parties of civil society in resisting the capitalistic and neoliberal approach during both governance periods: the British colonial rule and the SAR.

This case study presents the replacement of the 10-year-old Pre-primary Education Voucher Scheme (thereafter voucher scheme) by the Kindergarten Education Scheme in 2017 as an example to illustrate grassroots resistance and discusses the potentiality of transforming early childhood education in Hong Kong. With neoliberalism showing signs of unsustainability in global crises, to what extent may resistance bring transformation to the sector, as suggested by Roberts-Holmes and Moss (2021)? Built on my previous textual analyses of archival and current policy and media documents, as well as relevant local studies,

I begin by discussing the development of the private early childhood market under the colonial government's laissez faire approach. This is followed by a critical examination of the voucher scheme heavily grounded in the neoliberal notion of parent choice and the large-scale resistance movement that has brought it to an end. The last section presents a critique of the latest Kindergarten Education Scheme to facilitate deeper reflection on the possibility of transformation and the likelihood of more resistance. Before moving on, I want to clarify that early childhood education in the following discussion concerns mostly children aged 3–6 due to the focus of the policies discussed here.

Private early childhood market in transition: from laissez faire to neoliberalism

As previously stated, the private early childhood market in Hong Kong has undergone developments in two difference governance periods, with the British colonial rule adhering to laissez faire practices and the SAR administration showing more explicit endorsement of neoliberalism. The laissez faire doctrine, popular in the 19th century, differs from the neoliberal doctrine in its position of the State as non-interventionist in the private sphere while providing basic support to law and order. The neoliberal doctrine redefines the role of the State, expecting its active adoption of market logic to ensure a free economy (Foucault, 2008). Foucault (2008) wrote, "[n]eoliberalism should not therefore be identified with laissez-faire, but rather with permanent vigilance, activity, and intervention" (p. 132). Given the situated experience of early childhood education in Hong Kong, I argue that a discussion on its development with reference to the British colonial era of laissez faire is necessary. This discussion can offer a backdrop to contrast the notable changes instigated by the neoliberally conceived voucher scheme under the SAR government and to understand the advocacy agenda underpinning the resistance movement. It adds more appreciation of the daunting task to call for a reconfiguration of early childhood education as a public good to support children, parents, and teachers in Hong Kong.

The laissez faire approach to early childhood education enabled the colonial government to refrain from intervening in a private market of high demand. Official figures indicate a consistently high enrolment in kindergartens, from over 85% to around 95% between the 1980s and 1990s (Census and Statistics Department, 1996a; Llewellyn, Hancock, Kirst, & Roeloffs, 1982). On top of the economic and cultural reasons mentioned before, the high demand can be attributed to other factors, such as the necessity for parents to work to earn a living and the lack of support from extended families among mainland Chinese refugees (Sweeting, 1993). The high demand for early childhood education stimulated a continuous supply of kindergarten places, thus meeting one of the basic conditions that make markets work (Moss, 2009). When parents were willing to take responsibility for young children, why would early childhood education need government intervention? It has been argued that the colonial government made selective decisions on interventionist measures for social and economic developments, as demonstrated by its heavy involvement in public goods provision since the 1970s (Chan, 1997). Nonetheless, the government continuously reiterated its "positive non-intervention" stance to minimise "the colonial state's role as an active protector, provider and promoter of many community needs" and "to de-escalate the rising expectations of an increasingly affluent and modern society" (Chan, 1997, p. 574). By keeping government expenditure at bay, low taxation and a controlled growth of bureaucracy could be achieved to lure international businesses and at the same time encourage the private sector to take up a major share of responsibility to meet societal needs (Chan, 1997). In this light, low public spending on early childhood education, e.g. 0.5% and 0.8% of recurring education expenditure in 1986/87 and 1994/95, respectively (Census and Statistics Department, 1996b), could be rightfully justified decade after decade. Left to the private market by default of the laissez faire approach, early childhood education was relatively free from regulatory control by the colonial government. The high price in return was that kindergartens had to compete against each other to keep their businesses afloat, giving rise to different kinds of contention about the provision.

Increasing discontent about minimal government involvement gradually cultivated a sense of civic consciousness in bringing change to policy. I want to add here that the discontent concerned both the kindergarten and childcare sectors under the jurisdiction of the education and welfare units, respectively. Kindergartens regulated by the education unit typically operated in a bisessional mode (half day, 3 hours), whereas day nurseries under the welfare unit offered long whole-day places (10 hours, now called long-whole-day kindergartens). Both types of early childhood institutions provided similar educational elements, with day nurseries also serving children aged 2–3. The childcare sector has a very different trajectory of development which is beyond the scope of this discussion. This sector, however, has been an active member of grassroot movements since the earlier decades, mainly because of its repeated marginalisation by government policies. Regarding the prominent issues explicitly articulated through grassroot resistance, they reflect the constant struggle of covering teacher salaries and costs of provision improvement, the dilemma between increasing tuition fees to sustain operations (thus affecting market competitiveness) and making early childhood education less affordable to parents (Yuen, 2010), as well as the concern about disparities resulting from differences in key areas (e.g. access, funding, training, qualification) between the kindergarten and childcare sectors (Yuen, 2012). Disparities are common problems in early childhood systems involving two administrative roofs (Kaga, Bennett, & Moss, 2010). The bottom-up resistance to the laissez faire approach grew at a time when Hong Kong slowly moved away from quantitative educational expansion to qualitative development (Sweeting, 2004). It also emerged during a time when pressure groups and organisations became increasingly active in influencing government policy (Sweeting, 2004). At the turn of the 1980s, bilateral negotiations on Hong Kong's future arrangements after 30 June 1997 and preparations for the handover were underway. The sense of political uncertainty, including the spill-over effects of the Tiananmen Incident in June 1989, generated new momentum in democratic participation on matters affecting citizens and the society at large (Lo, 1998). All these significant moments foregrounded the awakening call for public provision to educate young children.

The quest for a public provision of early childhood education encountered numerous setbacks and often received something else in return. The analysis of archival materials shows the colonial government's strong insistence that a public provision would work against the existing policy and market operation. While questioning the economic value and efficiency of funding early childhood education, officials frequently maintained that public money could not be spent on for-profit kindergartens and that most public resources had already gone to other levels of education (Yuen, 2008, 2010). Mounting public pressure did force the colonial government to adjust its narrowly defined role from providing advice and in-service training only (Young, 1965), to ensuring "an expansion of pre-primary education in accordance with demand, at a price that people can afford and offering a suitable range of facilities and programmes" (Government Secretariat, 1981, p. 198). Rather than yielding to the quest for public provision, the colonial government introduced a means-tested fee remission scheme for parents in 1981, and for non-profit kindergartens, rent and rates reimbursement in 1981, and the Kindergarten Subsidy Scheme (voluntary participation with regulatory requirements, later becoming the Kindergarten and Childcare Centre Subsidy Scheme) in 1995. As shown, there was a long pause before the introduction of the first supply-side policy in the mid-1990s. The colonial government was not responsive to either the public demand or the recommendation made by an international panel of visitors to fully subsidise kindergartens (Llewellyn et al., 1982). A typical pattern can be observed in the ways that officials handled the contested issues, i.e. by means of improving the existing scheme(s) while loosening the tuition fee control and adjusting the recommended teacher salary scales at the same time. The SAR government resorted to a similar pattern. The conscious avoidance of a public provision points to an organised system of official resistance to contain bottom-up resistance and normalise early childhood education in the marketplace (Yuen, 2010). Immediately before the handover of Hong Kong to China in 1997, the colonial government made another successful detour by launching major initiatives concerning teacher education and professional development, legislation, and qualifications, arguing that these measures would support high-quality development of early childhood education in the private market (Yuen, 2008). The professionalisation of the early childhood workforce came a little late, but neoliberal rationalisation was already working its way into the education system.

Neoliberalism influenced public schools somewhat earlier, with early childhood education being affected at an accelerating speed after 1997. Into the 1990s, the colonial government made its initial attempts to reshape school governance structures and privatise education (Kwan, Li, & Lee, 2020). The neoliberal language of education as investment, value for money, effective and efficient use of funds, quality assurance, and managerial accountability was explicitly articulated in the policy address of Chris Patten, the last governor of the British colonial era (Governor, 1995). Since early childhood education was already in the private market, there was no urgent need to do more than what the laissez faire approach required. The colonial government largely stayed out of the early childhood market, letting the market do its job to shape the contractual relationships between parents as consumers and early childhood institutions as producers (Moss, 2009). Had there been no political change of governance, early childhood education would still have gone down the same neoliberal path as public schools. With the SAR administration moving into office and launching a large-scale education reform, the goal of building a new quality culture was set for early childhood education, and this goal was to be achieved through enhancing professional competence, quality assurance and monitoring mechanisms, and the transition to primary education (Education Commission, 2000). Interestingly, the mode of subsidy came last in the section. As explained in the reform blueprint, public provision would not necessarily ensure quality as resources and measures should be prioritised to enhance parent choice (Education Commission, 2000). The reform measures look relatively impressive when compared to the colonial period, especially in terms of the official recognition of early childhood education as the foundation of lifelong learning in the knowledge-based society of Hong Kong (Education Commission, 2000). These measures in effect marked the birth of a full-fledged neoliberal desire for a strong state role in the private early childhood market. They set the stage for introducing the voucher scheme, a cluster of nested measures which showcase, according to Roberts-Holmes and Moss (2021), the interwoven ideas of human capital, public choice, and new public management that constitute the grand narrative of neoliberalism to reconfigure subjects and institutions.

Voucher scheme and resistance movement

Both the voucher scheme and resistance movement were linked to two separate chief executive elections, involving the intentions of Tsang Yam Kuen to seek for his second term in 2007 and Leung Chun Ying to run for office in 2012. Different from the colonial era, the chief executive of the SAR government was subject to an electoral process every 5 years. Although the election was limited to a small committee of pre-selected members, the candidate was still expected to solicit support from these members and the wider community (Case, 2008). Embracing the neoliberal spirit of "big market, small government" (Tsang, 2007), Tsang announced the introduction of the voucher scheme in 2007 (Chief Executive, 2006) with limited sector-wide open consultation. Leung (2012) included free early childhood education as part of his election agenda, but he failed to deliver on his election promise. As a result, an alliance (Alliance on the Fight for Free

15-Year Education) was formed to launch the resistance movement, seeking to replace the voucher scheme with public provision of early childhood education.

The voucher scheme was a demand-side policy to promote parent choice. It was the first of its kind in the local education system. As a follow-up to the reform initiatives in 2000, the voucher scheme presented systemically organised measures to improve early childhood education. It came with an increase in recurrent education expenditure from 3.7% to 5.5% over a 10-year period (Education Bureau, 2012, 2019). Envisioning that all children aged 3–6 receive affordable and quality education, the voucher scheme provided a non-means-tested flat-rate subsidy directly to parents to reduce their financial burden when using half-day or whole-day places. Parents were expected to pay the tuition fee difference not covered by the voucher value. Officials rationalised their policy choice this way: "we wish to preserve the market responsiveness of the sector and to enhance quality at the same time" (Education and Manpower Bureau, 2006, p. 3). Henceforth, the scheme was also designed to tighten control and liberate the entrepreneur self in parents and service providers to enjoy greater freedom of choice and competition in the early childhood market. The specific design included: (1) limiting participation (voluntary) to non-profit kindergartens staying within the maximum tuition fee caps set for half-day and whole-day places; (2) removing the supply-side Kindergarten and Childcare Centre Subsidy Scheme and recommended teacher salary scales, to give kindergartens full discretion on salary decisions, subject to market forces; (3) requiring participating kindergartens to disclose operation information online and meet the prescribed standards stipulated by the quality assurance mechanism for eligibility in the second policy cycle; and (4) including a training subsidy for teachers and principals to obtain a sub-degree and a bachelor degree, respectively, within the first 5-year policy cycle (Education and Manpower Bureau, 2006). The voucher scheme encapsulates both parents and teachers/principals as the neoliberal subject or *homo economicus*, under intensive external and self-governance, to perform the buyer and seller roles for preserving market responsiveness. Empowered by the voucher, parents as consumers were to be autonomous and independent in making informed choices using the online information (e.g. kindergarten operation, quality review reports). To attract parents with the voucher to enrol in their kindergarten, teachers and principals were to be responsive to their needs and demands to stay competitive while being held accountable to the positivistic notion of quality through standardised measures. Whether as buyer or seller, the neoliberal subject is a rational and self-interested individual, always seeking to get the most out of the economic transaction for the least possible cost (Roberts-Holmes & Moss, 2021). The hasty implementation of the voucher scheme, in the absence of democratic participation in policy consultation processes, is prone to criticism and resistance.

The voucher scheme was heavily criticised and contested for its inherent problems that neglected care responsibilities and reproduced structural inequalities in early childhood education and society. Though welcoming the additional financial support, parents soon realised that they did not receive the full amount of money as stated, due to the inclusion of the teacher training subsidy in its value. The removal of the supply-side subsidy for kindergartens brought new fee hikes, and the annual increase in voucher value lagged behind the rising costs of operation and living (Yuen, 2012). The voucher value was never a calculation of the actual unit cost, as shown by the removal of the recommended teacher salary scales. As a whole, the design of the scheme reflected both gendered and classed assumptions about the care of young children. Arguing that care is complex and relational rather than natural to women or a standardised commodity, Tronto (2013) problematised the underlying patriarchal power structures of government policy. These power structures often position care responsibilities as merely universal, with limited concern about particular situations and thus outcomes that affect the moral quality of care. The voucher scheme privileged half-day over whole-day provision based on the familiar arguments that young children needed no more than half-day formal education and that it would be better for parents to spend more time with their children (Working Group on Review of the Pre-primary Education Voucher, 2010). The flat-rate voucher and per-head subsidy calculation added more competitive edges to bisessional half-day kindergartens (two student groups, morning and afternoon) while disadvantaging kindergartens that offered whole-day places (one student group) and admitted fewer children. Generally small-scale long-whole-day kindergartens, relocated to the education unit in 2005, were therefore hit hard by the voucher scheme. Challenging the neoliberal notions of choice and competition embedded in the policy, Yuen (2015) found mothers' strong preference for convenience in making their kindergarten choices and its significant association with socioeconomic status, and identified issues of access linked to market failure. An earlier study of over 10,000 parents by Yuen and Yu (2010) shed similar light on the significant relationship between the use of whole-day provision and socio-economic status, i.e. whole-day provision was commonly used by parents with lower socioeconomic status who needed to work full- or part-time. The voucher scheme failed to attend to how parents, especially mothers and those of lower socioeconomic status, cared for their young children. Being silent about the inherently unequal nature of markets and taking for granted the structural processes that frequently determine distributive patterns of resource allocation in society (Young, 2011), the voucher scheme invariably benefited mothers of higher socioeconomic status more (Yuen & Lam, 2017). Unlike resource-bounded families, these mothers also tended to spend the money saved from the voucher on interest classes and other learning opportunities for their children (Yuen & Lam, 2017). Another local study yielded similar findings (Wong & Rao, 2020). This unintended impact of the voucher scheme is another important concern. It points to the uneasiness and insecurity of parents when caring for children in uncertain local and global economic times.

Parents experienced a drastically different economic landscape after the handover in 1997. Some of the major crises have already been mentioned. Concerns about the upward and downward trends of social mobility were once the talk of the town, especially among the middle class (e.g. Lui, 2011) and within the government (e.g. Commission on Poverty, 2007). This economic insecurity fuels the education race through intensive parenting on the one hand, and the commodification of early childhood education (e.g. academic curriculum, English lessons taught by native speakers, offering interest classes, children's portfolios as a tool for ensuring customer satisfaction) on the other hand. By holding parents responsible for the care of young children, the voucher scheme enabled the government to limit its role to the mere construction of market conditions and standardised measures to enhance the quality of early childhood education. Informed by their studies with parents participating in the voucher scheme, Fung and Lam (2008) as well as Wong and Rao (2020) cast doubt on the official rhetoric of quality built upon a child-centred pedagogical approach. Parental expectations of academic learning and child-centred practices seemed to be contradictory to each another. In examining the interactions of parent choice, professional practices, and the voucher scheme, Yuen and Grieshaber (2009) identified the market notion of quality being constructed in the vicious cycle. This vicious cycle constrains what parents, teachers, and society can possibly imagine for early childhood education, to dampen the adverse impact of the education race on young children, to facilitate alternative constructions of all those involved in early childhood institutions, and to resist the hegemony of neoliberalism. Though sitting uncomfortably with economic uncertainty, parents do not necessarily think and act like neoliberal subjects. The overwhelming demand of parents for free provision is a case in point (Yuen & Lam, 2017; Yuen & Yu, 2010). Mothers of different socioeconomic and employment statuses in the study of Yuen and Lam (2017) shared the view that free provision was a must, not only for benefiting parents, children, and kindergartens in economic, emotional, and relational terms, but also for addressing equity and quality issues in the early childhood market, as well as societal issues like the rich-poor gap. One middle class mother, in particular, expressed the emotional drain caused by market competition for kindergarten places. When talking about policy enactment, Ball (2015) suggested the importance of making subjectivity into an individual and collective site of struggle in order to resist problematic practices while being intensively governed by neoliberalism. Ball (2015) wrote, "[i]f we take Foucault seriously, we must confront the problem of standing outside our own history, outside of ourselves and do ethical work on ourselves" (p. 310). It is this spirit that has cultivated a solid ground for endless grassroots efforts and eventually the launch of the large-scale resistance movement in 2013 to bring down the voucher scheme.

During the two 5-year policy cycles of the voucher scheme, there were ceaseless public protests. The tensions involved the exclusion of for-profit kindergartens from participation, various policy measures affecting kindergarten operation, and the unsatisfactory and yet familiar responses of the government after being pushed to conduct an early review of the scheme in the first policy cycle (Yuen, 2012). Fully subsidised provision re-emerged as the focal point of public attention, growing in momentum together with the perceived window of opportunity associated with the chief executive election in 2012. Three early childhood educational bodies joined to form the 15-Year Free Education Alliance for the purpose of facilitating discussions on the advocacy agenda and lobbying for support from the candidates of the election campaign. In January 2013, Leung announced in his first policy address that the feasibility of fully subsidising the sector had to be further examined by a specifically formed committee. This announcement triggered furious outcries, causing the former alliance to transform into the Alliance on the Fight for 15-Year Free Education in February 2013.

The resistance movement, spearheaded by the Alliance on the Fight for 15-Year Free Education, made a significant mark in the local history of early childhood education. I was directly involved with the alliance as the convenor, working with 30 organisational members to advocate for a comprehensive policy framework to support public provision of quality early childhood education. It is both the development and use of this comprehensive framework that have made the advocacy experience vastly different from the past. This framework was informed by several local studies on the voucher scheme, such as those mentioned before, from the perspectives of education equality and children's rights. It reconceptualised the meaning of early childhood education to cover children aged 0–6 and the relationship between early childhood and compulsory education, proposing a systemic approach to support sustainable educational developments (Alliance on the Fight for Free 15-Year Education, 2014; Working Group of Free 15-Year Education, 2012). The position underpinning the comprehensive framework and advocacy of the alliance was a rejection of the market approach. We attempted to raise public awareness about the values and assumptions made neutral in government policy instead of focusing on micro issues of a specific policy like in the past. The conscious construction of an alternative discourse for early childhood education also included a distancing from the common economic argument about a high rate of return yielded from education investment in young children. Interestingly, international experts like James Heckman and John Bennett were brought to Hong Kong by the government to facilitate policy discussions on the subject. Heckman's economic perspective attracted much public attention. On the side, I worked closely with John Bennett to shape the expert panel's policy recommendations to the government (I pay tribute to John for his passionate and genuine contributions to early childhood education in Hong Kong). As an insider who also served on one of the subcommittees under the government's Committee on Free Kindergarten Education, I saw this resistance experience in terms of activism as a process of becoming. The alliance began with a determined goal and an overarching direction, but it could never control what might happen in the process and how things might go in the end, especially when the grassroot movement had to sustain its efforts for an extended period of time (Yuen, 2018).

The resistance movement lasted for more than 3 years, involving massive mobilisation of bodies and resources within the sector, across levels of education and beyond (e.g. social service), at legislative and government levels, and in the media and general public (see Yuen, 2018, for details on the processes and dynamics of negotiation). The organisational membership of the alliance covered a wide range of professional and political backgrounds, including three leading educational bodies as well as various early childhood associations and groups. There was one parent group made up largely of those using long-whole-day kindergartens. This loosely organised group was a deliberate strategy to amplify the marginalised voices of parents in early childhood education policy, especially those who needed more than the half-day provision to meet the needs of various work and/or family situations. Ad hoc in nature, the parent group was backed by school sponsoring bodies and long-whole-day kindergartens once developed under the welfare unit as mentioned before. Due to the persistent marginalisation of long-whole-day provision, an activist trajectory can be clearly observed among all those involved. A review of the three public hearings organised by the Panel on Education (2013) and Subcommittee to Study the Implementation of Free Kindergarten Education (2015) of the Legislative Council showed the steady and continuous participation of parents, kindergartens, and school-sponsoring bodies of long-whole-day provision throughout the policy consultation period. Certainly, the demand for free and quality early childhood education was not limited to a particular group of parents. The alliance members indeed mobilised parents across operation modes, sometimes on a large scale, to participate in resistance of different forms (e.g. signature campaigns, protests, Facebook photo postings, press conferences) at various times. It was the contributions made by multiple players, including the media, that helped sustain the momentum of resistance long enough to ensure the removal of the 10-year-old voucher scheme (Yuen, 2018). The voucher scheme was eventually replaced by the Kindergarten Education Scheme in 2017.

Transformation or more neoliberalism and resistance

The supply-side Kindergarten Education Scheme (initially called Free Quality Kindergarten Education Scheme) is considerably a triumph of the resistance movement, at least from the viewpoint of stabilising and sustaining developments. Deep down, however, it is another camouflage of neoliberalism or in Connell's (2013) term, rationing of education resources. The new scheme has not made education for children aged 3–6 a public good. The government's scepticism towards a fully subsidised provision is evident in its defence of its official position. As before, familiar reiterations such as inefficient use of public funding, good enough resource allocation for quality provision, tightened control measures, and maintaining operation flexibility were repeated (Education Bureau, 2016). In brief, the Kindergarten Education Scheme provides direct subsidy to participating (voluntary) non-profit kindergartens, the calculation of which is based on half-day operation (per student head count). Kindergartens providing whole-day and long-whole-day places receive additional subsidies using the formulas of 1:3 and 1:6, respectively. The direct subsidy calculation also references new salary points (minimum-maximum point, not salary scales) set for teachers and principals (Education Bureau, 2016). The scheme has led to an increase of recurrent education expenditure to 7.1% (Education Bureau, 2019). Effectively speaking, the underlying premise of the design is no different from that of the voucher scheme, i.e. competing for students for more resources and parents responsible for covering the tuition fee difference, as before, the latter affecting mostly those using whole-day and long-whole-day places. Under the new scheme, half-day provision is largely free, except for kindergartens that have to charge parents for rental payments not covered by the official subsidy (Education Bureau, 2016). A critical examination of the specific details of various measures stipulated in the scheme revealed a more sophisticated structure of neoliberal governance. This basic structure, first developed for the voucher scheme, grew in magnitude to allow a return of the neoliberal imaginary and manifestation of the *homo economicus* (Yuen, 2021). Connell (2013) highlighted the paradox of neoliberalism, i.e. seeking to resolve problems created by neoliberalism by implementing neoliberal solutions. The supply-side Kindergarten Education Scheme does not redistribute resources to ensure equality and equity among historically marginalised groups, namely, young children, women, and the socially disadvantaged (Yuen, 2021). It reproduces the prevailing power structures in early childhood education and society at large, making it hard for the profession to transform practices to care for children's well-being, especially in current crises.

Facing the vastly complex crises stemming from the Covid-19 pandemic and the uncertain political situation of Hong Kong, the early childhood profession shoulders escalating pressure in protecting young children from adverse impact while confronting the market practices of commodification. Before these crises, the well-being of Hong Kong children and youth already caused serious concern (Hong Kong Paediatric Society, 2017). The pandemic simply added more problems to their vulnerable status, with the disadvantaged more adversely affected than others (Tse & Kwan, 2021). Riding alongside the changing pandemic situation are the unpredictable political developments of the city which have induced sweeping changes in all aspects of life at an unprecedented speed. Education is standing at the crossroads, struggling to reposition itself to support students' learning and well-being (Lo, 2021) and implement government directives related to national security education in kindergartens and schools. Teachers are expected to receive specific training in the same regard. Roberts-Holmes and Moss (2021) stressed the importance of becoming a critical thinker to resist neoliberalism and transform early childhood institutions through alternative perspectives. The rapidly disappearing civil society and democratic space in education and Hong Kong society seem to suggest that the possibilities for resistance and critical thinking will become far more daunting than before, if not totally unimaginable. In a caring democracy, citizens can care for each other if government support is committed to ensuring justice, equality, and freedom for all members of society (Tronto, 2013). As Hong Kong is in crisis, it is difficult to contemplate the idea of a caring democracy at this moment in time or it may be a good time to reimagine a caring democracy in the changed context.

Conclusion

Early childhood education in Hong Kong is uniquely situated in a specific political, economic, social, and cultural trajectory for examining the capitalistic impact of both laissez faire and neoliberalism. By tracing the development of the private early childhood market under the laissez faire approach of the British colonial government and contrasting it with the faithful adoption of neoliberalism by the SAR government, the dominant beliefs, values, and assumptions deeply entrenched in structures, practices, and languages of governance can be vividly exposed. This nuanced understanding is considered critical to analysing how parent choice has moved to the centre stage of the voucher scheme and become the invisible building block of the Kindergarten Education Scheme. The massive grassroot movement orchestrated to resist the web of neoliberal control expanded through the voucher scheme offers an encouraging message that policy change is possible when all those involved in the care of young children consciously confront their neoliberal subjectivities. The collective resistance has at least facilitated a temporary disruption of the consumer and producer subjectivities, enabling parents and early childhood institutions to play an activist role for young children. Early childhood advocacy in the past has witnessed the coming together of people for social justice causes. This coming-together is never easy. It requires a dedication to make the awakening calls, a willingness to problematise the dominance of neoliberalism in the capitalistic context of Hong Kong, and the courage to take an activist stance. Along the road, there are always bodies and minds (e.g. better resourced parents preferring vouchers, kindergartens enjoying the freedom of a market approach) that embrace the neoliberal subjectivities more than others. As discussed, the new supply-side policy is another manifestation of the neoliberal imaginary, far more sophisticated than before. Whether there will be further resistance is subject to how neoliberalism and the political developments of Hong Kong dance to each other's tune.

The "crèches parentales" in France

Marie-Laure Cadart

Parents who are not consumers but actors in childcare: utopia or reality? The question may seem incongruous. However, for 50 years, there have been nurseries in France where committed parents jointly participate in the care and the education of children with professionals, and where they are also responsible for the management of the nurseries. Even as for-profit companies increasingly take a hold of the field of early childhood, these parent-led initiatives persist and thrive. Solidarity, cooperation, flexibility, and local belonging replace competitiveness, customer service, modelling, and standardisation. The originality of these *"crèches parentales"* is also in how they perform various functions: a service function (the care of young children); a business function (managing the staff); a social inclusion function (hosting internships for vulnerable people in a process of labour market integration); and an initiation into active citizenship. They are living places, but also spaces of resistance against the commodification of early childhood. Many of them adhere to the umbrella organisation ACEPP, *Association des Collectifs Enfants, Parents, Professionels* (Association of collectives of children, parents, and professionals) which is intimately linked to their history and their development. Today, ACEPP represents 800 childcare centres (about one hundred of them are crèches parentales strictly speaking), 39,000 families, and 9,000 childcare professionals (www.acepp.fr).

After having contextualised ECEC in France and sketched a concise history of this movement, I will analyse the characteristics of the crèches parentales, the values that underpin them, the audiences they reach, the territories where they are established, and their relations with governmental institutions. What are the issues and challenges they face in these times of neoliberalism where humans are too often sacrificed on the altar of profit?

Childcare in France

The early childhood sector has undergone significant changes in recent decades. In 2000, by decree, nurseries (*crèches*) moved from childcare centres based on a hygienist model – focusing on hygiene, dominated by a medical discourse with little attention paid to the educational and emotional needs of children or their parents – to places of care and education for young children, whose educational project must "guarantee welcoming, care, development, experiences, and well-being" (Décret n°2000-762). The psychological life of the baby and the importance of her living environment for her development are taken into account, requiring staff qualifications in the educational field and an adapted adult-child ratio. The parents who had been confined outside the doors of the crèches until 1975 finally received a place. The crèches parentales have been formalised since then, allowing parents to manage early childhood centres and to actively participate in childcare alongside professionals. Each childcare centre is expected to create a pedagogical project that includes both an educational and a social project. This project must describe the integration (or anchorage) of the crèche in the neighbourhood and how the needs of vulnerable populations will be taken into account. In relation to this reform, a funding reform was meant to allow each child to be included, whether their parents were working or not and regardless of family income. As soon as they were legally recognised, parental crèches benefitted from the same funding as other childcare centres. It needs to be noted that the comparatively generous French family allowance policies, established in 1945, have always followed societal evolutions as they have allocated substantial funding to childcare centres and have given incentives to local municipalities to create childcare places.

Until 2004, the early childhood sector was protected from market laws and priority was given to creating new places, ensuring access to all children and improving the quality of care. The training of professionals integrated up-to-date knowledge in the psychological and educational fields. The opening up to competition, announced in 1994, when the World Trade Organisation (WTO) was created, was part of a larger movement to deregulate and privatise all public services, including health services, education, and early childhood (Cadart, 2008). Up to 2004, crèches could solely be managed by public authorities, health insurance funds, or by non-profit organisations, funded by the CNAF (the national organisation responsible for family policies). Being non-profit was compulsory. When the field of ECEC opened up to the for-profit sector, it was quickly taken over by childcare companies building new crèches and taking over existing ones. Among them, some large groups have up to 1,800 nurseries; in 2020, one of them was bought by an investment fund. However, they receive the same public funding as other childcare organisers, allowing some of the for-profit providers to have built up real estate assets with public funds. At present, the commercial sector continues to increase its share of what has become "the early childhood market." In recent years, it has created more than half of the new places and already manages 17% of the existing childcare places (compared to 7% in 2012) according to the French Federation of Nursery Companies (FFEC), the umbrella association of for-profit providers (Shahshahani, 2020). In 2016, a study by the CNAF nevertheless showed that the operating cost of non-profit associations (that include crèches parentales) was 20% lower than that of private for-profit childcare. In addition, in 2018, the FFEC extended its influence, obtaining – under the employers' federation (MEDEF) – a seat on the board of directors of the CNAF where the various childcare plans are approved, while representatives of the social and non-profit sector, including ACEPP, are not represented, despite repeated requests over 10 years (Delhon, 2021).

Since 2006, resistance movements appeared in France to protect ECEC, in an environment that so far was not politicised and little inclined to revolt. Initiated by professionals, they rallied many citizens and continue their mobilisation today, attempting (and sometimes succeeding) to influence public policies marked both by strong regulation and a neoliberal context of openness to competition. In 2006, the collective *Pas de 0 de conduite pour les enfants de 3 ans* (No zero for conduct of 3-year-old children) launched a major movement against the screening of what the then government labelled as "predelinquant children" in nurseries and gathered 200,000 signatures in two months, mobilising professionals, scientists, and civil society. It was followed in 2014 by the creation of the collective *Construire ensemble la politique de l'Enfance* or *CEP-Enfance* (Constructing early childhood policy together), allying over 100 national and local organisations by warning about "a childhood in a state of emergency" in a book to which

60 organisations contributed (CEP-Enfance, 2021). In 2011, the collective *Pas de bébé à la consigne* (No babies in the luggage storage) brought together more than 50 organisations to protest against measures aimed at reducing childcare quality for young children, such as reduced child-adult ratios, for the benefit of managerial profitability. Today, if the still active movement includes above all professionals whose mobilisation has not weakened, more and more voices are being raised among elected officials and even within certain departmental family allowance funds (CAF) to denounce the use of public money in the private for-profit sector. In 2017, following the Giampino (2016) report, a national body defined the common framework, the principles, and the essential values to be shared by professionals in the care of young children. Among them, themes dear to the ACEPP parental movement: collaboration with families; parent-professional cooperation in a non-normative approach; sharing knowledge between parents and professionals; the role of parents in decision-making bodies in a spirit of participation which excludes consumerist logics; and the integration and anchoring of childcare in the local community. This framework was included in the national charter for the care of young children legislation in 2021.

The history of the crèches parentales and of ACEPP

The crèches parentales emerged in the slipstream of the movement of May 1968, at a time when nurseries places were scarce and parents were perceived as ignorant by professionals who claimed a monopoly of expertise. The crèches parentales were created by parents wanting to have a say and to actively participate in the education of their children in the nurseries. These parents critically questioned the hygienic obsessions that prevailed at the time, such as the paramedical training of nursery nurses, the exclusion of parents for hygienic reasons, or the general lack of educational debates. They also wanted to free themselves from a family model made up of constraints and traditions, to choose for themselves how they wished to educate their children. Priority would therefore be given to the educational dimension of childcare based on a privileged relationship with children and a climate of trust in adults. Advances in paediatrics, the decline in infant mortality, discoveries about infant psychology, and the importance of early relations and of the first years of life on later development and on the constitution of personality, were revolutionising the way children were viewed. The status of the young child changed from an object into a subject. The references to psychoanalysis were important, as embodied by Françoise Dolto who influenced the movement (for instance Dolto, 1995). Very quickly emerged what would become the slogan of the crèches parentale movement: "the parent is the child's first educator." Professionals, who initially were absent from the very first "crèches sauvages" (wild nurseries), would soon become indispensable alongside parents, with a dedicated place to explore: establishing an alliance and sharing their knowledge about children, while respecting parents' educational methods. The profession that best met the aspirations of parents is that of the *éducateur de jeunes enfants*, a bachelor's degree in early childhood education that is also related to social work, as opposed to the traditional *puericulture*, that is a branch of nursing.

In the 1970s, it was no longer only intellectual and artistic circles that were interested in the crèches parentales, but parents in search of a different, more flexible form of childcare. Parents allied in "parent child collectives" (with an NGO status) to collectively care for their children during the day. They prioritised small centres in comparison to the traditional crèches (only 10–20 children) and favoured the presence of parents to comfort their children. The parent child collectives supported individual attention for each child without any pre-established educational aims and opened the nurseries to the outside community and the neighbourhood.

These collectives came together to create ACEP (association of parent and children's collectives) around strong educational values: collaboration between parents and professionals; acceptance of different educational attitudes towards children; the duty to interfere in the face of parental attitudes deemed irresponsible; respect for children; the importance of the group; the role of the father in early childhood; the relationship of trust with between parents and professionals; and an organisation of the room and the materials corresponding to these values.

In 1982, the report *"L'enfant dans la vie, une politique pour la petite enfance"* (The child in life, an early childhood policy) (Bouyala & Roussille, 1982) outlined the broad guidelines of the political left, which had recently come to power, for their broad early childhood policy, including, but not limited to, childcare. In addition to increasing the number of childcare places and improving their quality, the report acknowledged the vision of the parental crèches and promoted social innovation.

Development and recognition

The crèches parentales developed while diversifying their actions and have mushroomed since 1985. The number of associations that adhered to the ACEP increased from 10 in 1970 to 700 in 1998, with much creativity and dynamism in their participatory approach, searching for how each parents could use their talents and how to realise the inclusion of all parents. In some nurseries, parents with similar ideas who wanted to share common educational values and practices came together without seeking an opening to the outside world. In others, on the contrary, the pedagogical project was that of openness, diversity, and belonging to the community. Yet everywhere, through their active involvement in ECEC, parents became civic actors in the life of the neighbourhood or village, in a dynamic of local social development. What constitutes the originality of a crèche parentale is the connection with the neighbourhood or the rootedness in the local territory; the involvement of parents in ways that they deem fit, without any pre-established model of participation; and the strength of belonging to a social network to support them when life becomes too heavy. In 1998, while professionals took on an important role in order to ensure the sustainability of these parental structures, ACEP became ACEPP, adding the P for professionals to its name, officially recognising the place of professionals alongside children and parents. Both the national and the departmental federations of ACEPP remained faithful to the original organisation in a network without hierarchy and tried to remain as closely aligned as possible to local concerns. The fight for governmental recognition of parental crèches eventually led to their official recognition in the decree of August 1, 2000.

Diversification of actions and parent support

From its inception, the parental crèche movement has been marked by innovative initiatives, combining a proactive approach, knowledge of the field, and partnerships with local institutions and partners. Many of these initiatives served as a spur to improve ECEC, to anchor themselves in a territory, and to welcome diversity. In addition to childcare in which parents participate, many other actions have originated from this movement, corresponding to the needs of a territory: meeting places for parents and children, family daycare networks, mobile drop-in centres, toy libraries, and artistic activities. At the national level, alliances were made with actors in the domain of social economy. The movement influenced parent support policies, contesting the dominant deficit view of parents ("*parents démissionaires*"), and developing a concept of parents as citizens. According to Saül Karsz,

> Parenthood comes to the fore (because) families are asked to perform the imposing and unachievable task of remedying what the society in place no longer offers [...] they must repair what the predominantly liberal society tears apart in terms of solidarity, attention to others, and respect for the 'paupers of the earth'.
>
> *(in Cadart, 2006, p. 148)*

At the ACEPP association, the idea of parenthood is associated with collective coeducation with a particular vigilance against the possible stigmatisation of certain parents whose educational model seems too far from the dominant model and resistant to the idea that these parents need interventions and programmes that would force them to adhere to dominant mainstream model of parenting. Parental initiatives were multiplying and notably, in 2005, the first *Université Populaire des Parents* (Popular Parents University, UPP) was created in which groups of parents conducted research with the help of a facilitator and the methodological support of an academic on a theme they chose in relation to parenthood and with the explicit aim of influencing the political discussion on parenthood. In this period, three sustainable programmes emerged in the movement: in 1986, the intercultural programme in low SES neighbourhoods; in 1988, the programme for the qualification of future professionals; and in 1991, the development of parental initiatives in rural areas. We will return to these programmes after sketching the present situation.

The crèche parentale today

Today, a crèche parentale is a formally recognised structure, managed by an association of parents that can accommodate a maximum of 25 children from 2 months to 4 years (or even 6 years). According to the procedures defined by the association, parents commit to participate, on a regular basis, in the life of the nursery by taking turns ensuring the care and education of the children, with the help of qualified professionals. In addition to their time with the children, parents carry out other tasks (management, maintenance, stewardship, organisation of the physical space, relations with the outside world, ...). The professionals, under the responsibility of a technical manager, guarantee the quality of daily care. For the most part, parental crèches are subject to the same conditions as other childcare centres, with some peculiarities: the inclusion of parents in the adult-child ratio and the function of the technical manager which replaces that of the director in other crèches. As local children's services driven by the values of solidarity, these structures have adapted to the real needs of families, taking into account the reconciliation of professional and family life and local social life. They must be open to all children and their families while respecting social and cultural diversity. If the nursery is above all a welcoming place for young children, it also offers a space of conviviality, sharing between parents and professionals, and networking. Families are recruited according to their adherence to the pedagogical and social project, their willingness to commit, and their availability to participate in the care and education of the children (very variable depending on the establishment, ranging from 2 hours monthly to 2 1/2 days per week) as well as associative tasks. However, in some areas with a scarcity of childcare places, parents may have to choose this type of childcare by default. Some will then happily invest in it and testify to the changes it made in their lives, while others do not find their way and may leave as soon as they find another mode of childcare that better suits them. In Paris, parents should ensure on average 1/2 day of working with the children (around 2 hours one day) per week to which are added associative tasks (management, cleaning, shopping, and meal preparation) in different ways depending on the crèche. Parents also discuss and work with pedagogy, not in a rigid and imposed way but as discussions about different approaches: pedagogy of diversity, Montessori, Emmi Pickler, an ecological approach,... Not all parents are able to invest in this way during the first 3 years of their child's life.

Since the officialisation of parental crèches in 2000, some crèches are only "parent managed": parents do not participate in the care of children but manage them by sitting on the board of directors. They draw up the pedagogical and social project, set the priorities of the crèche, and are in charge of employee management and relations with institutional partners. It is not easy to improvise as a manager and the ACEPP offers members an optional service to help with associative management. Other nurseries abandon parental management because of increasingly complex procedures and regulations that consume too much time, to the detriment of reflection on the educational project and practices. An ACEPP parental label has been created to help them maintain their "parental project" and adherence to the values of ACEPP. It includes a series of criteria: being not-for-profit; aiming for quality as a primary concern; parent-professional collaboration on the pedagogical and social project; respect for each child's personality and each family's home practices; openness to all and respect for diversity; the participation of all families in the management and organisation of the material space; civic responsibility and solidarity towards the local environment.

While there are now only about 150 crèches parentales in France with 2,400 places (or 0.5% of the children who attend ECEC) (Observatoire national de la petite enfance, 2020), it should be noted that many points defended since their creation have been integrated into legislative texts: coeducation; the role of the parent as the first educator; and the inclusion of all children. Some nurseries have existed for more than 30 years and continue their original and quality work. Let us now return to the three programmes initiated by ACEPP.

From the intercultural programme in disadvantaged neighbourhoods to welcoming diversity

The crèche parentale "*Arc en Ciel*" in Vénissieux, a low SES suburb of Lyon, established in 1987, was one of the first crèches of the intercultural programme in disadvantaged neighbourhoods. In 1986, it was aspired that small crèches in social housing districts with significant ethnic minority populations could enable children to socialise in contact with the culture of the country where they lived and that mothers could emerge from their isolation and forge links with each other. This crèche was created by women who refused the stigma imposed on their neighbourhood that had experienced urban violence. The programme put in place was expected to make it possible to establish close ties in spaces where they did not previously exist, offer an opportunity for young children to develop, especially when the family environment is in difficulty, and play a real preventive role. Mothers and parents would participate in the care of children alongside professionals; the educational practices of families would be discussed and connected with those of professionals. It was expected that the dialogue would help to negotiate cultural differences that otherwise could be experienced as strange or even shocking. For almost 35 years, this 15-place parental crèche has been welcoming children and their families in this social housing district. The meeting with ACEPP allowed parents to develop their project. The management and the rules of the crèche are simple and the participative constraints are light to allow each family to belong: participate in the care of children for at least 2 hours each month and contribute to the monthly cleaning of the nursery. The involvement of parents in other tasks is encouraged according to their skills, possibilities, and availabilities. Only families who live in the neighbourhood are welcomed in order to respect the rootedness of the crèche in the neighbourhood. An inquiry by ACCESS showed that parents who participated in the crèche testified (Cadart, 2006):

> This makes parents aware that they have value. It is very ungrateful to be a stay-at-home mother.
> For us African women, it is especially our mother who is there to help us and I was alone. When I came here, I learned a lot from other moms who had children before me. It helped me a lot.
> We meet other parents who bring other solutions, other ideas, another culture, it is a mosaic that changes all the time, moving colours like the kaleidoscope.
> It makes it possible to live with the differences of others and to accept them.
> When you go to the nursery, you have prejudices about education, food, the relationship with the child. We always have the impression that our model is the best. We learn that it is only different. Difference is perceived as a wealth not as a danger.
> I had a hard time accepting that my child was clumsy. The professionals have made me understand that a child does not think like an adult. At first, I didn't understand. I felt listened to. It's important to be listened to. It allowed me to accept my role as a mother, the place of the child. I was afraid of the eyes of others.
> We share a lot of things with parents. We meet the people that we see in the nursery outside also.
> This is the first time that I have been involved in an associative environment. It is good to give your opinion, to say what you think.
> Each passing parent leaves something of himself to the others. Everyone leaves their mark and realizes that it serves others.
> Initially, I was a little scared. Because I have black skin, am I going to be rejected? No, it wasn't that. I took all the children, I carried them; there wasn't a single mom who didn't want me to.
> Our children also see different cultures, different skin colours, so they don't have to be afraid. I tell myself that they are lucky to meet people from all over the world.

A former child testified: I think it has taught us to respect people who come from far away (in Cadart, 2006).

These testimonies also show the importance of a welcoming culture in a space and a shared place to which everyone can belong. It is a shared space with a mixed population, yet thanks to the richness of the diversity of family cultures and the knowledge of each family member, the culture of this nursery is a practice of citizenship. This requires not only communicating about cultural shocks caused by certain family practices in confrontation with those of professionals but also thoroughly working on these issues, and that allowed parents and professionals to step back and find a space for negotiation between adults that is beneficial for the child(ren). Initial training in the early childhood profession did not sufficiently prepare future professionals for dialoguing with families and for complex intercultural confrontations. However, the crèche was successful in elaborating its pedagogy of diversity and in inscribing these values in the pedagogical and social project and bringing it to life. Faced with the Covid-19 epidemic that led to a 2-month lockdown in Spring 2020 and the abrupt closure of all childcare centres, the solidity of the links and the complicity with the families made it possible to remain in touch with each other. Samia Zemmit, technical manager for almost 20 years, testified about the creativity of the team and the strength of the collective,

> Everyone has been responsive and responsible, focusing first on the children so that they can grow up in an environment that is as stress-free as possible with adults performing their roles, despite some tense family situations finding themselves without resources. We were forced to close the curtains but we didn't close the nursery! We stayed in the nursery for two days to call all the families, and then we called them every day.

This has had a preventive effect. The lockdown having been extended by a month after the first month announced, the team improvised a kind of "toy library-drive-in," with a loan of toys to keep the link for the duration of the closure. The team reflected on the needs of children and this is how the toy library appeared as fundamental: it was essential to think together, to keep the link! It was through material things, but it wasn't about materiality. The crisis has served as an indicator of the pedagogical project. In this ordeal, the nursery was part of the family, with great professionalism. It is the framework of the solid and flexible pedagogical project that has made it possible to be "professionally familiar."

In rural areas

In rural areas, ACEPP's early childhood projects became the gateway to revitalise rural territories that were becoming deserted. For 20 years, at the request of several national partners, ACEPP has been engaged in local development actions to support the quality of life of inhabitants, and social cohesion in rural areas. It is necessary to adapt to each context, to rely on the reality of the territory and especially on the active participation of parents in local life. For families to remain in a region, they must feel welcome and experience a sense of belonging. It is essential to allow them to meet other parents, to build networks of solidarity and, of course, to be able to access childcare. The actions have borne fruit in terms of the creation of early childhood services and the revitalisation of the territories that promote the belonging of new families. The APEMAC program (*Accueil parents enfants en Massif Central*: Welcoming Parents and Children in the Massif Central), carried out between 2008 and 2014, aimed to promote the welcoming of new families and to revitalise territories affected by aging and demographic decline. Early childhood services were undeniable assets in this effort. Thus, the settlement of families in a given territory supported the local economic fabric and the maintenance of services, including schools. Creating provision close to families in a spirit of community building that empowers citizens is way beyond a vision of parents as consumers of a service. In rural areas, the associative dynamic has led to a co-construction of projects of local general interest in a wide variety of areas, including ECEC.

The qualifying training scheme

ACEPP's qualification training scheme with subsidised jobs aims to enable young people without any qualifications and people who have long been excluded from the labour market to socially reintegrate. The challenge of this system is to train early childhood professionals with a real policy of integration through employment by alternating training and internships. Professionals trained "à la carte" in the parental network are a fundamental advantage for the sustainability of these initiatives and for the transmission of values that they can maintain, regardless of their future workplace. While most childcare centres use such social economy projects for budgetary reasons (the jobs of these apprentices being subsidised), ACEPP moves a step further. It makes the inclusion of this often low-educated future workforce a spearhead for the dissemination of their specific conception of what working in ECEC may mean and for the adherence to its values. The departmental associations of ACEPP therefore relate to the formal training institutions and support parents as mentors of the trainees. An *Éducateur de Jeunes Enfants (EJE)* (an early childhood educator with a bachelor's degree) that currently works as the leadership of a crèche parentale testifies: "I did not have the baccalaureate (the diploma that gives access to post-secondary education in France); it was very important for me not to miss my entry into training; I received significant moral support." ACEPP considers it their mission to support the success of the next generation of professionals by supporting them in the preparation of the formal (state) exams, providing support for employers and tutors, organising regular collegial meetings that bring together all the partners, and linking preservice training and the parental crèches as workplaces.

Strengths and weaknesses of crèches parentales

Although each parental nursery is unique and cannot be replicated, this analysis reveals undeniable advantages as well as challenges. The advantages for children are quite straightforward. The child is at the heart of the concerns. The parental nursery allows the baby to spend quality time with their parent while simultaneously benefiting from the social advantages of group care and this allows them to grow up in emotional security and to separate more easily later. The educational project, safeguarded by the professionals, plays an essential role. An audit of parental nurseries commissioned by the Paris' municipal government noted that "great care is taken for the well-being of children with constant concern for their safety and development." Moreover, the small living spaces are adapted to the scale of the children. Life in the nursery is based on a living group, warranting an internal solidity ensured by the pedagogical project. Children learn to live in a community with confidence, continuity, and educational coherence despite different family cultures. Creativity and the importance given to cultural and artistic awakening are present from an early age.

There are also multiple advantages for the parents. In parental crèches, it is not the children who are enrolled but the parents who are recruited around a project and values to which they adhere, a concern for care and pedagogy that associates them in an open and non-dogmatic approach. The care is flexible and attentive to everyone. Parents' skills are put to work, allowing the association to function, each one investing his or her aptitudes in associative life. It is a community where parents find recognition, resources, and reciprocity. Coeducation takes its full meaning: "Co-education is simply to be together!" summarises an educator (Cadart, 2006). The group fosters belonging. Solidarity is enhanced between parents, who are involved in social relations at the nursery that continue thereafter. For some families, especially those who have just arrived in a community, the nursery can become an anchor, allowing them to emerge from isolation. Eventually, it is a space of active and civic parenthood allowing parents to dare to engage in other societal actions.

The professionals equally benefit from this approach. The social role and the effort made by ACEPP's training policy to train unqualified staff in early childhood professions matter. The social project of certain crèches enhances the inclusion and training of people benefiting from employment support contracts. The aid received for these staff allows the crèches to have lower ratios, which contributes to a good atmosphere that is also beneficial to the children. This also makes it possible to transmit values and practices that professionals will maintain regardless of their future workplace. Professionals are the keepers of the pedagogical and social project, its implementation, and transmission. In addition, they value the creativity. Artistic interventions are present and all the more appreciated by parents as no operational objective is expected. Art is an essential part of life from early childhood.

Finally, there are institutional and political advantages. The culture of the local civil service remains far removed from the knowledge of associative dynamism and its contribution to the richness of the social life of a territory. To combat this, ACEPP has done innovative work on mutual recognition between parents, professionals, and partners by creating training (Cadart, 2006). Thus, when institutional and political partners adhere to and understand the approach, they become fervent advocates and users who understand the richness of this contribution in a territory.

The multiple advantaged do not exclude important challenges. Major challenges are the considerable investment in time, the increasing complexity of management, the frequent renewal of parents and the requirement of transmission (the passage of a child in a nursery rarely exceeds 3 years), as these are sources of fragility, which can lead to discouragement.

There is the weight of these small institutions affiliated to the social economy that is very unequal compared to the behemoths of the for-profit private sector, large associations operating as companies, or the public sector. It is a constant challenge to reflect upon their own pedagogy and the rules and to re-examine to what extent these may exclude families, due to restrictions or due to the time that is demanded from parents.

In conclusion

Despite their limited number, parental crèches have shown to be a sustainable model, in relation to their solidarity. The priority given to quality care for each child, coeducation between parents and professionals, local development rooted in a territory, citizen parenting, social integration and respect for diversity, creativity and innovation are the assets of parental crèches. Breaking with the loneliness of exclusive parental responsibility, parental crèches offer an alternative where the collective makes sense in a shared responsibility towards children. Here, the "free choice" of the parent as a consumer is replaced by belonging to a collective, gathered around common values. Participating in childcare, reflecting on the educational values at work and accepting different educational models, giving one's precious time, finding shared gratitude and pleasure outside the monetary system, learning to live together and feeling good are assets that show that another way of being in the world is possible. The crèche is then a shared "common" and not a commodity, a convivial place of belonging for all, of learning and transmission, a place beyond consumentality for citizens; a political place in the noble sense. These are places of resistance in the face of the commodification of early childhood. Their adherence to a militant network that links them together, supports them and evolves according to their needs, mitigates their fragilities. As part of the social economy, they bring a breath of fresh air in France, albeit still only to a limited number of children and parents.

Community-based preschools in Chile

Pablo Rupin

What does community mean for a community-based preschool? Can we call upon this notion of community and this particular educational configuration, in order to propose alternative pathways in the face of the neoliberalisation and commodification of early childhood education? I propose some avenues for the analysis of the issue, based on the results of research on parental participation in Chile. This research was carried out in early childhood centres that use parental participation as a structural element of their functioning, while at the same time becoming part of the local community fabric. I present various contextual and cultural factors that can have an influence on the development of democratic, participatory, parental, family, and more broadly community logics in community-based early childhood settings.

A non-formal or community-based Latin American preschool

In Latin American literature, the terms "out of school," "non-formal," "unconventional," "alternative," and "communal" are used (Blanco, Umayahara, & Reveco, 2004; Fujimoto, 2000; Peralta & Fujimoto, 1998) to report on a type of early childhood institutions that are "facilitating the educational task of families in their daily environments" (Fujimoto, 2000, p. 5). Their main characteristic seems to be the sharing of the role of educator between early childhood professionals and other community workers or *agentes educativos locales* (local educational agents) (Ramírez, Nava, Ávila, Barrios, & Vázquez, 2012) – among them the mothers of the children themselves or other *madres monitoras* (mother instructors) (Bernard van Leer Foundation, 2001). These are mainly women volunteers from local communities, who follow a qualifying training process and, in many cases, ensure the overall management of the projects. The description of these programmes emphasises the positive impact of these characteristics for the construction of holistic educational processes (Ramírez et al., 2012).

Services of this nature thus seek to translate the informal learning of children within their living space into an explicit and shared educational project. Hence, the close contact that these programmes seek to establish with the inhabitants and organisations of the neighbourhood, in order to strengthen the spaces of learning and discovery for children. This pattern of operation leads professionals to encourage the participation of families and local agents and to adopt a posture of relative withdrawal, facilitation, or coordination of the learning dynamics (Peralta & Fujimoto, 1998). These features are most often developed in contexts of poverty or vulnerability, such as neighbourhoods that face a lack of resources on the part of the State. They are initiated in the context of broader actions aimed at the social development of local communities. In this sense, some have defended the contribution of such early childhood services as a means to combat poverty (Fujimoto, 2000). Beyond the objectives strictly related to the *educare* of children (Kaga, Bennett, & Moss, 2010), a broader conception of community-based practices in the field of youth, health, promotion of women's rights, and others would aim at improving the living conditions of the populations at hand (Pérez, Abiega, Zarco, & Schugurensky, 1999). That implies an orientation that considers the educational institution as a fundamental actor in the reconstruction of the social fabric of communities. The social role of educational institutions is strongly emphasised here, while at the same time re-emphasising the importance of integration into local project networks and coordination with other organisations working with children (CEC, 2006). In this vein, the participation of parents and more broadly of local communities in the upbringing of children is considered an essential factor contributing to social cohesion (Ramírez et al., 2012). On the other hand, the contribution of these programmes could be viewed in terms of inclusion, in the sense of a greater accessibility to educational services by parts of the population from which many children are traditionally excluded. It can be noticed that these arguments are also critically questioned. Rosemberg's (2010) analysis points to the construction of a system strongly marked by inequalities in access to quality services, which results in "poor early childhood education for the poor" and in a charity rather than a rights-based approach. In this critique, it is argued that far from contributing to overcoming poverty, the "unconventional" pre-school care facilities may contribute to its reproduction: insufficient responses, especially with few resources and poorly qualified staff, are offered for children and families who need quality care more than others.

The field of study

Two types of Chilean community-based preschools were part of the study, based on observations and interviews, and three services of each type were selected. A first group is that of the preventive health, the *Programa de Mejoramiento de la Atención a la Infancia* (Programme for the Improvement of Childcare), designed to operate at the local level through projects developed and implemented entirely by parents, with government support in terms of training and funding. In the absence of early childhood professionals, committed families are expected to organise themselves in order to develop a shared educational project adapted to their needs, defining the early childhood provision (managers and workers, the space to be used, the days and hours of operation) (JUNJI, 2008). Inspired by the principles of popular education (PIIE, 2008), this programme explicitly aims at the development of learning processes not only in children but also in participating adults (Venegas & Reyes, 2009). It is mainly the children's mothers who develop the early childhood service, sometimes with the support of other local organisations (a local church, a school, the municipality, an NGO, a nearby kindergarten), and who follow a qualification process. They also call on the involvement of people whose collaboration may be requested for specific pedagogical functions – the *agentes culturales clave* (key cultural agents) – or to participate in the realisation of coordination or management activities – the *colaboradores* (collaborators).

On the other side, there are the kindergartens of the *Red de Centros de Educación Comunitaria* (Network of Community Education Centres) (CEC), which is a space for collaboration and sharing of experiences between the managers of the different centres that are part of the network. Their history refers to a variety of unconventional pre-school education experiences: kindergartens that are staffed by professionals and mothers in continuing education, but also experiences run solely by local community women. Beyond their various pedagogical orientations and origins, they have in common the fact of sharing an approach, focused on popular education and parental, family, and community participation in educational processes. As part of a broader framework of support for the needs of families, some of these centres offer services for youth and for women.

The community and the community approach: several dimensions

Taking into account the local community is a central feature to all the centres under study. Several interviewees, including professional educators, also speak explicitly of an *enfoque comunitario* (community approach) that guides and gives meaning to their work, whether it is in relation to care, pedagogy, or local actions beyond what is traditionally associated with *educare*. More than just a contextual feature, the local community is the material and cultural basis, the irreplaceable preliminary reference point that gives meaning to experiences. Not only is this element inscribed in the documents that present the theoretical design and basic orientations of the different ECEC provision (JUNJI, 2008; PIIE, 2008; CEC, 2006), it is also present in the narratives of educators and parents. But beyond the recurrence in the use of the term, what does the community mean for these services? What does it mean to "work" with the community and how is this work done?

The origins of a community approach and its development

In the narratives of the interviewees, the community character of the services refers largely to their original conception. The effort of a shared construction with the local community is well-noted by most of the leaders. The ECEC centres studied are all presented as localised and relevant responses that have risen from the needs of the populations more than from an external institutional mandate. However, taking into account the processes of organising the ECEC does not seem to be enough to grasp this local anchoring. One should also consider the dynamics that are developed in the subsequent functioning, particularly in terms of extending the centre's task beyond children's education to other activities, equally conceived as components of a single community project. For many, wanting to be a community project means developing approaches beyond the usual childcare or preschool for children who are not of the official age to register for primary school. It means supporting actions for the most disadvantaged families (such as the case of a centre that intervenes with the municipality to help families in precarious housing situations). At the same time, it also means opening the centre to local meetings, for example, workshops for the prevention of drug abuse aimed at mothers together with their older children.

Integration into broader networks of work concerning childhood is seen as fundamental; not only for obtaining resources, but also for the legitimation and recognition of the ECEC centre. In a preschool like *Illimani* [the name of the centre], this orientation seems so developed that the centre became a space for meeting and establishing networks for children and families, including the sponsorship of other less developed or formalised childcare structures, the identification of various social problems, linking users to other social services, etc. It is an image of an ECEC centre that resonates with that of the public kindergarten as a privileged place for the development of a global community approach (Universidad de Chile, 2007).

The "popular" anchoring of ECEC structures

The weight of a shared history and culture allows us to better understand the anchoring of a "communitarian – participationist" discourse in many of these ECEC programmes, in connection with values that are specific to the sociohistorical and cultural context (Tobin, Wu and Davidson, 1989; Brougère and Rayna, 2000; Brougère, 2002). All the centres under study are located in relatively poor urban or semi-rural neighbourhoods and municipalities, characterised in the present or the past by limited access to basic services. One needs to be aware of the significant urban segregation of the city of Santiago (Sabatini et al., 2001), the high level of centralism in the national government (Waissbluth et al., 2007) and the resulting differences in access to social, cultural, and leisure services. On the basis of these characteristics, the municipalities include populations that are part of the vast majority that is still relatively deprived of the benefits promised by economic development and the modernisation of Chilean society (Ferreiro, 2012; Moulian, 1997; UNDP, 1998). In this vein, the contexts in which the programmes under study emerged, correspond to what the literature describes as a "popular" world or culture. Hence the interest in noting certain sociocultural and political dynamics that have developed within or in close contact with the popular world in recent decades in Chile, and which contribute to reflecting on the approach developed by these centres.

The sociopolitical dimension

A first element relates to the dynamics of action and sociopolitical organisation of the Chilean *poblaciones*. The term *poblador* (the one who inhabits) refers to the inhabitants of Chilean *poblaciones*, poor urban, or semi-rural neighbourhoods but not necessarily peripheral in the spatial sense of the term. The term close to *campamento* – which may refer to the notion of "slum" in English – is often used to designate a situation of increased precariousness, especially in the youngest poblaciones or those under construction and whose housing, consisting for the most part of light equipment, is the result of the *tomas de terreno* (taking land): the illegal occupation of land (Espinoza, 1988; Garcés, 2002).

From the 1950s, various forms of local or community popular organisation appeared in Chile as responses to their precarious situations in a context of great poverty. These actions concerned, in particular, problems of access to housing during a period of strong rural exodus (Garcés, 2002), but also because of the lack of supply or the inadequacy of various types of services for the promotion or protection of social rights (Hardy, 1987). The popular organisation could also include the intention to respond collectively to emergencies associated with impoverishment in basic subsistence conditions, such as food (Hardy, 1986). For Cornejo, González, and Caldichoury (2007), this aspect of the local community constituted an important space of political resistance and struggle for democracy during the 1980s. Espinoza (1988) and Garcés (2002) note the figure of the *poblador* and the new form of subjectivity that he or she embodies, born of a series of new practices of self-construction and peripheral urbanisation, expressed in the proliferation of *campamentos* and in particular in the phenomenon of *terreno tomas* (taking or reclaiming land). For Palma (1998), the participation in such initiatives causes the actors to fundamentally change their attitudes and predispositions to act in the public domain. Bringing together these experiences in the network of the Community Education Centres (CEC, 2006) testifies to this dynamic and shows the features of a popular anchoring both in cultural and in sociopolitical ways. It is clear from their documentation that the development of this type of experience is precisely situated between the 1970s and 1980s, within popular associative initiatives led in particular by *pobladoras* women and aimed, among other things, at the establishment of alternatives for the care of young children, allowing mothers to access the world of work. Many "popular kindergartens" were thus born in the heart of poblaciones and campamentos. As presented by the director of the "Illimani" kindergarten, the document of the CEC network (2006) emphasises that the educational processes were intimately linked to the *tomas de terreno* and other experiences of association and popular struggle from the beginning. For many of the centres in the CEC network, the organisation of educational projects began just after the return to democracy in Chile. If a feeling of nostalgia sometimes appears in the interviews, regretting the relative weakening of a kind of participatory disposition of the families involved, there is always the evocation of a desire to promote the autonomous "power to act," the empowerment of the inhabitants, as an important long-term objective. More broadly, the narratives speak of a form of ideology of collective action (Sabatini, 1995) always present in the popular milieu. These elements are consistent with the postulates of the so-called *educación popular* (popular or folk education), an approach that this network seems to share (CEC, 2006). The same applies to the development of projects that did not have a predetermined goal or a fixed approach at their onset, but were built on the basis of dialogue with the populations concerned.

Dreams and altruism: categories to identify and distinguish oneself

For all centres, it is also personal involvement, the stated commitment of several people in charge and their backgrounds, that needs to be taken into account to fully understand the characteristics of the provision. This is, for instance, the case of two kindergarten directors who arrived in the local communities as university students; yet, it is also the case of preventive health project managers, having been involved in a task that is not part of their previous interests or activities, as well as of a secretary and several housewives involved in the project. Faced with a situation considered interesting because of its challenges and potentialities but also for concerns about the injustices and inequalities that it raised, all these people discovered a vocation and committed to it. Some interviewees also stressed the importance of adopting an altruistic and supportive attitude that cannot dissociate oneself from the work done. Some of them testified about their commitment taking the form of long-standing volunteer work. Many women educators criticised the merely economic motives that prevail in most private childcare facilities. In short, the importance of a form of altruistic commitment seems to define the singularity of the experiences put in place for many. This is a feature which, for many parents, is significant for the quality of the ECEC centres and even for their superiority over other centres.

Another dimension inherent to the community approach, conceived as the result of a shared construction, is related to the establishment of a framework of democratic and egalitarian relations not only with parents but also among team members. The same applies to the effort to convey to parents the image of a non-hierarchical organisation, as explicitly pointed out by the director of the Illimani kindergarten.

All these elements speak of a categorisation and differentiation on the part of educators and managers, with the identification of criteria against which to judge the value of the work done. This work defines the traits of people and structures that are situated in a similar approach, belonging to the same broader reference group: that of engaged professionals and educators who, working in a popular context, try to go beyond the rationale of charity, to encourage parental participation, and to promote the empowerment of local actors. A kind of utopian rhetoric is present in the discourse, especially in the ECEC centres of the CEC network. These are allusions to a shared dream and to the faith that must be maintained to persevere in the task developed. The analysis of the commitment of the actors allows the establishment of joint ventures (Wenger, 2005), around shared objectives, by diverse people whose backgrounds are sometimes very contrasted and shows a dynamic that testifies more broadly to the meeting of "worlds" or fields that go beyond the strict framework of education and childcare.

Variations and tensions of community care

Before talking about parent participation, the educators of the centres under study referred to the development of a crucial arrangement that seeks to make room for families, their practices, and their knowledge. This openness also includes the explicit statement of a sustained attitude to acknowledge and take into account the expectations and needs of families in differentiated ways, with personalised care for children. Many parents stressed the presence of this attitude. Worrying about the daily details, keeping in touch with families' experiences, being open to negotiation, and developing diverse educational and care practices, seemed to be the best indicators of a different posture, an attitude "that we do not see everywhere else," according to many. This means that the community approach is also related to the *care* model they develop. The concept of care (Tronto, 2009) can be understood as a constitutive concept for the field of ECEC, as a set of concrete and located practices of attention and care given to children, but also to parents and professionals themselves. The explicit self-conception of certain projects as being "community organisations" goes hand in hand with a desire for adaptation and a stated conception of pre-school institutions as agents at the service of the primary educational role of the family, trying to make the operating framework of the structure more flexible:

> We are here to serve the needs of families; I do not want to act as a "family educator" organization, but rather support what they decide. If the child is in bed at 11:00 p.m., because he does not have the opportunity to see his father before that, and if after that, he gets up late, are we going to deprive him, because of the kindergarten timeframe of something that is more important?
>
> *(Director, Kindergarten CEC)*

On this matter, many mothers who were interviewed referred to their previous experiences in institutional care for their children. These experiences were often described as negative, due to situations of abuse or lack of communication with the ECEC staff. Others evoked a recurring feeling of suffering and helplessness in the face of the difficulty of finding a childcare system adapted to both their needs and their financial possibilities. Hence, perhaps, the strength with which many women expressed their sense of gratitude towards the ECEC centres. The child's enrolment seems in some cases to be lived as an unexpected experience of respect for their rights: the right of children to be welcomed and educated in a formal and collective environment, but also the right of parents to be welcomed and supported in their role. A lived experience that could well be described as being unusual in the Chilean preschool system, identified as commodified, marketized, and closed upon itself, as well as unconcerned about families' needs. This explains the strong support that some of these community-based centres seem to generate in their members. For many of the parents interviewed, they appeared to be real lifelines in a hostile context. Parents who share not just a story of suffering, but an entire journey: "We all have a story […] of struggle behind us."

(Laura, mother at the kindergarten Niño Jesús)

However, beyond these positive evaluations, one can ask about the limits of the negotiation of *educare* practices. On what aspects can disagreement be accepted, or even incorporated into a compromise? The leaders themselves point out the resistance that emerges within their teams. The question of the flexibility of opening hours is an example of this: respecting family choices or constraints can imply a loss of harmony in the functioning of centres, the daily dynamics of work becoming less "neat and orderly" (Director, Kindergarten "Illimani"). Several interviewees referred to the divergence of opinions between parents and professionals on what could be the most appropriate educational and care practices for children. These discrepancies sometimes became evident for educators through daily observation of parenting practices in the ECEC centre. For some, this explicitly took the form of a tension to be resolved, a balance that must be constantly restored between different notions of "good practices," but the most complex challenge seems to relate to how the problem should be framed. Framing the issue as a critique about particular parental attitudes or behaviours would seem most problematic for some of the educators. Others refuse to take on an "expert" position, hierarchically above the parents; and still others place greater emphasis on professional expertise and stress the different roles of parents and professionals and their necessary complementarity. The desire to maintain an attitude of respect and dialogue towards families and their knowledge is highlighted, but at the same time, some stress the importance of questioning practices from a reflexive perspective: "That we can at least question the parents, make them think" (Cecilia, director of kindergarten "Niño Jesús"). The narratives of the educators testify to a reflection around what authors like Tronto (2009) identified as the risks of care related activities, understood as the generic activity that includes everything we do to maintain, perpetuate and repair our "world," so that we can live there as well as possible. The risk is the infantilisation of recipients and the development of asymmetrical relations. If we follow Mozère (2004), any concern for the other necessarily implies a position of asymmetry, a position of power. The community-based ECEC centres are no exception to this concern, but at the same time, it seems that educators are aware of this situation, as they do not underestimate it and instead seek to counteract it. They strive to adopt an attitude concerned with the admissibility of care practices (Mozère, 2004): not only caring for others, but doing so adequately, so that this concern suits the other and new forms of care can emerge during the interaction. For parents, the support that educators provide also seems to be a form of care. Broadly and beyond certain formal arrangements aimed at parent support or parent education, this support is understood as the daily *accompagnement* (guidance, support in a non-hierarchical sense) of the lived experiences of the adults involved, sometimes in relation to their parental function, sometimes beyond this aspect, including their relational life, the integration in the labour market, and other experiences. Moreover, a condition for possibilities for parent participation seems to be that certain forms of sociability are established: that the ECEC centre is perceived as a place to meet and to share daily life, as well as a place to develop a multiplicity of informal relationships.

Variations and tensions of community education

The local communities in which the ECEC centres are integrated represent, especially for educators and managers, a major resource for children's learning processes. This is the objective of mobilising the material and symbolic resources present in the nearby environment to build a localised curriculum and develop significant learning processes that are experiential and relevant, because they are in connection with the daily experiences of children and their families. Involving – certainly with variations and also resistance –local educational agents is also consistent with a pedagogical approach that seeks to "better bring together the knowledge, feelings, and values of the community" in the educational project that is developed for the centre (to quote the director of the kindergarten Illimani). It is also important to use local spaces as valid educational resources for educational work, as meeting places where children can discover a wider range of interactions and be recognised as actors in the life of the neighbourhood.

Thus, some parents may contribute to ECEC to present certain subjects to the children, for example, by talking about their own profession. It is also possible to engage in pedagogical approaches developed outside the ECEC centre, considering the role conferred on the community as a global educational body. Different types of activities – local parties, meetings, visits, outings – allow not only children to expand their opportunities for discovery, but also parents to take part in these educational events. Initiatives can be subject to laborious planning, requiring the preparation of several adults, or can follow a more fortuitous and informal model in daily interactions between children, family, and community:

> The duty of the child is not "fill this page," but "let's go to the square, let's find out what kind of tree we have there, who can we ask"… Then the children arrive with information that they find with their parents, valuing at the same time the knowledge of other people.
>
> *(Director Kindergarten)*

> I work there, opposite… For the anniversary of the kindergarten, my son's group came to see me (…) with drawings they had made, they left them in the store, glued them on the walls (…), and then after I showed them what I do, what I sell, clothes and everything.
>
> *(Mother, Kindergarten CEC)*

The opportunities for community participation more broadly allow the involvement of adults who are not directly related to children. The coordinator of the preventive health service *Puertas abiertas* emphasised in this regard the possibilities of a different learning through the discovery of other realities, beyond the trinomial children-peers/parents/professionals. In the words of this leader, these meetings promote the capacity for socialisation in children and contribute to developing their identity and integration in the community. This narrative expresses the interest in socialisation beyond the usual spaces shared by the members of the centre. However, the community-based pedagogical orientation does not allow itself to be understood in an unambiguous way and the identification and valorisation of socialisation spaces, considered for the most part enriching, are not free from ambivalences. According to the opinion of some parents, children certainly develop a kind of self-confidence or self-esteem that can only be celebrated, as it shows the development of critical thinking. At the same time, however, the children develop behaviours that are considered inappropriate by their parents in that they challenge elements of traditional family education, such as speaking to adults using less distant and respectful terms. Moreover, if the ECEC centre is presented as a space for sharing and meeting not only for children but also for adults, should we separate the services for children and adults? A preventive health coordinator raised this question, relativising what would be a typical fear in early childhood settings: inappropriate relations and discussions according to the ages of the children. In her perspective, it would not be desirable to hinder these moments or to isolate the children, since this is a dimension specific to their daily lives, which they can benefit from in terms of learning, provided that adults pay attention to the way they discuss certain subjects.

Parents' views on the community and the community approach

In general, the parents interviewed spoke less than the educators about the local community or the community approach in the ECEC centres. However, they seem to be essentially in line with the guidelines put forward by those responsible, and some provide clarifications that enrich the issue. Thus, for example, for the parents of the kindergarten *Alicura*, the moral development of the children and their ethical education, in particular the transmission of values such as respect and solidarity, constitutes one of the main educational objectives of the centre. The pedagogical transmission of values can hardly be conceived without relating it to the symbolic and even spiritual dimension of the pedagogical approach, as this facilitates the development of a sense of belonging in children. Thus, not only are children taught what the community in which they live is, but it is also a process of identity building. As it is a place where children and parents learn to identify and take responsibility, the kindergarten is more than childcare, it is a socio-educational model based on an ethic. Moreover, the community character of the centre is not just a matter of enhancing the community. In the eyes of these parents, it is also the opposite movement that counts: the community itself values, respects, and appreciates the ECEC centre. One element to highlight is that the ECEC centre is perceived as a structure that transmits its sensitivity and thus helps to trigger broader processes of cultural transformation on various aspects: family practices, the educational role of men, the participation of parents and families in children's educational processes, the valorisation of children as social actors, and raising awareness of the richness of popular and indigenous cultures.

Finally, for many parents and in a transversal way, there is the question of the legitimisation of educators, a legitimation that is largely based on their local belonging. They are in a relatively horizontal relationship, since they share a common reality with families. The constant references to proximity, to the humane and affectionate treatment on the part of those responsible, are elements that reinforce this dimension.

Conclusion

In the field of early childhood education, the term *communities* could raise reservations about the possible idealisation of realities and contexts to which one refers, since the term is systematically used in social discourse in a positive sense (Williams, 1976). For some, on the contrary, the term would evoke the defence of values that oppose an ethnocentric universalism. Indeed, the notion of community frequently refers, in a European context, to that of *communitarianism*, a true "operator of illegitimisation" that is frequently opposed, in a pejorative sense, as much to republicanism as to secularism, nationalism, universalism, or individualism. But in the construction of this "false problem," we seem to forget the central philosophical observation in the origin of the neologism, in the United States in the early 1980s: that the individual does not exist independently of his belongings, be they cultural, ethnic, religious, or social. It is precisely in this sense that the community-based ECEC discussed here is essentially social in nature and an alternative to the individualistic nature of parent-professional relations in the neoliberal realm.

It is this belonging that matters here, specifically in terms of being part of a *territorio* (territory), of a local community understood as a common living space full of educational resources, rich in opportunities for collaboration, with an irreplaceable material and cultural base that gives meaning to experiences. The recognition of these elements explains the effort to build ECEC that is produced in dialogue with the populations concerned; to recruit local educational agents sharing the same living environment as the parents; and to maintain democratic and egalitarian relations with them. More broadly, various elements of these community initiatives seem to oppose the market approach of early childhood education and to offer an alternative. First, we have illustrated how many educators explicitly criticise the purely economic motivations of most private structures. The importance of a form of altruistic commitment on their part also seems to be linked to the stories of parents who tell us how their presence in the provision is an experience of respect for the rights of children and families. Some explain the link between this commitment and values that, like solidarity, seek to be developed in children, in a process of ethical upbringing that is not only an identification with the local community, but also a matter of accountability for the problems and realities of the community. These elements also testify, for parents, to the quality of the early childhood centres, even to their superiority compared to others, in particular in terms of a model of care that targets not only children, but also parents and families. Their value, according to the users, is expressed in an explicit and sustained attitude of welcoming the expectations and the needs of everyone in a way that is both differentiated and respectful of their diverse knowledges and contexts. This attitude of the educators is not unrelated to the recognition by the educators of the legitimacy of parents to "inhabit" the early childhood centre, and to know it. This means that, for participation to develop, the participation first needs to be recognised as legitimate.

Indeed, the research focused on the notion of parent participation as a collective construction, rather than an individual one. And beyond the diversity of visions on what participation and "co-education" may mean (Rayna, Rubio & Scheu, 2010), the collective participation in early childhood centres is first and foremost expressed by how parents are allowed to "be there," where the child is. From this possibility, different pathways of participation can take shape. These pathways may relate to the formal educational orientations and goals of the centre, but they can also go beyond these, giving rise to questioning, reorientation, and enrichment of practices. More broadly, some participatory dynamics may affect the possibilities of power-sharing, allowing parents to have an impact on the decision-making processes concerning the early childhood centre, in a context of local action and social struggle where the empowerment of actors is thought of as a fundamental component, in the form of citizen or political awareness. In this vein, the participation of parents – or with parents – also goes beyond the formal participation mechanisms put in place, since it resides in daily encounters with the other and the gradual discovery of the other. Sometimes understood as collaboration, as a cooperative relationship, these words highlight all the complexity and risks of participation. Doing something with others can certainly enrich the work but can also cause conflicts, or even make conflict an essential moment in practice. This perspective is contrary to the idea that it would be possible to standardise or even regulate the parental participation and disseminate it in general terms.

On another level, one could wonder how parental participation is related to the development of a synergy and a dynamic where the participatory processes of adults reinforce those of children and vice versa, and how opening spaces for some make it possible to envisage new possibilities of discovery for others. Some of the narratives in the study provide interesting insights into this question, in that they evoke the presence of spaces for children's socialisation which, while allowing the pedagogical intervention of parents beyond the school, as well as other people not necessarily related to children, also promote the visibility of children as actors in the local life. In so doing, the participatory synergy we are talking about is of an entirely different nature than the consumentality. In contrast with the neoliberal approach, the meaning of ECEC is not reduced to individual achievement of future citizens but relates to the educational resources offered by the community.

Noting the richness of these processes can be a way of reconsidering the potential of ECEC that is the result of its environment, in contact with the local community, with a variety of people and experiences present in the environment.

It is not a question of adopting a militant attitude that ignores the precariousness in which many of these community childcare services develop or the inequality of access to quality early childhood education in these fragile communities. What is at stake is to propose other avenues of analysis regarding what constitutes "quality," based on the expectations and experiences of the actors concerned. It is a matter of not evaluating early childhood with decontextualised standards intended to be universal, but of the construction and negotiation of meaning (Wenger, 2005) between the actors concerned, in their specific contexts. Finally, it is a way of contributing to the scientific debate but remaining a critical participant in these issues, by questioning the dominant paradigms of preschool education that aim to promote economic development, as an exclusive business of experts, and as a separate enterprise from other spheres of social life.

From individualised to shared responsibilities

The commodification of ECEC has been a process with far reaching consequences, as it also influenced the image of the parent, as well as nature of the parent-professional relations. In terms of Gramsci, explained in the introduction chapter, the parent as a consumer is a cultural hegemony, meaning a construction or an image that is not merely imposed upon parents, but that parents may also actively co-construct. However, the different cases also show how this image can be de-constructed.

Changing the image of the parent and of parent-professional relations, as Gail Yuen writes in her case study about Hong Kong, can be a matter of increasing civic consciousness in bringing change to policy, through the role of grass-roots organisations in mounting public pressure. The deconstruction and re-construction can be nourished by the role of (often feminist and leftist) movements in Italian regions that lacked municipal and state initiatives to provide childcare and that have contributed to share the educational responsibilities in the community. The different cases illustrate that there is no place for fatalism or determinism, a position that is joined by Paulo Freire and his pedagogy of hope (Vandenbroeck, 2020), as well as by a series of intellectuals in critical pedagogy (Giroux, 2010).

The four narratives of resistance, described in this chapter, took place in very different parts of the world: Italy, Hong Kong, Chile, and France. The cases of France and Chile are illustrative of what civil society may mean. According to Cox (1999), civil society is the realm in which those who are disadvantaged by globalisation of the world economy can mount their protests and seek alternatives. This can happen through local community groups that reflect diverse cultures and evolving social practices worldwide. Looking beyond local grass roots initiatives, as is illustrated by the contribution of Tullia Musatti, is the project of a "civic state," or what she labelled as *gestione sociale*, a new form of political authority based upon participatory democracy. It is not a matter of naïve beliefs or a dichotomous opposition between civil society and the State. As Foucault

(1990) reminds us, we need to remain critical about the reference to civil society as opposed to the State, a dichotomous thinking that afflicts the notion of "State" with a pejorative connotation while idealising "society" as a good, living, warm whole. Foucault rightly remains circumspect with regards to a certain way of opposing civil society and state, and to any project for transferring to the first a power of initiative and decision that the second is seen as having annexed in order to exercise it in an authoritarian fashion. After all, civil rights can only be warranted by public responsibilities and provision. Nevertheless, the (re)emergence of civil society is at the heart of the changes in the stories from Hong Kong, Chile, and France that are narrated in this section. In the case of Hong Kong, it is an alliance of professionals and scholars as well as parents who take up their role of critical citizens and activists. They successfully challenged the voucher system that is legitimised by a discourse on parental choice, but that has increased inequality in two ways: it consistently benefited mothers of higher socioeconomic status more and these mothers spent the money saved through the vouchers on additional learning opportunities for their children, reinforcing the educational race. But the Alliance for the Fight for Free 15-year Education did more than that: it brought together parents and professionals refusing their role as offering a commodity and as consumers in a market, profoundly reflecting on the role of early childhood education and their responsibility. The policy that came into place after the successful rejection of the voucher system did not really offer a radical alternative to neoliberalism, yet the Hong Kong case shows that policy change is possible.

The cases of the community-based early childhood centres in Chile and the *crèches parentales* in France, on the other hand, did succeed in creating sustainable and radical alternatives to the commodification of ECEC and alternatives to neoliberal imaginaries. They are even more representative of what a civil society may be, when it is not configured in opposition to the State. The Chilean community-based early childhood centres and parent-led childcare in France both originated from discontent with their social and political contexts: a context of profound and inacceptable inequality in Chile, where *poblador* had to seize land to be able to live and where public provision was lacking; and a context where childcare was dominated by a hygienist approach in France, leaving parents at the doorstep, condemning them to be spectators to the education of their child. In both cases, early childhood provision has become part of civil society in the way that Dahlberg, Moss, and Pence (1999) described: fora where children, parents, and professionals meet in projects with a cultural, social, political, and economic meaning. They have become community institutions, places of social commitment with a strong symbolic meaning. These centres have little to do with the language of choice or other languages of consumentality as parents are not consumers and ECEC is not a commodity. It is a place where educational responsibilities are shared and debated. That is also the case in Italy, especially in northern and central Italy. Education is considered a common good and therefore a shared responsibility. The participation of parents and its embeddedness in the community offers ECEC the possibility of being an agent in the cultural renewal of social life. The Italian case, as analysed historically by Tullia Musatti, also shows how concepts need to change and adapt to changing realities. That is both the strength of democratic practices and their vulnerability in present neoliberal times.

The value of disagreement

The community-based early childhood centres in Chile, as well as the parent-led childcare in France, and the concept of *gestione sociale* in Italy are examples of places and times where moments of democracy can emerge. As Pablo Rupin notes, it would be naïve to think that this all runs smoothly and without quarrels and that these centres are the best of possible worlds. There are few issues where disagreement is so pronounced as the theme of children's needs. With Woodhead (1997), we note that children's needs are an adult cultural construction and, consequently, opinions on what these needs are and what the responsibility of adults and of the community in relation to these needs are, may substantially vary according to one's beliefs, parental ethnotheories (Bruner, 1996), and contexts. People tend to fundamentally disagree on what is good for children, on how to educate them, and even on what to educate them for. In their seminal work *Preschool in three cultures*, Tobin and colleagues (2009; 2013) showed how opinions on what is good for children may vary substantially, not only across cultures, but also within cultures. They illustrate that some parents challenge the ideas of "progressive" or "liberal" educators who argue for a play-based, holistic approach of children, and ask for a more adult-centred academic approach, preparing their children for compulsory school. This is confirmed by Li and colleagues (2021), investigating expectations of parents towards early childhood education in rural China. These authors found that parents with high socio-economic status agree with the teachers on a play-based curriculum, yet send their children to leisure time activities where they are prepared for compulsory schooling. Lower SES parents want a more academic curriculum, while their demands are regarded as outdated by the teachers. Curriculum is probably not the only area of disagreement. It is highly unlikely that a group of parents would agree on when and how to punish children or even if children are to be punished at all; on how much freedom to allow a 4-year-old; on when to start or stop potty training; on how to deal with multilingualism and translanguaging; on what is a healthy meal; on what is developmentally appropriate; on when and how children need to learn to share; on gender-neutral education; or even on simple matters such as what should be considered decent children's books or how important outdoor play is. It is precisely these disagreements and, even more so, the ways we deal with them, that form the basis of democracy. As Mouffe (2005) aptly argues, overall consensus is deadly for democracy as a forced consensual thinking forms the basis for extremisms. It is on the basis of daily negotiations that we learn to explore insights and perspectives other than our own, and that we can move from individual private wants to common needs, and that, Biesta (2011) argues, is when moments of democracy emerge.

A precondition for democratic education is that we move away from the monolithic idea of parents as consumers, as if there were no alternatives. Democratic education is only possible in contexts of disagreements, diverse perspectives, or antagonisms, as these urge us to think about a fundamental question: education for what? It is not the sum of individual parents' desires, opinions, or expectations, as neoliberal consumentality holds out to us. It is not parental satisfaction with the services on offer. On the contrary, it is essentially about the communality, about the social, about what parents and professionals construct together and that serves the common good. It does not come as a surprise that Chilean community-based early childhood education is not only concerned about children's development, but also about women's rights, the labour market, sanitation, drug abuse, and many other aspects of what a human life in dignity may mean. Neither is it surprising that the French *crèches parentales* were the cradle of many other initiatives, including the *Université Populaire des Parents*. These initiatives were a reaction against the framing of parents as deficient (after the 2005 riots in the French suburbs). Importantly, they were initiatives by groups of parents from the *crèches parentales* with professionals who claimed that research on parenting was too important and, above all, too political, to be left to researchers and policy makers. In a spirit of "nothing about us without us," they decided to contact universities and do research together on the themes that parents themselves deemed important and with the explicit aim of enhancing dialogue between groups of parents and policy makers. All the cases described in this section are salient examples of what Freire meant by *conscientização*: the conscientisation or politicisation of education. Once the question of "education for what" is posed, or the question of what is meant by "socialisation," we cannot help but discuss the social, cultural, and structural conditions in which education takes place and thus reflect about what is fair, what is right, and what is essential for the good life. That is when the taken-for-granted narrative of common sense (in the Gramscian sense) makes place for counter-narratives that dismantle the hegemony of neoliberalism. With Manojan (2019), we can argue that education offers a regime where resistance can be inaugurated and established to critique cultural domination and that here the task of the critical educator is to become a transformative intellectual and to shape learners as organic intellectuals for counter-hegemonic actions.

Early childhood education and care as a transitional space

When ECEC is conceptualised as a commodity, a product, then parents are conceptualised as consumers. Commodification forces parents into a passive and individualised role, as the only agency of the consumer resides in the alleged free choice and the possibility to change to another brand of the same product. That is to say: if there is competition, which is usually not the case in ECEC. But even if there were competition, parents are denied the possibility to actively participate in shaping or co-creating their children's educational environment. In the neoliberal realm, there is very little room for the private domain to interfere with the public domain. Parent involvement is all too often reduced to a form of participation that is defined without any form of parent involvement. It is the provider who defines what parents need to be involved in, just as it is the provider who defines what areas of satisfaction will be surveyed. In contrast, parenting has become a policy domain and what parents do in their homes is increasingly the subject of trainings, programmes, and screenings. In other words, while there is hardly any penetration of the private in the public domain, there is increased penetration of the public in the private domain.

The resistance and the rejection to this neoliberal trend is not to inverse the order but to move beyond the dichotomy of private versus public responsibilities, as the French, Chilean, and Italian examples demonstrate. The response to the privatisation of ECEC is not to hand everything over to the State. In these contexts, it is to share educational responsibility between the private and the public domains. In that sense, ECEC centres can become transitional spaces, where private concerns, wishes, dreams, or anxieties can be shared with others and can be dealt with in a public space, a forum that belongs to the community. When communities of parents actively co-construct ECEC provision, it is not a matter of parents handing over their responsibilities to communities, not of communities taking over individual responsibilities. It becomes a matter of citizens taking up their public responsibility.

This process of politicisation or democratisation asks for professionals who are able to warrant the continuity of the democratic educational project, considering that parents come and go, as Marie-Laure Cadart describes in her case study, yet that remains open to renegotiate the social and educational project time and again. The combination of continuity and change can be quite challenging and unpredictable. Therefore, the daily work needs individuals who take a stand and refuse commodification, but also communities that support each other in fostering their dreams. Then ECEC can move way beyond being a service to children and become a place of community development, of cultural renewal and cultural heritage, of social support and social cohesion, of adult education, and many other possibilities. What early childhood education is (and what it is for) is, after all, a matter of choice. And this can be a deliberate choice to reconnect education to the broader structures of society.

4
RESISTING THE ALIENATION OF THE WORKFORCE

Linda Mitchell, Michel Vandenbroeck, and Joanne Lehrer

With the collaboration of:

Sonja Arndt, Donella Cobb, Nicole Cummings-Morgan, Lisa Johnston, Raella Kahuroa, Olivera Kamenarac, Stig G Lund, Alana Powell, Brooke Richardson, Dwi Purwestri Sri Suwarningsih, and Marcy Whitebook

Introduction

Neoliberalism impacts most strongly on the workforce in contexts where marketisation and privatisation are at an extreme, and where business interests have become dominant values in provision of ECEC. In these contexts, teachers/educators are treated as commodities, recruited and bought according to utilitarian calculations about cost and profit-making. Since staffing costs are a high item of expenditure within ECEC, there is strong motivation by for-profit providers to decrease staffing costs in the interests of making profit. This happens through employment of less qualified and experienced staff (who are cheaper to employ), and through economising on staff pay and conditions, made more possible where wage and salary bargaining arrangements allow employment agreements to be negotiated or decided by individual employers. Where government funding does not adequately cover and is not targeted to staffing costs, there are further consequences for pay rates. Low rates of pay for ECEC educators/teachers, which are inequitable in relation to teachers within the wider education sector and incommensurate with the worth of their work, are a long-standing feature of ECEC. The undervaluing of the work is further exacerbated by historical views that ECEC is "women's work" and what mothers do naturally, and as such is regarded as justifying low remuneration. As a consequence, those working in ECEC are alienated by societal norms, government policies, and corporate practices that consistently undervalue the complexity of their work, and its worth.

DOI: 10.4324/9781003218104-5

Within a commodified system, those who work in ECEC are increasingly portrayed as technicians, producing predetermined outcomes that are intended to serve in the interests of future economic growth. These outcomes present a standardised one-world view of education that is often narrowly confined to subject-based learning areas and essential skills of the school, and that are devoid of situated understandings of context. Moreover, where competition is a dominant ethos, the market exerts strong pressure to teach to specified outcome measures that can be used as "evidence" of "quality." In these ways, teachers/educators become alienated from their own professional identity, as they face enormous barriers in using their understandings of children and pedagogical knowledge within their ECEC setting.

This chapter discusses the impact of commodification on the workforce, explaining the complex interplay between ways in which ECEC is organised and provided, and the valuing and identity of the ECEC teacher/educator. It begins with an historical overview that discusses some reasons why divisions between concepts of "care" and "education" originated and produced different ways of organising ECEC, as split systems ("care" services as separate from "education" services) or as unified systems under the umbrella category of "care and education." Comparative data on teachers/educators' pay, working conditions, and qualifications across a range of countries highlight consequences of commodification for the ECEC workforce. We discuss discourses associated with views of the ECEC teacher/educator as "substitute mother" and "technician" that have served to undervalue the complexity of ECEC work, constrain professional agency and justify inequitable pay and employment conditions. By contrast, an image of the teacher/educator as critical pedagogue and researcher is held out as offering a pathway for resisting commodification. We end with case studies of collectively organised actions and individual acts of resistance to neoliberalism from Ontario, US, Aotearoa New Zealand, Nusa Tenggara Timur, and Denmark, demonstrating alternative conceptualisations of the ECEC workforce and the purpose of ECEC.

Historical underpinnings of ECEC and organisation of the ECEC system

Accounts of the state of the ECEC workforce in many parts of the world highlight ways in which the historical contexts under which ECEC in many countries originated and stereotypical views of women and children prevailing at that time produced divisions between concepts of "care" and "education," which became embedded in ECEC systems in many countries. A split system of care and education, in particular, produces differentials in qualifications, pay and employment conditions, with low pay and stressful working conditions linked to staff turnover. These divisions are reflected in the composition, pay and employment conditions of the ECEC workforce, and have continued in many countries. The devaluing of "childcare" has been furthered as "childcare" went from private in the home to private in the market, although this devaluing is also furthered by public systems whereby those (gendered) staff responsible for care (physical bodies and emotional well-being) receive less professional respect. Neoliberalism, and associated marketisation and privatisation of ECEC, has sustained and deepened inequities within the ECEC workforce and between the ECEC workforce and the school sector workforce. The role of the state and whether wage bargaining is collective or individual is also linked to pay and employment conditions. Underpinning the inequities and differences highlighted in this chapter, are values held at individual and government levels, about the rights of the child, the status of ECEC as a public or private responsibility, the construction of the ECEC educator/teacher and gender equity in employment.

In order to understand the construction, status, and valuing of the ECEC workforce and the influence of neoliberalism on provision and workforce matters, it is helpful to look back to the origins of ECEC, and features that have endured in many countries (see the chapter on Resisting children as human capital). Formal centre-based ECEC originated in the 19th century in many Western and affluent countries, usually divided among types of settings between "childcare" for the children of poor working families and "education" for older children, usually over 3 years and in years before starting school. Moss (2006) has discussed ways in which this conceptual divide is embedded in ways of thinking, at public, policy, and practitioner levels, and is also very evident in the structural organisation of systems of ECEC. Therefore, in many countries, "childcare" or "daycare" settings, providing all-day ECEC, mainly for children of families in paid employment, are administered by a different government ministry, often social welfare, from the ministry that administers "educational" ECEC settings, often education. While all-day ECEC emphasises the "care" of the child, "educational" settings sometimes had names denoting a connection to the idea of schooling, such as public preschools and école maternelles. Within these split systems were different underlying values, different ideas about the purposes of ECEC, different goals for the programmes, and different workforce profiles that were attributed different statuses.

New Zealand and the Nordic countries were the first countries to remove a split administrative system. Value-based decision-making influenced the development of systems of education integrated under one administration in these countries. In New Zealand, the recommendation for integration of childcare within an educational administration was first put forward by women during the 1976 International Women's Year, and subsequently promoted by the women's movement in the following decade, coming into effect in 1986 (McDonald, 1981). These women wanted their children to attend good quality educational settings in all-day provision, while they themselves took part in the paid workforce. They saw "care" and "education" as inextricably linked. The goals and values from women's perspectives were that breaking the artificial division between care and education settings was in the best interests of children, promising a holistic care and education focus in all ECEC settings. In addition, they were highly critical of the inequalities in funding, staffing, programming, and resourcing between care settings, poorly served under a social welfare administration, and education settings, somewhat better served under an education administration. Integration was intended to offer a basis for a good quality education for all children in whatever service they attended, but needed other policy (e.g., curriculum, staffing, advisory support, and funding) to support this goal. In the Nordic countries, where integration fits with a social democratic philosophy, it was also women's participation in the paid workforce, as well as the idea of sharing education and care between public and private institutions, that was the catalyst for provision of safe and high quality ECEC during the 1970s (Karila, 2012). Integration is now recognised as one of the core elements of a successful ECEC policy (OECD, 2001, 2006). A 2010 UNESCO report (Kaga, Bennett, & Moss, 2010, p. 13), analysing country case studies of integration, showed that ECEC can be integrated within a number of policy domains, with benefits including (1) universal entitlement, (2) affordable access, (3) a unified and well-educated workforce, (4) enhanced learning for all ages, and (5) smoother transitions for young children. The authors argued, with examples from the case studies, that the education sector is more likely to deliver such benefits.

However, in many countries, the administrative split remains. The 2019 Eurydice Report (European Commission/EACEA/Eurydice, 2019) of ECEC systems in 38 European countries described two main ways in which ECEC settings in these countries are organised:

1. Separate settings for younger and older children with a transition usually around the age of 3. Typically, provision for the under-3s has a childcare focus, while pre-primary schools for older children emphasise educational goals.
2. Unitary settings for the whole age range, up until the start of primary education. Both care and early education form an integral part of the provision in unitary settings (p. 13).

With some exceptions, where there are separate settings for younger and older children, responsibility for ECEC is split between two different ministries. In countries with unitary settings, responsibility for ECEC tends to lie with a single government ministry, often education, but again with exceptions.

The split is reflected in the composition of the workforce and pay and employment conditions. The ECEC workforce in OECD countries is described as "homogeneous, composed of mostly female, young workers and from the majority ethnic group" (OECD, 2012, p. 190). Educators in settings with a "childcare" focus are generally paid less than educators in services with an educational focus, and have less favourable employment conditions, such as access to professional development and non-contact time when they are not counted in the ratios. They tend to be less well-qualified and employed in all-day ECEC settings, home-based care, and family daycare, compared with qualified educators employed in "education" settings.

In addition, two types of staff may work together within a setting, teachers or pedagogues with higher qualifications, and a second group, who may be assistants, with lower or different or no formal qualifications. Van Laere, Peeters, and Vandenbroeck (2012), in their analysis of data from 15 European countries, undertaken as part of the European "Competence Requirements in Early Childhood Education and Care" (CoRe) research project, found that even when there are unitary systems in a country, "a hierarchy between care and education can exist, embodied in the relationship between core practitioners and assistants" (Van Laere et al., 2012, p. 536). The education and care split may be further reinforced through these divided roles, with greater value placed on "education" and lesser value on "care," when the aim is for a holistic education that interweaves care and education. The differential valuing is reflected in differentials in the pay and employment conditions of core practitioners and assistants in the workforce. The hierarchy may also limit how staff see their role and what are appropriate tasks and activities for them to undertake, with consequences for interactions with children and families.

The ECEC workforce

Comparative data on teachers/educators' pay, working conditions, and qualifications highlight ways in which those who work in ECEC are treated as commodities in a largely privatised market. This section highlights inequitable and low pay, and variable qualifications that are found in ECEC centres in a wide range of countries. Links are made to the type of provider, i.e. commercial for-profit providers, non-profit and public providers, and the dominant values of these providers, as well as industrial bargaining arrangements and government funding.

Compilations of data on the ECEC workforce have been gathered and compared across many countries. These are useful in showing commonalities and differences, and the influence of context-specific factors. The *Systems of Early Education and Professionalisation in Europe* (SEEPRO) study, followed up in 2018, as the SEEPRO-R study (Oberhuemer & Schreyer, 2018), provides a systematic description of the ECEC workforce in 30 European countries, located within a synopsis of country-specific aspects of the ECEC system. Each country profile was written by "co-operation partners" who were experts from within that country. The report is valuable in providing comparative data about the composition of the workforce, qualification requirements, pay, and selected working conditions of ECEC practitioners, systems of initial professional education, and continuing professional development, alongside reform initiatives and research.

Analysis across the 30 country reports shows common trends. In most countries, the pay of ECEC practitioners is lower than the pay of school teachers. Conditions of employment, including noncontact time and holidays, are also usually less favourable for ECEC practitioners compared with conditions for teachers in schools. An exception in several countries is that kindergarten/pre-primary teachers in particular settings, for example, école maternelles in France, public scuole dell'infanzia in Italy, éducation précoce classes in Luxembourg's public education system, are paid the same as primary teachers. These ECEC settings come within the public education system; within these same countries, ECEC teachers in private settings are employed with lower rates of pay.

In all countries, lower salaries are paid to practitioners in the "childcare" sector, and conditions of employment are usually poorer. The differentials in salary can be linked to a range of factors that vary according to country context. As discussed above, some countries have split systems of education and care, where "care" services are administered by a welfare or health or employment ministry, and education services by an education ministry, and where education services are better funded and supported and practitioners are better paid. Furthermore, variations in pay may be linked to the age of the child catered for within the ECEC service, with teachers/educators of older children earning more than teachers/educators of infants and toddlers, reflecting a view of teachers/educators for infants and toddlers as mother substitutes. See the next section for an exploration of this problematic conceptualisation.

The ownership of the ECEC service (public, community not-for profit, and private for-profit) and arrangements for wage bargaining exert a strong influence on salary differentials. These are encapsulated within many ECEC systems, where privatised provision is widespread. For example, in Luxembourg, differentials linked to both ownership and wage bargaining are evident in a hierarchy, in which staff in the formal sector are paid better than staff in the non-formal sector. Staff in the not-for-profit sector, with a collective agreement, are generally paid better than those in commercially run settings who are paid on individual agreements determined by their for-profit provider (Oberhuemer & Schreyer, 2018).

For-profit ECEC centres make financial gains and distribute these to members. They include corporate businesses operating as publicly listed companies and private equity firms, which first and foremost, act in the interests of business profits. Government funding, parent fees, and savings made on staffing costs are a lucrative source of profits. Two recent reports (Simon et al., 2022; United Workers Union, 2021) into corporatised for-profit ECEC providers exposed common practices of companies paying exorbitant salaries to owners and executives and avoiding tax by paying the parent company offshore and registering a debt. Key findings from both studies were the low wages paid to ECEC educators in comparison with wages paid by not-for-profit providers. The financial case study analysis in the study, *Acquisitions, mergers and debt: The new language of childcare* (Simon et al., 2022), found that staff costs could be as much as 14 percent lower than the not-for-profit company sector.

Not only are pay rates poorer in the for-profit sector, but conditions of work are often less favourable. Those working in for-profit centres tend to have poorer levels of staffing (more children to staff and larger group sizes), less non-contact time, and less opportunity for professional development. In some situations, teachers/educators are treated as expendable in situations where they are employed on short-term contracts and made redundant after the contract period. A 2016 survey of pay rates across the ECEC workforce in Ireland found many staff delivering the Free Preschool in ECCE Programme are on short-term contracts for the 38 weeks of the year that the Programme runs, and are made redundant outside those weeks. They may then need to live on social welfare payments and reapply for their jobs in the following year (Oberhuemer & Schreyer, 2018). The power imbalance in favour of the employer contravenes the rights of the worker to ongoing employment, further exemplifying treatment of the worker as a commodity. It is easier to pick off workers and breach their rights when they are not organised collectively, such as within a trade union.

A key feature distinguishing for-profit from not-for-profit providers is the vision held for the ECEC centre and those who work in it. In Danish ECEC, where democracy is an explicit value, a qualified pedagogue earns "minimally less" than a school teacher (Oberhuemer & Schreyer, 2018, p. 280). ECEC services come under the auspices of one ministry, are regulated by the same law, and have the same pedagogical philosophy and the same professional staff. By contrast, a commitment to profits contributes to a view of educators as commodities and a justification for low wages and poor working conditions.

All the settings in the SEEPRO-R study were in European countries. The same trends can be seen across many English-speaking countries. In the US marketised and privatised ECEC systems, there is little uniformity either across states or within states with respect to programme standards and levels of funding. These differences are driven by the perceived purpose of the service ("childcare" or "early education"), the age of children served (3- and 4-year-olds or infants and toddlers), whether the programme is universal or targeted to children living in low-income families, the setting (centres or schools or private homes), the source(s) of funding, regulations governing teacher qualifications, adult/child ratios, and other programme requirements.

Problems in recruiting and retaining qualified ECEC teachers/educators are common and are directly associated with the low pay, poor working conditions, and insufficient recognition of the complexity of teachers' work (Irvine, Thorpe, & McDonald, 2018; Nutbrown, 2021; Oberhuemer & Schreyer, 2018; OECD, 2012). Nutbrown (2021, p. 237) references several reports, academic analyses, and commentary on ECEC qualifications and the early childhood workforce in the UK to encapsulate these connections:

> The recruitment and retention crisis will persist until there is a proper and formal recognition of the stresses, long hours, unequal pay, lack of career structure and recognition, and lack of qualifications that enable educators to develop deep understanding of children's learning and development. All these factors contribute hugely to the recruitment and retention problems of the workforce, as does the achievement of a representative balance of gender and ethnicity.

Writing of "workforce supply," the Organisation for Economic Co-operation and Development (OECD) also noted a major challenge in many countries is to secure a high quality ECEC workforce:

> Chronic shortages of ECEC staff are observed, especially in remote and disadvantaged areas. Furthermore, lower qualification levels of the workforce especially in the childcare sector, often raise concerns among parents and policy makers about the quality of the services. [...] The main reasons for the shortages are often cited as: low wages, low social status, heavy workload and lack of career progression paths [...].
> *(OECD, 2012, p. 190)*

Maternal discourses and image of the teacher/educator as "substitute mother"

The low valuing of ECEC, reflected in low rates of pay and poor working conditions, has been attributed to a conceptualisation of the ECEC practitioner as a substitute mother, with a stereotype of women in the home as the main caregiver of the child. Helen May has pointed out that because of its close alignment to "mothering," ECE has been seen as "fulfilling custodial, emotional or social needs as opposed to the presumed intellectual functions of the rest of the education system" (May Cook, 1985, p. 85). The gendered nature of the workforce reinforces this stereotype, which coexists alongside other images. Peter Moss (2006) argued that this positioning requires qualities and competencies that are thought to be "innate" to women and acquired through domestic work, rather than specialist education.

Maternal discourses are hard to withstand and move beyond. In New Zealand, for example, maternal discourses continue, despite New Zealand's progress in developing an integrated system of ECE within an education ministry, taking steps towards employing a fully qualified teaching workforce in ECE, and adopting an enlightened early childhood curriculum that has "holistic development" as a core principle (Ministry of Education, 2017, p. 19). In a recent New Zealand doctoral thesis, Jane Ewens (2019) found that discourses which position the teacher as "mothering" were the most dominant discourses shaping the 15 teachers in her study. Associated with this was "the prioritisation of the care and custodial functions of teaching and subsequent prioritisation of affective qualities in teachers" (Ewens, 2019, p. 133). These teachers, influenced by maternal discourses, tended to over emphasise the socialisation of children and teachers, rather than offering a balanced curriculum.

Powell, Langford, Albanese, Prentice, and Bezanson (2020) point out that in order to participate in the workforce and gain economic empowerment, women need to access childcare services. By "freeing" women from the "maternal care burden," the burden of care becomes the educator's responsibility. These authors argue that

> Further, the outsourcing of the maternal care burden to early childhood educators positions them as 'substitute mothers' (Moss, 2006), rather than professionals in their own right. As Moss (2006) describes, this view draws on a gendered understanding of care, wherein care comes naturally to women and requires no education or formal training. This discourse obfuscates the value of the work of early childhood educators and compounds their marginalization.
> *(Powell, Langford, Albanese, Prentice, & Bezanson, 2020, p. 160)*

The "quality" of ECEC settings is traditionally defined in terms of "process quality" – the emotional and educational aspects of children's interactions in ECEC (Leseman, 2009; Mitchell, Wylie, & Carr, 2008; van der Werf, Slota, Kenis, & Leseman, 2020) – and "structural quality," structural features including practitioner qualifications, reasonable salaries, high staff:child ratio, small group size, and staff stability (Leseman, 2009; Mitchell et al., 2008; NICHD Early Child Care Network, 2002). These features are in turn linked to children's learning, well-being, and development. Competent teachers/educators, who are appropriately educated and experienced, are essential in this process, but need to be supported by facilitating environments that provide structural conditions for the kinds of teaching and learning that are linked to meaningful learning experiences for children. Access to ongoing professional development and a collegial and inclusive work climate are further features that are facilitating at an organisational level (Mitchell et al., 2008; van der Werf et al., 2020).

Likewise, the European *Competence Requirements in Early Childhood Education and Care* (CoRe) project found that rather than competence being an individual characteristic, systemic conditions for developing, supporting, and maintaining competence are necessary at all layers of the early childhood system (Urban, Vandenbroeck, Lazzari, Van Laere, & Peeters, 2012a; Urban, Vandenbroeck, Van Laere, Lazzari, & Peeters, 2012b).

> At the level of the individual practitioner, being and becoming 'competent' is a continuous process that comprises the capability and ability to build on a body of professional knowledge and practice and develop professional values. Although the 'knowledge' and 'practice' are critical, practitioners and teams also need reflective competences as they work in highly complex, unpredictable and diverse contexts. A competent system requires possibilities for all staff to engage in joint learning and critical reflection. This includes sufficient paid time for these activities.
> *(Urban et al., 2012,, p. 512)*

A competent system requires a broad vision of education as a public good and a site for democratic participation, and valuing of the workforce reflected in fair remuneration and professional support. Furthermore, competent system thinking interrupts gender essentialism as it recognises the structural conditions necessary for good care to occur (rather than leaving it to the gendered, poorly paid, ever-giving educators). Where ECEC is privatised and treated as a commodity, and where commercial values dominate, altruistic aims of fully supporting aspirational goals for the public good are overshadowed or diluted by individual interest in protection of private gain (Press & Woodrow, 2005).

Impact of commodification on the ECEC workforce

Privatisation and corporatisation of ECEC services have increased dramatically since the 1970s when neoliberalism became a dominant ideology in much of the world. An increasing percentage of ECEC services (particularly childcare and home-based or family daycare) in neoliberal countries, rather than being valued and provided as a community and public responsibility and asset, have become business ventures. In the UK, large companies now own over half of the childcare "market." Helen Penn (2011) writes:

> For-profit entrepreneurs making money out of providing childcare may exploit not only the parents paying for the service but the workers delivering it, unless sufficiently stringent regulatory conditions are in place-such as capping fees at around 15-20% of household income, or imposing high level competencies for staff.
>
> *(p. 2)*

When education is commodified and privatised, interests in profit-making for business owners compete with and override democratic goals around the best interests of children, families, teachers, and community. There are clear indications in studies carried out over time and in different countries that for-profit providers spend less on staffing and are rated as poorer on indicators of "quality" than non-profit providers. Aims to make profits for business owners and shareholders impact especially on the pay and employment conditions of practitioners, since these are the biggest cost items in an ECE service. Paull and Xu (2019), in a study of childcare costs in England, found 78 percent of costs were for staffing. A similar percentage of revenue (70–80 percent) was spent on staff by large not-for-profit providers in Australia (United Workers Union, 2021). Yet, in that same Australian study, large for-profit providers were spending only 54 percent on staff. Reducing labour costs can be made by employing fewer staff, employing less qualified and therefore cheaper staff, and offering minimal rates of pay and employment conditions. Studies across different countries, e.g., New Zealand, Canada, US, and UK, have found that on average, rates of pay are lower and employment conditions are worse in the for-profit sector compared with the public or community sectors, and particularly poor in large childcare corporations (Cleveland & Krashinsky, 2004; Lloyd & Penn, 2012; Sosinsky, Lord, & Zigler, 2007). Non-profit ECEC centres have been found to have higher staff qualification levels and lower ratios of children to staff compared with for-profit centres (e.g., Cleveland & Krashinsky, 2004; Sosinsky et al., 2007). These structural measures of "quality" link to more positive and responsive pedagogy. More recently, Brooke Richardson's (2018) comparison of licensing compliance between corporate (Brightpath) and non-profit regulated childcare settings in Alberta found twice as many licensing inspection visits and four times as many provincial non-compliances with provincial childcare regulations in corporate compared with non-profit centres. Brightpath had ten times more numerous complaint investigations as well.

Corporate chains have been defined by Langford (2011) as including "more than 4 centres with a minimum aggregate capacity of 200 children" (cited in Richardson, 2017, p. 161). Richardson (2017) adds:

> Corporate childcare is further characterized by its financial backing by related and/or unrelated industries (usually real estate), diverse business interests (such as linked companies and/or ancillary services), the operation of at least twenty centres, and its potential to be publicly traded on the stock exchange.
>
> (p. 160)

Corporate businesses expect to make a profit for individual owners and, if they are publicly listed companies or private equity firms, for shareholders. The enormity of profiteering was illustrated in a recent Australian report (United Workers Union, 2021), where the "big five" corporate chains in Australia – G8, Affinity, Guardian, Busy Bees, and Only About Children – were said to account for 20 percent of long daycare centre revenue. These big five companies reported combined earnings of $292 million in 2020. Four of these were owned by Private Equity (PE) firms, and only one paid tax.

> Tax avoidance is practiced through transfer pricing and related party transactions, in which cash generated within a business is remitted to the PE firm or another company within the group. This is often facilitated through use of tax havens. PE buyouts are often highly leveraged – debt incurred to fund an acquisition is transferred to the target company after purchase – meaning companies are unlikely to report a profit, even if they are profitable.
>
> (United Workers Union, 2021, p. 6)

The report also provided information on the huge salaries paid to CEOs and profits for owners.

The increase in for-profit providers is influenced by economic arguments that leaving ECEC provision to the market within a competitive environment will be more cost-effective than state involvement in provision. These values are in direct opposition to acting in the public good, in the best interests of the ECEC community.

Michael Apple (2005) argues that educational reforms that have centred around a commitment to the market have "marked a dangerous shift in our very idea of democracy – always a contested subject – from "thick" collective forms to "thin" consumer-driven and overly individualistic forms" (p. 11). The shift engenders risks that employees will change from an allegiance to collective understanding and public service to an allegiance to working for profits for owners and investors. In the New Zealand case, Olivera Kamenarac discusses how teachers in corporate ECEC services needed to "wear two hats" and "juggle between being teachers and business managers," while being asked to align with managerial professionalism and business identities.

What is valued lies at the heart of resistance to neoliberalism, and associated marketisation and privatisation, and is a recurrent theme in this chapter. Michael Sandel (2013) gave an example of how, in a study by Gneezy and Rustichini (2000), fines for late pickups of children from daycare increased rather than reduced the number of parents arriving late. He explains that rather than seeing their lateness as imposing a disadvantage and inconvenience on the teacher, parents saw it as "a fee for services." In this instance, money corrupted or crowded out nonmarket attitudes and norms, and changed the nature of the activity that was commodified. Sandel argues that the market is reaching into places where it does not belong. Commodifying and putting a price on every human activity erodes certain moral and civic virtues. Rather, these virtues are "more like muscles that develop and grow stronger with exercise" (Sandel, 2013, p. 138).

Economic arguments and identity of the teacher/educator as "technician"

When economic arguments are foregrounded as a main rationale for governments to invest in ECEC, not only is the purpose of ECEC narrowed, but without strong resistance, the identity of the teacher/educator is affected. Influenced by cost-benefit analyses showing that through provision of good quality ECEC services, employment and tax revenues are increased, and savings are generated in educational and social expenditure (Mitchell et al., 2008), ECEC is increasingly conveyed as a solution to economic problems. Economist James Heckman and others have argued that investing resources in ECEC for very young children is a good investment. In a review of 153 studies of empirical literature on skills formation, Cunha, Heckman, Lochner, and Masterov (2005) developed a formal model of the economics of investing in "human capital" that describes two mechanisms: self-productivity and complementarity. These are multiplier effects which explain how "skills beget skills." Self-productivity says that skills that develop in one period persist into future periods; skills are self-reinforcing.

Complementarity implies that early investment has to be followed up by later investment in order for the early investment to be productive. Cost-benefit analyses are particularly limited in measuring only some quantifiable outcomes. Many studies on which they hinge are longitudinal studies carried out in particular country contexts and not generalisable across time, context and country. Penn et al. (2004), in their systematic review to address the question, "What is known about the long-term economic impact of centre-based early childhood interventions?" identified just three studies that met their inclusion criteria. These were the well-known Abecedarian Study, Perry Preschool Study, and Chicago Child Parent Study carried out in the USA with African American children in "deprived" inner city communities in the late 1960s and early 1970s. The authors point out the difficulty and high cost of such exercises and the likely problems of generalisability, as well as the lack of measures of children's wellbeing in the here and now.

Associated with a dominant economic rationale for investing in ECEC is an understanding of the ECEC practitioner as a producer of outcomes that attract economic returns. In particular, the practitioner is a person who provides childcare for working families (predominantly mothers), promotes school readiness and educational achievement, and addresses inequities in child outcomes, e.g. as promoted in policy goals of "narrowing the gap" and "diminishing the difference." Peter Moss labels the understanding of the worker produced through economic discourses as "the worker as technician" (Moss, 2006, p. 35).

Curriculum and assessment become overprescribed by government and management, and the practitioner produced under this discourse has less of an ability to exercise professional judgement. These trends to manage and control outcomes of ECEC are alive today in the OECD International Early Learning Study (IELS) (OECD, 2016, 2017), initiated to develop internationally comparable assessment tools in the areas of literacy, numeracy, and socioemotional competence, and discussed in the chapter on children. Significant international concern about the study has been voiced by leading early years scholars and educators around the world for the potential of narrowly defined internationally standardised outcome assessment to shrink democratic possibilities for education. In a united statement, early childhood professors from nine countries – the UK, Sweden, Australia, Italy, Aotearoa New Zealand, Canada, France, the USA, and Belgium – opened a colloquium in the *Contemporary Issues in Early Childhood* journal (Moss et al., 2016) to highlight concerns about the proposed study's assumptions, practices, and possible negative effects. In its documentation for the IELS, the OECD positions "early childhood education and the proposed study as if they are purely technical exercises" (Moss et al., 2016, p. 346), but does not acknowledge the political nature of education or argue for the political choices on which it is based. The writers discuss the failure of the IELS testing regime to accommodate and welcome diversity and the likelihood one effect will be "a growing standardisation and narrowing of early childhood education" (Moss et al., 2016, p. 349). These trends position the early childhood practitioner as a technician, meeting demands of externally imposed requirements, that constrain and shape what they do. Helped by critique from academics and others, the IELS was resisted in all but Estonia, UK, and US, but the pressure for internationally comparative standardised assessment remains a challenge.

In combination, the forces of neoliberalism, the commodification of ECEC, and the narrowing of the purpose of education to meeting economic goals have served to alienate the ECEC workforce. These forces have precluded teachers/educators from having a full say in decision-making about matters that affect them and minimised their capacity for making professional judgements about the curriculum and assessment that lies at the heart of their practice. Privatisation, a for-profit business ethic, and the low valuing of the complexity of the work of teachers/educators have resulted in further alienation as teachers/educators are treated as commodities to be bought at competitive prices. Hope lies in organised actions through collectively organised trade unions and community organisations, as well as "micro-resistances" through courageous actions undertaken by individuals, as case studies in this section will demonstrate. At societal and global levels, more wide-reaching solutions are discussed in the conclusion to this workforce section.

Democratic values and image of the teacher/educator as critical pedagogue and researcher

Values have been a common thread through what has been written so far. They are evident in the gendered and stereotyped constructions of the ECEC teacher/educator as a "substitute mother," the limited understanding of the complexity of the role of working in ECEC, and the low valuing of the workforce exemplified in low pay and poor employment conditions. Privatisation and the proliferation of for-profit entrepreneurs as providers of ECEC in many countries indicate a view of ECEC, not as a public good, but a private responsibility. Economist, Mariana Mazzucato (2018), argues that a contested debate about values for the betterment of humanity is needed. A starting point, advocated by Peter Moss and Pat Petrie (1997), is for a public debate about fundamental questions and issues concerning aspirations for children; values about childhood and the place of children and childhood in society; and relationships between children, parents and society. These authors argued that at a local and community level, early childhood education institutions as community institutions can provide opportunity for a wide group of participants to be engaged in debating these issues. Rather than as a private good, an alternative conception of ECEC is to take as its foundational values that children are citizens, and that education is valued as a public good and a child's right. ECE services are conceptualised as community organisations playing an important role in fostering a democratic society (Mitchell, 2007).

How we conceptualise children and ECEC interrelates with constructions of practitioners and their roles. Another image is of the practitioner as a researcher. Peter Moss (2006, pp. 36–37) characterises the practitioner as researcher as constantly seeking deeper understanding and new knowledge; a learner herself, co-constructing knowledge and identities; a reflective and dialogic practitioner, and embodying values – including understanding knowledge as being perspectival, partial and provisional, being open to the unexpected, being open to dialogue and listening. Pamela Oberhuemer (2005) used the term "democratic professionalism" as a concept based on participatory relationships and alliances, and emphasising co-operation and collaborative action with others in the local community. These conceptualisations offer ideas for pathways to resisting neoliberalism in pedagogical practice.

Stories

In the following, we give examples from five different countries, of collectively organised actions and individual acts of resistance to neoliberalism that offer alternative conceptualisations of the ECEC workforce and the purpose of ECEC. In all examples, practitioners played a lead role in the resistance, often working collectively and partnering with allies who shared similar values and concerns. Authors described themselves for this introduction. Authors of the first case, located in Ontario are: Brooke Richardson, a critical childcare and child protection policy scholar and advocate; Alana Powell, early childhood educator and activist committed to honouring care and achieving decent work, Nicole Cummings-Morgan, a Black, proud, ECE who leads the AECEO's Community of Black Early Childhood Educators in Ontario; and Lisa Johnston an educator, scholar, activist, and community leader who is deeply concerned about the lives of early childhood educators in Ontario. The case shows ways in which educators, through their professional association, AECEO, purposefully worked together to support and link with each other, to understand, name, and call out oppressive structures and practices, and to organise action to disrupt and transform these. The second case is analysed by Marcy Whitebook, currently Director Emerita of the Center for the Study of Child Care Employment (CSCCE) at the University of California at Berkeley, founding member of the Worthy Wage campaign in the US, and former teacher and longstanding ECEC activist. This case is located in the US, where the ECEC system, described as "inequitable by design," is at the extreme end of marketised and privatised systems, and educator pay and working conditions are abysmally poor. The case tracks the national Worthy Wagers grassroots movement, organised and led by early educators in the last quarter of the 20th century and their efforts to gain equitable pay, and looks forward to challenges in the current context of Covid-19. "Storying as resistance: Tales from an ECE teacher mentoring programme," was written by Donella Cobb, Sonja Arndt, and Dwi Purwestri Sri Suwarningsih, who worked with teachers in Kupang, Nusa Tenggara Timur, on a teacher mentoring programme. Through the programme, teachers created children's picture books in home languages and became empowered to resist enacting the standardised and centrally governed ECE curriculum. From Aotearoa New Zealand, Olivera Kamenarac, a scholar advocating for a more socially just and sustainable early childhood education and the world, Raella Kahuroa, an activist researcher within the early childhood sector in Aotearoa New Zealand, and Linda Mitchell, writing from my previous role as early childhood union official, offer three examples of resisting neoliberalism for the Aotearoa New Zealand case. Olivera Kamenarac conveys an individual teacher's resistance to a company's enterprise interests through deliberately choosing a different "moral" option of advocating for children's and families' best interests. Raella Kahuroa's example from a New Zealand kindergarten analyses ECE teachers as critical thinkers and agents of change, who intentionally work with children to ensure equitable outcomes for all. The third example is an ongoing story of deliberate strategising, collective action, community support, and advocacy organised through the union to achieve parity of pay for ECE teachers with the pay of primary school teachers. Finally, from Denmark, Stig G. Lund, an international ECEC expert and trade unionist, presents how BUPL – a Danish trade union for pedagogues – through professionalisation, has secured a public ECEC system.

Resisting commodification through community building: reflections on the work of the Association of Early Childhood Educators Ontario, Canada

Brooke Richardson, Alana Powell, Lisa Johnston and Nicole Cummings

Introduction: who are we?

The Association of Early Childhood Educators Ontario (AECEO) is the professional association for early childhood educators (ECEs) in Ontario, Canada. The AECEO was established in 1950, when group childcare programs in Ontario, and much of the world, were coming into being. Since that time, our role and mandate has changed, reflecting the different needs of early childhood educators, children, families, and the sector more broadly. What has always remained consistent however is our commitment to furthering the integrity and respect of ECEs while advocating for the material/structural conditions necessary to support educators, and therefore children and families', well-being.

Ontario is unique from other Canadian provinces, and many other international jurisdictions, in that a College of Early Childhood Educators (CECE) was formally legislated in 2007. Since 2009, any person practicing as an early childhood educator in Ontario is legally required to be registered with the CECE. Like professional colleges in other disciplines, the CECE's mandate is to "regulate and govern ECEs in the public interest." This is pursued primarily through outlining professional ethics and standards of practice and a corresponding, legally sanctioned, complaints and discipline process. In recent years, the CECE has also implemented mandatory Continuous Professional Learning (CPL) whereby ECEs are required to document active engagement and reflection on professional learning opportunities. Despite this shift to "professionalisation" through the establishment of the

CECE, the wages and working condition of ECEs remain poor. Approximately half of Registered ECEs (RECEs) earn less than $20/hour (AECEO, 2017).

The establishment of the CECE in 2007 required a clear delineation of roles between the AECEO (professional association) and CECE (regulatory body). Given that membership with the AECEO is optional and registration with the CECE is not, we have had to carve out a unique space for ourselves in the childcare landscape in Ontario. Today, the AECEO's primary purpose is to build a strong collective voice for early childhood educators (ECEs) so they can participate in and influence positive change that benefits ECEs, children, families, and communities. We do this work in a number of ways including public education, leadership building, creating and organising low/no cost professional learning opportunities for ECEs, policy analysis, development, and dissemination, community organising, and advocacy at all levels of government in Canada (municipal, provincial, federal). As a voluntary membership-based organisation, we have remained viable by seeking out opportunities to partner with allied community-based organisations, foundations, and researchers who share our passion and commitment to prioritising the gendered work of early childhood educators at a practice and public policy level. But the real strength of our organisation stems from our members – early childhood educators whose passion and commitment to providing meaningful care experiences to children and families motivates and inspires us.

For the past several years, our key focus (and funding) has been related to conceptualising and advocating for decent work with and for ECEs. Because we represent the underpaid, predominantly female and racialised ECE workforce that neoliberal state structures (and/or lack thereof) systematically under value, we take our responsibility to think critically about *how* and *with whom* we do our work seriously. The AECEO believes that the experiences and knowledges of ECEs are vital to identifying, articulating, and advancing policy and funding solutions that reflect what children, families, educators, and communities need. We actively resist neoliberal logic, including the commodification of care, through spending time listening and being with ECEs. ECEs' stories, experiences, and voices guide our work, point us in new policy directions, and constantly remind us why this work matters. It is through listening and reflecting on their stories that we are motivated to disrupt, challenge, and transform oppressive structures and practices that continue to marginalise ECEs.

Resisting the commodification of childcare during the COVID-19 pandemic and beyond

At a global and local level, the pandemic revealed the necessity of robust social infrastructure in place to support care – from long-term care to medical care to childcare. The impact of neoliberally driven erosion of social infrastructure in favour of market provision over the past several decades was felt by almost everyone, and certainly anyone in a caregiver or care-receiver role (i.e. all of us in some way). In Ontario, early childhood programs and educators were left in the dust as the pandemic wreaked havoc across the province. Even though most childcare programs remained open for the majority of the pandemic (save the initial pandemic onset), ECEs were notably absent from the policy agenda. Similarly, the provincial government did take the initiative to fund emergency childcare for essential workers in the province, but ECEs were never recognised as "essential" and therefore did not qualify for the emergency wage subsidies other care professions received. Perhaps most surprising was the fact that ECEs were left out of priority access to the vaccine, even though they work in direct contact with unmasked, young children for upwards of 8 hours a day.

We were, and continue to be, deeply troubled by the extent to which ECEs are excluded from policy dialogue and political spaces, effectively silencing their/our voices and experiences. We fought and continue to fight harder than ever in our government relations and advocacy work to pull at the threads of exclusion by bringing ECEs as directly as possible to the policy/political table. In response to proposed regulatory changes, new funding opportunities, and curricula reviews, we have created openings for ECEs to share their perspectives, feedback, and stories that problematise government (in)action in these areas (see our ongoing Rising Up for Child Care Campaign).

In the context of the pandemic and now moving beyond it, our grassroots way of working has been incredibly important. Alongside our members, partners, and allies, we have produced a number of key reports and policy recommendations that address the impacts of the COVID-19 pandemic on the childcare sector and ECEs (for example, Powell & Ferns, 2020a, 2020b; Powell, Ferns, & Burrell, 2021). These reports and recommendations have been products of slow, intentional collaboration that captures and advances the stories of ECEs through surveys, consultations, public webinars and conversations, and our Communities of Practice (more on these below). In these reports, we weave the narratives, lived experiences, and ideas of ECEs into policy recommendations that envision another way forward. We work in the tension of where we are (a neoliberal market system) and where we need to go (a collective and caring future) that respects and responds to the precarious material conditions ECEs work/live within and the marginalisation of care and care work more broadly.

A closer look at our community organising work

A foundational component of all of the work at the AECEO are our Communities of Practice (CoPs). Supported through foundation funding for our Decent Work Project, our CoPs provide the much-needed space for ECEs to connect with each other, with us, and with our allies. Overseen by our Executive Coordinator (Alana) and Community Organiser (Erin), our CoPs are spaces run by and for ECEs in localised spaces and places. They are a place for educators to come together to connect, support, and mobilise. Activities may include staying updated on policy/funding issues, reading groups, organised action, or creating professional learning opportunities. CoPs may also simply provide a space where

ECEs debrief, share ideas, and/or feel seen/heard. We consider our CoPs a fundamental component of transformational systems change as they are a key mechanism through which we create opportunities for ECE voices and stories to be centred in our work, heard by the public, and responded to by decision makers. What matters deeply to ECEs matters deeply to us.

We also recognise that it is unsustainable to resist neoliberalism's hypermarketisation and individualisation alone. In coming together and being/acting collectively, we are enabling the only sustainable antidote to this thinking: responsive, meaningful, caring relations with each other. As ECEs connect, share, and hear from one another, they come to understand their challenges not as individual inadequacies but systemic failures (for example, having no planning time, having to take on a second job to make ends meet, feeling burnt out). This creates opportunity for ECEs to actively resist oppressive forces (like the commodification of care and/or an audit culture of professionalisation) through naming and disrupting these phenomena. Once "the problem" is not taken on as an individual burden and educators feel supported by and with each other, there becomes both motivation and space to imagine and transform what *is* to something more equitable and more caring.

In the remaining space of this case, two ECEs and CoP leads, Lisa Johnston and Nicole Cummings, will discuss their experiences establishing, facilitating, and leading CoPs.

Lisa Johnston: lead of early years rise up! Toronto

My foray into advocacy was the result of a number of colliding events. Over the 15 years that I worked as a RECE in a college lab school, I experienced the professionalisation of the sector which brought with it an increase in regulations and expectations without the support of extra time to meet them. My stress steadily grew alongside the increasing demands. During this time, I was also completing an undergraduate degree part time in a School of Early Childhood Studies. In the middle of all of this, I was also offered an opportunity to teach a night course in an Early Childhood Education diploma program at a local college. The title of the course was Advocacy and Policy Issues in ECE. I always had a desire to engage in advocacy but after putting all of my energy and passion into my daily work as an educator in-program, I did not have much left to give to advocacy. I also had no idea where to begin. Taking on this teaching opportunity was the catalyst I needed to kickstart my involvement in advocacy as well as address my growing frustrations working in a childcare program that demanded more and more of me with no additional support.

Around the same time, I met Lyndsay Macdonald, a passionate, inspiring childcare advocate who quickly became a dear friend and mentor. While she had been involved with the AECEO for some time, she had recently been hired as the Executive Coordinator. Lyndsay was instrumental to both conceptualising and actualising steps towards the ECE-led childcare advocacy movement we continue today (and Lyndsay is now on the AECEO Board of Directors!). Alongside a key community-based partner (the Ontario-based Institute for Change Leaders), the AECEO embraced a project that involved mentoring ECEs in how to use their public narratives to create change as well as how to practically organise and campaign for policy change. Engaging ECEs in this leadership opportunity is how the CoPs came into being and how I came to lead one in Toronto (Ontario, Canada).

Our group started out small and for 3 years, it ebbed and flowed with members, a few remaining constant. We met once a month at a local pub or coffee house and planned some events together. We learned how to canvas door to door and how to meet with our elected officials. We grew closer as we created a community of support as well as action. When the pandemic hit, we found this community as a space of refuge and the support that we built together carried us through those dark and uncertain first months. We began to meet weekly as most of us were either working from home or not working at all because the childcare centres were closed. Widespread uncertainty in the sector meant that many people were reaching out to the AECEO for guidance and support. We organised a few monthly Coffee and Conversation gatherings and invited the sector to join, to come and ask questions, share resources, and feel connected. Our group grew exponentially from these virtual dialogues and many people began to join our regular weekly meetings.

I have learned a great deal about being in a leadership role through this project. I am most energised and inspired when members of the group are able to speak up with strong voices and demand change. We have cried and laughed, celebrated, and lamented, together. We have accomplished many firsts through overcoming our fears (of public speaking and/or speaking to politicians for example). This group is a refuge and a source of strength, creativity, and passion. I am honoured to hold this space and to be a part of this growing movement where others are seeing their work as intensely political and potentially transformative

Establishing a space where ECEs can support and empower each other and themselves as active agents in making policy change is one-way CoPs resists the commodification of early childhood education and the commodification of ECEs. A market model of childcare provision thrives on competition rather than cooperation, whereby being "better than" others is prioritised over working well with others. Similarly, a market model situates children, parent, and educator's needs in opposition to each other (i.e. for example, educator wages are dependent upon parent fees, the former being too low and the latter too high). As we fight for decent wages and working conditions for ECEs, we must also understand how our lack of decent wages and working conditions are directly tied to neoliberalism and ongoing settler colonialism. In an effort to make these connections, we gather once a month to read scholars that question discourses of neoliberalism, child development, and ongoing settler colonialism in early childhood education and education more broadly.

Unlike the neoliberal, hyper-individualised agenda, our goal is to build solidarity among ECEs, children, and families whereby we have the tools, resources, and strength to identify oppressive forces and actively resist them. My own studies in graduate school (I am currently pursuing a PhD) have helped inform my research and advocacy work, including critically examining neoliberal discourses of quality, accountability, standardisation, human capital development, and economic returns of investment in the early years. Through our reading and discussions together we are becoming aware of how these discourses reproduce the neoliberal status quo. More importantly, through naming these discourses, we begin to actively dismantle them, creating space to think together about what early childhood education would look and feel like as an ethical and political project.

Nicole Cummings: lead of the community of black ECEs

> Here we go again. Another White woman talking to a room filled with People of Colour about how to get involved in an association filled with White women. I'm tired of this. How do they expect me to care about an organization that doesn't seem to care about me?

These were my thoughts as I sat listening to the white woman (Alana) talk about how important it was for me and my fellow classmates to become involved in childcare advocacy. But as she continued speaking, something shifted in me. I decided to approach her.

I said to her: "I don't mind joining, but I don't see myself up there. There are no members that look like me. How can I join an organization that has only white women on their board?" And her make-or-break response was, "Well that's why we need people like you to join so we CAN reach others like you!"

This is how I became involved with the AECEO. While some may view my presence on the board as tokenistic, I see myself as the beginning of change. I knew Alana was right about needing people like me, but I also knew that I wouldn't be enough. It felt overwhelming to be responsible for encouraging other Black ECEs to join this organisation that has been predominantly white for decades. While I was nervous, I had a great feeling that my decision would be the beginning of something amazing to come. And it has been.

In May 2020, at one of the board meetings, we were discussing the tragic story of George Floyd and all the issues surrounding anti-Black racism that were being highlighted in the media. The idea to start a committee to address anti-Black racism was put forward. Again however, I was worried about tokenism. I didn't want this to be just another committee. It needed to be a place where Black ECEs could come together, discuss *our* issues in early childhood education, encourage and support one another, and address the unique needs of the Black children and families we were working with. So instead of an anti-racism committee, I took the first steps towards establishing a new CoP: A community of Black ECEs. In my mind, I wanted this to be a space for Black ECEs like myself to come together, share our experiences, truths, challenges, and triumphs. I wanted it to be a space where our work together would be seen and heard in the political space.

Because the AECEO already had CoPs set up, it seemed most logical to establish a CoP focused specifically on the needs and experiences of Black ECEs. Practically, our work has occurred through monthly meetings, a WhatsApp group, and other social media platforms. Unlike other CoPs at the AECEO, we are not geographically located. Given that our group came together during the pandemic and all meetings and events have been virtual, we are an open group, truly welcoming any Black ECE who feels she/he/they would like to participate.

Like many ECEs, we often feel undervalued, disrespected, and unimportant because our work is not seen as a profession but a "job." The intersection of blackness seems, to us, to make those feelings even more prominent. It is most painful when we feel disrespected and/or are treated poorly by white ECEs, teachers, parents, supervisors, professors, policy-makers, and even children. We repeatedly feel like we don't matter. Like Lisa described in her CoP, a re-occurring topic we discuss in this group is our low wages. It is difficult to understand how our work is discursively constructed as so valuable (i.e. "children are the future" and "children deserve the best") yet materially we are compensated barely above poverty-level wages. We are working to tease apart how and where race fits into this, both in terms of our experiences and at a broader systemic level.

Thankfully, this group holds space for us, where we can safely come together, talk, and facilitate critical conversations that are meaningful to us. We network, share resources, listen to each other, and act with one another. We share strategies on how to cope with racist environments; ideas on how to address racist people and children. The Community of Black ECEs is ultimately a place of hope, as we are working together to insist our voices are heard at the program and policy level. And we know that we are just getting started...

Wrap-up

Resisting the ongoing commodification of care is a tall task for ECEs. Within a predominantly private system, where our/their employment and therefore material well-being is often dependent on private childcare providers (increasingly corporate), ECEs take on real risk as individuals who "speak up" or "speak out" regarding wages, working conditions, and/or practice concerns. It is also intimidating to publicly oppose dominant neoliberal discourses/policy "reform" that serves corporate, rather than human, interests – especially if your own paycheque depends on it. That caring for children is increasingly accepted as a commodified "product" should be extremely alarming for all citizens. Yet, public policy in Ontario continues in this direction.

What we do know is that we are stronger together. While an individual voice can easily be drowned out by those already in positions of power, a chorus of diverse voices who have thought deeply about the value and positioning of care in society is harder to ignore. While there is often little, if any, immediate policy gratification in our work, we are in it for the long haul. Our purpose is to create spaces and places for ECEs to not only feel like they matter, but to actually matter and influence change. And a big piece of our work is also to be with and support each other through the process. We may or may not ever make it to our destination of a publicly funded and delivered childcare system where ECEs have decent work and children and families have access to affordable, meaningful care experiences. But in the process, we are committed to holding each other up, calling out oppression, and witnessing the struggle play out. Even though we are a provincially based organisation, we welcome anyone who shares our passion and commitment to be a part of our community.

Forging a way to equitable pay: The US early educator-led movement for worthy wages in the late 20th century

Marcy Whitebook

In the US ECEC market-based system, financed primarily by parent fees, with only a limited mix of government investment, educators focus simultaneously on preserving and expanding government funding, organising on-the-job, and advocating for public policies to improve their working conditions and economic security. This case discusses a national grassroots movement organised and led by early educators in the last quarter of the 20th century, a period when privatisation of the ECEC system intensified. The movement emerged following the defeat of major reform, in the context of the Reagan years, when other advocates were in retreat. The case explores how educators in this era understood the barriers they faced and discusses the strategies they pursued to navigate around or dismantle them. It concludes with a brief discussion of the relevance of those barriers and strategies, nearly a quarter of a century later when privatisation continues to spread through the ECEC system, and following the Covid-19 pandemic assault on an already precarious ECEC system and the undervalued and underpaid workers on which it relies.

ECEC in the US today: inequitable by design for families and the workforce

Services for children from infancy to age 5 operate primarily in the private market with limited publicly subsidised provision restricted to children living in families with low incomes. With the exception of public kindergarten for children 5 and older which is offered as part of public, free schooling, and universal public pre-K programs available in a handful of states and cities, early care and education in the US is neither a public good nor a right for children and families. Although public pre-K is sometimes part of the public school system, more typically, depending on state or local policy, it is offered in privately operated centres in the community. Most centres are small non-profit organisations or private businesses, with an average of ten employees. School sponsored services and corporate run services are typically larger employers but represent a smaller share of programs (National Survey of Early Care and Education, forthcoming). Family child care providers who operate child care businesses in their homes also play a large role in provision, particularly for the youngest children.

Family resources determine whether children have access to services and the quality of services they receive in the private ECEC market. Children living in families with fewer resources are least likely to have access to regulated home or centre-based care, and those children are disproportionately of colour and living in immigrant families. Among children residing in low-income families, further inequities exist due to insufficient and unequal funding. The majority of children who qualify for federally subsidised care are barred from participating because the programmes are oversubscribed. In addition, because there are no uniform qualifications for early educators set at the federal level or across program types, children may find themselves in ECEC settings with teachers who have very different levels of preparation. Depending on the state in which they live, their families' resources, and the supply of services in their communities, their teachers may have no training at all or a bachelor's degree or higher (McLean, Austin, Whitebook, & Olson, 2021).

The historical and pervasive undervaluing of labour performed by people of colour and women in the United States, combined with reliance on a market-based system has made ECEC one of the most underpaid fields in the country. Early educators face severe pay penalties for working with younger children in all states, with poverty rates an average of 7.7 times higher than for teachers in the public K-8 system (McLean et al., 2021). Further, while wages paid to early educators overall are low, additional disparities within the workforce itself cause greater harm to certain populations.

Across different types of settings and job roles in the sector, wage disparities are linked to funding source, age of children, and racial discrimination (Whitebook, McLean, Austin, & Edwards, 2018). At every level of education, there is a pay differential based on program sponsorship and funding, typically in the range of $4 to $6 per hour. Wage disparities also drive turnover across program types, as educators seek out employment in the publicly funded programs, especially those that are school sponsored, as they are more likely to offer pay parity with teachers of older children (McLean & Caven, 2021).

Among centre-based teachers, those working full-time exclusively with infants and toddlers are paid up to $8,375 less per year than those who work with preschool-age children. And this disparity is especially harmful to Black women working in centres, as they are more likely than their peers to work with infants and toddlers, and to Black, Latina, and immigrant women working in home-based settings, where a large share of infants and toddlers are in care. The pay gap is more than doubled for Black educators who work with preschool-age children ($1.71 less per hour compared with their White peers) compared with the pay gap for Black educators who work with infants and toddlers ($0.77 less per hour compared with their White peers) (Austin, Edwards, Chávez, & Whitebook (2019).

Low pay is compounded by a lack of access to basic health and well-being supports like health insurance and paid sick leave. Several studies conducted across local communities and states have reported high levels of economic worry, including worrying about paying monthly bills, housing costs, routine health care costs, and the ability to feed their families, among early educators. In these same studies, educators report a lack of workplace and professional support that influence teaching practice, such as dedicated time for observation, planning, and reflection with colleagues, materials and resources, and sufficient staffing to work with individual children or to take their breaks during the day as required by agreements (McLean, Austin, Whitebook & Olsen, 2021). The federal government does not address workplace standards, nor has it endorsed or offered guidance to states based on the International Labour Organisation Policy Guidelines or the US-based Model Work Standards for Centers and Homes developed by the Worthy Wage Campaign, and updated in 2019 (International Labour Office, 2013; Center for the Study of Child Care Employment, 2019).

Fighting for a better way: late 20th century early educator activism in the US: the era of the Worthy Wage movement

In the mid to late 1970s, teachers from local groups in Boston, MA, New York City, New Haven, CT, Madison, WI, Minneapolis, MN, Ann Arbor, Michigan, and the San Francisco Bay Area became aware of one another by word of mouth, from handouts and newsletters circulated by mail or shared at annual and regional conferences of the National Association for the Education of Young Children (NAEYC), the umbrella professional organisation for the early childhood field. At the 1981 NAEYC Annual Conference, representatives of these local teachers' groups formally established themselves as the Child Care Employee Caucus. The aim was to create a collective voice for teacher members of NAEYC to advocate for a greater focus on teachers' needs within NAEYC with regard to internal policies and external activities (Boston Area Day Care Worker United News, January-February, 1982; Child Care Employee News, V1 N1 January 1982; Whitebook, 2001).

Caucus meetings, convened annually at the NAEYC national Conference, provided a space for the cross-state groups to formulate their demands and present them to the NAEYC Governing Board and professional staff. The meetings also served as a forum to learn from local efforts to transform early care and education jobs, and over the next decade the Caucus forged a long-term collective strategy for change throughout the sector.

Initially the Caucus was composed largely, though not exclusively, of female White, college-educated centre-based teachers. More family child care providers and educators of colour joined the Caucus over time. Many members were left-leaning politically, veterans of the anti-war, civil rights, and women's movements. They shared a commitment to gender and racial justice, and considered high quality early care and education as a means to advance their aims for all children and families, particularly those from marginalised communities. They were strongly committed to challenging gender and racial stereotypes and viewed creating environments for young children that were intentionally anti-bias as a core value. Most viewed it as their responsibility to upend status quo attitudes, policies, and social structures, and were generally comfortable with challenging authority through collective action (Whitebook, 1994).

At the same time, they were deeply committed to their practice as teachers, to each other as fellow teachers and caregivers with whom they could share and learn, and to children and families, always considering how their actions in the classroom or in the political arena would affect those they served. Structured similarly to women's consciousness raising groups of the period, these groups often evolved from teachers discussing the problems they encountered as individuals on the job as well as in larger feminist and social movement circles. Through these groups, they came to recognise the commonalities and political nature of their individual problems, a recognition that served as a springboard for activism. While encouraged by the widening circle of fellow teachers who shared their concerns, they also came to recognise how individual and community differences among them–from job role, educational background, race and ethnicity, to settings and the policy context in which they worked, shaped the characteristics of their groups, and the strategies they prioritised. This diversity spurred learning but also created tensions within the group about the process and strategy that they necessitated.

It did not take long for Employee Caucus members to come to a shared understanding that there was no quick solution or one size fits all strategy to achieve the rights, raises, and respect all agreed were needed and deserved. Success depended on breaking the link between what parents could afford to pay and what teachers and providers earned, and that required increased public investment, a very hard sell given the growing dominance of anti-public spending ideology and its impact on child care policies.

And even if public funding could be secured and expanded, Employee Caucus members recognised from direct experience in their communities that designing and gaining support for progressive workforce policies was a daunting task. Because each state determines qualifications, ratios, and other workforce policies with minimal parameters set by the federal government, uniform policy solutions for the workforce as a whole across states were challenging to conceive and achieve (Boyer, Gerst, & Eastwood, 1990). Additionally, members were aware of a mismatch between traditional workplace organising strategies and the structure of an industry dominated by small sites with high turnover, entrenched anti-unionism in some states, and growing attacks on the labour movement. With the exception of corporate chains, there were no excess profits to bargain over, and concerns remained over strategies, such as strikes and work stoppage, that would disrupt services for families and children.

Recognising that not all early educators had the same opportunities to organise, resource materials were developed and widely distributed to help teachers address common problems or propose new practices. These covered a wide range of topics around model contracts and working conditions: instituting grievance procedures, developing salary scales, establishing substitute policies, informing one another about legal breaks and federal pay standards. Materials were also developed offering guidance about working with parents, e.g. dealing with parents late to pick up their children, and other issues related to classroom practices. The nationally circulated Child Care Employee News, published quarterly from 1981 to 1993, compiled and circulated resources drawing heavily on materials and newsletters developed by local teacher groups. Conference workshops and drop-in clinics were also conducted on these topics.

Additional fronts in the struggle demanded members' attention and energy, requiring creative approaches to organising others in the field, external allies and less sympathetic players in the larger political arena. Public consensus held that working with young children was unskilled work undeserving of higher pay, especially if it would raise costs. Thus, the Employee Caucus recognised that there was a great deal of work to be done to change perceptions and beliefs in order to mobilise allies for the cause. Documenting the problems teachers and providers faced through salary and working condition surveys became a widely employed strategy used by local groups, and eventually led to a national child care staffing study led by the Child Care Employee Project, the California group that served as the coordinator of the Caucus (Whitebook, 2001). *Who cares? The national childcare staffing study* linked compensation and working conditions to the quality of care children received (Whitebook, Phillips, & Howes, 2014).

The NAEYC leadership was composed mainly of academics, researchers, professional advocates, and program administrators. Most were not currently teachers and some had never worked directly with young children, the very people who comprised the Employee Caucus and much of NAEYC's membership. Generally, the leadership and many members adhered to an ethos that it was unprofessional to raise concerns about compensation and working conditions, the motivating force behind the Caucus. These opposing views gave rise to increasing conflict within the organisation and spurred the Caucus to consider fresh strategies which led to the development of a national grassroots Worthy Wage Campaign.

Despite their marginalised positioning and the enormity and complexity of achieving their goals, those who comprised the emerging early childhood teacher movement were unwavering in their commitment to their goals. Most were prepared for a long struggle to topple or circumvent the barriers they faced related to: organising to improve conditions at their workplace; changing the status quo field leadership; establishing their collective presence and power in a complicated policy arena; and building their own capacities individually and collectively to learn, lead, and sustain one another in these efforts. After a decade, most Caucus members recognised the futility of their attempts to get NAEYC to use its political clout on behalf of those working with young children, claiming their mission was to support young children, not teachers. Judging that they could count on the support of their fellow teachers, at the 1991 Annual conference, Caucus leaders announced the 5-year national Worthy Wage Campaign which would launch on Worthy Wage Day the following April.

The Worthy Wage Campaign was a nationally coordinated effort to disrupt the status quo of low wages, poor working conditions, and the lack of public respect for, and recognition of the work of, caring for our nation's young children. Intentionally inclusive of the ECEC sector, the Worthy Wage Campaign Principles state:

> Whether we call ourselves child care workers, family child care providers, preschool or early childhood teachers, teacher assistants or caregivers, we are working in a field where most employees are underpaid and undervalued—a field that is continually losing its best workers because of poor wages and benefits.

Conceived as a 5-year Campaign, and announced at a national early childhood conference in 1992, it was organised around three principles:

1. To create a unified voice for the concerns of the early care and education workforce at the national, state, and local levels;
2. To increase the value and respect for those who provide early care and education through improving their wages, benefits, working conditions, and training opportunities;
3. To promote the accessibility and affordability of high-quality early care and education options that meet the diverse needs of children and families.

Worthy Wage Day, an annual spring event, became a national focal point of the campaign. To demonstrate its pervasiveness, at its peak, 35 states documented local and/or state-wide activities on Worthy Wage Day. Over the course of the Campaign, 45 states organised Worthy Wage activities, with more than half holding events in more than one city each year. While there is no longer an organised Worthy Wage Campaign, many communities continue to acknowledge Worthy Wage Day on May 1 every year.

The decade that followed was one of public demonstrations and protests, media campaigns, political engagement, and heightened community organising. The outstanding feature of the Campaign was that it was "teacher-led" — meaning that those working directly with young children (primarily women who were child care teachers and family child care providers) developed the principles that guided the Campaign and designed and implemented its activities. To this end, it focused on intentional learning, leadership development, and policy formulation by teachers and providers themselves.

For example, in the 1990s, as improving the quality of child care became a focus of policy makers and other stakeholders, the Worthy Wage Campaign asserted the importance of establishing work standards for all programs, regardless of funding source, ages of children or setting. Coordinated by the Worthy Wage Campaign staff, postcards were used to solicit feedback from hundreds of campaign members around the country about changes needed to their work environments. Committees of centre-based teachers, family child care providers, and school-age workers used the feedback to develop specific Model Work Standards for centre-based, home-based and school-age child care programs in 1999 (Center for the Study of Child Care Employment, 2019). They were designed to be helpful at individual work sites, to inform collective bargaining agreements, and potentially to be incorporated in quality rating and improvement systems being developed by state early childhood program administrators in accordance with federal directives.

The Worthy Wage Campaign successfully mobilised the field and many allies, and elevated serious discussion about the workforce into the public discourse about improving child care and early education. The attention it drew allowed teachers and providers in some states to propose and win public policies that offered some financial support and reward to the workforce in the form of stipends and bonuses. Importantly, it succeeded in breaking the silence around educator pay and working conditions among early educators themselves and empowered many to speak up on their own behalf. Despite these accomplishments, the Campaign formally came to an end in 1999, because it lacked the financing to continue, let alone transform itself into a sustainable organisation home dedicated to teachers and providers, a role it had assumed during the height of the Campaign.

The Worthy Wage Campaign would not, and could not, have happened without the work that began in the late 1970's up until the inception of the campaign in 1991. Like all movements, there was a spontaneity in how it grew out of small efforts in local communities that became larger ones, creating momentum for ever-larger impacts. And like other movements, lives were transformed because the movement itself was driven by the power of the people most intimately impacted by the problem and most invested in solutions (Haack, Vardell, & Whitebook, 2021).

Post Covid: imperative for educator activism and system reform

The impact of Covid layered onto the severe consequences of the pervasive and long-standing economic precarity of early educators has meant that since early 2020, many centre-based teachers and home-based family child care providers have had to choose between a pay cheque or their own health and safety and that of their families. Others have been laid off, had their hours reduced, or lost their jobs permanently as the programs in which they worked, already operating on razor thin margins, lost enrolments or incurred higher costs in response to public health mandates (Doocy, Kim, Montoya, & Chávez, 2021).

In contrast to teachers of children aged five and above in public schools, only a narrow swath of the early education and care workforce were paid and continued to receive benefits during lockdowns and surges of the epidemic. Typically, these were workers employed in the more generously publicly funded programs, which are the most likely to be among the small percentage protected by collective bargaining agreements. The chronic staffing shortage in ECEC that existed long before the onset of the pandemic has only deepened, now impeding maternal employment and economic recovery. Recovery has been slower in ECEC than other sectors, and is further challenged as teachers walk away for higher pay at Big Box (a large chain store) and other jobs (McLean & Caven, 2021).

Often overlooked is the increased pressure the pandemic has placed on early childhood teachers and providers in the face of the public health threat. They were forced to abandon many well-honed and often cherished classroom practices. And they were forced to rethink what good practice would be, try it and change what did not work. Changes in the job predate the Covid crisis as well. In the 20 years since the organised Worthy Wage Campaign ended, educator autonomy has been eroded by commercial curricula, and expectations that teachers routinely conduct regular assessments and prepare reports on children. State preschool program standards and QRIS (Quality Rating and Improvement Systems) identify research- or evidence-based curricula as indicators of quality. They are more prescriptive than teacher-led approaches to curricula in the past, and are purchased and used to guide teacher training and practice. For example, Creative Curriculum was developed and continues to be distributed by Teaching Strategies (for website see https://teachingstrategies.com/), a for profit company. It is widely used in federal Head Start programs. No accommodation in working conditions and schedules have been made for performing these tasks, often limiting teachers' interactions with children (McLean, et. al. 2020) Those working with young children are subject to more oversight of their work and professional development than their late twentieth century counterparts, at the same time as their economic security has declined.

The near collapse of early care and education services during 2020, and its failure to fully recover, fuels support for reform. It underscores the problems teacher activists identified nearly a half century before, as had others before them. Whether the sector will ultimately rebound remains to be seen, but most certainly it won't without massive public investment. Building Back Better, the Biden administration's social and economic policy agenda, includes the most ambitious ECEC reform proposal in generations, but it constitutes only a down payment on the full cost of an equitable system for all children, affordable for their families, and one that concretely values their teachers and caregivers (Austin, Whitebook, & Williams, 2021). While it does set a living wage (as yet undefined) as a floor for all teachers and calls for pay parity for early childhood teachers with equivalent qualifications to elementary school teachers, there is as yet no clarity on whether the money will get into the hands of teachers, especially the majority who remain unrepresented (Austin et al., 2021).

New threats to organising also loom, as corporate child care, often run by private equity firms and/or underwritten by venture capital, pursue their stated plans to expand in the aftermath of Covid (Hinchleffe & Aspen, 2021). With business and policy makers desperate to rebuild and expand supply to get mothers back into or to stay in the labour market, few appear to recognise the threat they pose to unorganised child care employees or family child care workers. Anecdotally, non-disclosure agreements about program operations and curriculum, as well as agreements for staff to turn down employment in competing companies appear to be standard practice. These are contractual agreements that certain information will remain confidential. Perhaps most disturbing, the companies have firmly established their place as providers of subsidised services since being allowed to receive government funds as a result of policy reforms in the 1990s. Their legitimacy within government circles now extends to contracts with federal and state agencies for their ancillary training and administrative services extending their reach beyond the programs they operate and further integrating profit extraction in the sector.

On a more promising note, family child care providers' inclusion in the subsidy system has been firmly established over the last three decades, and family child care providers serving subsidised children have won the right to bargain with state authorities over rates and other working conditions in several states. Represented by SEIU (Service Employees International Union), AFSME (American Federation of State, County and Municipal Employees) and American Federation of Teachers (AFT), some of the most influential unions, family child care providers' leverage in the political arena has been successful, most recently in California. Similarly, with the expansion of public preschool during this period, teachers have expanded opportunities to join unions if they work in school-based programs, and for those who work in community-based publicly funded preschools, to organise for parity with their counterparts in schools.

Alternative organising strategies among early childhood teachers and providers are once again sprouting in local communities, often in coalition with parents working on funding to make child care affordable and to improve pay and working conditions. Ole, a non-profit grassroots membership organisation in New Mexico, successfully advocated for Covid relief dollars to be paid directly to teachers and providers. They have successfully advocated to create a monthly meeting of teachers, without directors present, to share their concerns with the state administrators designing and implementing ECEC policy. They have spearheaded a proposal to create a wage-pass-through for teachers working in subsidised programs, attempting to create strategies that raise the ongoing pay of early childhood workers. In North Carolina, a new Worthy Wage Campaign has launched based on work over several years to develop a state salary schedule and to secure funding to enable programs to raise wages. Advocates in one North

Carolina county have successfully secured funding to enable programs to implement key aspects Model work standards over the next 3 years.

Should the Biden reform under debate in Congress in 2022 pass, their teachers and providers' mobilisation will be critical to influence how any new program will be implemented and continue to fight for more resources and policies that address their concerns. Early educators today continue to face many of the same barriers identified by the Worthy Wagers, even as they face an arguably harder reality. There remains an ongoing need for an organisational home where they can join together to learn as individuals and as a group how best to sustain themselves and make progress toward securing their long overdue worthy wages and the rights and respect that should be theirs.

Storying as resistance: tales from an ECE teacher mentoring programme

Sonja Arndt, Donella Cobb and Dwi Purwestri Sri Suwarningsih

Introduction to educational reform in Indonesia

The focus on educational reform is not new in Indonesia. Despite this, early childhood education and care (ECE) teachers continue to experience poor working conditions, low pay, and poor status, enduring a continuing devaluation of their professional autonomy (Newberry & Marpinjun, 2018). In this case study, we demonstrate how an ECE teacher mentoring programme in Kupang, Indonesia used the creation of children's picture books to resist a dominant often Euro Western control of teachers, pedagogies and curriculum foci, to strengthen teacher agency and sense of autonomy. We show how mentoring empowered teachers to make curriculum decisions that respond to the needs of children and the cultural aspirations of their local communities, and demonstrate how teachers' increasing agency helped them resist the enactment of a standardised and centrally governed ECE curriculum. We first examine factors that have shaped current working conditions for teachers in Indonesia through policies that de-professionalise and commodify teachers' work. Then we introduce the teacher mentoring programme in Kupang to illustrate how peer mentoring can offer a powerful way to resist the de-professionalisation of Indonesia's ECE teaching workforce by drawing on local knowledges, languages and identities.

We were all involved in the design and implementation of this mentoring programme in Kupang, Nusa Tengarra Timur from 2016 to 2020 in slightly different ways. Suwarningsih was a local ECE officer experienced in working for UNICEF in Indonesia. She offered local ECE, policy and cultural insights into the leadership of the programme, and is now enrolled as a PhD candidate at the University of Waikato. Arndt and Cobb were invited by the New Zealand Aid Programme on the basis of their expertise in ECE and cross cultural identity and policy studies to develop the mentoring programme, guided by Suwarningsih's local knowledge and expertise. Our involvement in the programme took place between June 2018 and November 2019, with mentors, lead teachers and teachers. Our work in this initiative gave us first-hand insights into the tensions and challenges teachers experienced in navigating extremely difficult working conditions, limited resources, and poor (if any) remuneration. Throughout, we were struck by teachers' willingness, enthusiasm, and commitment to their own professional learning and development. For many, the mentoring programme presented their first opportunity to engage in professional conversations about their teaching with teachers from other centres. Teachers walked for miles to attend their monthly cluster meetings, to learn from each other, share their teaching experiences and discuss the implementation of educational ideas and pedagogical strategies. The mentoring programme created a professional learning community which resisted the isolation and resulting de-professionalisation of ECE teachers by encouraging and valuing their professional autonomy and collaborative learning. It unsettled dominant approaches intended to raise accessibility by offering teachers new approaches to designing what quality ECE might mean in their local Indonesian context.

The ECE workforce in Indonesia

The proliferation of neoliberal ideologies throughout Indonesia's education systems has been well-scrutinised and documented (Newberry & Marpinjun, 2018; Octarra & Hendriati, 2018). While it is not our intent to replicate this substantive body of work, a brief contextual overview demonstrates how neoliberal ideologies have shaped Indonesia's ECE workforce. Indonesia is classified as a lower-middle income country, however economic growth has been unevenly experienced, particularly in Eastern Indonesia, where high rates of poverty and unemployment persist (UNDP, 2021; see also the Indonesian case in the section "Resisting children as human capital" in this book). Over the past two decades, education has been presented as a panacea to address growing poverty and inequality by international aid organisations such as the World Bank (Hasan, Hyson, & Chang, 2013; Octarra & Hendriati, 2018). The World Bank's continued investment in Indonesia's economic development has seen the embedding of human capital discourses in education policies in a bid to produce economically productive citizens (Formen & Nuttall, 2014; Octarra & Hendriati, 2018; Yulindrasari & Ujianti, 2018). In this economistic gaze, ECE is presented as an important foundation for skill development, future employability and, consequently, poverty alleviation (Formen & Nuttall, 2014; Hasan et al., 2013; Yulindrasari & Ujianti, 2018), and teachers are the tool with which this is to be achieved.

ECE in Indonesia, or PAUD (*Pendidikan Anak Usia Dini*) as it is referred to locally, was officially recognised in the education system in 1950 when the Ministry of National Education (MoECRT) was established to oversee PAUD (Thomas, 1988). Initially, PAUD involved kindergartens and play groups in informal centres, however these centres were generally only accessible in urban areas to middle- and upper-class families (Thomas, 1988). Initially, the Indonesian government was primarily focused on the development of primary and secondary education so PAUD was largely developed by private institutions, such as women's groups, religious-based organisations, or village governments (Newberry, 2010). PAUD continued to lack investment and attention from the MoECRT until 2004 when a nation-wide education reform saw the introduction of a bill for ECE and the establishment of the Directorate General of Early Childhood, Non-Formal and Informal Education (PAUDNI) (United Nations Organization for Education, Science and Culture [UNESCO], 2005). This was followed by the introduction of a national ECE curriculum and national ECE standards (Formen & Nuttall, 2014). Despite this merger, long-standing divisions, for example, between the Ministry of Education, Culture, Research and Technology (MoECRT), and the Ministry of Religious Affairs (MORA) remain (Qoyyimah, 2018). This compartmentalisation of PAUD services is further exacerbated by the division of responsibility within the Ministry Directorates, for example, the ECE Directorate is responsible for the development, design, and delivery of the national PAUD curriculum, while the National Accreditation for ECE and Non-formal education Body (Badan Akreditasi Nasional PAUD dan PNF) holds responsibility for the training, accreditation, and regulation of teachers.

These administrative complexities are compounded by the Ministry's two-tiered governance structure, which is split between the national MoECRTRT and the regional districts. Such a decentralised approach is reflective of the broader neoliberal reforms implemented over the past two decades, which promised to promote greater community involvement in local education by giving power to local District Education Offices to make administrative, policy, and management decisions (Luschei & Zubaidah, 2012). In some ways this decentralised governance structure did succeed in creating regional autonomy (Octarra & Hendriati, 2018), yet in other ways it created a complex system lacking financial and regulatory transparency (Octarra & Hendriati, 2018) and lacking clear support and guidance of PAUD teachers. These decentralisation policies have also created uneven access to and provision of PAUD services throughout the country, leading to tensions and contradictions in the way PAUD is understood and positioned (Formen & Nuttall, 2014). The fractured nature of PAUD services and resources between numerous agencies, has led to poor management and coordination between policy initiatives (UNESCO, 2005).

The rollout of the government's privatisation policies and reduced state funding for PAUD services strengthened engagement from the private sector, largely removing the development of PAUD from the public domain (Newberry & Marpinjun, 2018). Only 2% of PAUD are public (e.g. funded by the government), for example, whereas 98% are considered to be private. These private PAUD providers include community or village government preschools, self-funded centres or those funded by private donors (Ministry of Education and Culture [MoECRT], 2021). On the one hand, this has enabled some private actors to develop PAUD to advance their own interests, agendas, and objectives (Formen & Nuttall, 2014; Newberry, 2010), on the other hand it has provided villages and communities access to PAUD services and encouraged greater community involvement where this may not have been otherwise possible. Notably, the quality of PAUD provision within the private sector varies significantly, with many PAUD severely under-resourced and largely reliant on mothers fulfilling the teaching roles without experience, qualifications, professional development, or training (Newberry & Marpinjun, 2018). Furthermore, this situation exacerbates the divisions between Ministerial governance and responsibility referred to above (Qoyyimah, 2018).

The complex arrangement of PAUD governance and privatisation has significantly impacted the nature of teachers' work. The 2021 data shows that the total number of ECE teachers is 669.845 (7% are civil-servant teachers and 93% non-civil servants (Ministry of Education and Culture, 2021, Yulindrasari & Ujianti, 2018). Many PAUD charge minimal fees to attract families and this amounts to little, if any, funding for teachers' salaries (Yulindrasari & Ujianti, 2018), and leads to a stratified workforce with public teachers receiving a larger salary, more opportunities for professional development, and greater status than teachers in the private sector (Qoyyimah, 2018). With no formal qualifications, limited financial means to pursue formal qualifications, and few opportunities to engage in professional learning and development (Luschei & Zubaidah, 2012; Qoyyimah, 2018), there is a dependence on women's "unpaid, community-based care labour" (Newberry & Marpinjun, 2018, p. 31). Only 32.4% of PAUD teachers are qualified (e.g. with a Bachelor of Arts degree in ECE), while 20.6% have a Bachelor of Arts degree outside of ECE, and 47% have no formal qualifications (e.g. high school or junior high school graduates) (Ambarukmi, 2022). This has subtly eroded teacher professionalism, reinforcing PAUD teachers as largely unskilled and uneducated (Newberry & Marpinjun, 2018). From this basis, teachers are seen to have limited capacity for professional decision-making, and are consequently given few opportunities to exercise professional agency and autonomy (Qoyyimah, 2018).

In 2008, the government established a regulatory system in an attempt to enhance the quality of the teaching profession (Yulindrasari & Ujianti, 2018). This saw the standardisation of teacher competencies, qualifications, professional development, and management practices. A professional allowance was also introduced, regulating certification through the introduction of performance-based pay. Certified teachers were required to take an annual test and be regularly assessed by the principal to retain their certified status and receive a monthly allowance (Yulindrasari & Ujianti, 2018). Rather than enhancing the quality of teaching and elevating the status of teachers, research suggests that performance-based pay led to the de-professionalisation of the teaching workforce, shaping teachers as "technicians" who deliver a standardised curriculum bound by imposed requirements rather than local and pedagogical insights (Yulindrasari & Ujianti, 2018). Such centralised evaluation practices contradict the intent of the national curriculum. For example, national policy guidance promotes the diversification of curriculum and greater teacher autonomy to enact the curriculum in a way that reflects local needs and culture (Luschei & Zubaidah, 2012; Qoyyimah, 2018). Yet, the evaluation of curricula implementation at District level tends to overlook this, expecting rigid adherence to the implementation and enactment of a narrow interpretation of the national curriculum (Luschei & Zubaidah, 2012; Octarra & Hendriati, 2018). This opposition to teacher autonomy stems from the belief that teachers lack the ability to "interpret, adapt and adjust" (Qoyyimah, 2018, p. 576) the curriculum to reflect the needs and cultural specificities of children in their local context. In addition, research suggests that the lack of professional development opportunities in the private sector has a significant impact on teacher agency and autonomy. Without a sustained programme of professional learning, teachers are likely to avoid opportunities to exercise agency, preferring to replicate practices and strategies despite their lack of effectiveness and responsiveness to children's needs (Qoyyimah, 2018). Limited opportunities for sustained professional learning have consequently played a role in devaluing teachers' professional autonomy (Luschei & Zubaidah, 2012; Qoyyimah, 2018).

In the teacher mentoring programme in Kupang, teachers' continuing professional learning and development became a highlight, offering opportunities to resist the alienation of the workforce. In response to recent increased regulation in the government's reform agenda which further accelerated the de-professionalisation narrative, one of the elements of this programme was to enhance teachers' sense of self and personal and cultural abilities to develop locally informed and meaningful curricula. We used the creation of children's picture books for teachers to exercise agency to enact the curriculum in a holistic way that responded to children's learning needs in contextually and culturally relational ways. Strengthening teachers' capacity for decision-making and sense of professional knowledge in the local context was an active attempt to decommodify ECE.

Teacher mentoring in Kupang

An objective of the New Zealand Aid Programme is to improve knowledge, skills and basic education in the Indo-Pacific region. In 2016, the New Zealand Ministry of Foreign Affairs (MFAT), UNICEF Indonesia, and the Indonesian MoECRT formed a collaborative partnership to fund a pilot 4-year teacher mentoring programme. Its aim was to improve access for children in 100 PAUD centres in the Nusa Tenggara Timur (NTT) province. NTT is defined as a poor region by size of Gross Domestic Product (GDP) (Aba, Yussof, & Mohd, 2015), where access to pre-primary education is a significant challenge with a gross enrolment rate of children aged 3–6 in 2016/2017 of 56,32%, compared to 70.06% at a national level (Ministry of Education and Culture [MoECRT], 2016). The quality of ECE in NTT is far from adequate, with large numbers of unqualified teachers, a prevalence of didactic pedagogical practices, and limited opportunities for children's learning (UNICEF, 2015, 2017). In Kupang, only 19% of teachers have a Bachelor's degree and 16% of those have a Bachelor of Arts degree in ECE and receive little, if any, formal training (UNICEF, 2017). Remuneration for PAUD teachers is extremely low, with many teachers working in a voluntary capacity (UNICEF, 2017). Consequently, a 2015 UNICEF report determined that enhancing the quality of teaching was the most critical factor needed to strengthen ECE in NTT (UNICEF, 2015).

This mentoring programme offered a way to enhance teaching capacity and quality. 24 local mentors were selected from their villages and employed by UNICEF to provide continuous professional learning and development opportunities to clusters of approximately four PAUD centres each. The mentors had a range of tertiary qualifications at degree level, however not all were in ECE. A community of practice design was introduced, where mentors and lead teachers worked together to implement peer mentoring practices and facilitate monthly cluster meetings. The programme involved mentor training workshops led by UNICEF and ourselves providing mentors and lead teachers with pedagogical understanding and strategies to facilitate peer mentoring practices in their PAUD clusters. These workshops were attended by mentors, lead teachers, as well as representatives from the District Education Offices, National Ministry of Education, and the local university to ensure that all key stakeholders involved in the evaluation and training of teachers had the same opportunities to learn about peer mentoring practices. Mentors also attended monthly mentor meetings and quarterly mentor training with UNICEF, where additional support and guidance was offered. Another key feature of this programme was its strong support from national, regional, and local government through the MoECRT's National Directorate for ECE and Non Formal Education, the Kupang District Education Office, and the Bupati Office (Head of District). This ensured that all levels of government were involved in key decision-making, to ensure coherence and collaboration around key initiatives.

Through the mentor training, mentors and lead teachers learned how to facilitate peer mentoring relationships in their PAUD centres. They were taught strategies to engage in professional learning conversations, reflect on their own teaching practice, observe each other's teaching practice, and provide strengths-based and formative feedback. While these tools assisted the mentors and lead teachers to identify and respond to children's learning needs, they also encouraged them to build a professional agency and autonomy that followed and responded to local cultural specificities and needs. By encouraging peer reflections and questioning mentors and teachers became increasingly confident not to negate outright, but to work within the dominant Western influences with which they were often surrounded in locally relevant and meaningful ways. The professional learning from the workshops was transferred into PAUD centres, allowing teachers to draw on collaborative experience, expertise, and insight, strengthening individual and collective practice. Peer mentoring thus empowered teachers to become agents of their own professional development by instilling confidence in their professional decision-making. The dominant forces affecting the professionalism of the teaching workforce were disrupted in a number of ways through this mentoring programme. In the next section we illustrate how teachers themselves shaped and drove this resistance to dominant narrowing and commodification of the ECE workforce through the development of local language picture books and associated pedagogies and cultural knowledges.

Exercising agency through storying

A baseline study conducted at the beginning of the programme revealed that few PAUD centres had picture books, and that teachers seldom read stories to children or asked children questions to extend their language development (UNICEF, 2017). Local languages were rarely used in PAUD centres, with the national vernacular, Bahasa Indonesian, used as the medium of instruction. These challenges offered an opportunity to strengthen teachers' professional knowledge and understandings through mentoring, and the creation of children's picture books as a tool through which to teach peer mentoring strategies. During our first training workshop, we asked mentors and lead teachers to retell a traditional story or legend from their village. For some, this meant talking with elders and community members as the retelling of these traditional stories had been lost over the years. In small groups, mentors and lead teachers shared these stories with one another, with peers providing positive and constructive feedback to further enhance the presentation of these stories. From there, we co-constructed criteria for writing "a great" children's picture book. Mentors and teachers were provided with basic materials (scrap books, water colours and crayons) and we set the challenge for them to turn their local story into a children's picture book, using their local language. Throughout the training workshop we had been teaching specific mentoring strategies such as giving and receiving feedback, followed with opportunities for mentors and lead teachers to practice enacting these strategies. The co-constructed picture book criteria gave mentors and lead teachers opportunities to practice giving and receiving feedback on each other's picture books. They gave feedback to enhance the quality of the picture books, and on how to use picture books to further extend children's language and literacy development.

At the conclusion of the workshops, mentors and lead teachers went back to their PAUD clusters and mentored local teachers to create their own picture books, based on their local stories and written in their local language. 135 picture books were written and illustrated by teachers – an incredible outcome for first-time authors. We observed how the process of creating picture books gave teachers agency to use available resources to make their own learning materials, and most importantly, to value their own cultural identities and knowledges. Until now, many teachers believed that resources such as books were either beyond their reach or written in non-local languages. Many lacked confidence in their ability to present, let alone write, a picture book. Being mentored by their peers, however, empowered teachers to extend their own professional knowledge and understandings, and importantly, was not focused on the increasingly neoliberal dominant commodification of the resources for the field. In this instance the value of the books was in the local knowledges they embodied.

Eventually, all 135 picture books were submitted to a local picture book competition and thirty books were selected for publication. The selected authors (teachers) were then mentored by an established local author to further prepare their stories for publication. Once published, all 100 ECE centres in the mentoring programme received 30 picture books each, the first picture books in their centres to be written in local languages (Figure 4.1). Furthermore, the MoECRT published all 30 picture books on their website, making these stories accessible to teachers and children throughout Indonesia (see for example http://repositori.kemdikbud.go.id/23383/1/Cerita_1.pdf?fbclid=IwAR2wX4CR9X-eh61V_Tx280zPiFpFkDKspoVbh0muS_8ZDsOEBVgJ1cvvLifw). We observed

FIGURE 4.1 30 teacher-authored local language picture books

(and shared) the excitement, joy, and incredible pride that teachers felt when their picture books were published. Not only were these unqualified teachers now published authors, but they were recognised on the Ministry website as contributing professional and cultural knowledge to enhance ECE teaching. They had become agents of change first of all within themselves, and also in their centres, their communities, and now, their nation.

Conclusion

This brief outline has illustrated how a small group of teachers in Kupang, NTT began to subvert the pervasive powers of the neoliberalisation and the dominant Westernisation of the ECE sector in their region of Indonesia. Rather than a pre-prescribed formula for how ECE should be performed, the mentoring programme which the three of us designed and led, sought and elevated teachers' participation in constructing their learning in ways that were relevant, locally informed and culturally specific to their communities. What was culturally knowable or appropriate for us, after all, was likely far from appropriate for them. Narrating their cultural stories, sharing their languages, and supporting each other with pedagogical feedback foregrounded the importance of teachers' cultural identities and understandings in their own pedagogies. Even more significantly, the experience of recognition, empowerment, and shared learning through the power of story was – and continues to be – immense among their PAUD and colleagues. The national recognition of cultural and linguistic knowledges as pedagogically and professionally valuable raised the confidence and capabilities of the mentors and lead teachers in our programme and the teachers they influenced in their PAUD centres. From within the Kupang area these picture books and pedagogies offer a critical experience of listening to and valuing local insights as a grass roots resistance to dominant de-professionalisations of the teacher workforce.

Stories of advocacy and activism from within the New Zealand ECE sector

Olivera Kamenarac, Raella Kahuroa, Linda Mitchell

Neoliberal commitment to the market has had a profound effect on early childhood education (ECE) and accountability systems in New Zealand, where private owners of education and care (childcare) centres have set up to produce profits for themselves and their investors from their business undertakings. Within this model, resources intended for education have been siphoned off for profits for individual business owners and, in some corporations, shareholders. Competition between ECE centres for children has led to an inequitable distribution of ECE provision, where economically richer communities and families who can pay more have been best served. There has been a steady increase in the percentage of privately owned education and care centres from 45 percent of the total in 2002 to 72 percent of the total in 2020 (Ministry of Education, 2021).

Yet, adoption of neoliberal principles is at odds with the social justice foundations and empowerment principles of New Zealand's renowned early childhood curriculum, Te Whāriki. It is also at odds with the operation of community-based ECE services (kindergartens, Pasifika centres, playcentres, community education and care centres) where emphasis is placed on collectivity, community participation in decision-making, and the idea of education institutions as community assets, where full funding from government resources goes into educating the child and supporting their family (May & Mitchell, 2009).

This case provides three examples illustrating how commodification of ECE has affected the workforce in New Zealand, and how ECE staff have individually and collectively employed counter-discourses to resist this impact. The first example coveys a strong message of hope and possibility of resisting neoliberalism in ECE through making deliberate choices for advocating for children and families' best interests, despite a company's enterprise interests. The second example illustrates a positioning of teachers as agents *for* change within a kindergarten that is deliberately established in a culture of social justice, a community financial model and democratic, respectful approach to all. The third is an ongoing story of collective action and advocacy organised through the union to achieve parity of pay for ECE teachers with the pay of primary school teachers.

A moment of a possibility: resisting for-profit priorities in a business early childhood centre

This example draws on a study on how teacher professional identities have been (re)constructed in response to the shifting discourses in New Zealand early childhood education (ECE) policies and practices over the last two decades (Kamenarac, 2019). The central topic of discussion is Joana, a manager of a for-profit ECE centre owned by one of the largest "ECE business companies" in New Zealand. The centre was located in a low-socioeconomic status community in an urban area of the country. Most of the children attending the centre came from families who could not afford ECE without the Government's support. However, teachers believed that children would benefit from staying longer than 20 hours in their ECE centres, which is the number of hours fully funded by the Government. Parents also wanted their children to stay longer in ECE, but their financial circumstances were the main barrier preventing them from affording the cost of the ECE service.

Under pressure to meet the requirement for profit-making (i.e. "a business side of the job") and supporting children (i.e. "a social side of the job"), teachers and managers in for-profit services found themselves in "a very challenging position." Their work and professional identities were torn between tensions created in the interplay of the enterprise discourses, driving a "business operation" of their organisations, and democratic discourses, underpinning their "moral obligation to help families who cannot afford to pay the extras." Teachers needed to "wear two hats" and "juggle between being teachers and business managers" while also being asked to align with managerial professionalism and business identities (Kamenarac, 2021).

Despite demands for making monetary gains, rather than operating primarily as a public education service, Joana argued that by employing her "moral obligations," she was still able to balance between the "social and business side of the job." The concept of "moral obligations" emerged as a critical feature in the balancing act between profit-making and advocating for the best interests of children and family and created a moment of a possibility for contesting neoliberal practices in a for-profit ECE centre.

To occupy the position of children's advocates, Joana explained that teachers and managers needed to "understand the funding [system of their company] *really, really* well." The understanding required the "knowledge of what [their centre] incomes will be from the Government and parents" and "what [their] moral obligations are." Joana's confidence in knowing the operating system of the company and opposing discourses underpinning the system (i.e. "business," "social," "democratic") appeared crucial for proposing decision-making practices that were not entirely aligned with the company's for-profit priorities. The critical awareness of how the opposing discourses construe and constrain teaching practices and Joana's commitment and persistent struggle to occupy a position of children's advocate created space for micro-resistance in a rigid neoliberal ECE context. Joana explained:

> [w]hen a family comes, it is a case by case; I can say to my centre business manager: "Look, this is how much money we will get from the Government funding. This is how much parents' portion would be. So, do you mind if we, for a certain person, say, 'We understand your situation [referring to issues experienced by the low socio-economic status community], so you can come here for free of charge"? It is something I do.

While Joana's advocacy and agency were limited in scope and not as effective as resistance mobilised through systemic politicised practices, yet the example pictures a moment of a possibility for teachers and managers in for-profit ECE spaces to deliberately choose to think, be and do ECE differently. This act of resistance results from self-consciousness engagement with the opposing discourses and commitment to demonstrating that neoliberal practices and identities are a choice, not a necessity.

Furthermore, Joana unpacked how her "moral obligations" allowed the positioning of children's advocate to come into existence within neoliberal places and spaces restricting it. In a conversation with her business manager, Joana argued for two babies to stay free of charge in the centre for a short period while convincing the manager that the decision would not create a budget deficit.

Joana exposed that in situations where the for-profit and democratic emphases are in conflict, her "moral obligation comes in." She said that "advocating for children is what I do from my heart" and "it is what I feel we all [referring to the for-profit ECE] need to do."

Notwithstanding the circumstances (i.e. no budget deficit) that allow teachers and managers to be children's advocates, Joana persistently argued that by "employing [their] moral obligations" and "doing [their work] from the heart," they "can still" advocate for children even in a for-profit centre. Joana's statements provoked responses from participants not having an opportunity and often even not imagining nor trying to challenge neoliberal practices and choosing to act as children's advocates. The discussion made it evident that the "business side" was crucial in defining whether or not teachers and managers could take up the positioning of children's advocate. However, there was still an agreement among participants that "the social side [of their] job is the reason why [they] are in ECE" and they "always do best [they] can for children with what [they] have got."

While highlighting apparent barriers that limit teachers to be and act as children's advocates in a for-profit ECE centre, Joana's story gives hope that the tensions between "the business and the social side of the job" could be used as a starting point for challenging, disrupting, and refusing decision-making driven by profit-making principles. It also sheds light on the power of the deliberate commitment to professional ethics and the persistent struggle for creating alternatives that put the well-being of children and families before enterprise interests.

Teachers as agents for change: empowering children to seek their own change

This example comes from a study that explored critical pedagogy approaches in an ECE setting (Kahuroa, 2021). A particular emphasis in the study was exploring how critical pedagogy approaches could be implemented with young children. The setting for the study was a non-profit community-based kindergarten in South Auckland, working with children aged 2–5 years.

The team leader at the kindergarten took the position that education itself was inherently political (Kincheloe, 2008). Using a Freirean critical pedagogy lens (Freire, 1970/2018), she and the teaching team consciously sought to initiate socially just learning opportunities.

This positioning is exemplified by the work of Tina, a member of the teaching team. Tina identified a need to support every child she worked with to "have a voice" – even where that child was predominantly non-verbal, learning English as a second language, or shy. Tina identified key actions she could undertake to hear the unique "voices" of children. Tina interpreted the expression of a child's "voice" multimodally, a recognition that children communicate in many different ways (Ministry of Education, 2017). Her approach focused on supporting a child's unique communicative competencies, in order to provide equitable opportunities for them to contribute to the kindergarten community through group projects, discussion, and new initiatives.

Tina's work with Derek is an illustrative example of her equitable approach to hear (and include) all children's voices in her group project work. Derek, who was learning English as an additional language, preferred gestural communication over verbal interactions. In a project to build a friendship seat, Tina used the picture he had drawn of the friendship seat as a reference point to both check on his ideas with him, and to also share those ideas with the small group working on the seat's design. This approach meant Derek could respond gesturally rather than verbally, again using the picture. This mediated exchange was so successful that Derek was even able to take on the role of project manager as the group proceeded to create a prototype of the seat, using his picture as a plan. Other children in the group followed Tina's lead, pointing to aspects of the picture and asking Derek for confirmation. His face shining and animated, Derek's ideas were implemented without him having to say a word. Tina's work with Derek is one example of many, and is illustrative of the overall approach taken by the collective teaching team as effective teachers (Muñoz & Powell, 2016).

In the last phase of her work Tina widened her inquiry, moving from a focus on her own practice, to working with children on creating opportunities for recognising how each child's voice could be acknowledged. Using a video clip that showed a previous interaction, Tina invited small groups of children to both identify who in the clip had a voice, as well as sharing their own ideas about how the group could support quieter children to be "heard." The three groups she worked with all had their own ideas that looked at how they could make learning more accessible for their peers.

Work of this depth and complexity is able to develop at the kindergarten because the kindergarten culture empowers teachers to act. Tina does not have to fight to be an agent for change; this role emerges naturally from a kindergarten environment that has a culture of social justice, a community-based financial model rather than profit-driven one, and a democratic approach to teacher autonomy. Teachers who are themselves empowered, and have a vision of social justice, seek to create real opportunities for children to engage with their own empowerment (McAllister-Flack & McAllister, 2016). All these aspects support teachers to pursue equitable outcomes *with* children, rather than *for* them. In the broader scheme of commodified ECE, the kindergarten's position is a personalised response emphasising how lifelong learning encompasses more than learning content knowledge (Papa, Eadens, & Eadens, 2016). This case study offers a vivid example of how teachers, working in an environment that provided facilitating conditions for democratic practice, resisted the alienation of the workforce by weaving a curriculum relevant to that time and place. This was a curriculum that went beyond narrow economic imperatives and standardised outcomes, and incorporated social justice values within the goals for children.

Collective advocacy for pay parity

ECE services are run, staffed and used predominantly by women. Ninety-eight percent of early childhood staff are women; a percentage that has changed little since ECE services were established in New Zealand in the 1890s. Despite the integration of childcare within an education administration in 1986, ECE continued to be regarded by many as a "care" service, undertaken by women whose work is systematically undervalued. As May (2005) writes "At a deeper level there are deep seated issues associated with society's negative perception of paying women to 'work with – teach – care for' young children; a task that mothers do for love" (p. 148).

Traditionally the rates of pay for teachers in the early childhood sector have been very low and well below those of teachers in the school sector. In 1999, experienced registered teachers with a degree employed on the best union negotiated collective agreements in the childcare sector (Consenting Parties Early Childhood Teachers' Collective Employment Contract) and kindergarten sector (Kindergarten Teachers' Collective Employment Contract) earned 52 percent and 46 percent respectively below comparable teaching positions in the school sector (Mitchell, 2005). Many early childhood teachers in the childcare sector earned much less than this. In this context, the union, NZEI Te Riu Roa, developed strategies for negotiating pay parity for teachers in the early childhood sector with the pay of teachers in schools. Unlike equal pay arguments, which compare skills qualifications and experiences of a predominantly female occupational group with skills, qualifications, and experience of a predominantly male occupational group, the case for pay parity used internal comparisons with the largely female primary teacher workforce. This case focuses on pay parity for kindergarten teachers and discusses the wider progress made on pay parity for teachers in the education and care sector.

Kindergarten teachers pay parity

The times were the mid to late 1990s, following an era of cost cutting when government funding for kindergartens had been virtually frozen, and rules changed so that kindergartens could charge fees. Teachers' pay rates stagnated. There was no palatable source of funding for kindergartens. Communities were pushed to the limit in their ability to fundraise and fee charging would compromise the strongly-held philosophy of universal access to kindergarten.

Kindergarten teachers were a unionised workforce – over 90 percent of teachers belonged to the union. The union strategy was to address the inadequate funding levels as a first step to pay parity, first, through a 17-month campaign for increased kindergarten funding so that money would be available for pay increases. Campaign plans were decided nationally, and given a local flavour as teachers decided what they would do to capture the imaginations and support of their families, communities, and local politicians. Actions included petitions presented by teachers and parents to almost every local politician in the country, with identical wording calling for increased kindergarten funding. The MP was then obliged to read out the petition in the House of Parliament, so the message was continuously being brought to politicians' attention. The public supported these claims in each community because they were articulated well and discussed with real examples by local teachers. In 1997, significant policy change was won "against the odds" of these times (Wells, 1991) – a funding increase for kindergartens and a pay increase for teachers (Mitchell, 2019). And importantly, an agreement was reached to compare the skills, experience, and qualifications of kindergarten teachers relative to those of primary teachers through an independent job evaluation.

After this victory, in a vicious backlash, the government passed legislation under urgency to remove kindergartens from the State Sector Act, thereby flinging them into the private sector. In this context, kindergartens were left to bargain without input from the state. New Zealand's harsh anti-union employment legislation, the Employment Contracts Act, made it especially hard to engage in collective bargaining, and the national kindergarten teachers' employment contract splintered into 18 separate contracts, as kindergarten employers decided to do their own bargaining.

Yet, the job evaluation was carried out and showed similarity in job size and qualifications of kindergarten teachers relative to primary teachers and "no justification for difference in salary at any time of the salary levels" (Burns, 1999, p. 5). A new and sympathetic government, whose politicians had been lobbied at national and local levels, was elected in 1999. It was willing to act. Kindergarten teachers were reinstated to the State Sector Act in 2000. In the government's second term, pay parity was agreed in August 2002, with a 4-year phase-in. The Secretary for Education was a party to this agreement, binding the government into negotiating and paying for the pay parity settlement.

Pay parity in the education and care sector

In the largely privatised education and care sector, progress towards pay parity has been slow and only partially achieved for a small percentage of education and care centres. The same funding campaign described above, was inclusive of teachers in education and care centres. The union agreed to a pay parity settlement in 2004 with the New Zealand Childcare Association, an umbrella organisation representing some willing employers ("consenting parties"), but rates payable were conditional on funding. A new government ECE funding formula linked higher rates of funding for qualified teachers to the Consenting Parties Collective Employment Contract rates, but only at the first step of the scale. Hence, pay parity for teachers in education and care centres was only ever partially supported by government funding and requirements.

Some reasons for this include the fact that, unlike kindergarten teachers, teachers in education and care centres had never been part of the state sector and the government had never been responsible for negotiating and paying their salaries. Reinstating that connection with the state had been key to achieving an enduring pay parity settlement for kindergarten teachers. In addition, there was a very low level of union membership, so collective organisation was difficult. "A good number of private employers were deeply antagonistic to union membership and to having to abide by collectively bargained awards" (Mitchell, 2019, p. 118). Finally, pay for teachers diminished financial returns for private business owners and shareholders.

The New Zealand government in 2021 is offering higher funding levels for employers paying the first six steps of kindergarten teachers' 11-step pay scale. But, unlike for kindergarten teachers, there is as yet no presence of the government in pay negotiations, no stipulation that employers abide by a nationally negotiated pay scale, and little scrutiny of spending or accountability for public funding.

Concluding thoughts

The case study offered three different stories on how ECE staff have collectively and individually employed counter-discourses to resist the impacts of commodification in New Zealand ECE.

The first example highlighted the complexities of working in a for-profit centre, demanding that ECE staff make monetary gains rather than primarily operating as an education service, publicly available for all children and families. Under pressure to align their work with the principle of "what works best for profit-making, the story captured a moment of a possibility for contesting neoliberalism in ECE through making a deliberate choice for advocating for children and families" best interests. Joana showed that it was possible to think and act differently if/when ECE staff employ their "moral obligations" and consciously decide to view neoliberal discourses as a choice, not a necessity.

The second example highlights that empowering working conditions in an ECE setting combined with its culture, rooted in a longstanding commitment to democratic practice, is a key in creating possibilities for teachers to get on with the job of teaching and offering a foundation for transformational work in ECE. Moreover, by ensuring that teachers have a real opportunity to seek change, they can bring acts of collective resistance and empowerment into the early childhood setting, making it a democratic place for all children.

The third example is an ongoing story of collective action and advocacy organised through the union to achieve parity of pay for ECE teachers with the pay of primary school teachers. It showed that achieving pay parity for kindergarten teachers required an understanding of the policy context; an analysis of the legitimacy of the case for pay parity for kindergarten teachers; strategic thinking – timing action around key political events when there was greater effect; government politicians who supported the claim; and intervention by the state to enact pay parity. Persistence was crucial. Collective organisation and advocacy were most important. A central argument is that effective unions are essential in a participatory democracy. The unions provided a means to organise, give voice to, and persist in a collective effort to progress pay equity for teachers.

Taken together, the examples reinforce that to combat neoliberal ECE policies and practices, ECE staff individually and collectively need to see themselves as ethically obliged and persistently committed to contributing to the vision of ECE as a universal right of a child. For this to happen, they need to position themselves as political beings individually and collectively responsible for insisting upon the right to work in democratically governed places and spaces and go beyond personal and individual (often for-profit) gains into the sphere of the public good. Furthermore, the third example emphasised the power of collective agency and advocacy in ECE and the union's vital role as a source of persistent collective actions for more socially just and equitable working conditions. Finally, while giving the hope that combating neoliberalism is to some extent possible in some ECE spaces and places, a broader need is for the government to take responsibility for legislating and financing ECE services to establish a democratic, socially just, and equitable ECE system for all children and families no matter their circumstances.

Denmark – the union as a social and professional partner

Stig G Lund

BUPL – The Danish Union of Early Childhood and Youth Educators – organises more than 55,000 pedagogues and leaders working in ECEC, leisure time centres (out of school childcare), youth clubs and some other pedagogical jobs in the Danish social welfare society. Pedagogues have a professional Bachelors degree of 3½ years study. The degree includes practice studies of 3 months in the first year, and 6 months in each of the second and third years in different fields of the pedagogical labour market, including special education, for example, for adults with special needs in residential centres. The education to become a pedagogue is quite popular – with the highest number of applicants among higher education for many years – and with more than 25 percent of the students being men. But the male pedagogues typically don't apply for jobs in ECEC after graduation; they prefer jobs with older children. More than 80 percent of pedagogues belong to the union, and are organised by BUPL.

The salary level for a pedagogue is still the lowest among all professions with a Bachelor's degree in Denmark. It is a "hangover" from 1969 when the Parliament fixed the salary level for public servants, and at that time considered this female dominated group as not belonging to the main bread-earning persons in the family. BUPL still works intensely to have the Parliament to change this unjust decision together with other female dominated professions.

BUPL is a member of the Danish Trade Union Confederation, the European Trade Union Committee on Education (ETUCE) and Education International (EI). BUPL has a special status internationally due to the fact that we are an independent trade union in the field of ECEC and leisure time facilities, and not just as is common, a section in a teacher trade union. Because of that, BUPL has represented ETUCE twice on the European Commission's working group on ECEC (2012–2014 and 2018–2020).

ECEC in Denmark is regulated by the Act on Day Care Facilities covering nurseries, kindergartens, age-integrated centres, leisure time centres and youth clubs, and public supervised childcare provided in private homes. The latter today only exists for children aged 0–2 years as more and more children in this age group attend age-integrated centres for 0–5 year olds. The state decides how much money is provided for the municipalities to run the ECEC centres, because the municipalities are responsible for providing ECEC for all children whose families ask for a place. Parents have maternal/paternal leave for up to 1 year, so most children start around the age of 10–12 months. The coverage for 1–2 year-old children is 86 percent, and for children aged 3–5 years, close to 100 percent. At the age of 6, children start in the kindergarten-class – an integral part of the primary school. Fees for parents are 25 percent of the total costs of ECEC, but grants are also available for low-income families. Most centres in Denmark are public, run by the municipalities, but also quite a lot of independent centres exist, established by welfare organisations, parents, etc. – all of them are non-profit centres. The independent centres have to have an agreement with the local municipality in order to get funding and have to follow all requirements just like the municipal centres.

Introduction of private ECEC in 2005

A major change to the ECEC system in Denmark occurred in 2005. A liberal-conservative Government introduced in the legislation for child care the option to establish private ECEC – even including the option of profitmaking. The political argument was the idea of giving parents "a free choice" to choose, like a consumer, between taking care of their children at home, or to choose between a public or a private service. The change was ideologically supported by traditional conservative views on families' individual responsibility for the care and upbringing of young children. The economic argument for the change was to promote competition between public and private services in order to raise quality and effectiveness in child care – and to reduce public costs.

BUPL criticised the change as being a general attack on public financed welfare. We didn't see any reason for the private option as long as the establishing of independent non-profit services existed within the legislation. Also, we saw the introduction of private centres as a marketisation of ECEC that would be an open invitation for private national and international companies for profitmaking in the ECEC field, as we had seen in countries abroad.

Municipalities, due to the new legislation, could contract out the operation and management of existing public ECEC centres. The Danish worldwide cleaning company, ISS, was quick to take on these contracts in order to make profits through administering and running ECEC centres. Besides criticising the change from public to private centres, BUPL reacted by raising requests for agreements with ISS in order to secure the salaries and working conditions of the staff in the centres. Together with the general public debate on privatisation, ISS had to give up their activities in the field after a few years. ISS publicly said that the resistance from BUPL was the reason to drop their investment in private for-profit centres. (https://www.dr.dk/nyheder/penge/iss-opgiver-drive-boernehaver-i-danmark)

In regard to other private for-profit centres, BUPL also had success in putting pressure on the owners in order to negotiate agreements to safeguard our members' social and professional rights.

Generally, with these experiences in mind, and because the public ECEC system was well established in Danish society and in the general public, BUPL did not expect that private for-profit centres would flourish. So, besides a general criticism of the privatisation ideology, the main focus of BUPL has been to secure salary and working conditions for pedagogues in the private centres.

Nevertheless, private centres have grown ever since, although most of these are non-profit. The reason for this growth was related to general public cuts on welfare services that made municipalities shut down small public ECEC centres and replace them with much bigger entities to achieve a cheaper and more economically efficient ECEC system. But, a typical reaction from parents has been to establish their own private centre when municipalities have closed down the local kindergarten because parents prefer to keep child care in their neighbourhood and to be able to influence the centre according to local needs. Staff typically continue to work in the now private kindergartens and they often find several advantages, such as more freedom in pedagogical planning and a closer cooperation with parents. Unsurprisingly, these examples of parent-initiated private centres are non-profit, and BUPL has negotiated agreements on salaries and working conditions for the staff equal to the public agreements.

Today, 70 percent of private centres are in practice run like the independent centres – i.e. without profit – whereas the rest have the option to withdraw profit. In 2018, the profit was approximately 27,000 €for each of those private centres that did pay out profit (Ministry of Education and Culture, 2018).

Figures from 2019 shows that public centres are still the most common, with almost 3,000 centres compared with 500 private centres. Most of them – although private – are established as non-profit services. Many of them are connected to the independent and private primary schools who all, by legislation, are not allowed to withdraw profits, whether they are schools or ECEC services.

An end to for profit-ECEC?

The former liberal-conservative Government lost the elections in 2011 and a coalition of the social democratic party with a left-wing and a social-liberal party formed a new government. Unfortunately, the latter party was not in favour of changing the legislation to end the for-profit ECEC option. So nothing changed, and in 2015 once again a liberal-conservative government was elected in Denmark.

At the most recent election in 2019, the social democratic party decided to form a minority Government supported by two left-wing parties and the social-liberal party. One important political initiative of the new majority in Parliament was to propose improved minimum ratios in ECEC. The initiative was based upon BUPL's strong advocacy in the public debate over many years to raise ECEC quality through better child-adult ratios.

So, in December 2021, the Parliament passed the new legislation on ratios (read details later) and also included the private centres in the legislation. But in order to ensure that the funding of the new tax-paid improved ratios should not be taken out as an extra profit in private for-profit centres, the Government and the three other political parties agreed that new legislation should be followed by regulations for private centres to change their legal statutes from for-profit to non-profit. The private centres would have the option to either become an independent non-profit centre, or, if they preferred to continue as a private centre, then they would have to document that they will not take out any form of profit. This would be monitored and controlled by the municipalities.

Unfortunately, the social-liberal party suddenly, in January 2022, jumped from the agreement it had made with the Government and the other two parties to stop for-profit private centres in Denmark in the future. So, the current situation is that, as the Act on minimum ratios has been legislated, the private for-profit ECEC centres, now unhindered, can continue to take out profit, including the extra funding intended for better ratios for the children! Of course, BUPL is now lobbying the Parliament and the social-liberal party to try to have this absurd situation reversed.

From a two-leg strategy to a profession strategy

Way back in the 1980s, BUPL decided to unify traditional trade union activities on salary and working conditions with professional issues concerning pedagogy. This strategy was announced as a "two-leg strategy." It was recognised by BUPL that improvement of working conditions is not only about the will to fight and strike, but equally also requires a public acknowledgement that pedagogues are professionals who advocate and work in favour of children's rights and well-being. BUPL invested in pedagogical courses for members and got involved in public debates with national and local authorities, parents, as well as the municipal employers on the content and values of ECEC pedagogy.

Also, cooperation with researchers began and BUPL employed more people in the union to work with pedagogical issues, with the education of pedagogues, and to lobby the Parliament, policy makers, employers and other stakeholders in the field about the need for better conditions for staff in order to improve the quality of children's education and care.

BUPL Congress 2004 decided to work on strategies for the development of a profession in order to define what categorises the pedagogue's work with children. During the following years, until today, a professional strategy was established that involved a holistic approach to high quality pedagogy, ethics, working conditions, and the right of pedagogues to define the profession through BUPL. These issues require knowledge about the profession. This led BUPL to focus on research as a tool for pedagogues to take power over their profession and to disseminate accounts of everyday experiences from ECEC centres. During the last 10 years, BUPL has published books, research reports, analyses, and articles about the profession and working conditions and organised educational workshops for members to share knowledge and experiences.

The latest Congress of BUPL (2020) adopted a renewal of the original profession strategy from 2018: "A Strong pedagogue profession on the move" with the aim of strengthening the involvement of individual ECEC centres, pedagogues, and leaders. The local branches of BUPL are closely connected with the headquarters in order to coordinate national and local lobbying. Engaging all members with their experiences and knowledge in developing a professional solidarity and community is a priority.

The strategy aims, besides strengthening the profession and improving the working conditions, to avoid commodification of ECEC, to empower professional judgement, to improve the education of pedagogues, and to produce solutions for a future welfare society. We will do this by empowering the profession through mutual, collective exchange of experiences, through training the union representatives in the workplaces both in educational and working rights issues, and through a massive use of social media, campaigns, etc. BUPL will build up a unified professional and trade union stronghold aimed at keeping multinational companies from entering the Danish ECEC field, along with fixed educational programmes and concepts of pre-academic training, and any initiative to privatise the existing ECEC system.

Onwards to 2030 the strategy will function as a guideline for the activities in the Union to develop the profession's mutual knowledge based on pedagogical practice and research – in order to have a societally recognised profession and so pave the road ahead for better salary and working conditions.

Below the major initiatives and the first results from the profession strategy are described.

Research and developmental activities funded by BUPL

A general shift in BUPL's strategy to gain power over the profession and to receive higher societal recognition was decided at BUPL's Congresses through the professional strategy over the last 15 years. Knowing that a profession needs to produce its own knowledge, BUPL began to use membership fees to fund research and to give financial support for members who would perform developmental work in their centres in 2008. The object of this permanent professional strategy was to show Danish society that the pedagogue profession and the union can provide relevant solutions to current societal issues and problems and that the profession must be listened to because we have answers from practice as well as research and investigations. Also, the dissemination of knowledge to members through the union journal and special publications, and later by videos, podcasts and other social media, is a central initiative offered since 2011.

Though prioritising this strategy, the trade union continued to work and argue for improvement in working and salary conditions – so the former two-leg strategy was kept in principle. Still, the low payment of pedagogues has been raised and fought every third year during the general collective negotiations that we have with one unified municipal employers' association (Local Government Denmark, representing all 98 municipalities in Denmark), as well as the daily, continued debate on the child:staff ratio, and any other aspect that influences pedagogues' activities and well-being in ECEC centres.

So BUPL began to produce analyses on different aspects of pedagogical work and working conditions based on its research and developmental work, and published suggestions on how to improve the quality of ECEC, pedagogue education and the working environment. This was and still is disseminated both to the public and to local and national administrative and political decision makers. So BUPL has developed a strong public media policy. Besides our Union Journal, dissemination happens through our website (www.bupl.dk), Facebook, podcasts, videos and newsletters, as well as data sheets with facts and figures on, for example, the quality level of ratios and group sizes in ECEC.

Research projects

Researchers are openly invited to apply for research funding (up to 100,000 €for a single research project) for a project on one of the issues decided by the BUPL's National Council every second year. The applicants' projects are later selected by the Council. The selected themes are connected to the current strategic considerations of BUPL, for example, for 2021–2022 to raise awareness about children and young people's lives in a society with a growing focus on achievement, and for example, to further an attitude of critical practice on gender and diversity.

The work of the researchers is independent of the Union so that the results are seen as objective and trustworthy, and can be used by BUPL in favour of the profession in dialogue with the public. The researchers are mostly connected to universities and research centres. The total amount for research funded by BUPL in 2021–2022 was 800,000 €.

One research project, connected to decommodification, investigated the growing use of evidence-based educational concepts and programmes in ECEC that have been imposed on pedagogues by municipalities. (https://bupl.dk/wp-content/uploads/2018/05/filer-programmering_paedagogikken_2.pdf). Many of these concepts and programmes are developed and sold by national and international companies and are expensive. Although some pedagogues find these helpful on a busy day, they also think that the use of concepts with predefined procedures and fixed methodologies reduces their autonomy and pedagogical reflection. The risk of using these concepts and associated methods is that you only focus on the data the programme requires (for example, number of words learned) but these data might be irrelevant to the actual pedagogical situation (for example, it may be more important to note children's use of language when playing with other children, rather than number of words used). The research also exposed the high costs of buying these concepts and programmes – expenses that could have been used better – for example, on continuous professional development selected by the pedagogues themselves in order to strengthen their professional judgement. Research like this has strengthened the resistance among pedagogues to the commercialisation of their profession.

Developmental projects

Funding for members' own initiated projects on pedagogical issues (up to 15,000 € per project) has the aim that members can investigate a specific pedagogical theme. The funding covers substitutes for the involved pedagogues – who only can receive the funding if they are a union member – and for some external consultancy. Some projects are carried out by single centres – others involve several centres in one or more municipalities.

Among the themes selected for the next 2 years is one called: "Your own dream-project." The project offers an opportunity for pedagogues in a local area to raise debate and empower engagement, for example, about imagination and visions of a future high quality public ECEC or how to promote democratic sustainability or children's voices and rights. Just like the research themes, the themes are decided by BUPL and the applicants are selected by the union as well. The total amount granted to the development projects is 300,000 € for 2021–2022.

The Danish Centre for Research in Early Childhood Education and Care (CeDif)

To support the development of research in ECEC, BUPL took the initiative to establish, together with Roskilde University, a centre for research in ECEC facilities in 2015. The aim of the centre is to research children's lives, pedagogy and development of the pedagogue profession in nurseries, kindergartens, and age-integrated centres for 0–6-year-old children. The central point of the centre is to strengthen and provide a stronger knowledge base for professional work in ECEC and to support children's good life. BUPL is a member of the board of the centre and contributes financially to its operation (600,000 € for 2021–2022).

The ECEC Curriculum debate

The revised Act on ECEC facilities introduced a pedagogical curriculum in 2004. A divide occurred between pedagogues in favour of the curriculum because they saw it as marking a growing understanding of the importance of ECEC, and others in opposition who thought a curriculum was a threat to professional autonomy and to children's play and self-initiated activities, by introducing specific themes the centres had to work on and by requiring reports on children's progression.

BUPL's position in this debate was a bit difficult as both opinions were relevant depending on the focus. Therefore, the union, in dialogue with the Parliament, Government, and political parties, argued for professional liberty in the centres when implementing the pedagogical curriculum, and that the conditions to do so needed to be improved.

The reformed pedagogical curriculum

The curriculum was changed in 2018 after a thorough debate in which BUPL played an important role. A master group was established in 2016, in which BUPL was invited by the Ministry to participate. A central focus for BUPL in the master group was to minimise the influence of narrow academic curriculum concepts and fixed teaching and assessment methods introduced by private companies and often imported from abroad and far away from Danish pedagogical philosophy. BUPL had experienced how some municipalities had instructed their ECEC centres to use specific measurable systems that incorporated these concepts and methods, thus reducing the pedagogues' professional autonomy. We also fought against the idea of introducing narrow academic learning activities in the curriculum. So, for BUPL, it was crucial to prevent formal assessment of children's academic performance from becoming part of the pedagogical curriculum. Instead, BUPL advocated for the fundamental role of children's play in ECEC to be highlighted in the curriculum.

As a result, BUPL succeeded in convincing the members of the master group to make the importance of children's rights and play a priority, together with a much broader understanding of what learning is in an ECEC context: to create "pedagogical learning environments, with the play as fundamental, and with a starting point in a child perspective" (Act § 7). Also, *dannelse* (*bildung* in German which in English/French is somehow an approximation to *formation*) (see also the chapter Resisting Children as Human Capital) and autonomy as well as well-being, became fundamental principles in the reformed curriculum known as the "strengthened pedagogical curriculum."

National funded research on ECEC

In parallel with BUPL's own funded research, we have argued for national engagement – to have a specific PhD Council to promote PhD studies in the 0–6 years field. Therefore, BUPL welcomed the current government's agreement in Parliament in October 2020 to spend almost 7,000,000 € every year from 2021 to 2024 on nationally funded research in the 0–5 years field. The funding will, for example, favour PhD studies that investigate, through research and knowledge generation, how to create relationships between young children, to make them feel safe, to stimulate them and encourage their development, so they are nurtured and learn – they are educated. The research on the one hand would be practice oriented, on the other it would strengthen the education of pedagogues and enhance the understanding of municipalities so that their support for ECEC is given greater priority.

The Minister of Higher Education and Science, in presenting the decision to raise the level of funding for research in ECEC, stated that she looks forward to developing and increasing the research capacity in ECEC through this funding. Therefore, the Minister would further the education of PhDs so they can contribute to the teaching of pedagogue education. The implementation of the funding will include BUPL, together with universities, municipalities, colleges, and other stakeholders.

Minimum child/staff ratios

For a very long time after the 2008 financial crisis, general cuts in public spending happened every year due to national fixed budgets that the local municipalities had to follow – including ECEC that local municipalities are responsible for providing. BUPL, along with the parents' associations, fought against these cuts and, in order to illustrate vividly the impact of these cuts, every year BUPL published a map showing the impact on child/staff ratios for every local municipality.

We realised that a change in the situation required nation-wide legislation and introduced the demand for a minimum of one staff to three children aged 0–2 and one staff to six children aged 3–5. The claim was presented together with pedagogical arguments such as time for planning, reflection, evaluation, and of course time for doing activities with children. Other important aspects were time in favour of prevention, for example supporting "children at risk," children with special needs, supporting immigrant children's language etc.

Unsurprisingly, the parents and their associations were active, held demonstrations, and presented a nationwide campaign using the slogan, "Where do we have an adult?" in order to criticise and illustrate the poor staff:child ratios. The slogan is translated directly from Danish into English and pinpoints that often parents experienced that too few staff members (adults) were available in the centres. And so, parents supported BUPL's idea of a minimum ratio to ensure more staff in ECEC centres.

BUPL's demands for better ratios were closely connected to the issue of high-quality education and care for children, as well as for pedagogues' working conditions. Through lobbying and communication based on research and learning stories from everyday practice in ECEC, BUPL succeeded in persuading the current government and three political parties in 2019, to introduce a minimum ratio in ECEC. The claim of BUPL for ratios 1 to 3 and 1 to 6 was accepted by the government as the basis for future ratios in ECEC, with total implementation planned for 2025 – later this was changed to 2024. The improved ratios and funding will provide full-time employment for 5,000 extra persons. https://www.retsinformation.dk/eli/lta/2021/2594).

Already today – in 2021 – some municipalities by themselves have decided to implement the new ratios though they haven't yet received the full government compensation. Even conservative municipalities have made this decision, which indicates that minimum ratios have won general public approval.

The improved ratios have now raised a new issue: the shortage of pedagogues. Today only 58 percent of staff in ECEC have a pedagogue education – the other staff are typically untrained young people with some having a vocational assistant education. The parliament's agreement on minimum ratios is aimed at keeping at least the current balance between pedagogues and other staff, whereas BUPL and some of the political parties are aiming for a pedagogue percentage of 80 percent. Recognising the problem, the agreement on minimum ratios also included special funding – 27,000.000 € – to increase the percentage of pedagogues, for example by educating assistants to become pedagogues.

So, in 2021, BUPL, the Ministry of Children and Education, and other stakeholders are reviewing pedagogue education and looking for more ways to attract and recruit students to these education courses. Once again, BUPL was involved in the process as a social and professional partner with our specific knowledge of the field.

Next steps

BUPL looks forward to having the salary level of pedagogues raised due to the growing recognition of the importance of pedagogues' work with young children based upon our professionality, research-based knowledge, documentation, and commitment to a Danish welfare society. Over the last decades, BUPL changed from being a traditional trade union to establishing itself as a professional association to promote high quality ECEC, as well as a union who fights for improved working and salary conditions. Though generally trade unions have a strong platform in Danish society, BUPL is well aware that pedagogue students have selected the education because they want to work with children – not because they want to be members of BUPL. During their studies and when they enter the pedagogical field after graduation, they learn that BUPL safeguards, supports, and develops workplace conditions as well as their professional interests. The old two-leg strategy is in fact still alive today.

You could call this strategy a modern comprehensive form of solidarity for professionals. Solidarity with the people we as pedagogues meet and to whom we have a professional responsibility – children, young people, adults, parents. A solidarity with colleagues to support each other to develop our mutual knowledge and practice of high-quality professionalism. Solidarity to fight for better working conditions and in favour of the societal recognition of the importance of the profession. And solidarity to a democratic welfare society in favour of all people.

Conclusion: working in solidarity for democratic ECEC

Solidarity is a theme running through all five cases in this chapter. The ideology of a democratic welfare society cultivates a broad concept of solidarity, as not only connecting practitioners as members of a group who have a common purpose that crosses lines of race, gender, and class, but also connecting with allies and the wider public. Coming together to share personal experiences and views created bonds among those working in ECE and with allies, and offered opportunities for them to become aware and critical of injustices. It was through these processes and finding a common vision that ECEC practitioners transcended individual needs and wants, and, in their organised associations and unions, found pathways to resisting neoliberalism and commodification. Despite very different contexts in the US, Denmark, New Zealand, Nusa Tenggara Timur and Ontario, these were common, unifying ideas. Resistance makes a difference, and holds out hope for a fairer and more humane world in which ECEC plays a vital role.

A main message from research and stories of participants in ECEC is that marketisation and privatisation exacerbate inequities for children, families, and teachers/educators in ECEC, and magnify differences in opportunities and remuneration for the workforce across different sectors and racial groups. Within publicly listed corporate ECEC companies, marketisation and privatisation are at the extreme in skewing the valuing of ECEC as a public good and an institution in civil society, to a means for making financial returns for individual owners and shareholders. Mark Carney, a former Governor of the Bank of England and now UN Secretary-General Special Envoy for Climate Finance, in the 2020 Reith lectures, discussed how financial values have come to be prioritised over human values.

> Values and value are related but distinct. Values represent principles or standards of behaviour, their judgements of what is important in life, such as fairness, responsibility, sustainability, solidarity, dynamism, resilience and humility. Value is the regard that something is held to deserve, its importance, its worth, its usefulness. Value isn't necessarily constant but, rather, specific to time and situation.
>
> *(Carney, 2020, p. 9.23)*

At the heart of resistance in the five cases, were overarching values about the purpose of education and the value of the workforce. These values of solidarity, integrity, and commitment to teaching, children, families, and society shown by ECEC teacher/educators/pedagogues in the cases presented here, are distinctly at odds with the low pay and poor working conditions of the ECEC workforce, the lack of value placed on the workforce. The Danish union, BUPL, held a vision of "solidarity to a democratic welfare society in favour of all people" and a recognition of pedagogues as "professionals who advocate and work in favour of children's rights and wellbeing." In Nusa Tenggara Timur, teachers were empowered within a mentoring programme to "resist the enactment of a standardised and centrally governed ECE curriculum" in favour of "curriculum decisions that respond to the needs of children and the cultural aspirations of their local communities." Synthesised from the New Zealand examples, was a vision for "a democratic, socially just, and equal ECE system for all children and families no matter their circumstances." Associated with that, the New Zealand stories of individual and collective resistance underlined a responsibility for teachers to see themselves as "ethically obliged and persistently committed to contributing to the vision of ECE as a universal right of a child." In Ontario, a vision was held for "a collective and caring future." Early childhood educators sought "a publicly funded and delivered childcare system where ECEs have decent work and children and families have access to affordable, meaningful care experiences." Similarly, in the US, advocacy was for "an equitable system for all children, affordable for their families, and one that concretely values their teachers and caregivers." And focusing on the underpaid and marginalised ECEC workforce, priorities were "securing their long overdue worthy wages and the rights and respect that should be theirs."

A common theme was that the practitioners working in ECEC, as people who know the realities of their work, who are deeply committed to their children, families, and communities, and to principles of a "good education," are best equipped to identify and articulate workforce issues, challenges, and policy solutions to resist neoliberalism and commodification. When, as practitioners, they organise collectively towards a common vision of what might be possible in a fairer world, significant advances can be made, even in very hostile environments. In the US, where privatisation and marketisation of ECEC is at an extreme, the Worthy Wage Campaign succeeded against the odds in raising public discussion and awareness of quality child care and early education, educator pay and working conditions, and measures needed to improve these. In some states, tangible policy advances were made around reward for the workforce, in the form of stipends and bonuses. Further examples of collective action show how practitioners working through their unions (Denmark and New Zealand) and professional association (Ontario), united to form coalitions pursuing their own locally constructed aims for an ECEC system that is equitable for all those participating in it. In Nusa Tenggara Timur, teachers worked together to resist de-professionalisation that an agenda of neoliberalism and privatisation had promoted. In all the coalitions and campaigns, the aims went beyond individual self-interest to incorporate wider goals for workers, families, children, and society. It was through sharing their experiences and stories that individuals came to set their individual circumstances within a wider context, see that change was possible, strategise, and take constructive action.

In the AECEO case in Ontario, the authors described a process somewhat akin to Freire's (1970/2018) concept of *concientização* (conscientisation), as members of AECEO within their collective immersed themselves in educators' stories and experiences, and as educators moved beyond their personal circumstance to become critically aware of the reality of oppressive ECEC structures and practices. This provided opportunities to recognise the "problems" and take action to resist and disrupt them, whether it was an audit culture that eroded professionalism or commodification and the impacts of corporate childcare. Opening the membership to a diversity of groups, as happened when the Black EC educators in Ontario set up a Community of Practice, was crucial in analysing and starting to address the intersection with racism. Similarly, the Employee Caucus of teachers and caregivers, described by Marcy Whitebook in the US case, began with a similar structure to women's consciousness raising groups of the period. The groups often started with discussion of the problems the teachers and caregivers encountered on the job and in wider movements, enabling recognition of common problems and their political nature. It was this conscious awareness and sense of collectivism that then served as a catalyst for Employee Caucus members to take political action.

Resistance to neoliberalism and activism was made possible through collaborative sharing of expertise and knowledge to come to new, contextually relevant, and creative ways to promote a common vision. The opening of advocacy to others outside the ECEC workforce was a feature in many of the cases. It was foregrounded in the Danish case, where BUPL formed strong alliances with researchers and funded research and development activities. This aligned with the BUPL strategy to unify traditional trade union activities on salary and working conditions with professional issues concerning pedagogy. Brought into discussion of pedagogical matters was a much wider group that included researchers, local and national authorities, and families. In New Zealand, teachers in their campaign for increased funding and pay parity enlisted support from local families and community, and, in a less common alliance, with their employer national body. The union and employer organisation funded an independent job evaluation. The AECEO in Ontario "partnered with allied community-based organisations, foundations, and researchers who share our passion and commitment to prioritising the gendered work of early childhood educators at a practice and public policy level."

In each of the organisations, problems were carefully analysed and research undertaken to explore issues and back up claims and advocacy. The Danish union, BUPL, regarded research as "a tool for pedagogues to take power over their profession" and "to disseminate accounts of everyday experiences from ECEC centres." Research funded by BUPL covered wide ranging aspects of pedagogy, with research project topics decided by nationally elected representatives, along with some individual member-initiated projects. The research brief of the BUPL had a big visionary aim: to produce solutions for a future welfare society. Salary and working conditions surveys were used widely by local groups from the Employee Caucus in the US, and the national child care staffing study (Whitebook, 2001), that linked compensation and working conditions to the quality of care children received, is still widely referenced and used in advocacy outside US. In the US,

> Recognizing that not all early educators had the same opportunities to organise, resource materials were developed and widely distributed to help teachers address common problems or propose new practices. These covered a wide range of topics around model contracts, working conditions: instituting grievance procedures, developing salary scales, establishing substitute policies, informing one another about legal breaks and federal pay standards. Also late pickup [fees charged if parents come late to pick up their child].

In the absence of a strong supportive union, resources for teachers to advocate on their own behalf were a crucial support. Likewise, in the New Zealand case, a commissioned job evaluation comparing the job size and qualifications of kindergarten teachers relative to primary teachers was used to justify pay parity between the teachers in the different sectors, and was highly influential. AECEO in Ontario, through "slow, intentional collaboration" carried out surveys, consultations, public webinars and conversations, to "weave the narratives, lived experiences, and ideas of ECEs into policy recommendations that envision another way forward." In all cases, goals were clearly articulated and backed with reasoned evidence, and widespread support was gained through planned campaigning.

The conditions for a democratic association or union of ECEC practitioners require leadership by practitioners themselves and structures to enable knowledge to be co-produced and widely dispersed. Advocacy is weakened and skewed when these structures are not embedded within the organisation, and others make decisions and "speak for" this workforce. This was graphically illustrated in the US case that discussed how the Employee Caucus claims for improved compensation and working conditions were hijacked by the NAEYC leadership, most of whom were not currently teachers.

The case study examples show ways in which bringing those working in ECEC settings together created networks and bonds that were of benefit in offering, in the first instance, mutual support and opportunities for empowerment, in the sense of personal control and influence that broadened into political understanding and activism. In Nusa Tenggara Timur, teachers came together in a mentoring programme where they created a professional learning community, learning from each other, discussing educational ideas and pedagogical strategies, and subsequently extending to mentoring others. In the Danish case, Stig G Lund explained that pedagogue students chose teacher education because they wanted to work with young children, not because they wanted to be members of the union, BUPL. Through involvement in the professional activities of the union, they realised a wider view of the role of the union in safeguarding and developing both professional and employment interests. Lisa Johnston and Nicole Cummings from AECEO each offered their personal accounts of ways in which belonging to their Communities of Practice created a community of support which became a catalyst for political action. For Lisa, the CoP offered her "a refuge and a source of strength, creativity, and passion." More than this, Lisa learned a lot through her involvement about being in a leadership role, and overcoming fears, such as fears of public speaking and speaking to politicians. For Nicole, initiating a Community of Black Early Childhood Educators enabled the creation of a community that could focus on the unique needs and experiences of Black ECEs, "tease apart how and where race fits into this both in terms of our experiences and at a broader systemic level" and insist on visibility and action at both programme and policy levels. Through the Employee Caucus groups in the US, commonalities and differences and the political implications of the issues faced were uncovered, offering "a springboard for activism."

Two of the New Zealand examples were of individual resistance to neoliberalism. Olivera Kamenarac exemplified a teacher in a corporate for-profit setting, where making a profit for business owners was a primary management motivation, and illustrated how deliberate commitment to professional ethics underpinned the teacher's actions to prioritise the interests and well-being of children and families over enterprise interests. In doing so, the teacher needed to be informed about and understand the ECE funding system, and be willing to make a compromise by balancing tensions between business and social priorities. Raella Kahuroa gave a snapshot of how teachers were able to work as critical pedagogues within a community kindergarten, to provide equitable opportunities for each child to contribute, and moreover, for children themselves to consider and identify how all children could be heard. The image of the teacher in this scenario is closely aligned to that of teacher as researcher and critical pedagogue, outlined in the introduction. Her example illustrates the affordances of facilitating environments to support critical pedagogy.

The policy context

Funding

The acts of resistance described in the cases were set within each country context, political structure, and policy frame. A strong message is that resistance was made more potent through a careful and well-researched analysis of the systems and structures that were problematic and concrete proposals on how resistance and advocacy might effect change. The following policy issues were a focus: funding mechanisms and levels; employment legislation and freedom of association; the country's curriculum framework; and overarchingly, the role of the state in regulating, funding and providing ECEC.

The levels of government funding and the ways in which it is allocated have a direct impact on what is spent on staffing. Funding is often categorised as demand-led or supply-led. (for the fundamental difference between demand-led and supply-led funding, see the Chapter 1, On Commodification and Decommodification)

Demand-led funding is paid directly to parents, to enable them to choose and pay for ECEC in the private market, through tax credits or tax incentives, or a voucher system. Supply-led funding is a subsidy that is paid directly to the provider, usually on a per capita basis, providing regulatory requirements are met (Penn, 2013). In a supply-led system, funding can be contingent on delivery of requirements, such as teacher pay and employment conditions. This cannot be done through funding in a demand-led system because the ECEC setting does not receive the funding directly; rather it comes through parents who use the funds to pay for the ECEC service of their choice. Another source of funding is parent fees. Some countries have a fee cap. In 2013, Helen Penn found that in many European countries this is around 15–20 percent of household income.

The cases illustrate the impact of government (federal/regional/municipal) funding amounts and funding mechanisms on teacher pay and employment conditions, and what may be achieved through advocacy to improve these. In New Zealand, the campaign for kindergarten teachers' pay parity with school teachers' pay began with advocacy for improved funding levels, after several years during which government funding levels had stagnated while costs increased. The only palatable way to achieve the high pay increases needed for pay parity was to pressure the government to increase funding levels in the first instance. Otherwise, the cost of pay parity would have had to come from payments by families and community, who were already financially pressed, and which was incompatible with teacher beliefs about government responsibility for early childhood education. Consistent with the union vision for ECEC to be treated as a public service and on a par with schools, was the belief that the government should be responsible for meeting the costs of paying and professionally supporting early childhood teachers. The union was successful in lobbying for increased funding, but in retribution, the government of the day severed connection with the state by removing kindergartens from the State Sector Act. This effectively cut off government responsibility for kindergarten teachers' pay and looked grim for future negotiations. It was not until kindergartens were reinstated to the State Sector Act under a sympathetic new government, that these teachers, through their union, achieved pay parity. The story highlights the vision held by the union and its teacher members about the status and valuing of ECEC, their ability to think about the issue of teacher remuneration in a wider policy context, and the careful analysis and planning that went into the advocacy. It also illustrates that the path of resistance is a long game, and that sympathetic government allies are necessary. By contrast, the US system of limited government funding and a mainly demand-led funding mechanism (financed primarily by parent fees, with limited government investment) created obstacles that multiplied the difficulties in achieving equitable pay within the ECEC sector and across education sectors.

Although supply side funding is better able to be targeted to improving staffing, when management is given discretion to use the funding as it wishes, and in the absence of a collective employment agreement, there is no guarantee that funding will be spent on staffing, unless there are policy requirements about how it is spent. Direct salary funding by the state (for example, through teachers' employment as public servants on a government payroll) is a mechanism to prevent funding intended for salary purposes being siphoned off for other spending purposes, a clear likelihood when there is a large number of for-profit providers.

In Denmark, there is a close connection with the state on content and curricular issues and the union bargains salaries with the municipal employers on a 3-year basis. ECEC pedagogue salary levels are marginally lower than those of school teachers, a quirk of an older sexist Act of Parliament that viewed women's work as being of lesser value because women were not the "main breadwinner." The advocacy described in the Danish case was around improving staffing ratios. As in the New Zealand case, it was timed to coincide with a sympathetic government that contributed to improvement in ratios and the government's radical decision to deny public funding for improved staffing ratios to for-profit settings, unless they became independent and abided by municipality rulings.

By contrast, writing of the recent *Building Back Better* initiative, the Biden administration's social and economic policy agenda, Marcy Whitebook pointed out that

> While it does set a living wage (as yet undefined) as a floor for all teachers and calls for pay parity for early childhood teachers with equivalent qualifications to elementary school teachers, there is as yet no clarity on whether the money will get into the hands of teachers, especially the majority who remain unrepresented.

In conclusion, resistance to privatisation and marketisation and the flow-on effects to the pay and conditions of the ECEC workforce, needs to address big and complex issues: levels of government funding sufficient to pay a well-qualified, professionally supported workforce; supply-side funding and mechanisms to ensure funding for pay and employment conditions reaches these intended destinations; negotiation of collective employment agreements; and a hands-on role for the state.

Privatisation, employment legislation, and freedom of association

Global corporate actors who have promoted the commercialisation and privatisation in and of education have been a focus of campaign resistance by Education International, the Global Union Federation that represents teachers and organisations around the world (Sorensen, Grimaldi, & Gajderowicz, 2021). Education International has argued that the presence of corporate actors weakens collective bargaining and its solidarity and equity impacts. This has certainly been evident in the cases in this chapter, where high levels of privatisation, particularly in the US, pitted teachers/educators against individual owners whose priority was profit-making for their corporate body. The New Zealand case illustrated acts of individual resistance to enterprise interests in a corporate ECE setting, but this was by a single individual acting alone, required considerable courage, and lacked the power of collective resistance to bring about change beyond the individual context, as important as this was. Similarly, arguing for the power of the collective, the Ontario case noted that "Once 'the problem' is not taken on as an individual burden and educators feel supported by and with each other, there becomes both motivation and space to imagine and transform what *is* to something more equitable and more caring."

Another crucial policy element affecting employment conditions is the country's employment legislation, and in particular, rights to freedom of association and the right to bargain collectively. Freedom of association is a human right recognised within the *Universal Declaration of Human Rights*, and in the context of the ECEC workforce, refers to workers having the right to participation and have a voice in economic and social policy, and their right to form and join organisations, including trade unions. Collective bargaining is a right enshrined in the 1998 ILO *Declaration on Fundamental Principles and Rights at Work*.

Examples from the Danish case demonstrated the powerful influence when pedagogues, working through their union, BUPL, and in alliance with researchers and parent associations, had the right to participate in government forums to determine professional matters affecting them and their ECEC services. In the US, the Worthy Wage campaign made use of the International Labour Organisation Policy Guidelines to develop its own *US- based Model Work Standards for Centers and Homes*. The work of the Campaign happened against the odds of an unsympathetic federal government that neither supported these workplace standards nor offered guidance.

Curriculum and assessment

The influence of commercial providers on the development of curriculum resources and management principles based on neoliberal logic were further areas of resistance exemplified in the cases. These were starkly described in the US where "educator autonomy has been eroded by commercial curricula, and expectations that teachers routinely conduct regular assessments and prepare reports on children." Stig G Lund, in the Danish case, outlined the dangers of an audit culture of professionalisation, resisted through naming and disrupting these phenomena. BUPL had a significant influence on the development of curriculum, where it worked to "minimise the influence of concepts and fixed methods introduced by private companies and often imported from abroad and far away from Danish pedagogical philosophy." Its commissioned research exposed the use of commercially produced curriculum programmes and educational content that lacked responsiveness to local context, were narrowly focused on academic goals, and undermined pedagogue judgement and autonomy. In particular, BUPL resisted the kinds of measurable assessment of children's academic performance that would detract from a broad and holistic understanding of children's learning and right to play. BUPL was successful because it had a voice as a participant in curriculum reform, drawing on and communicating research and its members' expertise and experience. BUPL not only reacted to government agendas for curriculum reform, it also influenced agendas through its partnership with researchers and support for members to undertake research on themes that BUPL determined. Perhaps the most forward-looking theme was the invitation to members to research their own "dream-project" intended to open up pathways to local powers of innovation and imagination about "big" topics as diverse as visions for high quality public ECEC, democracy, and children's rights.

In Kupang, Nusa Tenggara Timur, where teachers were afforded little professional autonomy and limited curriculum materials were available only in Bahasa Indonesia, a small group of teachers participating in a mentoring programme, co-constructed their own culturally relevant picture books in local languages. The experiences of participating in the mentoring programme, extending the programme by becoming mentors of other teachers, and having their pedagogical understandings recognised and affirmed at local and national levels, were enormously influential in helping teachers resist a dominant, Euro and Western perspective of quality and de-professionalisations of the teacher workforce.

As a story of hope, Raella Kahuroa's example in the New Zealand case showed how teachers, working from a critical theory perspective, supported and provoked the young children in the kindergarten to think critically and ethically about their relationships with each other and to develop working theories about how environmental and social issues in their context might be addressed. Her example illustrates the affordances of facilitating environments to support critical pedagogy. Teachers were supported in their work of by "competent systems" at every level. They held a social justice vison for a democratic community and worked within New Zealand's curriculum framework, a permeable curriculum that enables possibilities to democratise education in ways envisaged by Freire (Mitchell, 2020, p. 175). The kindergarten was not-for-profit, with the full funding from government going into educating the child and supporting the family. The community management trusted the professional judgement of teachers and supported their work through conducive employment conditions. The image of the teacher in this community kindergarten is aligned with the image of the teacher as critical pedagogue and researcher.

Conclusion

Lisa Johnston encapsulated core problems of neoliberalism when she wrote: "A market model of childcare provision thrives on competition rather than cooperation, whereby being "better than" others is prioritised over working well with others." Taken together, the examples in this chapter reinforce our conviction that ECEC practitioners can work individually and collectively to resist and combat neoliberal ECEC policies and practices that promote inequities and divisions. A central argument is that effective unions and community associations are essential in a participatory democracy. The unions and associations provide a means to organise, give voice to, and persist in a collective effort to progress a democratic vision for ECEC as a public good, a professionally supported, qualified, and well-remunerated ECEC workforce, and autonomy for practitioners to work in the best interests of children, families and society.

In Canada and the US, the Covid-19 pandemic has highlighted the inadequacy of social infrastructure, weakened by decades of neoliberalism, and the precarious position of ECEC practitioners whose employment rights worsened during the pandemic. In Ontario, practitioners were left out of priority for the wage subsidy. In the US, return to work threatened practitioners' health, and others were laid off, had hours reduced, or were made redundant. This was not the case in New Zealand, where government funding continued to be paid during lockdowns, and careful health and safety measures were put in place in ECEC settings (Mitchell, 2020; Mitchell, Hodgen, Meagher-Lundberg, & Wells, 2020; Mitchell, Meagher-Lundberg, & Wells, 2020).

To end, a hope is that the Covid-19 pandemic will provoke new thinking about how the world should be and what a meaningful ECEC system would look like within a reimagined world. In a reimagined world, ECEC will be understood as a public good, a right of the citizen child, and the concept of education will be understood in its broadest sense. The capacity of teachers/educators to think and act critically will be developed to the fullest. There is some resonance in these ideas with Gramsci's concept of the "organic intellectual," whose role is to "mediate between the good sense of subaltern groups and the formation of a counterhegemonic consciousness that can read the contextually specific and historically conjunctural contradictions inherent in society" (Fischman & McLaren, 2005, p. 434). Giroux (2020) makes a case for educators as "public intellectuals willing to connect pedagogy with the problems of public life, a commitment to civic courage, and the demands of social responsibility" (p. 4). Likewise, Broström (2013) has argued that curricula are needed to help children "act in a future society as critical-democratic subjects" (Broström, 2013, p. 254).

> Animated by a sense of critique and possibility, critical pedagogy at its best, attempts to provoke students to deliberate, resist and cultivate a range of capacities that enable them to move beyond the world they already know without insisting on a set of fixed meanings.
>
> *(Giroux, 2020, p. 88)*

In realising this hope, advocacy is needed to bring about change in the values and valuing of ECEC, and the structures and systems that oppress, so that new imaginaries of what ECEC could possibly be can be sustained.

5
CONCLUSIONS

Michel Vandenbroeck, Joanne Lehrer, and Linda Mitchell

Peter Moss' introduction to this book, *From the Politically Impossible to the Politically Inevitable*, reminded us that neoliberalism and commodification, or the *economisation* of everything, is a grand narrative that hides in plain sight, presenting itself as inherent and natural, incontestable. In Chapter 2, *On Commodification and Decommodification*, we showed how the continuing belief in childcare markets as being in the best interests of children, parents, educators, and society is false, and that the continuing belief in commodification by policy makers cannot be understood other than as an ideological choice. We sought to examine the micro and macro politics involved in the commodification of children's day-to-day realities in diverse early childhood care and education (ECEC) contexts across the globe, in order to shed light on the problems and processes inherent in this disturbing trend. More importantly, we sought to amplify inspirational examples of resistance. We insist that the commodification of ECEC is not inevitable, and we hope that the three sections that followed, *Resisting Children as Human Capital; Resisting the Consumentality of Parents;* and *Resisting the Alienation of the Workforce,* and specifically the case studies within them from diverse local contexts, can help to imagine multiple alternatives to the hegemonic commodified vision of ECEC and its actors, as we stutter and stumble our way towards a post-neoliberal world.

Good sense and counter-hegemony

In Chapter 2, *On Commodification and Decommodification*, we presented Gramsci's work as an attempt to understand and theorise how the neoliberal vocabulary and the commodification of ECEC became perceived as the only show in town. The language of children's outcomes; the language of parental choice; or the language of cost reduction when speaking about ECEC staff; are all examples of language that oppresses and limits the possibilities of those children, parents, and staff that it oppresses. Gramsci proposed the concept of cultural hegemony to understand how subalterns may contribute to their own subaltern status, and how such oppressive language may be adopted by those it oppresses. Gramsci therefore also presents the concept of *common sense* with a meaning that substantially differs from what we usually mean when using that term. For Gramsci, *common sense* is the constellation of spontaneous beliefs and opinions of the *common people*, the feelings, intuitions, or ideas of everyday existence in a given society and epoch. Common sense is, according to Gramsci, by no means consensual, monolithic, or homogenous. Quite conversely, it is contradictory in character and always contains elements of adaption and subordination, as well as satire, protest, and transformation (Patnaik, 1988). It is fragmentary, incoherent, and inconsequential. It is through common sense that the status quo is reproduced, but nevertheless, it also contains what Gramsci labels *good sense*: a conception of reality that has gone beyond common sense and has become a *critical* conception. For Gramsci, the *senso commune* (common sense) is one of the most characteristic forms of collective ensembles of subaltern opinion. It is also the terrain on which any progressive movement must engage with the existing hegemony: where good sense exists entangled with common sense that is "crudely neophobe and conservative" (Crehan, 2016, p. 186). Concrete examples of the contradictive nature of common sense are to be found in online discussions amongst parents in the many chat groups that exist on parenting issues. A study by Geinger, Vandenbroeck, and Roets (2014), for instance, showed that in their narratives on Zappy Baby, an online chat room on parenting, the participants were both co-constructing *and* resisting the concept of individualised parental responsibility and of a deficit approach to parenting. Subaltern knowledge emerges in fragmented, often chaotic form, but the good sense embedded within it represents the embryonic beginnings of a genuine alternative to the existing hegemony, an alternative that is an indispensable element in the creation of a new economic and political order, according to Crehan (2016). The previous chapters have been illustrated with such examples of microresistance, where Indigenous and religious visions of childhoods that are neither measurable nor predictable have been used to design alternate curricula, organise settings for children and families, and resist the insistence on testing and measurement of children; where parents and citizens have created and maintained childcare networks and structures that are an integral part of their communities and that reimagine the role of the ECEC centre in community life; and where professionals, working in the straitjacket of for-profit ECEC, resisted cost-benefit logics. Examples can also be found amongst ECEC staff, where working conditions can be accepted and at the same time critically deconstructed. Research has shown how ECEC professionals in general and family day care providers in particular adhere to their profession being described as "what mothers naturally do" or even as "second best to what mothers do," yet at the same time, they resist the gendered and oppressive nature of their job being described in those terms, and strive for the recognition of their public and professional status (Dalli, 2002; Lim, Kim, & Lee, 2021; O'Regan,

Halpenny, & Hayes, 2019). Similarly, as described in Chapter 2, Islamic religious discourse in Indonesia and the inclusion of religious and spiritual development in early childhood curricular frameworks promote reflection on values and attitudes to foster in children that resist a neoliberal framing of young people as human capital to be assessed and measured. At the same time, this discourse positions the women who educate and care for children as volunteers fulfilling their religious duties, and therefore without the right to protest the unjust working conditions and low pay they are subjected to. In Chapter 3, Chilean community-based preschools in poor neighbourhoods included mothers as educators alongside trained professionals. While a sense of belonging was centred in these programs, the structural inequalities in access to ECEC and the use of mothers as volunteer educators were not addressed. In Chapter 4, private for-profit ECEC owners in New Zealand were described as having an overarching concern with their business operations and individual and company profits. At the same time, a teacher described both teaching within this business world and actively using its language to oppose its principles and "make exceptions" to value humans above profit.

It is precisely that contradictive nature of cultural hegemony and common sense that provides the possibilities of opposition and counter-hegemony. Good sense can emerge from common sense by renovating and making critical what already exists (Gramsci, 1971 in First, 2016). For Gramsci, good sense is not a matter of scientific reasoning, a privilege of intellectual elites, but rather generating good sense is entrenched within the everyday and is therefore within reach of all social groups (First, 2016). It is therefore not surprising that the possibilities of change and resistance are elaborated by neo-Gramscian thinking, stressing the possibility of agency within structure and a reflection on the role of civil society as a place in which hegemony is based, but also as the ground on which new and challenging counter-hegemonies can arise. In that sense, the civil society is "both shaper and shaped, an agent of stabilization and reproduction, and a potential agent of transformation" (Cox, 1999). Chapters 2, 3, and 4 documented different ways in which civil society is shaped as a movement of resistance.

In the case of Australian children attending long day care, the children themselves acted as agents, reproducing neoliberal framings while performing competition and belonging within ECEC, and resisting, passively and actively, such framings. In the case of the Kōhanga reo, community members created an entire movement contesting colonialism and affirming Māori cultural identity and self-determination that privileges the *mana* or self-determination of the children. In the case of Norway's Kindergarten uprising, educators and parents resisted the way that developmentalism and commodification impact conceptions of children and their well-being. In the case of the Indigenous curriculum in various African countries, including Nigeria, indigenous knowledges, similar to the Islamic ECEC discourse in Indonesia, reclaim traditional values about what attitudes and dispositions the community wants to nurture in children that cannot be measured or decontextualised from daily life. The implementation of this curriculum, despite the resistance it has received from those entrenches in globalised neocolonial discourses of developmentalism and neoliberalism, affirms the self-determination of Indigenous people and the importance of contextualised and culturally relevant control of ECEC content and structure.

In the case of the struggle against commodification in Hong Kong, the civil society is a collective where parents and professionals joined forces in common actions for education as a public good. In the cases of the French *crèches parentales* or the Chilean community ECEC, these organisations form a civil society in itself, joining educational aims to social renewal, contesting not only the commodification of ECEC in particular but neoliberal identity in general. The Italian example of *gestione sociale* also serves as an interesting case. Here, civil society is not conceptualised as an entity that is supposed to be in opposition to the State, but as a shared responsibility between the (local) public authorities and families. *Gestione sociale,* or social governance, is how, in the Italian context and in that precise historical era, early childhood education became a place that is both the result of democratic decision-making and contributing to democratic citizenship. This historically viable and democratic approach to including parents and the wider community in the management of all aspects of schools for young children leaves no place for commodification.

Civil societies of teachers/educators were formed by the unions in Denmark and New Zealand, and the associations of teachers/educators in Ontario and the US. Here, teachers/educators joined together in collectives that were structured to enable democratic deliberation, decision-making, and action by members of the workforce themselves. Within these structures, members found opportunities for their own self-empowerment that were transformative for some educators personally, as the Ontario case illustrates. More especially, through their combined advocacy, these organisations sought to overturn entrenched societal attitudes about the worth of the ECEC professional as a "substitute mother" or a "technician," and the role of ECEC as following narrow economic imperatives to produce predetermined child outcomes. Their advocacy resisted neoliberal imperatives, and asserted that the value of ECEC professionals should be reflected in equitable pay and conducive working conditions. It is notable that advocacy went beyond workforce employment conditions, to "big" questions about the role of education in a democratic society, arguments for ECEC as a public good, and questions of social justice for children and families, as in the "microresistance" shown by the teacher employed in a for-profit centre in New Zealand. The civil society formed through unions and teacher/educator associations was often conceptualised as having a broad membership of associated community organisations and individuals, researchers, and parents, who were able to organise together to bring about new thinking. The case of Denmark exemplified the power of a coalition of union and research organisations to change conceptions of a commercialised curriculum and promote a curriculum that was educationally expansive and contextually relevant. The example of the Norwegian childcare rebellion has now begun to inspire a civil movement of childcare workers and parents in Flanders to ask for respect for their educational value and demand better working conditions. Teachers in Nusa Tenggara Timur showed possibilities for resisting the enactment of a standardised and centrally governed ECE curriculum when, working in collaboration with professional development facilitators, they co-constructed their own culturally and linguistically appropriate picture book resources. In so doing, these teachers became empowered and willing to use their experiences and understandings in mentoring other teachers to also resist the standardised curriculum resources. A challenge is to maximise the potential of such coalitions to critically question and change the fundamental structural relationships within societies so that those who dominate politically do not hold the power to assert neoliberal solutions.

With Manojan (2019), we argue that education offers a regime where resistance can be inaugurated and established to critique cultural domination and that here, the task of the critical educator is to become a transformative intellectual and to shape learners (here children, educators, parents, and community-members) as organic intellectuals for counter-hegemonic actions. This transformative intellectual, as Gramsci describes it, is not an individual possessed of certain skills who engage in recognisably intellectual activities. Gramsci totally rejects this conventional understanding, insisting that it is the social relations that organise the production of authoritative knowledge on which we should focus (Crehan, 2016).

Quality as a social project

What the many cases of resistance described in the three main sections of this book have in common is that the educational is not to be separated from the social and that what constitutes the social is not the mere addition of individual wants, of individual parental "choices," but of a common societal project, an attention to the common good. What this societal project may be is the result of a common reflection, and is deeply embedded in the local, historical, geographical, and political context. In Chile, the social and educational project is related to claims of the land and the struggle for a life in dignity for the *poblador*. In some regions in France, the project is related to the concern for social cohesion in the suburbs of major cities, but also to the concern about the depopulation of rural villages. In Italy, the social project is based on the reconstruction of a new era after the Second World War. In Norway, and Denmark, it is a social movement protesting the commodification of education and struggling to share educators' and parents' personal experiences in order to articulate the importance of maintaining their own social pedagogy traditions and resisting the imposition of a neoliberal and globalised vision of standardisation. In Aotearoa New Zealand, kōhanga reo is a movement resisting colonisation and subsequent loss of Māori language and culture, loss of lands, and cultural alienation within a monocultural society. Kōhanga reo are Māori immersion whānau (family) programmes for young children from birth to six years of age to be raised within their whānau (Māori social networks), where the language of communication is Māori. All the cases documented in the

Conclusions 219

previous chapters have in common a strong awareness of what there is to oppose: the rejection of the fascist history as well as of the dubious role that the church played during the dark days in Italy; the injustice of blatant inequality in Chile; the hygienist rulings of ECEC that exclude parents in France; the colonial history including the denial of the language and cultural heritage of the Māori populations in Aotearoa or the Yoruban Indigenous culture in Nigeria.

The local embeddedness as well as the dialogical approach and the crucial role of civil society inevitably means that quality cannot be defined beforehand, as an abstract concept, unrelated to these social contexts or to the societal projects of which the ECEC is an integral part. On the contrary, it is important to recognise the democratic right of groups to choose the content of their learning and the process by which this would be transmitted. The idea that quality is necessarily a social construct does not mean that it is an invalid concept and that we should do away with it. There may even be aspects of quality that are valid in many, if not all, different contexts, such as the fact that children should be safe and well-fed, what constitutes *meaningful interactions* between adults and children, or that what is meaningful encompasses *emotional support* and *educational support*. As Lemay and colleagues (2017) argue, a hybrid approach between Dahlberg et al.'s (2007) concept of sense-making and universal quality standards as measured by some quantitative checklists like the ECERS or the CLASS is possible, if one were able to agree upon the universal aspects of quality and be able to measure this "quality" without losing sight of local and contextual subjective visions of what ECEC should be and what it is for. Pagani (2021) proposes an integrated framework that adds a qualitative dimension to standardised assessment, in order to explore the meanings and interpretations of local practitioners as they react to these assessment tools. These attempts to reconcile these two seemingly contradictory aims of quality assessment mean that quality can never be reduced to basic universal concepts or narrowed down to what quality measurement scales aim to measure. In fact, the focus on measuring quality as opposed to adequately and sustainably funding ECEC programs, and ensuring that they are accessible to all, is a questionable use of resources. Quality measurement scales can document a state of affairs, and therefore their use can contribute to the necessary debates on public investments in ECEC for instance. A salient example is that the use of quality measurements has documented that the quality of ECEC decreased after the commodification of childcare in The Netherlands (van der Werf, Slota, Kenis, & Leseman, 2020), Quebec (Bellemare, 2019) as well as elsewhere (Whitebook, Kipnis, & Bellm, 2007). The risk is, however, that quality is reduced to what quality scales measure, as this would deny the social project of ECEC and that social project is the provisional assemblage that results from dialogue, dispute, resistance, and – more positively – dreams, projects, and struggles of both private and public operators. Inevitably, what constitutes quality will change from place to place and from time to time. It will also mean that some crucial aspects of quality will not be measurable. Creativity, empathy, aesthetics, solidarity, ecological concern, respect for diversity, emancipation, equity, altruism, kindness, and love may be central concepts of the social project of ECEC but cannot (and should not) be included in any quality measurement. That doesn't mean that these concepts cannot be experimented and documented. Nor does it mean that more traditional concepts such as educational and emotional support in the adult-child interaction, healthy food, or clean toilets would lose their significance as quality indicators. But it does mean we need to remain critical about what Stephen Ball in the foreword of the book on neoliberalism by Roberts-Holmes and Moss (2021, p. xvi) names "the metier and modalities of neoliberalism, both its *modus operandi* and *modus vivendi*, (...): visibility, accountability, transparency, measurement, calculation, comparison, evaluation, ratings, ranking, indicators, metrics and indices." It is presented to us that only what is measurable is valid and that it is the calculators, the measurers, the league tables that define what quality is.

The cases presented in this book show that this is not the case. They document that communities, practitioners, parents, and civil society can be well-equipped to define what ECEC is for and to deliberate what quality may mean in their situations and localised contexts. Therein resides an important responsibility for the research community. Early childhood scholars are tempted to look for measurable outcomes as these may be easier to publish in highly ranked journals and bibliometric (indeed quantifiable) criteria matter for career prospects. As a result, it is tempting to restrict research in ECEC to issues that reinforce the idea that quality can only be studied in terms of regression analyses, quasi-experimental studies, meta-analyses, with instruments created in the United States and which contribute to the marketisation not only of the instruments themselves, but also of the researchers who profit from them. Other choices are possible. These may be more risky, tentative, qualitative, provisional, as they include participatory trajectories with parents and practitioners, as well as with children. Such choices matter, as they bear the possibility to showcase how diverse social constructions of quality are possible, feasible, and sustainable. They also centre the voices and perspectives of those whose lives are impacted by decisions made at all other levels, from purchasing curriculum to evaluating and renumerating educators, from seeing parents as partners instead of consumers, to listening to children and exploring their ideas instead of following a commercial program for teaching English as a foreign language to prepare children for later educational success. These are the choices that many of the contributors in this book have made. They illustrate that research may contribute to the necessary debates on the decommodification of early childhood education and critical resistance to neoliberalism. In so doing, they form what Gramsci labels the intellectuals that foster counter-hegemonies.

ECEC professionals as social agents

ECEC professionals are mainly female, often low paid and working under poor conditions, diverse in their qualifications, and holding low status and insufficient recognition for the complexity of their pedagogical work. This common profile has been the result of historical and stereotypical views that have devalued ECEC as "women's work" and that became further entrenched within countries where split systems of "childcare" and "education" existed. Neoliberalism, marketisation, and privatisation have magnified inequities in pay and working conditions, as private providers have worked to recruit staff at the lowest possible cost, in order to make financial returns for themselves, their shareholders and/or their private equity companies. In these ways, ECEC professionals are treated as commodities and alienated through societal and managerial undervaluing. Further alienation has occurred through the imposition of standardised curricula and assessment measures that have treated educators as technicians and bypassed their capacity to make their own professional judgements within their local contexts.

Together with Nieuwenhuis and Van Lancker (2020), we argue that a whole set of multilevel policies (international organisations, central and local governments) ultimately affect individual professionals' choices, opportunities, constraints, and capabilities. Yet, as they also claim, what professionals do is not simply a matter of trickle-down policies with the highest levels deciding and the other levels following suit. There is constant interaction and influencing is also bottom-up, with practitioners and communities influencing policy. It is well-known for instance that what professionals actually do is not necessarily what is prescribed in the early childhood curricular frameworks applying to them. Sylva, Ereky-Stevens, and Aricescu (2015) showed that official curriculum documents only tell a fraction of the story, as other factors determine how national mandates are implemented in practice. These authors mention, for instance, acts and decrees, non-legislated curriculum guidelines, financial resources for staffing and salary, pedagogical monitoring and support. In addition, however, we need to add the discretion of practitioners as a determining factor.

The ECEC professionals in our illustrative cases have in various ways resisted the discourses that, at their extreme, position ECEC and themselves as commodities. They have shown themselves as able to interpret the discourses that stifle their professionalism, to see potential within local and national policies, and to work individually and collectively as social agents of change. They are well-positioned for advocacy work, bringing a wealth of understanding and knowledge from their own education, their everyday interactions and relationships with children and families, and their connections with local communities and other educators. This puts them in a place where it is possible to form alliances with others, who, like themselves, are prepared to undertake acts of resistance directed towards social change. By uniting amongst themselves to constitute a force, these alliances can have a powerful impact, as our case studies have illustrated.

The examples of microresistance from Denmark, Norway, Aotearoa New Zealand, Ontario, and US show the value of trade union and professional organisations in offering democratic structures to bring professionals together collectively, to articulate and address issues that trouble them, and reasons for these. These are not confined to issues of low pay and poor employment conditions. Through collective structures and building alliances, ECEC professionals have become agents of social change in promoting imaginaries of what ECEC might possibly be, and the status of ECEC as a public responsibility. In promoting collective values and goals, social change has been supported by an astute analysis of the shortfalls in levels of government funding for ECEC and the need for funding to be delivered so that it reaches intended purposes within ECEC, rather than for the private gains of providers. In these ways, resistance has begun to challenge the competitive and economic ethos that has been a hallmark of neoliberalism.

ECEC as a social project

ECEC is situated at the crossroads of diverse policy fields, including (but not necessarily limited to) family policies, gender policies, educational policies, social policies, identity politics, nationalistic policies, and labour market policies. ECEC policies are therefore deeply connected with visions about what constitutes the social. In the neoliberal realm, there is little room for thinking about what constitutes the social, as there is only space for the individual, the economical, and the technical. As Roberts-Holmes and Moss (2021) have aptly analysed, this is an ideological choice amidst other possible choices and there are many other languages to speak about ECEC. Throughout an analysis of the impact of commodification on children, parents, and professionals, as well as by documenting alternative pathways, we have argued for ECEC as a social project. This vision on ECEC implies debates on what images of the child we prefer to advance, what images of the parent and the professional speak to us and our vision of a good and just world, of being with children in the present, while also preparing them for the future. It also implies a public debate on what the social and societal meanings of ECEC are. We imagine public ECEC as an integral part of an adequately and sustainably resourced social project where ECEC spaces allow children to grow; allow children, families, and educators to build relationships and to feel that they belong to a community; and allow us as a society to encourage values that we hold dear, such as conflict resolution, openness to diversity, equity, and respect for gender diversity, where our cultural values are shared with as well as shaped by future generations of citizens.

In the introduction to this book, Moss asserted that the end of neoliberalism is inevitable. We hope that this book inspires readers to start thinking about, discussing, and organising for what comes next. According to Peter Moss in the introduction of this book, this is "a public system of early childhood education, fully integrated and based on democratic and solidaristic values and on an ethics of care and an ethics of an encounter." We wonder about a post-economic world, a world where clean water, healthy fresh food, a warm home, a safe neighbourhood, access to nature, and quality ECEC are universal rights for everyone, not commodities to be bought and sold and skimped on because governments either leave them to the private sphere or attempt to invest as little as possible into them.

REFERENCES

AA.VV. (1972). *La gestione sociale nella scuola dell'infanzia*. Roma: Editori Riuniti.

Aba, F. X. L., Mohd, S. B., Yussof, O. M. (2015). Analysis of economic structure in poverty eradication in the province of East Nusa Tenggara Indonesia, *Procedia – Social and Behavioral Sciences, 211*, 81–88. DOI: 10.1016/j.sbspro.2015.11.013.

Adesina, S. (1988). *The development of modern education in Nigeria*. Ibadan: Heinemann Educational Books (Nig) Limited.

Adriany, V. (2017). The internationalisation of early childhood education: Case study from selected kindergartens in Bandung, Indonesia. *Policy Futures in Education, 0*(0), 1–16.

Adriany, V. (2018). The internationalisation of early childhood education: Case study from selected kindergartens in Bandung, Indonesia. *Policy Futures in Education, 16*(1), 92–107. DOI: 10.1177/1478210317745399

Adriany, V. (2019). Negotiating local and glocal discourse in kindergarten: Stories from Indonesia. *Journal of Pedagogy, 10*(1), 77–93.

Adriany, V., & Newberry, J. (2021). Neuroscience and the construction of a new child in early childhood education in Indonesia: A neoliberal legacy. *Current Sociology, 70*(4). DOI: 10.1177/0011392120985875.

Adriany, V., Yulindrasari, H., & Tesar, M. (2019). Satu Desa, Satu PAUD unpacking the meaning of children's participation within ECE policy and provision in Indonesia. In J. Murray, B. B. Swadener, & K. Smith (Eds.), *The Routledge international handbook of young CHILDREN'S rights*. Oxon and New York: Routledge.

AECEO. (2017). "Ontario's Early Childhood Sector Decent Work Charter." Retrieved June 1, 2020, from https://www.aeceo.ca/ontario_early_childhood_sector_decent_work_charter.

AECEO. (2017). *Professional pay & decent work*. Association of Early Childhood Educators of Ontario. https://www.aeceo.ca/professional_pay_decent_work_for_all

Akgunduz, Y. E., & Plantenga, J. (2014). Childcare in the Netherlands: Lessons in privatisation. *European Early Childhood Education Research Journal, 22*(3), 379–385.

Aksoy, N., & Eren Deniz, E. (2018). Early childhood education in neoliberal, religiously conservative times in Turkey. *Policy Futures in Education, 16*(1), 108–123.

Alliance on the Fight for 15-year Free Education. (2014). *Recommendations submitted to the Committee on Free Kindergarten Education* (in Chinese). https://www.legco.gov.hk/yr14-15/chinese/panels/ed/ed_fke/papers/ed_fke20150117cb4-360-4-c.pdf

Ambarukmi, S. (2022). *Tata Kelola pendidik dan guru PAUD di desa sebagai pondasi layanan PAUD yang berkualitas* [Paper presentation]. Seminar Kepala Desa Webinar, Jakarta, Indonesia. http://bit.ly/3JzDXea

Anttonen, A. (1994). 'Hyvinvointivaltion naisystävälliset kasvot' ['Women-friendly face of welfare state'], in A. Anttonen, L. Henriksson and R. Nätkin (Eds.), *Naisten hyvinvointivaltio* (Women's Welfare State) (pp. 203–226). Tampere: Vastapaino.

Anttonen, A. (1999). *Lasten kotihoidon tuki suomalaisessa perhepolitiikassa* [Child home care allowance in Finnish family policy]. Sosiaali- ja terveysturvan tutkimuksia. Helsinki: KELA.

Apple, M. (2005). Education, markets, and an audit culture. *Critical Quarterly, 47*(1–2), 11–29. https://doi.org/10.1111/j.0011-1562.2005.00611.x

Are, A. (2007). *An international workshop on the role of early childhood education for a sustainable society.* Göteborg University.

Atkin, W. (2001). "Playing together as Canadians": Historical lessons from the West end creche. In S. Prentice (Ed.). *Changing child care: Five decades of child care advocacy and policy in Canada.* Fernwood.

Austin, L.J.E., Edwards, B., Chávez, R., Whitebook, M. (2019). Racial Wage Gaps in Early Education Employments. Berkeley, CA: Center for the Study of Child Care Employment, University of California, Berkeley. Retrieved from https://cscce.berkeley.edu/racial-wage-gaps-in-early-education-employment/.

Austin, L. J., Whitebook, M., Dade, A., & Williams, A. (2021). *The American rescue plan: Recommendations for addressing early educator compensation and supports.* Center for the Study of Child Care Employment. Berkeley: University of California. https://cscce.berkeley.edu/arpa-reccomendations-ece-workforce

Austin, L. J., Whitebook, M., & Williams, A. (2021). *Early care and education is in crisis: Biden can interview.* Center for the Study of Child Care Employment. Berkeley: University of California.

Balduzzi, L. (2015). Beyond 'transition' from home to early childhood services. The Italian approach of *ambientamento*. 5th Meeting of the Transatlantic Forum on Inclusive Early Years, Dublin, January 22th-28th.

Ball, S. J. (2013). *Foucault, power and education.* London: Routledge.

Ball, S. J. (2015). What is policy? 21 years later: Reflection on the possibilities of policy research. *Discourse: Studies in the Cultural Politics of Education, 36*(3), 306–313.

Ball, S. J. (2016). Subjectivity as a site of struggle: Refusing neoliberalism?. *British Journal of Sociology of Education, 37*(8), 1129–1146.

Ball, S. J. (2017). *The education debate* (3rd ed). Bristol: Policy Press.

Ball, S. J. (2021). Preface. In G. Roberts-Holmes and P. Moss, *Neoliberalism and early childhood education: Markets, imaginaries and governance.* Abingdon: Routledge

Bambra, C. (2005). Cash versus services: "worlds of welfare" and the decommodification of cash benefits and health care services. *Journal of Social Policy, 34*(2), 195–213.

Barnehageopprøret. 2021. "Then it's finally zero hours". https://barnehageoppror.com/ Barnehageopprøret- info. "Kjære Barnehageopprørere II disse to årene har situasjonen gått fra vondt til verre for barnehagesektoren. Bemanningskrisa vi nå ser". Facebook. https://www.facebook.com/bhgoppror2016/

Barnett, A. (2020). Out of the Belly of Hell: COVID-19 and the humanisation of globalization. openDemocracy. www.opendemocracy.net/en/opendemocracyuk/out-belly-hell-shutdown-and-humanisation-globalisation/.

Barry, E., & Sorenson, M. S. (2018). In Denmark, harsh new laws for immigrant 'ghettos' *New York Times*, July 2, 2018 https://www.nytimes.com/2018/07/01/world/europe/denmark-immigrant-ghettos.html

Becker, G. (2002). *Human capital*. Paper given at the University of Montevideo. (www.um.edu.uy/docs/revistafcee/2002/humancapitalBecker.pdf

Bellemare, G. (2019). *Le contexte des services de garde au québec: Vers une logique d'entreprise réseau hiérarchisée*. Quebec: Université du Québec en Outaouais.

Beresford, P. (2005). Redistributing profit and loss: The new economics of the market and social welfare. *Critical Social Policy*, 25(4), 464–482.

Berman, S. (2019). 'Interregnum or Transformation', blog for *Social Europe*, 9 December 2019. (www.socialeurope.eu/interregnum-or-transformation).

Bernard van Leer Foundation. (2001). La participación de padres y madres en programas de desarrollo infantil temprano. *Espacio Para La Infancia*, 16(Enero 2001). Retrieved from http://www.bernardvanleer.org/La_participacion_de_padres_y_madres_en_programas_de_desarrollo_infantil_temprano

Bernazzani, O., Côté, C., & Tremblay, R. E. (2001). Early parent training to prevent disruptive behavior problems and delinquency in children. *The Annals of the American Academy of Political and Social Science*, 578(1), 90–103.

Bettio, F., & Plantenga, J. (2004). Comparing care regimes in Europe. *Feminist Economics*, 10(1), 85–113.

Bezanson, K., Bevan, A., & Lysack, M. (2020). From stabilization to stimulus and beyond: A roadmap to social and economic recovery. *First policy response*. https://papers.ssrn.com/sol3/papers.cfm?abstract_id=3580746

Bhabha, H. K. (1994). *The location of culture*. London: Routledge.

Bhambra, G. K. (2014). Postcolonial and decolonial dialogues. *Postcolonial Studies*, 17(2), 115–121. DOI: 10.1080/13688790.2014.966414

Biesta, G. J. J. (2011). *Learning democracy in school and society: Education, life-long leanring and the politics of citizenship*. Rotterdam: Sense Publishers.

Billett, S. (2004). Working participatory practices : Conceptualising workplaces as learning environments. *Journal of Workplace Learning*, 16(5/6), 312–324.

Billett, S. (2008). Les pratiques participatives sur le lieu de travail : Apprentissage et remaniement de pratiques culturelles. *Pratiques De Formation/Analyses*, 54, 149–164.

Bishop, R., Berryman, M., Tiakiwai, S., & Richardson, C. (2003). *Te Kōtahitanga: The Experiences of Year 9 and 10 Māori Students in Mainstream Classrooms*. Retrieved from New Zealand: https://www.educationcounts.govt.nz/publications/maori/english-medium-education/9977/5375

Blanco, R., Umayahara, M., & Reveco, O. (2004). *Participación de las familias en la Educación Infantil Latinoamericana*. Retrieved from http://unesdoc.unesco.org/images/0013/001390/139030s.pdf

Blau, D. M. (Ed.) (1991). Introduction. In *Economics of child care* (pp. 1–9). New York: Russel Sage Foundation.

Bloch, M., Holmlund, K., Moqvist, I., & Popkewitz, T. S. (Eds.) (2003). Global and local patterns of governing the child, family, their care and education: An introduction. In *Governing children, families and education: Restructuring the welfare state* (pp. 3–34). Springer.

Bloom, P. (2013). Fight for your alienation: The fantasy of employability and the ironic struggle for self-exploitation. *Ephemera: Theory & Politics in Organizations*, 13(4), 785–807.

Bockel, J. M. (2010). *La prévention de la délinquance des jeunes. Rapport à Monsieur le Président de la République*. Paris: Secrétaire d'Etat à la Justice.

Boston Area Day Care Worker United News. (January–February, 1982). https://drive.google.com/drive/u/0/folders/1WpcsgxajhTn1jakQcSfAbfajC-yWN-0p

Bourdieu, P., & Passeron, J. C. (1970). *Le reproduction. Eléments pour une théorie du système d'enseignement*. Paris: Editions de Minui.

Bouyala, N., & Roussille, B. (1982). *L'enfant dans la vie, une politique pour la petite enfance*. Paris: La documentation française.

Bove, C. (2007). Parent involvement. In R. S. New & M. Cochran (Eds.), *Early childhood education: An international encyclopedia* (pp. 1141–1145), 4, Westport CT: Praeger Publishers.

Boyer, M., Gerst, C., & Eastwood, S. (1990). *Between a rock and a hard place: Raising rates to wage raises*. Minneapolis Child Care Worker Alliance.

BrightPath (2022). Brightpath. https://brightpathkids.com/home/

Brogaard-Clausen, S., & Ringsmose, C. (2017). The professional identity of the Danish pedagogue: Historical root in an education with focus on democracy, creativity, Dannelse and a 'Childhood Logic'. In *Nordic social pedagogical approach to early years* (pp. 237–252). Cham: Springer.

Brookes Publishing. (2022). Teaching Pyramid Observation Tool https://brookespublishing.com/product/tpot/.

Brostrom, S. (2013). Understanding *Te Whāriki* from a Danish perspective. In J. Nuttall (Ed.), *Weaving te whāriki. Aotearoa New Zealand's early childhood curriculum document in theory and practice*. (2nd ed., pp. 239–257). Wellington, New Zealand: New Zealand Council for Educational Research.

Brougère, G. (2002). L'exception française: l'école maternelle face à la diversité des formes préscolaires. *Les Dossiers Des Sciences De l'éducation*, 7, 9–17.

Brougère, G., & Moreau, A. (2014). Participation parentale, pratiques partagées et diversité. In S. Rayna & G. Brougère (Eds.), *Petites enfants, migrations et diversités* (pp. 137–164). Bruxelles: P.I.E. Peter Lang.

Brougère, G., & Rayna, S. (2000). *Traditions et innovations dans l'éducation préscolaire. Perspectives internationales*. Lyon: INRP.

Brown, W. (2016). Sacrificial citizenship: Neoliberalism, human capital and austerity politics. *Constellations*, 23(1), 3–14.

Bruner, J. (1996). *The culture of education*. Harvard University Press.

Burman, E. (1997). Psychology: Market, metaphor and metamorphosis. *Culture & Psychology*, 3(2), 143–152.

Burman, E. (2008). *Deconstructing developmental psychology*. East Sussex: Routledge.

Burns, J. (1999). *Kindergarten and primary teachers. A comparison of their work*. Top Drawer Consultants.

Cagliari, P., Castagnetti, M., Giudici, C., Rinaldi, C., Vecchi, V., & Moss, P. (2016). *Loris Malaguzzi and the Schools of Reggio Emilia: Selected writings and speeches 1945–1993*. Abingdon: Routledge.

Cameron, C., & Moss, P. (Eds.) (2020). *Transforming early childhood in England: Towards a democratic education*. London: UCL Press.

Cannella, G. S., & Viruru, R. (2005). Childhood and cultural studies: Section introduction. *Journal of Curriculum Theorizing*, 21(3), 131.

Carney, M. (2020). The Reith lectures: How we get what we value. Retrieved from https://downloads.bbc.co.uk/radio4/reith2020/Reith_2020_Lecture_1_transcript.pdf

Carr, M., Mitchell, L., & Rameka, L. (2016). Some thoughts about the value of an OECD international assessment framework for early childhood services in Aotearoa New Zealand. *Contemporary Issues in Early Childhood*, 17(4), 450–454. https://doi.org/10.1177/1463949116680705

Center for the Study of Child Care Employment. (2019). *Creating better child care jobs, model work standards.* https://cscce.berkeley.edu/creating-better-child-care-jobs-model-work-standards/

Center for the Study of Child Care Employment. (2020). *California child care at the brink data snapshot.* Center for the Study of Child Care Employment.

Cleveland, G., & Krashinsky, M. (2002). *Financing ECEC services in OECD countries. OECD Occasional Papers.* Retrieved fromhttps://www.oecd.org/education/school/28123665.pdf

Cleveland, G., & Krashinsky, M. (2004). *The quality gap: A study of nonprofit and commercial child care centres in Canada.* http://www.peelearlyyears.com/pdf/Research/CANADA%20EARLY%20YEARS/.pdf

Child Care Employee News, V1 N1. (January 1982). https://cscce.berkeley.edu/wp-content/uploads/2022/06/Child-Care-Employee-News-Jan-March-1982.pdf

Childcare resource and research unit (CRRU). (2021). *For-profit Child Care Quebec Profile.*

Christie & Co. (2020). 'What does Covid-19 mean for the childcare market?' (https://www.christie.com/news-resources/blogs/what-does-covid-19-mean-for-the-childcare-market/)

City of Toronto. (2020). *Assessment for Quality Improvement.* City of Toronto. Retrieved November24fromhttps://www.toronto.ca/community-people/community-partners/early-learning-child-care-partners/assessment-for-quality-improvement-aqi/

Cadart, M. L. (2006). *Des parents dans la crèche: Utopie ou réalité?* [Parents in the nursery: utpy or reality?]. Toulouse: Érès.

Cadart, M. L. (2008). *Les crèches dans un réseau de prévention précoce.* [Childcare centres in a network of early prevention]. Toulouse: Érès.

Case, W. (2008). Hybrid politics and new competitiveness: Hong Kong's 2007 chief executive election. *East Asia, 25*, 365–388.

CASIOPE. (2022). Les outils CLASS® et formations https://casiope.org/class/

CEC. (2006). *Participación : Aportes para una Educación de Calidad. Sistematización de Experiencias de la Red de Centros Comunitarios de Educación.* Santiago: Red de Centros Comunitarios de Educación.

Census and Statistics Department. (1996a). *1996 population by-census: Summary results.* Hong Kong: Government Press.

Census and Statistics Department. (1996b). *Hong Kong annual digest of statistics.* Hong Kong: Government Press.

CEP-Enfance. (2021). Enfance, l'état d'urgence. Toulouse: Erès.

Chan, M. K. (1997). The legacy of the British administration of Hong Kong: A view from Hong Kong. *The China Quarterly (London), 151*, 567–582.

Chang, H.-J. (2011). *23 things they don't tell you about capitalism.* London: Penguin Books.

Chief Executive. (2006). *2006-07 policy address.* https://www.policyaddress.gov.hk/06-07/eng/policy.html

Chief Executive. (2013). *2013 policy address.* https://www.policyaddress.gov.hk/2013/eng/index.html

Clarke, J. (2005). New labour's citizens: Activated, empowered, responsibilized, abandoned? *Critical Social Policy, 25*(4), 447–463.

Clausen, S. B., & Ringmose, C. (2017). The professional identity of the Danish pedagogue: Historical root in an education with focus on democracy, creativity, Dannelse and a 'childhood logic'. In C. Ringsmose and G. Kragh-Müller, (Eds.), *Nordic social pedagogical approach to early years,* (pp. 237–252). Copenhagen, Denmark: Springer.

Cleveland, G. (2008). *If it don't make dollars, does that mean that it don't make sense? Commercial, nonprofit and municipal child care in the city of Toronto*. Toronto: Department of Management, University of Toronto Scarborough.

Collectif, L. (2006). *Pas de zéro de conduite pour les enfants de 3 ans!*. Ramonville Saint-Agne: Érès.

Collectif CEP-Enfance. (2021). *Enfance, l'état d'urgence, nos exigences pour 2022 et après*. [Childhood, a state of emergency. Our demands, for 2022 and beyond]. Toulouse: Erès.

Commission on Poverty. (2007). *Report of the Commission on Poverty*. Commission on Poverty. https://www.povertyrelief.gov.hk/archive/2007/eng/report.htm

Connell, R. (2013). Why do market 'reforms' persistently increase inequality? *Discourse: Studies in the Cultural Politics of Education, 34*(2), 279–285.

Cornejo, R., González, J., & Caldichoury, J.-P. (2007). *Participación e incidencia de la sociedad civil en las políticas educativas: El caso chileno*. Colección Libros FLAPE, Foro Latinoamericano de Políticas Educativas. Buenos Aires: Fundación laboratorio de Políticas Públicas.

Cox, R. W. (1999). Civil society at the turn of the millennium: Prospects for an alternative world order. *Review of International Studies, 25*(1), 3–28.

Crehan, K. (2016). *Gramsci's common sense. Inequality and its narratives*. Durham: Duke University Press.

Cryer, D., & Burchinal, M. (1997). Parents as child care consumers. *Early Childhood Research Quarterly, 12*, 35–58.

Cunha, F., Heckman, J. J., Lochner, L., & Masterov, D. (2005). Interpreting the evidence on life cycle skill formation. *British Educational Research Journal, 30*(5), 713–730. https://doi.org/10.3386/w11331

Dahlberg, G. (2003). Pedagogy as a loci of an ethics of an encounter. In *Governing children, families, and education* (pp. 261–286). New York: Palgrave Macmillan.

Dahlberg, G., & Asen, G. (2002). Evaluation and regulation: a question of empowerment. *Rethinking Welfare: A Critical Perspective*.

Dahlberg, G., & Moss, P. (2005). *Ethics and politics in early childhood education*. Abingdon: Routledge.

Dahlberg, G., & Moss, P. (2007). Au-delà de la qualité, vers l'éthique et la politique en matière d'éducation préscolaire. In G. Brougère & M. Vandenbroeck (Eds.), *Repenser l'éducation des jeunes enfants* (pp. 53–76). Bruxelles: Peter Lang.

Dahlberg, G., Moss, P., & Pence, A. R. (1999). *Beyond quality in early childhood education and care: Postmodern perspectives*. Psychology Press.

Dahlberg, G., Moss, P., & Pence, A. R. (2013). *Beyond quality in early childhood education and care: Languages of evaluation*. Routledge.

Daley, M., & Bray, R. (2015). Parenting support in England. The bedding down of a new policy. *Social Policy & Society, 14*(4), 633–644.

Dalli, C. (2002). Being an early childhood teacher: Images of professional practice and professional identity during the experience of starting childcare. *New Zealand Journal of Educational Studies, 37*(1), 73–85.

Dalli, C., Miller, L., & Urban, M. (2012). Early childhood grows up: Towards a critical ecology of the profession. In *Early childhood grows up* (pp. 3–19). Dordrecht: Springer.

Daly, M. (2013). Parenting support policies in Europe. *Families, Relationships and Societies, 2*(2), 159–174.

Daly, M. (2015). Parenting support as policy field: An analytic framework. *Social Policy & Society, 14*(4), 597–608.

Day, K. (2016). *Religious resistance to neoliberalism: Womanist and Black feminist perspectives*. Springer.

De Swaan, A. (1972). *Een boterham met tevredenheid. Gesprekken met arbeiders.* Amsterdam: Van Gennep.

Décret n°2000-762 du 1er août 2000 relatif aux établissements et services d'accueil des enfants de moins de 6 ans. [Decree of August 1st 2000 on early childhood centres for children below 6 years of age].

Delannoi, P., Taguieff, A., & Trigano, S. (2004). *Le « communautarisme »: vrai concept et faux problèmes.* Conference organised by Groupe d'études et d'observation de la démocratie & Cevipof), Paris.

Delhon, L. (2021). *Crèches privées, les dérives d'un business biberonné à l'argent public.* [Privae childcare. Abuse of public money]. Médiapart 15/07/2021. www.mediapart.fr

Deleuze, G., & Guattari, F. (1988). *A thousand plateaus: Capitalism and schizophrenia.* Bloomsbury Publishing.

Denboba, A., Hasan, A., & Wodon, Q. (2015). *Early childhood education and development in Indonesia: An assessment of policies using SABER.* Washington: The World Bank.

Department of Education, Employment and Workplace Relations (DEEWR). (2009). *Belonging, being and becoming: The early years learning framework for Australia.* Australian Government Department of Education, Employment and Workplace Relations for the Council of Australian Governments, Commonwealth of Australia.

Di Giandomenico, I., & Picchio M. (in press). Children's transition between home and ECEC services: Innovative practices during the COVID-19 pandemic. In L. Henderson, H. Ebrahim & K. Bussey (Eds.), *Early childhood education and care in a global pandemic: How the sector responded, spoke back and generated knowledge.* London: Routledge.

Devlieghere, J., Li, Y., & Vandenbroeck, M. (2020). Beyond the veil of parents: Deconstructing the concept of parental involvement in early childhood education and care. *Early Years.* DOI: 10.1080/09575146.2020.1840526

Diaz-Diaz, C., Semenec, P., & Moss, P. (2019). Opening for debate and contestation: OECD's International Early Learning and Child Well-being Study and the testing of children's learning outcomes. *Policy Futures in Education,* 17(1), 1–10.

Dolto, F. (1995). Destins d'enfants. Paris: Gallimard

Doocy, S., Kim, Y., Montoya, E., & Chávez, R. (2021). *The consequences of invisibility: COVID-19 and the human toll on California early educators.* Center for the Study of Child Care Employment. Berkeley: University of California.

Early Childhood Pedagogies Collaboratory. (2020). Conditions for Moving Beyond "Quality" in Canadian Early Childhood Education: an occasional paper. Ontario: Early Childhood Pedagogies Collaboratory.

Education Bureau. (2012). *Replies to initial written questions raised by Finance Committee Members in examining the estimates of expenditure 2012–13.* https://www.legco.gov.hk/yr11-12/english/fc/fc/w_q/edb-e.pdf

Education Bureau. (2016). *Policy on kindergarten education.* https://www.legco.gov.hk/yr15-16/english/panels/ed/papers/ed20160201cb4-542-1-e.pdf

Education Bureau. (2019). *Replies to initial written questions raised by Finance Committee Members in examining the estimates of expenditure 2019–20.* https://www.edb.gov.hk/attachment/en/about-edb/press/legco/replies-to-fc/19-20-edb-e.pdf

Education Commission. (2000). *Learning for life. Learning through life: Reform proposals for the education system in Hong Kong.* https://www.e-c.edu.hk/doc/en/publications_and_related_documents/education_reform/Edu-reform-eng.pdf

Education and Manpower Bureau. (2006). *Item for Finance Committee.* http://www.legco.gov.hk/yr06-07/english/fc/fc/papers/f06-29e.pdf.

Education Review Office. (1997). *What counts as quality in kōhanga reo?* Wellington, New Zealand: Author.

Edwards, C. P., Gandini, L., & Forman, G. E. (1993). *The hundred languages of children: The Reggio Emilia approach to early childhood education*. Ablex Publishing.

Edwards, S., Blaise, M., & Hammer, M. (2009). Beyond developmentalism? Early childhood teachers' understandings of multiage grouping in early childhood education and care. *Australasian Journal of Early Childhood, 34*(4), 55–63.

Ekpo, Selina Sunday (2018). Re-engineering human existence through foundation building. 64th Inaugural Lecture of the University of Uyo delivered on Thursday, August, 2018.

Esping-Anderson, G. (1990). *Three worlds of welfare capitalism*. Princeton University Press.

Esping-Andersen, G. (2009). *The incomplete revolution: Adapting to women's new roles*. Cambridge, UK Malden, Massachusetts: Polity.

Espinoza, V. (1988). *Para una historia de los pobres en la ciudad*. Santiago: SUR.

European Commission/EACEA/Eurydice. (2019). *Key data on early childhood education and care in Europe. Eurydice report*. Publications Office of the European Union.

European Commission. (2012). Communication of the Commission on the application of the European Union State aid rules to compensation granted for the provision of services of general economic interest. *Official Journal C8, 11/02/2012*.

Ewens, J. (2019). "You kind of have to be a bit superhuman". Early childhood teacher beliefs about what it takes to be a good teacher: A discourse analysis [Doctoral thesis, The University of Waikato, Hamilton, New Zealand]. Research Commons. http://researchcommons.waikato.ac.nz/

Fafunwa, A. B. (1967). *New perspectives in African education*. London: Macmillan Education Limited.

Fafunwa, A. B. (1974). *History of education in Nigeria*. London: George Allen & Unwin.

Farris, S. R., & Marchetti, S. (2017). From the commodification to the corporatization of care: European Perspectives and debates. *Social Politics, 24*(2), 109–131.

Fenech, M. (2012). Discerning childcare quality: Parents as potential informants of policy beyond regulation. *Critical Studies in Education, 53*(3), 327–345.

Ferreiro, S. (2012). *Retrato de la Desigualdad en Chile*. Senado de la República. Gestión Editorial y Diseño: COMUN & K Producciones Ltda.

First, A. (2016). Common sense, good sense and commercial television. *International Journal of Communication, 10*, 530–548.

Fischman, G. E., & McLaren, P. (2005). Rethinking critical pedagogy and the Gramscian and Freirean legacies: From organic to committed intellectuals or critical pedagogy, commitment, and praxis. *Cultural Studies ↔ Critical Methodologies, 5*(4), 425–447. DOI: 10.1177/1532708605279701

Forgacs, D. (2000). *The Gramsci reader*. New York: New York University Press.

Formen, A. (2017). In human-capital we trust, on developmentalism we act: The case of Indonesian early childhood education policy. In M. Li, J. Fox, & S. Grieshaber (Eds.), *Contemporary issues and challenge in early childhood education in the Asia-Pacific region* (pp. 125–142). Singapore: Springer Singapore.

Formen, A., & Nuttall, J. (2014). Tensions between discourses of development, religion, and human capital in early childhood education policy texts: The case of Indonesia. *International Journal of Early Childhood, 46*(1), 15–31. https://doi.org/10.1007/s13158-013-0097-y

Fossati, D. (2019). The resurgence of ideology in Indonesia: Political Islam, Aliran and political behaviour. *Journal of Current Southeast Asian Affairs, 38*(2), 119–148.

Foucault, M. (1978). *The history of sexuality. vol. 1, an introduction*. (Translated by Robert Hurley). New York: Pantheon.

Foucault, M. (1980). *Michael Foucault: Power knowledge*. Herrtfordshire: Harvester Wheatsheaf.

Foucault, M. (1990). *Politics, philosophy, culture. Interviews and other writings 1977–1984*. London: Routledge.
Foucault, M. (Ed.) (1994/2001). Le jeu de Michel Foucault. In *Dits et écrtis II* (Vol. 2, pp. 298–329). Paris: Gallimard.
Foucault, M. (2008). *The birth of biopolitics: Lectures at the Collège de France, 1978–1979*. New York: Palgrave Macmillan.
Fournier, A.-C. (2018). Le rôle de l'État dans les enjeux de formation issus de la coexistence des groupes professionnels des éducatrices à la petite enfance et des enseignantes à l'éducation préscolaire [the role of the state in training challenges due to the coexistance of professional groups of early childhood educators and preschool teachers]. *Canadian Journal for New Scholars in Education/Revue Canadienne Des Jeunes Chercheures Et Chercheurs En éducation*, *9*(1).
Fox, L., Hemmeter, M. L., & Snyder, P. S. (2014). *Teaching pyramid observation tool for preschool classrooms (TPOT). Research* Edition. Baltimore, MD: Paul H. Brookes.
Freire, P. (1970/2018). *Pedagogy of the oppressed* (M. B. Ramos, Trans.). Bloomsbury.
Friedman, M. (1962/82) *Capitalism and freedom* (1982 edn). Chicago, IL: University of Chicago Press.
Friendly, M., Forer, B., Vickerson, R., & Mohamed, S. (2021). COVID-19 and childcare in Canada: A tale of ten provinces and three territories. *Journal of Childhood Studies*, *46*(3), 42–53.
Friendly, M., & Prentice, S. (2009). *Childcare* (Vol. 2). Brunswick Books.
Fujimoto, G. (2000). *La Educación No-Formal: Experiencias Latinoamericanas de Atención a la Infancia: la No-escolarización como alternativa*. Retrieved from http://www.oei.es/inicial/articulos/educacion_noformal_alternativa.pdf
Fung, C. K. H., & Lam, C. C. (2009). The pre-primary education voucher scheme of Hong Kong: A promise of quality education provision? *Education Journal*, *36*(1–2), 153–170.
Furedi, F. (2001). *Paranoid parenting. Abandon your anxieties and be a good parent*. London: Penguin books.
Gallagher, A. (2018). The business of care: Marketization and the new geographies of childcare. *Progress in Human Geography*, *42*(5), 706–722.
Garcés, M. (2002). *Tomando su sitio. El movimiento de pobladores de Santiago, 1957–1970*. Santiago: LOM.
Gaunt, C. (2021). 'Nursery group sells freeholds in £34m sale-and-leaseback deal', *Nursery World*, 6 September 2021 (https://www.nurseryworld.co.uk/news/article/nursery-group-sells-freeholds-in-34m-sale-and-leaseback-deal)
Geens, N., & Vandenbroeck, M. (2013). Early childhood education and care as a space for social support in urban contexts of diversity. *European Early Childhood Education Research Journal*, *21*(3), 407–419.
Geinger, F., Vandenbroeck, M., & Roets, G. (2014). Parenting as performance: Parents as consumers and (de)constructors of mythic parenting and childhood ideals. *Childhood*, *21*(4), 488–501.
George, S. (1999). 'A short history of neoliberalism: Twenty years of elite economics and emerging opportunities for change', paper presented at conference *Economic Sovereignty in a Globalising World*, Bangkok, Thailand, 24–26 March 1999 (www.tni.org/en/article/short-history-neoliberalism).
Giampino, S. (2016). *Développement du jeune enfant, modes d'accueil, formation des professionnels.* [Early child development, childcare and staff training]. Paris: Ministère de la santé et de la solidarité. https://solidarites-sante.gouv.fr/IMG/pdf/rapport-giampino-vf_modif-17_08_16.pdf

Gillies, V., Edwards, R., & Horsley, N. (2017). *Challenging the politics of early intervention: Who's' saving' children and why.* Policy Press.

Gingras, L.; Audet, N., & Nanhou, V. (2011). *Enquête sur l'utilisation, les besoins et les préférences des familles en matière de services de garde 2009: Portrait québécois et régional.* Québec: Institut de la statistique du Québec.

Giroux, H. (2010). *On critical pedagogy.* New York: Continuum.

Giroux, H. (2020). *On critical pedagogy* (2nd ed.). London: Bloomsbury Academic.

Gneezy, U., & Rustichini, A. (2000). A fine is a price. *Journal of Legal Studies, 29*(1), 1–17.

Goodstadt, L. F. (1998). Hong Kong: An attachment to democracy. *Round Table (London), 87*(348), 485–503.

Government of British Columbia. (2019). *British Columbia Early Learning Framework.* Government of British Columbia. https://www2.gov.bc.ca/assets/gov/education/early-learning/teach/earlylearning/early_learning_framework.pdf

Government of Canada. (2020). Alberta Early Learning and Child Care Agreement https://www.canada.ca/en/early-learning-child-care-agreement/agreements-provinces-territories/alberta-2017.html

Government of the HKSAR Education Bureau. (2016). Education Bureau Circular No. 7/2016. Free Quality Kindergarten Education.

Government of New Brunswick. (2017). *New Brunswick Curriculum Framework for Early Learning and Child Care.* http://www2.gnb.ca/content/gnb/en/departments/education/elcc/content/curriculum/curriculum_framework.html

Government of Ontario. (2014). *How does learning happen: Ontario's pedagogy for the early years.* http://www.edu.gov.on.ca/childcare/HowLearningHappens.pdf

Government Secretariat. (1981). *The Hong Kong education system: Overall review of the Hong Kong education system.* Hong Kong: Government Press.

Governor. (1995). *Address by the right honourable Christopher Patten at the opening of the 1995/96 session of the legislative council on 11 October 1995.* Hong Kong: Government Press.

GovTribe. (2022). RFP - International Early Learning Study Pilot (iELS) - Solicitation https://govtribe.com/opportunity/federal-contract-opportunity/rfp-international-early-learning-study-pilot-iels-solicitation-edies17r0001

Gouvernement du Québec. (2021). Guide explicatif: Mesure d'évaluation et d'amélioration de la qualité éducative des services de garde à l'enfance – groupes d'enfants de 3 à 5 ans. https://www.mfa.gouv.qc.ca/fr/publication/Documents/Guide-explicatif-qual-educ.pdf

GRIT. (2022). Access, Support and Participation, Getting Ready Fort Inclusion Today. https://asapgrit.ca/about/

Growjo. (2022). Teachstone Revenue, Competitors and Alternatives https://growjo.com/company/Teachstone

GruppoCRC. (2021). *I diritti dell'infanzia e dell'adolescenza in Italia Risorse dedicate all'infanzia e all'adolescenza in Italia.* https://gruppocrc.net/tipo-documento/pubblicazioni.pdf

Haak, P., Vardell, R., & Whitebook, M. (2021, May 3). *Who Were the Worthy Wagers?* Center for the Study of Child Care Employment, University of California Berkeley. https://cscce.berkeley.edu/blog/who-were-the-worthy-wagers/

Hampton, M. (2016). *Hong Kong and British culture, 1945–97.* Manchester: Manchester University Press.

Hardy, C. (1986). *Hambre + Dignidad = Ollas Comunes.* Santiago: Programa de Economía del Trabajo (PET).

Hardy, C. (1987). *Organizarse para vivir. Pobreza urbana y organización popular*. Santiago: Programa de Economía del Trabajo (PET).

Harvey, D. (2005). *A brief history of neoliberalism*. Oxford: University Press.

Harvey, D. (2007). *A brief history of neoliberalism*. New York: Oxford University Press Inc.

Hasan, A., Hyson, M., & Chang, M. C. (Eds.) (2013). *Early childhood education and development in poor Villages of Indonesia: Strong foundations, later success*. Washington, D.C: International Bank for Reconstruction and Development/The World Bank. 10.1596/978-0-8213-9836-4

Haut Conseil de la famille, de l'enfance et de l'âge. (2018). *L'accueil des enfants de moins de trois ans. Tome I: Etat des lieux*. Paris: HCFEA.

Heberle, A. E., & Carter, A. S. (2020). Is poverty on young minds? Stereotype endorsement, disadvantage awareness, and social-emotional challenges in socioeconomically disadvantaged children. *Developmental Psychology, 56*(2), 336.

Heckman, J. J., & Masterov, D. V. (2007). The productivity argument for investing in young Children*. *Applied Economic Perspectives and Policy, 29*(3), 446–493. DOI: 10.1111/j.1467-9353.2007.00359.x

Hemmeter, M. L., Snyder, P., & Fox, L. (2018). Using the teaching pyramid observation tool (TPOT) to support implementation of social–emotional teaching practices. *School Mental Health, 10*(3), 202–213.

Henly, J., & Lyons, S. (2000). The negotiation of child care and employment demands among low-income parents. *Journal of Social Issues, 56*(4), 683–706.

Heydon, R., & Iannacci, L. (2008). *Early childhood curricula and the depathologizing of childhood*. Toronto, Buffalo and London: University of Toronto Press.

Hietamäki, J., Kuusiholma, J., Räikkönen, E., Alasuutari, M., Lammi-Taskula, J., Repo, K., Karila, K., Hautala, P., Kuukka, A., Paananen, M., Ruutiainen, V., & Eerola, P. (2017). *Varhaiskasvatus- ja lastenhoitoratkaisut yksivuotiaiden lasten perheissä: CHILDCARE-kyselytutkimuksen 2016 perustulokset* [Solutions on early childhood education and care in families with one-year-old children]. Helsinki: Terveyden ja hyvinvoinnin laitos (THL) [National Institute for Health and Welfare]. Työpaperi [Discussion paper] 24. https://www.julkari.fi/handle/10024/132438

Hiilamo, H. (2002). *The rise and fall of nordic family policy? Historical development and changes during the 1990s in Sweden and Finland*. Helsinki: Stakes.

Hiilamo, H., & Kangas, O. (2009). Trap for women or freedom to choose? The struggle over cash for child care schemes in Finland and Sweden. *Journal of Social Policy, 38*(3), 457–475.

Himmelweit, S., & Sigala, M. (2004). Choice and the relationship between identities and behaviour for mothers with pre-school children: Some implications for policy from a UK study. *Journal of Social Policy, 33*(3), 455–478.

Hinchleffe, E., & Aspen, M. (2021). *Are these companies the future of US child care?* Fortune Magazine Newsletter Broadsheet.

Hofferth, S., & Wissoker, D. (1992). Price, quality and income in child care choice. *Journal of Human Resources, 27*(1), 70–111.

Hong Kong Paediatric Society. (2017). *20 years review: Government's policies are unable to meet the needs*. http://www.hkpf.org.hk/download/20%20years%20child%20health%20policy%20review%20press%20release_Eng_20170621_HKPF.pdf

Hopman, M., & Knijn, G. C. M. (2017). *Happy children in the Netherlands - Positive parenting and problems to solve. Zeitschrift fur Familienforschung*, 2016/2017 (Special Issue 11), (pp. 257–272).

Hoshi-Watanabe, M., Musatti, T., Rayna, S., & Vandenbroeck M. (2015). Origins and rationale of centres for parents and young children together. *Child & Family Social Work, 20*(1), 62–71.

Humblet, P., & Vandenbroeck, M. (2007). Sauver l'enfant pour sauver le monde. Le care et la (re) construction de problèmes sociaux [saving the child to save the world. Care and (re)constructuction of social problems]. *Repenser l'éducation des jeunes enfants [Rethinking Early Childhood Education]*, 189–206.

Hytten, K., & Bettez, S. C. (2011). Understanding education for social justice. *Educational Foundations, 25*(1–2), 7–24.

Institut de la statistique du Québec (ISQ). (2004). Enquête québécoise sur la qualité des services de garde éducatifs 2003. https://statistique.quebec.ca/fr/document/enquete-quebecoise-sur-la-qualite-des-services-de-garde-educatifs-2003

Institut de la statistique du Québec (ISQ). (2015). Enquête québécoise sur la qualité des services de garde éducatifs 2014. https://statistique.quebec.ca/fr/document/enquete-quebecoise-sur-la-qualite-des-services-de-garde-educatifs-2014

Institut de la statistique du Québec (ISQ). (2022). Enquête québécoise sur la qualité des services de garde éducatifs (Grandir en qualité) 2003 et 2014. https://statistique.quebec.ca/fr/enquetes/realisees/enquete-quebecoise-sur-la-qualite-des-services-de-garde-educatifs-grandir-en-qualite

Institut National de la Recherche Médicale. (2005). *Troubles de conduites chez l'enfant et l'adolescent*. Paris: INSERM.

International Labour Office. (2013). ILO policy guidelines on the promotion of decent work for early childhood education personnel: Meeting of experts on policy guidelines on the promotion of decent work for early childhood education personnel: Geneva. International Labour Office. http://www.ilo.org/public/libdoc/ilo/2014/114B09_147_engl.pdf

International Labour Organisation (ILO). (2010). *ILO Declaration on Fundamental Principles and Rights at Work and its Follow-up*. Retrieved from https://www.ilo.org/declaration/thedeclaration/textdeclaration/lang–en/index.htm

Irvine, S., Thorpe, K., & McDonald, P. (2018). Low-paid 'women's work': Why early childhood educators are walking out. *The Conversation*. https://eprints.qut.edu.au/123027/

Jackson, M. (2016). Decolonising education. In J. Hutchings & J. Lee-Morgan (Eds.), *Decolonisation in Aotearoa: Education, research and practice* (pp. 39–47). Wellington, New Zealand: NZCER.

Janssen, J., & Vandenbroeck, M. (2018). (De)constructing parental involvement in early childhood curricular frameworks *European Early Childhood Education Research Journal, 26*(6), 813–832.

Janssen, J., Spruyt, B., & Vandenbroeck, M. (2021). Is everybody happy? Exploring the predictability of parent satisfaction with childcare in Flanders. *Early Childhood Research Quarterly, 55*, 97–106.

JUNJI. (2008). *Guía para la Construcción de Proyectos PMI*. Santiago: JUNJI.

Kaga, Y., Bennett, J., & Moss P. (2010). *Caring and learning together: A cross-national study of integration of early childhood care and education within education*. Paris: UNESCO. https://doi.org/10.1007/2288-6729-4-1-35

Kahuroa, R. (2021). *Critical pedagogy in early childhood education: Four case studies in Aotearoa New Zealand* [Doctoral thesis, The University of Waikato Hamilton, New Zealand]. Research Commons https://hdl.handle.net/10289/14527

References

Kamenarac, O. (2019). *Discursive constructions of teachers' professional identities in early childhood policies and practice in Aotearoa New Zealand: Complexities and contradictions* [Doctoral thesis, The University of Waikato, Hamilton, New Zealand]. Research Common. https://hdl.handle.net/10289/12363

Kamenarac, O. (2021). Business managers in children's playground: Exploring a problematic (or not!) Identity construction of early childhood teachers in New Zealand. *Contemporary Issues in Early Childhood*, 1–13. https://doi.org/10.1177/1463949121989362

Karila, K. (2012). A Nordic perspective on early childhood education and care policy. *European Journal of Education*, 47(4), 584–595. https://doi.org/10.1111/ejed.12007

Karsten, L. (2015). Middle-class childhood and parenting culture in high-rise Hong Kong: On scheduled lives, the school trap and a new urban idyll. *Children's Geographies*, 13(5), 556–570.

Kela. (2021). https://www.kela.fi/web/en/home-care-allowance-amount-and-payment.

Keller, J., & Kittay, E. F. (2017). Feminist ethics of care. In *The Routledge Companion to Feminist Philosophy* (pp. 540–555). Routledge.

Kemendikbud. (2020). *Statistik PAUD Pendidikan Anak Usia Dini 2019/2020*. Jakarta: Kemendikbud.

Kemendikbud. (2021). Tahun 2021, BOP PAUD Rp 4,01 Triliun untuk 6,6 Juta Siswa. Retrieved from https://anggunpaud.kemdikbud.go.id/index.php/berita/index/20210106100336/Tahun-2021-BOP-PAUD-Rp-401-Triliun-untuk-6-6-Juta-Siswa

Kennedy, D. (2002). The child and postmodern subjectivity. *Educational Theory*, 52(2), 155–167.

Kennedy, A. (2006). Globalisation, global English: 'futures trading' in early childhood education. *Early Years*, 26(3), 295–306.

Khanif, A. (2020). *Religious minorities, Islam and the law: International human rights and islamic law in Indonesia*. Routledge.

Kincheloe, J. L. (2008). *Critical pedagogy primer*. Peter Lang Publishing.

Kirschenbaum, L. A. (2013). *Small comrades: Revolutionizing childhood in Soviet Russia, 1917–1932*. Routledge.

Knijn, T., & Hopman, M. (2015). Parenting support in the Dutch "participation society". *Social Policy & Society*, 14(4), 645–656.

Knijn, T., & Ostner, I. (2002). Commodification and de-commodification. In B. Hobson, J. Lewis & B. Siim (Eds.), *Contested concepts in gender and social politics* (pp. 141–169). Edward Elgar Publishing.

Koh, A., & Ziqi, L. (2021). 'Start-up' capital: Cultivating the elite child in an elite international kindergarten in Shenzhen, China. *Oxford Review of Education*, 1–16.

Kolawole, D. O. (1989). *Nursery and early primary classes in Nigeria: A guide to effective teaching and organization*. Ibadan: Vantage Publishers.

Kumon Institute of Education. (2022). Kumon's History. https://www.kumongroup.com/eng/about-kumon/history/?ID=eng_about_report

Kuusisto, A. (2022). The place of religion in early childhood education and care. In *the Routledge international handbook of the place of religion in early childhood education and care* (pp. 1–16). Routledge.

Kwan, P., Li, B. Y. M., & Lee, T. T. L. (2020). Neoliberal challenges in public schools in Hong Kong: An East Asian model? In K. Arar, D. Örücü & J. Wilkinson (Eds.), *Neoliberalism and education systems in conflict exploring challenges across the globe* (pp. 29–42). New York: Routledge.

Lahtinen, J., & Svartsjö, M. (2020). *Kotihoidontuen ja yksityisen hoidon tuen kuntalisät ja palveluseteli* [Child home care allowance and private day care allowance and day care vouchers]. Selvitys kotihoidontuen ja yksityisen hoidon tuen kuntalisistä ja niiden maksatusperusteista sekä palvelusetelistä. Helsinki: Kuntaliitto. https://www.kuntaliitto.fi/sites/default/files/media/file/Kotihoidontuen-kuntalisat-2020.pdf

Lamont, M., & Pierson, P. (2019). Inequality generation & persistence as multidimensional processes: An interdisciplinary agenda. *Dedalus, 148*(3), 5–18.

Langford, R. (Ed.) (2019). *Theorizing feminist ethics of care in early childhood practice: Possibilities and dangers.* Bloomsbury.

Langford, R., Bezanson, K., & Powell, A. (2019). Imagining a caring early childhood education and care system in Canada: A thought experiment. *International Journal of Care and Caring.* https://www.ingentaconnect.com/content/tpp/ijcc/pre-prints/content-ijccd1900068.

Langford, R., Powell, A., & Bezanson, K. (2020). Imagining a caring early childhood education and care system in Canada: A thought experiment. *International Journal of Care and Caring, 4*(1), 109–115.

Langford, R., Prentice, S., Albanese, P., Summers, B., Messina-Goertzen, B., & Richardson, B. (2013). Professionalization as an advocacy strategy: A content analysis of Canadian child care social movement organizations' 2008 discursive resources. *Early Years, 33*(3), 302–317.

Langford, R., & Richardson, B. (2020). Ethics of care in practice: An observational study of interactions and power relations between children and educators in urban Ontario early childhood settings. *Journal of Childhood Studies, 45*(1), 33–47. https://doi.org/10.18357/jcs00019398

Langford, R., Richardson, B., Albaense, P., Bezanson, K., Prentice, S., & Jaqueline, W. (2017). Caring about care: Reasserting care as integral to early childhood education and care practice, politics and policies in Canada. *Global Studies of Childhood, 7*(4), 311–322. https://doi.org/10.1177/2043610617747978

Langford, T. (2011). From social movement to marginalised interest group: Advocating for quality childcare in Alberta. In S. Prentice (Ed.), *Changing child care: Five decades of child care advocacy and policy in Canada* (pp. 63–75). Toronto: Fernwood.

Lanyasunya, A. R., & Lesolayia, M. S. (2001). El-barta child and family project. Working Paper in early childhood development No. 28. The Hague, The Netherlands: Bernard van Leer Foundations.

Lears, T. J. J. (1985). The concept of cultural hegemony: Problems and Possibilities. *The American Historical Review, 90*(3), 567–593.

Lee, E. (2014). Introduction. In E. Lee, J. Bristow, C. Faircloth, & J. Macvarish (Eds.), *Parenting culture studies.* (pp. 1–22). London: Palgrave MacMillan.

Lemay, L., Lehrer, J., & Naud, M. (2017). Le CLASS pour mesurer la qualité des interactions en contextes culturels variés [the CLASS to measure interaction quality in varied cultural contexts]. *Les dossiers des sciences de l'éducation, 37,* 15–34.

Leseman, P. P. M. (2009). The impact of high quality education and care on the development of young children: Review of the literature. In European Commission (Ed.), *Tackling social and cultural inequalities through early childhood education and care in Europe* (pp. 18–49). https://doi.org/10.2797/18055

Leung, C. Y. (2012). *2012 chief executive election: Introduction to candidates* (in Chinese). https://www.elections.gov.hk/ce2012/pdf/Candidate1.pdf

Li, Y., Li, J., Devlieghere, J., & Vandenbroeck, M. (2021). What parents and teachers say about their relationships in ECEC: a study in rural China. *European Early Childhood Education Research Journal.*

Li, Y., & Vandenbroeck, M. (2020). Conceptualisations of parent involvement in early childhood education in China. *Asia-Pacific Journal of Research in Early Childhood Education, 14*(1), 169–192.

Lightfoot-Rueda, T. (2018). Education for a competitive Asia: Questioning the discourse of human capital. *Policy Futures in Education, 16*(1), 43–52. DOI: 10.1177/1478210317736208

Lim, S. (2017). Marketization and corporation of early childhood care and education in Singapore. In *Contemporary issues and challenge in early childhood education in the Asia-Pacific region* (pp. 17–32). Springer: Singapore.

Lim, M., Kim, J., & Lee, K. (2021). Subcontracted mothering: A discourse on professionalism in childcare in South Korea. *European Early Childhood Education Research Journal, 29*(6). DOI: 10.1080/1350293X.2021.1985560

Llewellyn, J., Hancock, G., Kirst, M. & Roeloffs, K. (1982). *A perspective on education in Hong Kong: Report by a visiting panel.* Hong Konh: Hong Kong Government Printer.

Lloyd, E. (2019). Reshaping and reimagining marketised early childhood education and care systems. *Zeitschrift für Pädagogik (Beiheft), 65*, 89–106.

Lloyd, E. (2012). Childcare markets: An introduction. In E. Lloyd & H. Penn (Eds.), *Childcare markets. Can they deliver an equitable service?* (pp. 3–18). Bristol: Policy Press.

Lloyd, E., & Penn, H. (Eds.) (2012). *Childcare markets: Can they deliver an equitable service.* The Policy Press. https://doi.org/10.1332/policypress/9781847429339.001.0001

Lloyd, E., & Penn, H. (2014). Childcare markets in an age of austerity. *European Early Childhood Education Research Journal, 22*(3), 386–396.

Lo, S. H. (1998). The politics of sustaining, reversing and constraining private democratisation in Hong Kong. *Australian Journal of International Affairs, 52*(3), 273–292.

Lo, S. H. (2021). Hong Kong in 2020: National security law and truncated autonomy. *Asian Survey, 61*(1), 34–42.

Lui, T. L. (2011). *Middle class worries: After the crisis.* Hong Kong: Up Publication Limited.

Luschei, T. F., & Zubaidah, I. (2012). Teacher training and transitions in rural Indonesian schools: A case study of Bogor, West Java. *Asia Pacific Journal of Education, 32*(3), 333–350. https://doi.org/10.1080/02188791.2012.711241

Maduewesi, E. J. (1999). *Early childhood education: Theory and practice.* Ibadan: Macmillan Nigeria Publishers Limited.

Maduewesi, E. J. (2005). *Benchmarks and global trends in education.* Benin city, Nigeria: Dasylva influence Enterprises.

Majebi, Idowu O., & Oduolowu, E. A. (2019). *Integrating culturally responsive practices into pre-primary and lower primary school as an innovative classroom practices for effective education in fundamentals of pre-school and primary school teacher preparation in Nigeria.* In Esther Oduolowu, I. A. Salami, & M. D. Amosun (Eds.), Department of Early Childhood and Educational Foundations. Nigeria: University of Ibadan.

Majebi, O. I., & Oduolowu, E. (2020). Concept of Ọmọlúàbí in pre-primary and primary school classrooms and sustenance of effective democracy in Nigeria. *Journal of Social Studies Association of Nigeria (SOSAN), 10*(2), 259–279.

Makovichuk, L., Hewes, J., Lirette, P., & Thomas, N. (2014). *Play, participation and possibilties: A early learning and child care curriculum framework for Alberta.* G. o. Alberta. http://childcareframework.com.

Malaguzzi, L. (Ed.) (1971). *Esperienze per una nuova scuola dell'infanzia.* Roma: Editori Riuniti.

Manojan, K. P. (2019). Capturing the Gramscian project in critical pedagogy: Towards a philosophy of praxis education. *Review of Development and Change, 24*(1), 123–145.

Mantovani, S. (1976). La gestione dell'asilo-nido: Significato educativo, legislazione, esperienze. In S. Mantovani (Ed.), *Asili-nido. Psicologia e pedagogia* (pp. 230–252). Milano: Franco Angeli Editore.

Mantovani, S., Bove, C., Ferri, P., Manzoni, P., Cesa Bianchi, A., & Picca, M. (2021). Children 'under lockdown': Voices, experiences, and resources during and after the COVID-19 emergency. Insights from a survey with children and families in the Lombardy region of Italy. *European Early Childhood Education Research Journal, 29*(1), 35–50. DOI: 10.1080/1350293X.2021.1872673.

Mantovani, S., & Musatti, T. (1996). New educational provisions for young children in Italy. *European Journal of Psychology of Education, 11*, 119–128.

Marin, A. (2014). *Careless about childcare: Investigation into how the ministry of education responds to complaints and concerns related to unregulated daycare providers*. Toronto, ON.

Martin, C. (2015). Parenting support in France: Policy in an ideological battlefield. *Social Policy & Society, 14*(4), 609–620.

May, H. (2005). *Twenty years of consenting parties: The 'politics of 'working' and 'teaching' in childcare 1985–2005*. NZEI Te Riu Roa.

May, H., & Mitchell, L. (2009). *Strengthening community-based early childhood education in Aotearoa New Zealand*. http://www.nzare.org.nz/portals/306/images/Files/May%20and%20Mitchell%20(2009)%20Report_QPECE_project.pdf

May Cook, H. (1985). *Mind that child*. Blackberry Press.

Mazzucato, M. (2018). *The value of everything: Making and taking in the global economy*. UK: Penguin Random House.

McAllister-Flack, E., & McAllister, G. (2016). Stories of social justice from the kindergarten classroom. In R. Papa, D. M. Eadens, & D. W. Eadens (Eds.), *Social justice instruction: Empowerment on the chalkboard* (pp. 139–146). Springer International. https://doi.org/10.1007/978-3-319-12349-3_13

McDonald, G. (1981). The story of a recommendation about care and education. In M. Clark (Ed.), *The politics of education in New Zealand* (pp. 160–173). New Zealand Council for Educational Research.

McLean, C., Austin, L. J. E., Whitebook, M., & Olson, K. L. (2021). *Early childhood workforce index – 2020*. Center for the Study of Child Care Employment. Berkeley: University of California.

McLean, C., & Caven, M. (2021). Why did the child care teacher cross the road? To get to higher pay. *The View of the Hill*. https://thehill.com/opinion/finance/557045-why-did-the-child-care-teacher-cross-the-road-to-get-to-higher-pay

McMillan, H. (2020). Mana whenua/Belonging through assessment: A kōhanga reo perspective. *Early Childhood Folio, 24*(1).

Meyers, M. K., & Jordan, L. P. (2006). Choice and accommodation in parental child care decisions. *Community Development, 37*(2), 53–70.

Miksic, M. (2019). *The value of early childhood educators. A pathway forward to salary parity for community-based organizations*. https://www.dccnyinc.org/wp-content/uploads/2018/05/DCCNY_SalaryParityReport2019.pdf

Ministero dell'Istruzione (2020). Commissione Infanzia e Sistema Integrato zero-sei (D.lgs. 65/2017), *Orientamenti pedagogici sui LEAD: Legami Educativi A Distanza. Un modo diverso di fare nido e scuola dell'infanzia*. https://miur.gov.it(web/guest/orientamenti-pedagogici-sui-lead

Ministry of Education. (1996). *Te whāriki: He whāriki matauranga mō ngā mokopuna o Aotearoa = early childhood curriculum*. Wellington, New Zealand: Learning Media.

References

Ministry of Education. (2017). *Te Whāriki a Te Kōhanga Reo.* Retrieved from https://www.education.govt.nz/assets/Documents/Early-Childhood/Te-Whariki-a-te-Kohanga-Reo.pdf

Ministry of Education. (2017). *Te whāriki. He whāriki mātauranga mō ngā mokopuna o Aotearoa. Early childhood curriculum.* https://www.education.govt.nz/assets/Documents/Early-Childhood/ELS-Te-Whariki-Early-Childhood-Curriculum-ENG-Web.pdf

Ministry of Education. (2021). *Pivot table: number of ECE service 2000–2021.* Education Counts https://www.educationcounts.govt.nz/statistics/services

Ministry of Education and Culture (MoEC). (2016). APK/APM PAUD, SD, SMP, dan SM (termasuk Madrasah dan sederajat) Tahun 2015/2016. Jakarta: Centre for Data and Statistics for Education and Culture-MoEC. Retrieved from: http://publikasi.data.kemdikbud.go.id/uploadDir/isi_45AA7918-EBDF-4594-98B2-7B2F44685926_.pdf

Ministry of Education and Culture. (2021). *Statistics early childhood education (ECE) 2020/2021.* Jakarta: Centre of Data and Information Technology (PUSDATIN) MoEC. Retrieved from: http://publikasi.data.kemdikbud.go.id/uploadDir/isi_C27BA606-9DC6-4915-B975-392598A7821C_.pdf

Mirowski, P. (2013). *Never let a serious crisis go to waste: Hoe neoliberalism survived the financial meltdown.* London: Verso.

Mitchell, L. (2002). *Differences between community owned and privately owned early childhood education and care centres: A review of evidence.* New Zealand Council for Educational Research. www.nzcer.org.nz

Mitchell, L. (2005). Policy shifts in early childhood education: Past lessons, new directions. In J. Codd & K. Sullivan (Eds.), *Education policy directions in Aotearoa New Zealand* (pp. 175–198). Thomson Learning.

Mitchell, L. (2007). *A new debate about children and childhood. Could it make a difference to early childhood pedagogy and policy?* (PhD Doctor of Philosophy thesis). Wellington: Victoria University of Wellington. http://researcharchive.vuw.ac.nz/handle/10063/347

Mitchell, L. (2012). Markets and childcare provision in New Zealand: Towards a fairer alternative. In E. Lloyd & H. Penn (Eds.), *Childcare markets: Can they deliver an equitable service?* (pp. 97–114). London, UK: The Policy Press.

Mitchell, L. (2019). *Democratic practices and policies in early childhood education and care. An Aotearoa New Zealand case study.* Springer Nature. https://doi.org/10.1007/978-981-13-1793-4

Mitchell, L. (2020). Early childhood education in Aotearoa in a post-covid world. *New Zealand Annual Review of Education, 25,* 39–56. DOI: https://doi.org/10.26686/nzaroe.v25.6913

Mitchell, L., Hodgen, E., Meagher-Lundberg, P., & Wells, A. (2020). Impact of Covid-19 on the early childhood education sector in Aotearoa New Zealand: Challenges and opportunities. An initial survey of managers. Retrieved from https://www.waikato.ac.nz/wmier/centres-and-units/early-years-research/where-have-we-published

Mitchell, L., Meagher-Lundberg, P., & Wells, C. (2020). Impact of Covid-19 on the early childhood education sector in Aotearoa New Zealand. Report 2: Interviews with managers. Retrieved from https://www.waikato.ac.nz/__data/assets/pdf_file/0006/567285/Impact-of-Covid-19_Report-2_Final_2020-12-09.pdf

Mitchell, L., Tangaere, A. R., Mara, D., & Wylie, C. (2006). *Quality in parent/whānau-led services: Summary report.* Wellington, N.Z.: Ministry of Education.

Mitchell, L., Wylie, C., & Carr, M. (2008). *Outcomes of early childhood education: Literature review.* Report to the Ministry of Education. http://www.educationcounts.govt.nz/publications/ece/25158/48867

Mocan, N. (2007). Can consumers detect lemons? An empirical analysis of information asymmetry in the market for child care. *Journal of Population Economics, 20*(4), 743–780.

Monbiot, G. (2016). *How did we get into this mess?: Politics, equality, nature*. London: Verso.
Moon, P. (2013). *Turning points: Events that changed the course of New Zealand history*. Auckland, N.Z.: New Holland.
Morabito, C., Carosin, E., & Vandenbroeck, M. (2016). What parents say about children's inequality of opportunities: A study in Mauritius. *Early Years, 37*(4), 423–437.
Morris, P., & Sweeting, A. (1991). Education and politics: The case of Hong Kong from an historical perspective. *Oxford Review of Education, 17*(3), 249–267.
Morton, K. (2021). 'Busy Bees Childcare moves into New Zealand', Nursery World, 22 October 2021 (https://www.nurseryworld.co.uk/news/article/busy-bees-childcare-moves-into-new-zealand)
Moss, P. (2006). Structures, understandings and discourses: Possibilities for re-envisioning the early childhood worker. *Contemporary Issues in Early Childhood, 7*(1), 30–41. https://doi.org/10.2304/ciec.2006.7.1.30
Moss, P. (2009). *There are alternatives. Markets and democratic experimentalism in early childhood education and care*. (Vol. 53). The Hague: Bernard Van Leer Foundation. https://files.eric.ed.gov/fulltext/ED522533.pdf
Moss, P. (2013). Need markets be the only show in town? In E. Lloyd & H. Penn (Eds.), *Childcare markets. Can they deliver an equitable service?* (pp. 191–208). Bristol: Policy Press.
Moss, P. (2014). *Transformative change and real utopias in early childhood education: A story of democracy, experimentation and potentiality*. Abingdon: Routledge.
Moss, P., & Cameron, C. (2020). From the state we're in to what do we want for our children. In C. Cameron & P. Moss (Eds), *Transforming early childhood in England: From childcare to a democratic education system*. London: UCL Press.
Moss, P., Dahlberg, G., Grieshaber, S., Mantovani, S., May, H., Pence, A., … & Vandenbroeck, M. (2016). The organisation for economic co-operation and development's international early learning study: Opening for debate and contestation. *Contemporary Issues in Early Childhood, 17*(3), 343–351.
Moss, P., & Pence, A. (Eds.) (1994). *Valuing quality in early childhood services: New approaches to defining quality*. Sage.
Moss, P., & Petrie, P. (1997). *Children's services: Time for a new approach*. London, England: Institute of Education, University of London.
Moss, P., & Urban, M. (2017). The organisation for economic co-operation and development's international early learning study: What happened next. *Contemporary Issues in Early Childhood, 18*(2), 250–258.
Moss, P., & Urban, M. (2019). The organisation for economic co-operation and development's international early learning study: What's going on. *Contemporary Issues in Early Childhood, 20*(2), 207–212.
Mouffe, C. (2005). *On the political*. London: Routledge.
Moulian, T. (1997). *Chile actual: anatomía de un mito*. Santiago: LOM.
Mozère, L. (2000). *Le printemps des crèches*. Paris: L'Harmattan.
Mozère, L. (2004). Le « souci de soi » chez Foucault et le souci dans une éthique politique du care. *Le Portique, 13–14*. Retrieved from http://leportique.revues.org/623
Muñoz, M., & Powell, P. J. (2016). Preparing early childhood professionals to meet the changing demography of the United States. In R. Papa, D. M. Eadens, & D. W. Eadens (Eds.), *Social justice instruction: Empowerment on the chalkboard* (pp. 23–31). Springer International.
Musa, M. M., Abubakar, I. B., & Danladi, N. Y. (2017). Early childhood education: Development, challenges and prospects in Nigeria. *International Journal of Education and Evaluation, 3*(10), 47–58.

Musatti, T. (2007). La signification des lieux d'accueil de la petite enfance aujourd'hui. In G. Brougère & M. Vandenbroeck (Eds.), *Repenser l'éducation des jeunes enfants* (pp. 207–224). Bruxelles: P.I.E. Peter Lang.

Musatti, T., Giovannini, D., S. Mayer, & Group Nido Lagomago (2013). How to construct a curriculum in an Italian nido. In L. Miller, & C. Cameron (Eds.), *International perspectives in the early years* (pp. 85–110). London: Sage.

Musatti, T., Hoshi-Watanabe, M., Rayna, S., Di Giandomenico, I., Kamigaichi, N., Mukai, M., & Shiozaki, M. (2016). Social processes among mothers in centres for children and parents in three countries. *Child & Family Social Work, 22*(2), 563–1127.

Musatti, T., Picchio, M., & Mayer S. (2016). Continuous professional and quality: The case of Pistoia. In M. Vandenbroeck, M. Urban, & J. Peeters (Eds.), *Pathways to professionalism in early childhood education and care* (43–56). London and New York: Routledge.

Mustafa, L. M., Yunus, N. K. Y., & Azman, M. N. A. (2014). An overview of private preschool in Malaysia: Marketing strategies and challenges. *Procedia-Social and Behavioral Sciences, 130,* 105–113.

Nelson, E., & Charteris, J. (2021). Student voice research as a technology of reform in neoliberal times. *Pedagogy, Culture & Society, 29*(2), 213–230.

New, R., Mallory, B. L., & Mantovani, S. (2000). Cultural images of children, parents and professionals: Italian Interpretations of home-school relationships. *Early Education & Development, 11*(5), 597–616.

Newberry, J. (2010). The global child and non-governmental governance of the family in post-suharto Indonesia. *Economy and Society, 39*(3), 403–426. DOI: 10.1080/03085147.2010.486217

Newberry, J. (2012). Empowering children, disempowering women. *Ethics and Social Welfare, 6*(3), 247–259.

Newberry, J. (2017). Interiority and government of the child: Transparency, risk, and good governance in Indonesia. *Focaal, 77,* 76–89.

Newberry, J., & Marpinjun, S. (2018). Payment in heaven: Can early childhood education policies help women too? *Policy Futures in Education, 16*(1), 29–42. DOI: 10.1177/1478210317739467

Neyrand, G. (2006). *Faut-il avoir peur de nos enfants? Politiques sécuritaires et enfance.* Paris: La Découverte.

Neyrand, G. (2012). *Soutenir et contrôler les parents. Le dispositief de parentalité.* Toulouse: Erès.

Ng, L. H. (1984). *Interactions of East and West: Development of public education in early Hong Kong.* Hong Kong: Chinese University Press.

NICHD Early Child Care Network. (2002). Child-care structure>process>outcome: Direct and indirect effects of child-care quality on young children's development. *Psychological Science, 13*(3), 199–206. https://doi.org/10.1111/1467-9280.00438

Nieuwenhuis, R., & Van Lancker, W. (2020). Introduction: A multilevel perspective on family policy. In R. Nieuwenhuis & W. Van Lancker (Eds.), *Palgrave handbook of family policy* (pp. 3–24). Cham: Palgrave Macmillan.

Nsamenang, A. B. (2004). *Cultures of human development and education: Challenges to growing up African.* New York: Nova Science Publishers.

Nsamenang, A. B. (2011). Towards a philosophy for African education in Nsamenang A. B., & Tchombe T. M. S. (Eds.), African educational theories and practices: A generative teacher education handbook. Yaounde, Cameroon, Presses Univeritairesd Afrique. Retrieved on 02-04-2022 from http://www.thehdrc.org/Handbook%20f%

Nutbrown, C. (2021). Early childhood educators' qualifications: A framework for change. *International Journal of Early Years Education, 29*(3), 236–249. https://doi.org/10.1080/0 9669760.2021.1892601

Närvi, J. (2014). Äidit kotona ja työssä – Perhevapaavalinnat, työtilanteet ja hoivaihanteet [Mothers at home and work – Decisions about family leaves, work life situations and ideals of care]. *Yhteiskuntapolitiikka, 79*(5), 543–552.

Närvi, J., Salmi, M., & Lammi-Taskula, J. (2020). Home care and early childhood education in Finland: Policies and practices of childcare. Teoksessa Katja Repo, Maarit Alasuutari, Kirsti Karila, Johanna Lammi-Taskula (toim.). *The policies of childcare and early childhood education. Does equal access matter?* (pp. 133–151). Cheltenham: Edward Elgar Publishing.

Oberhuemer, P. (2005). Conceptualising the early childhood pedagogue: Policy approaches and issues of professionalism. *European Early Childhood Education Research Journal, 13*(1), 5–16. DOI: 10.1080/13502930585209521

Oberhuemer, P., & Schreyer, I. (Eds.) (2018). *Early childhood workforce profiles in 30 countries with key contextual data*. www.seepro.eu/ISBN-publication.pdf

Observatoire national de la petite enfance (2020). *L'accueil du jeune enfant en 2019.* [Childcare in 2019]. Paris: Onape.

O'Connel. (2010). (How) is childminding family like? Family day care, food and the reproduction of identity at the Public/Private interface. *Sociological Review, 58*(4), 563–586.

Octarra, H. S., & Hendriati, A. (2018). 'Old, borrowed, and renewed': A review of early childhood education policy in post-reform Indonesia. *Policy Futures in Education, 16*(1), 80–91.

Ødegaard, E. E., & White, E. J. (2016). Bildung: Potential and promise in early childhood education. *Encyclopedia of educational philosophy and theory*. Singapore: Springer.

Oduolowu, E. A. (2000). *Introduction to the philosophy of nursery and primary education*. Ibadan: The Centre for External Studies, University of Ibadan.

Oduolowu, E. A. (2011). *Contemporary issues in early childhood education*. Ibadan: Franco-Ola Publishers.

O'Regan, M., Halpenny, A. M., & Hayes, N. (2019). Childminding in Ireland: Attitudes towards professionalisation. *European Early Childhood Education Research Journal, 27*(6), 757–775.

OECD. (2001). *Starting strong. Early childhood education and care*. Organisation for Economic Cooperation and Development. https://doi.org/10.1787/9789264192829-en

OECD. (2006). *Starting strong 11: Early childhood education and care*. Organisation for Economic Cooperation and Development.

OECD. (2012). *Starting strong 111. A quality toolbox for early childhood education and care*: http://dx.doi.org/10.1787/9789264123564-en

OECD. (2016). Call for tenders, International Early Learning Study. https://www.oecd.org/callsfortenders/CfT%20100001420%20International%20Early%20Learning%20Study.pdf

OECD. (2016). International early learning and child wellbeing study (IELS). http://www.oecd.org/edu/school/international-early-learning-and-child-well-being-study.htm

OECD. (2017). *The international early learning and child well-being study – The study.* http://www.oecd.org/edu/school/the-international-early-learning-and-child-well-being-study-the-study.htm

Organization for Economic Co-operation and Development (OECD). (2021). Early Childhood Education and Care. https://www.oecd.org/education/school/earlychildhoodeducationandcare.htm

Orcos, L., Hernández-Carrera, R. M., Espigares, M. J., & Magreñán, Á. A. (2019). The Kumon method: its importance in the improvement on the teaching and learning of mathematics from the first levels of early childhood and primary education. *Mathematics*, 7(1), 109.

Osanyin, F. A. (2002). *Early childhood education in Nigeria*. Lagos: Concept Publications Ltd.

Osanyin, F. A. (2012). *Once upon a child*. An inaugural lecture delivered at the University of Lagos on Wednesday 18th April, 2012.

Ostner, I., & Stolberg, C. (2015). Investing in children, monitoring parents. Parenting support in the changing German welfare state. *Social Policy & Society*, 14(4), 621–632.

Pagani, V. (2021). Behind the numbers. A mixed-methods study of the CLASS tool application in Italy. *Italian Journal of Educational Research*, 26, 46–56.

Palma, D. (1998). *La participación y la construcción de ciudadanía. Universidad ARCIS, Centro de Investigaciones Sociales, Documento de Trabajo n°27*. Santiago: ARCIS.

Panel on Education (2015). Subcommittee to Study the Implementation of Free Kindergarten Education. Premise-related issues. LC Paper N° CB(4)627/14-15(01).

Papa, R., Eadens, D. M., & Eadens, D. W. (Eds.) (2016). *Social justice instruction: Empowerment on the chalkboard*. Springer International. https://doi.org/10.1007/978-3-319-12349-3

Parramore, L. (2018). 'Meet the Economist behind the one percent's stealth takeover of America', blog for *Institute for New Economic Thinking*, 30 May 2018, (www.ineteconomics.org/perspectives/blog/meet-the-economist-behind-the-one-percents-stealth-takeover-of-america)

Patience O. Awopegba, Esther A. Oduolowu and A. Bame Nsamenang, 2013. *Indigenous early childhood care and education (IECCE) curriculum framework for Africa a focus on context and contents Addis Ababa*, UNESCO: International Institute for Capacity Building in Africa

Patnaik, A. K. (1988). Gramsci's concept of common sense: Towards a theory of subaltern consciousness in hegemony processes. *Economic & Political Weekly*, 23(5), PE2–PE10.

Paull, G. (2012). 'Childcare markets and government interventions', in E. Lloyd and H. Penn (Eds.), *Childcare markets: Can they deliver and equitable service?* (pp. 227–256). Bristol: Policy Press.

Paull, G., & Xu, X. (2019). *Early years providers cost study 2018*. https://assets.publishing.service.gov.uk/government/uploads/system/uploads/attachment_data/file/913076/Frontier_-_Childcare_Cost_Study2.pdf

Pence, A. (2004). ECD Policy development and implementation in Africa. UNESCO Early Childhood and Family Policy Series 9.

Pence, A. (2016). Baby PISA: Dangers that can arise when foundations shift. *Journal of Childhood Studies*, 41(3), 54–58.

Penn, H. (2002). The World Bank's view of early childhood. *Childhood*, 9(1), 118–132.

Penn, H. (2011). Gambling on the market: The role of for-profit provision in early childhood education and care. *Journal of Early Childhood Research*, 9(2), 150–161.

Penn, H. (2011). Policy rationales for early childhood services. *Korean Institute of Child Care and Education*, 5(1), 1–16. https://doi.org/10.1007/2288-6729-5-1-1

Penn, H. (2012). Childcare markets: Do they work?. In H. Lloyd & H. Penn (Eds.), *Childcare markets. Can they deliver an equitable service?* (pp. 19–42). Bristol: Policy Press.

Penn, H. (2013). The business of childcare in Europe. *European Early Childhood Education Research Journal*, 22(4), 432–456. doi:10.1080/1350293X.2013.7883300

Penn, H., Barreau, S., Butterworth, L., Lloyd, E., Moyles, J., Potter, S., & Sayeed, R. (2004). What is the impact of out-of-home integrated care and education settings on children aged 0–6 and their parents? In *Research evidence in education library*. EPPI-Centre, Social Science Research Unit, Institute of Education. University of London.

Peralta, V., & Fujimoto, G. (1998). *La Atención Integral de la primera Infancia en América Latina: Ejes centrales y los desafíos para el Siglo XXI*. Santiago: OEA.

Pérez, J., Abiega, L., Zarco, M., & Schugurensky, D. (1999). *Nezahualpilli. Educación preescolar comunitaria*. Centro de Estudios Educativos, A.C., México: Plaza y Valdés Editores.

Peyton, V., Jacobs, A., O'Brien, M., & Roy, C. (2001). Reasons for choosing child care: Associations with family factors, quality, and satisfaction. *Early Childhood Research Quarterly, 16*(2), 191–208.

Pianta, R., LaParo, K., & Hamre, B. (2007). *Classroom scoring assessment system (CLASS): Pre-K*.

Pianta, R. C., La Paro, K. M., & Hamre, B. K. (2008). *Classroom assessment scoring system™: Manual k-3*. Paul H Brookes Publishing.

Piattoeva, N., Silova, I., & Millei, Z. (2018). Remembering childhoods, rewriting (post) socialist lives. In *Childhood and schooling in (Post) socialist societies* (pp. 1–18). Cham: Palgrave Macmillan.

PIIE (Programa Interdisciplinario de Investigaciones en Educación). (2008). *Descripción del Programa de Mejoramiento de la Atención a la Infancia, PMI*. Retrieved from http://www.piie.cl/portal/index.php?option=com_content&task=view&id=118

Piquero, A. R., Farrington, D. P., Welsh, B. C., Tremblay, R., & Jennings, W. G. (2009). Effects of early family/parent training programmes on antisocial behavior and delinquency. *Journal of Experimental Criminology, 5*(2), 83–120.

Plantenga, J. (2012). Local providers and loyal parents: Competition and consumer choice in the Dutch childcare market. In E. Lloyd & H. Penn (Eds.), *Childcare markets: Can they deliver an equitable service?* (pp. 63–78). London, UK: The Policy Press.

Powell, A., & Ferns, C. (2020a). *From reopening to recovery: A plan for child care reopening in Ontario and moving to a publicly funded system*. Association of Early Childhood Educators of Ontario and the Ontario Coalition for Better Child Care. Ontario. Available online at: https://www.childcareontario.org/from_reopening_to_recovery_a_plan

Powell, A., & Ferns, C. (2020b). *Revisiting "From reopening to recovery": A child care plan for Ontario*. Association of Early Childhood Educators of Ontario and the Ontario Coalition for Better Child Care https://d3n8a8pro7vhmx.cloudfront.net/aeceo/pages/2572/attachments/original/1597697664/Revisiting_Reopening_to_Recovery.pdf?1597697664

Powell, A., Ferns, C., & Burrell, S. (2021). *Forgotten on the frontline: A survey report on Ontario's early years and child care workforce*. Association of Early Childhood Educators of Ontario and the Ontario Coalition for Better Child Care. https://d3n8a8pro7vhmx.cloudfront.net/childcareon/pages/2667/attachments/original/1621427998/Forgotten_on_the_frontline.pdf?1621427998

Powell, A., Langford, R., Albanese, P., Prentice, S., & Bezanson, K. (2020). Who cares for carers? How discursive constructions of care work marginalized early childhood educators in Ontario's 2018 provincial election. *Contemporary Issues in Early Childhood, 25*(2), 153–164.

Press, F., & Woodrow, S. (2005). Commodification, corporatisation and children's spaces. *Australian Journal of Education, 49*(3), 278–291. https://d3n8a8pro7vhmx.cloudfront.net/aeceo/pages/2559/attachments/original/1590578703/FROM_REOPENING_TO_RECOVERY.pdf?1590578703

Price Waterhouse Coopers & The Front Project. (2019). *A smart investment for a smarter Australia* https://www.thefrontproject.org.au/images/downloads/Cost-benefit%20analysis_brochure.pdf

References **245**

Prochner, L. (2000). *A history of early education and child care in Canada, 1820–1966.* In *Early childhood care and education in Canada: Past, present, and future* (pp. 11–65). Vancouver, BC: UBC Press.

Programme of Prime Minister Sanna Marin's Government. (10 December 2019). Inclusive and competent Finland – a socially, economically and ecologically sustainable society. http://julkaisut.valtioneuvosto.fi/handle/10024/161935 (accessed 23 June 2021)

Prout, A., & James, A. (2015). A new paradigm for the sociology of childhood?: Provenance, promise and problems. In *Constructing and reconstructing childhood* (pp. 6–28). Routledge.

Qoyyimah, U. (2018). Policy implementation within the frame of school-based curriculum: A comparison of public school and Islamic private school teachers in East java, Indonesia. *Compare: A Journal of Comparative and International Education, 48*(4), 571–589. https://doi.org/10.1080/03057925.2017.1334536

R. A. Malatest & Associates, Ltd., (2020). Evaluation of Early Learning and Child Care Centres, Annual Report (2018-19). https://open.alberta.ca/dataset/fab44a22-36e3-4515-b2f0-19cfb4ac6435/resource/1c37628f-9af6-42f2-bdaf-f88b7e87d1a0/download/cs-evaluation-of-early-learning-and-child-care-centres-annual-report-2018-19.pdf

Ramírez, D., Nava, L., Ávila, A. Barrios, G., & Vázquez, M. (2012). *Modelo para la Participación de Padres de Familia en la Educación Inicial y Básica del Conafe.* Retrieved from http://www.conafe.gob.mx/mportal7/acompaname/modelo-participacion-padres.pdf

Rantalaiho, M. (2010). 'Rationalities of cash-for-childcare: The nordic case', in J. Sipilä, K. Repo and T. Rissanen (Eds.), *Cash-for-childcare: The consequences for caring mothers* (pp. 109–142). Cheltenham, UK and Northampton, MA, USA: Edward Elgar Publishing.

Räsänen, T., Österbacka, E., Valaste, M., & Haataja, A. (2019). *Lastenhoidon tukien vaikutus äitien osallistumiseen työmarkkinoille* [The effect of child care subsidies on mothers' labour market participation]. Sosiaali- ja terveysturvan raportteja 14 [Social Insurance Institution of Finland, Social security and health reports 14]. Helsinki: Kela.

Raworth, K. (2017). *Doughnut economics: Seven ways to think like a 21st century economist*, London: Random House Business Books.

Rayna, S. ; Rubio, M-N. et Scheu, H. (dir.) (2010). *Parents-professionnels : la coéducation en questions.* Toulouse: Éditions Érès.

Readhead, Z., & DfE, U. R. N. (1996). Summerhill school. *Deschooling our lives*, 108–112.

Reedy, T. (2013). Tōku rangatiratanga nā te Mana mātauranga: "Knowledge and power set me free …". In J. Nuttall (Ed.), *Weaving te whāriki* (2nd ed., pp. 35–49). New Zealand: NZCER.

Repo, K. (2010). 'Finnish child home care allowance: Users' perspectives and per-ceptions', in J. Sipilä, K. Repo and T. Rissanen (Eds.), *Cash-for-childcare: The consequences for caring mothers* (pp. 46–64). Cheltenham, UK and Northampton, MA, USA: Edward Elgar Publishing.

Richardson, B. (2017). Taking stock of corporate childcare in Alberta: Licensing inspection data in not-for-profit and corporate childcare centres. In R. Langford, S. Prentice and P. Albaense, (Eds.), *Caring for children: Social movements and public policy in Canada* (pp. 119–140). Vancouver, BC: University of British Columbia Press.

Richardson, B. (2018). Taking stock of corporate childcare in Alberta. In R. Langford, S. Prentice, & P. Albanese (Eds.), *Caring for children. Social movements and public policy in Canada* (pp. 119–139). University of British Columbia Press.

Richardson, B. (2021). Commodification and care: An exploration of workforces' experiences of care in private and public childcare systems from a feminist political theory of care perspective. *Critical Social Policy, 42*(1), 1–22. doi.org/10.1177/0261018321998934

Rinaldi, C. (1984). L'elaborazione comunitaria del progetto educativo. In Vianello, R. (Ed.) *Stare con i bambini: Il sapere dell'educatore* (pp. 176–88). Bergamo: Juvenilia.

Rinaldo, R. (2013). *Mobilizing piety: Islam and feminism in Indonesia*. Oxford University Press.

Rizvi, F., & Lingard, B. (2010). *Globalising education policy*. London; New York: Routledge.

Roberts-Holmes, G., & Moss, P. (2020). *Neoliberalism and early childhood education: Imagineries, markets and pedagogies*. London: Routledge.

Roberts-Holmes, G., & Moss, P. (2021). *Neoliberalism and early childhood education: Markets, imaginaries and governance*. Abingdon: Routledge.

Romijn, B. (2021). Cultural inclusion in early childhood and primary education. PhD thesis. Utrecht: Utrecht University.

Rosemberg, F. (2010). Tendances et tensions de l'éducation de la petite enfance au brésil. *Revue Internationale d'éducation Sèvres, 53*, 119–128.

Royal Tangaere, A. (1997). *Learning Maori together: Kohanga reo and home*. Wellington, New Zealand: NZCER.

Royal Tangaere, A. (2012). *Te hokinga ki te ukaipo – A socio-construction of Maori language development: Kohanga Reo and home*. (Doctoral dissertation, University of Auckland, Auckland, New Zealand), Retrieved from https://researchspace.auckland.ac.nz/bitstream/handle/2292/13392/whole.pdf?sequence=2

Royal Tangaere, A. (2014). Te hōkinga ki te ūkaipō: Constructions of māori language development. In R. Higgins, P. Rewi, V. Olsen-Reeder, & Ngā Pae of te Māramatanga (Eds.), *The value of the māori language: Te Hua o te reo māori* (pp. 205–222). New Zealand: Huia Publisher.

Ruutiainen, V., Alasuutari, M., & Karila, K. (2020). Rationalising public support for private early childhood education and care: The case of Finland. *British Journal of Sociology of Education, 41*(1), 32–47.

Ruutiainen, V., Räikkönen, E., & Alasuutari, M. (2021). Socio-economic and attitude-related selectivity between public and private early childhood education and care services. Manuscript/(under review for publication).

Ruutianen, V., Räikkönen, E., Alasuutari, M., & Karila, K. (in press). Palvelunkäyttäjien valikoituminen varhaiskasvatusmarkkinoilla [the selectivity of clientele in early childhood education and care markets]. In P. Eerola, K. Repo, M. Alasuutari, K. Karila & J. Lammi-Taskula (Eds.), *Varhaiskasvatuksen ja lastenhoidon monet polut [the diverse paths of early childhood education and care]*. Gaudeamus: Helsinki.

Sabatini, F. (1995). *Barrio y participación. Mujeres pobladoras de Santiago*. Santiago: Ediciones SUR.

Sabatini, F., Cáceres, G. et Cerda, J. (2001). Segregación residencial en las principales ciudades chilenas: Tendencias de las tres últimas décadas y posibles cursos de acción. *EURE (Santiago), 27*(82), 21–42.

Sahlberg, P. (2012) 'Global Educational Reform Movement is here!', blog at *PasiSahlberg.com*. (https://pasisahlberg.com/global-educational-reform-movement-is-here/).

Säkkinen, S., & Kuoppala, T. (2017). Varhaiskasvatus 2016 [Early childhood education and care 2016]. National Institute for Health and Welfare (THL). Tilastoraportti [Statistical report] 29.

Säkkinen, S., & Kuoppala, T. (2018). *Varhaiskasvatus 2017* [Early childhood education and care 201t]. Tilastoraportti 32. THL [National Institute for Health and Welfare]: Helsinki. https://www.julkari.fi/bitstream/handle/10024/136962/Tr32_18.pdf?sequence=5&isAllowed=y

Säkkinen, S., & Kuoppala, T. (2020). *Varhaiskasvatus 2019* [Early childhood education and care 2019]. Tilastoraportti. Helsinki: Terveyden ja hyvinvoinnin laitos. https://www.julkari.fi/bitstream/handle/10024/140541/Tr33_20.pdf?sequence=5&isAllowed=y

Salazar, G. (2012). *Movimientos sociales en Chile. Trayectoria histórica y proyección política.* Santiago: Uqbar editores.

Salazar, G. et Pinto, J. (dir.) (1999). *Historia contemporánea de Chile. Volumen II: Actores, identidad y movimiento.* Santiago: LOM.

Salmi, M. (2006). Parental choice and the passion for equality in Finland, in A. L. Ellingsæter and A. Leira (Eds.), *Politicising parenthood in Scandinavia: Gender relations in welfare States* (pp. 145–168). Bristol: Policy Press.

Sandel, M. J. (2013). Market reasoning as moral reasoning: Why economists should reengage with political reasoning. *Journal of Economic Perspectives*, 27(4), 121–140.

Shahshahani, L. (2020). Le service public de la petite enfance, une réussite française en danger. [Childcare as a public service, an endangered French success]. *Le Monde Diplomatique, Février 2020.*

Shdaimah, C., & Palley, E. (2016). To fix America's childcare, let's look at the past. The Conversation. https://theconversation.com/to-fix-americas-child-care-lets-look-at-the-past-63913

Shlay, A., Tran, H., Weinraub, M., & Harmon, M. (2005). Teasing apart the child care conundrum: A factorial analysis of perceptions of child care quality, fair market price and willingness to pay by low-income, African-American parents. *Early Childhood Research Quarterly*, 20, 393–416.

Shonkoff, J. P., Phillips, D. A., & National Research Council. (2000). The developing brain. In *From neurons to neighborhoods: The science of early childhood development*. US: National Academies Press.

Siippainen, A., Repo, L., Metsämuuronen, J., Kivistö, A., Alasuutari, M., Koivisto, P., & Saarikallio-Torp, M. (2019*). Viisivuotiaiden maksuttoman varhaiskasvatuksen kokeilun ensimmäisen vaiheen arviointi. Varhaiskasvatukseen osallistuminen ja kokeilun järjestäminen* [The first phase of the evaluation of an experiment on free of charge early childhood education and care for five-year-olds. Participation in early childhood education and the organization of the experiment]. Julkaisut [Publications] 16. KARVI [Finnish Education Evaluation Centre]: Helsinki. https://karvi.fi/app/uploads/2019/09/KARVI_1619.pdf

Simon, A., Penn, H., Shah, A., Owen, C., Lloyd., E, Hollingworth, K., & Quy, K. (2022). *Acquisitions, mergers and debt: The new language of childcare – Main report.* London: UCL Social Research Institute, University College London. (https://www.nuffieldfoundation.org/wp-content/uploads/2022/01/The-new-language-of-childcare-Main-report.pdf)

Simon, J., & Smith, L. (Eds.) (2001). *A civilising mission? - Perceptions and representations of the New Zealand native schools system.* Auckland, New Zealand: Auckland University Press.

Sims, M. (2017). Neoliberalism and early childhood. *Cogent Education*, 4(1). https://www.tandfonline.com/doi/pdf/10.1080/2331186X.2017.1365411?needAccess=true

Smith, K., Tesar, M., & Myers, C. Y. (2016). Edu-capitalism and the governing of early childhood education and care in Australia, New Zealand and the United States. *Global Studies of Childhood*, 6(1), 123–135.

Snyder, P. A., Hemmeter, M. L., Fox, L., Bishop, C. C., & Miller, M. D. (2013). Developing and gathering psychometric evidence for a fidelity instrument: The teaching pyramid observation Tool–Pilot version. *Journal of Early Intervention, 35*(2), 150–172.

Sorensen, T. B., Grimaldi, E., & Gajderowicz, T. (2021). *Rhetoric or game changer: Social dialogue and industrial relations in education midst EU governance and privatisation in Europe*. Retrieved from https://www.ei-ie.org/en/item/23729:europe-study-on-industrial-relations-and-privatisation

Sosinsky, L., Lord, H., & Zigler, E. (2007). For-profit/non-profit differences in center-based child care quality: Results from the national institute of child health and human development study of early child care and youth development. *Journal of Applied Developmental Psychology, 28*(5), 390–410.

Spaggiari, S. (1997). Considerazioni critiche ed esperienze di gestione sociale. In A. Bondioli & S. Mantovani (Eds.), *Manuale critico dell'asilo nido* (pp. 111–134). Milano: Franco Angeli Editore.

Stiglitz, J. (2019). 'The end of neoliberalism and the rebirth of history', blog for *Social Europe*, 26 November 2019. (www.socialeurope.eu/the-end-of-neoliberalism-and-the-rebirth-of-history).

Sulkanen, M., Närvi, J., Kuusiholma, J., Lammi-Taskula, J., Räikkönen, E., & Alasuutari, M. (2020). *Varhaiskasvatus- ja lastenhoitoratkaisut neljävuotiaiden lasten perheissä. CHILDCARE-kyselytutkimuksen 2019 perustulokset* [Early childhood education and childcare solutions in families with four-year-old children. Basic results of the CHILDCARE survey 2019]. Työpaperi [Discussion Paper] 28. Helsinki: Terveyden ja hyvinvoinnin laitos [National Institute for Health and Welfare] (THL). https://www.julkari.fi/bitstream/handle/10024/140417/URN_ISBN_978-952-343-538-4.pdf?sequence=1&isAllowed=y

Sumsion, J. (2013). ABC Learning and Australian early education and care: A retrospective ethical audit of a radical experiment (pp. 209–225).

Sumsion, J., & Wong, S. (2011). Interrogating 'belonging' in belonging, being and becoming: The early years learning framework for Australia. *Contemporary Issues in Early Childhood, 12*(1), 28–45.

Sweeting, A. (1993). *A phoenix transformed: The reconstruction of education in post-war Hong Kong*. Hong Kong: Oxford University Press.

Sweeting, A. (2004). *Education in Hong Kong, 1941 to 2001: Visions and revisions*. Hong Kong: Hong Kong University Press.

Sylva, K., Ereky-Stevens, K., & Aricescu, A.-M. (2015). *Overview of European ECEC curricula and curriculum template*. Utrecht: Utrecht University – CARE Project.

Tawhiwhirangi, I. (2003). Iritana tawhiwhirangi. In P. Diamond (Ed.), *A fire in your belly - Māori leaders speak* (pp. 73–109). New Zealand: Huia Publishers.

Tawhiwhirangi, I. (2014). Kua tū tāngata e! Moving a critical mass. In R. Higgins, P. Rewi, V. Olsen-Reeder, & N. P. O. T. Māramatanga (Eds.), *The value of the Māori language* (pp. 33–52). New Zealand: Huia Publishers.

Taylor, C. L., Christensen, D., Stafford, J., Venn, A., Preen, D., & Zubrick, S. R. (2020). Associations between clusters of early life risk factors and developmental vulnerability at age 5: A retrospective cohort study using population-wide linkage of administrative data in Tasmania, Australia. *BMJ Open, 10*(4), e033795.

Te Kohanga Reo National Trust. (1995). *Te Korowai. Unpublished document. Chartered agreement between the ministry of education and Te Kohanga reo national trust on behalf of the kohanga reo whanau (1995–2008)*: Wellington: Te Kohanga Reo National Trust.

Te Kohanga Reo National Trust. (n.d). *Te Kōhanga Reo* Retrieved from https://www.kohanga.ac.nz

Te Kōhanga Reo National Trust (Producer). (2020). *Wererou Te Whāriki Tuatahi.* Retrieved from https://www.youtube.com/watch?v=DIca3jDUvrI

Teachtone. (2022). *Measure and Improve Teaching Quality with CLASS®.* https://teachstone.com

Terävä, J., Kuukka, A., & Alasuutari, M. (2018). Miten lastenhoidon ratkaisuja saa perustella? Vanhempien puhe 1–2-vuotiaan lapsensa hoitoratkaisuista [talk about childcare choices. Finnish parents' justifications for their childcare decisions]. *Yhteiskuntapolitiikka,* Special issue on Childcare Policies, *83*(4), 349–359.

Teymoori, A., Côté, S. M., Jones, B. L., Nagin, D. S., Boivin, M., Vitaro, F., ... & Tremblay, R. E. (2018). Risk factors associated with boys' and girls' developmental trajectories of physical aggression from early childhood through early adolescence. *JAMA Network Open, 1*(8), e186364.

The Ministry of Education and Culture Republic of Indonesia. (2014a). *2013 Curriculum of Early Childhood Education No 146.* Jakarta: Ministry of Education and Culture Republic of Indonesia.

The Ministry of Education and Culture Republic of Indonesia. (2014b). *Ministry of Education and Culture Republic of Indonesia Regulation No 137: National Standard on Early Childhood Education.* Jakarta: Ministry of Education and Culture Republic of Indonesia.

Thomas, R. M. (1988). Dividing the labor: Indonesia's government/private early childhood education system. *Early Childhood Development and Care, 39*(1), 33–43.

Thompson, C. (2015). The authority of bildung: Educational practices in early childhood education, *Ethics and Education, 10*(1), 3–16. DOI: 10.1080/17449642.2014.998031.

Tobin, J., Arzubiaga, A. E., & Adair, J. K. (2013). *Children crossing borders.* Russel Sage Foundation.

Tobin, J., Hsueh, Y., & Karasawa, M. (2009). *Preschool in three cultures. Revisited.* Chicago: The University of Chicago Press.

Tobin, J., Wu, D., & Davidson, D. (1989). *Preschool in three cultures – Japan, China and the United States.* New Haven, CT: Yale University Press.

Tooze, A. (2021). 'Has Covid ended the neoliberal era?', *The Guardian,* 2 September 2021. (https://www.theguardian.com/news/2021/sep/02/covid-and-the-crisis-of-neoliberalism)

Tor-Anyin, S. A. (2008). *Origin, growth and development of pre-primary education in Nigeria.* Makurdi Safer academic Press Ltd.

Tronto, J. (1993). *Moral boundaries: A political argument for an ethics of care.* New York: Routledge.

Tronto, J. (2009). *Un monde vulnérable. Pour une politique du care.* Paris: La Découverte.

Tronto, J. (2013). *Caring democracy: Markets, equality, and justice.* New York, NY: New York University Press.

Tronto, J. (2017). 'There is an alternative: *homines curans* and the limits of neoliberalism. *International Journal of Care and Caring, 1*(1), 27–43.

Truth & Reconciliation Commission of Canada. (2015). *Canada's residential schools: The final report of the truth and reconciliation commission of Canada* (Vol. 1). McGill-Queen's Press-MQUP.

Tsang, Y. C. D. (2007). *2007 chief executive election: Introduction to candidates* (in Chinese). https://www.eac.hk/pdf/chief/2007/2458921_LFT-2.pdf

Tse, W. W. Y., & Kwan, M. Y. W. (2021). Impacts of the COVID-19 pandemic on the physical and mental health of children. *Hong Kong Medical Journal, 27*(3), 175–176.

Tuori, K. (2021). *Asiantuntijaselvitys eräistä yksityisen varhaiskasvatuksen sääntelyyn liittyvistä oikeudellisista kysymyksistä* [Expert study of certain legal questions related to regulation on private early childhood education].Publications of the Ministry of Education and Culture 22. Helsinki. https://julkaisut.valtioneuvosto.fi/bitstream/handle/10024/162977/OKM_2021_22.pdf

UNDP. (2021). *About Indonesia*. About Indonesia. https://www.id.undp.org/content/indonesia/en/home/countryinfo.html#:~:text=Indonesia%20is%20now%20categorized%20as,is%20challenged%20with%20widening%20inequality

UNDP (Chile). (1998). *Informe desarrollo humano en Chile – año 1998. Las paradojas de la modernización*. Santiago: PNUD.

UNICEF. (2015). *Activity design document: New Zealand MFAT–UNICEF partnership for early childhood education in Eastern Indonesia*. UNICEF.

UNICEF. (2017). *Baseline study for Early Childhood Development Programme in Kupang District: NTT 2017* (p. 250). UNICEF and New Ministry of Foreign Affairs and Trade (MFAT).

United Nations Organization for Education, Science and Culture (UNESCO). (2005). *Policy review report: Early childhood care and education in Indonesia*. (The Section for Early Childhood and Inclusive Education Division of Basic Education No. 10; UNESCO Education Sector, Early Childhood and Family Policy Series). UNESCO.

United Nations. (1948). Universal Declaration of Human Rights. Retrieved from https://www.un.org/en/about-us/universal-declaration-of-human-rights

United Workers Union. (2021). "Spitting off cash": Where does all the money go in Australia's early learning sector? Retrieved from https://bigsteps.org.au/categories/release/stop-profiting-off-our-children/Universidad de Chile (Facultad de Ciencias Sociales) (2007). *El enfoque comunitario en la JUNJI*, Informe Final.

Universidad de Chile (Facultad de Ciencias Sociales). (2007). *El enfoque comunitario en la JUNJI*, Informe Final.

Urban, M. (2017). We need meaningful, systemic evaluation, not a preschool PISA. *Global Education Review, 4*(2).

Urban, M., & Swadener, B. (2016). Democratic accountability and contextualised systemic evaluation: A comment on the OECD initiative to launch an international early learning study (IELS). *International Critical Childhood Policy Studies, 5*(1), 6–18.

Urban, M., Vandenbroeck, M., Lazzari, A., Van Laere, K., & Peeters, J. (2012a). *Competence requirements in early childhood education and care. Research documents*. http://files.eric.ed.gov/fulltext/ED534599.pdf

Urban, M., Vandenbroeck, M., Van Laere, K., Lazzari, A., & Peeters, J. (2012b). Towards competent systems in early childhood education and care. Implications for policy and practice. *European Journal of Education, 47*(4), 508–526. https://doi.org/10.1111/ejed.12010

Ünver, Ö., & Nicaise, I. (2018). *Towards inclusive service markets through social investment in the EU. The case of early childhood education and care*. Leuven: HIVA.

Vabø, M. (2009). *New Public Management: the neoliberal way of governance*. (https://thjodmalastofnun.hi.is/sites/thjodmalastofnun.hi.is/files/skrar/working_paper_4-2009.pdf)

Valentim, S. (2016). *Entre gestion et éducation dans la petite enfance au Brésil et en France: des implications professionnelles sous tension*. Thèse doctorale. Cergy-Pontoise: Université Féderale Fluminense.

Van Bruinessen, M. (2002). Genealogioes of Islamic radicalism in post-soeharto Indonesia. *South East Asia Research, 10*(2), 117–154.

Van Bruinessen, M. (2011). What happened to the smiling face of Indonesia Islam? Muslim intellectualism and the conservative on post-Suharto Indonesia. *RSIS Working Papers*. Retrieved from http://hdl.handle.net/10220/7533

Vandenbroeck, M. (2006). The persistent gap between education and care: A 'history of the present' research on Belgian child care provision and policy. *Paedagogica Historica. International Journal of the History of Education, 42*(3), 363–383.

Vandenbroeck, M. (2019). Feasibility study for a child guarantee. *Policy paper on early childhood education and care. Unpublished report.* Brussels: European Commission.

Vandenbroeck, M. (2020). Discussion: Early childhood education as a locus of hope. In M. Vandenbroek (Ed.), *Revisiting Paulo Freire's pedagogy of the oppressed. Issues and challenges in early childhood education.* (pp. 186–202). London: Routledge.

Vandenbroeck, M., Boonaert, T., Van der Mespel, S., & De Brabandere, K. (2009). Dialogical spaces to reconceptualize parent support in the social investment state. *Contemporary Issues in Early Childhood, 10*(1), 66–77.

Vandenbroeck, M., De Visscher, S., Van Nuffel, K., & Ferla, J. (2008). Mothers' search for infant child care: The dynamic relationship between availability and desirability in a continental European welfare state. *Early Childhood Research Quarterly, 23*(2), 245–258.

Van der Werf, W. (2020). *Diversiteit, inclusie en kwaliteit in het hybride kinderopvangstelsel in nederland.* Utrecht: Universiteit Utrecht.

van der Werf, W. M., Slot, P. L., Kenis, P., & Leseman, P. P. M. (2020). Hybrid organizations in the privatized and harmonized Dutch ECEC system: Relations with quality of education and care. *Early Childhood Research Quarterly, 53*, 136–150. https://doi.org/10.1016/j.ecresq.2020.03.006

Van Laere, K., & Vandenbroeck, M. (2017). Early learning in preschool: Meaningful and inclusive for all? Exploring perspectives of migrant parents and staff. *European Early Childhood Education Research Journal, 25*(2), 243–257.

Van Laere, K., Peeters, J., & Vandenbroeck, M. (2012). The education and care divide: The role of The early childhood workforce in 15 European countries. *European Journal of Education, 47*(4), 527–541. https://doi.org/10.1111/ejed.12006

Vanpée, K., Sannen, L., & Hedebouw, G. (2000). *Kinderopvang in vlaanderen. Gebruik, keuze van de opvangvorm en evaluatie door de ouders.* [Childcare in Flanders. Its use, choice and evaluation by parents]. Leuven: Katholieke Universiteit Leuven - HIVA.

Venegas, P., & Reyes, M. (2009). El programa de mejoramiento a La infancia: La cultura local. *Serie educación parvularia 2000: Aportes a la reflexión y a la acción.* Santiago: MINEDUC.

Vintimilla, C. (2014). Neoliberal fun and happiness in early childhood education. *Journal of the Canadian Association for Young Children, 39*(1), 79–87.

Viruru, R. (2005). The impact of postcolonial theory on early childhood education. *Journal of Education, 35*(1), 7–30.

Visiting Panel. (1982). *A perspective on education in Hong Kong: Report by a visiting panel.* Hong Kong: Government Press.

Waissbluth, M., Leyton, C. et Inostroza, J. (2007). La descentralización en Chile 1990–2005: Asignatura pendiente. *Revista del CLAD Reforma y Democracia,* N° 37 (Feb. 2007).

Waitangi Tribunal. (2013). *Matua Rautia: The report on the kohanga reo claim.* Retrieved from Lower Hutt, New Zealand.

Walker, J. R. (1991). Public policy and the supply of child care services. In D. M. Blau (Ed.), *Economics of child care* (pp. 51–77). New York: Russel Sage Foundation.

Walker, R. (2016). Reclaiming Māori education. In J. Hutchings & J. Lee-Morgan (Eds.), *Decolonisation in Aotearoa* (pp. 19–38). Wellington, New Zealand: NZCER.

Walkerdine, V. (1998). Developmental psychology and The child-centered pedagogy: The insertion of piaget into early education. In J. Henriques, W. Hollway, C. Urwin, C. Venn, & V. Walkerdine (Eds.), *Changing the subject: Psychology, social regulation, and subjectivity* (pp. 153–202). London: Routledge.

Wells, C. (1991, September). *The impact of change – Against the odds* [Paper presentation}. The Fifth Early Childhood Convention, Dunedin.

Wenger, E. (2005). *La théorie des communautés de pratique. Apprentissage, sens et identité.* Québec: Les Presses de l'Université Laval [*Communities of Practice: Learning, Meaning, and Identity.* Cambridge: Cambridge University Press, 1998].

Whitebook, M. (1994). Advocacy to challenge the status quo. In J. Johnson & J. McCracken (Eds.), *The early childhood career lattice: Perspectives on professional development* (pp. 68–70). Washington, DC: National Association for the Education of Young Children.

Whitebook, M. (2001). *Working for worthy wages: The child care compensation movement, 1970–2001.* University of California Berkeley: Institute of Industrial Relations.

Whitebook, M., Kipnis, F., & Bellm, D. (2007). *Disparities in California's child care subsidy system.* Berkeley, CA: Center for the Study of Child Care Employment, University of California at Berkeley.

Whitebook, M., McLean, C., Austin, L. J. E., & Edwards, B. (2018). *Early childhood workforce index – 2018.* Center for the Study of Child Care Employment. Berkeley: University of California.

Whitebook, M., Phillips, D., Howes, C. (2014). *Worthy work, STILL unlivable wages: The early childhood workforce 25 years after the National Child Care Staffing Study.* Berkeley, CA: Center the Study of Child Care Employment, University of California.

Whitty, P., Lysack, M., Lirette, T., Lehrer, J., & Hewes, J. (2020). Passionate about policy, practice, and pedagogy: Exploring intersections between discourses, experiences, and feelings...knitting new terms of belonging. *Global Educational Review,* 7(2), 8–23.

Williams, R. (1976). *Keywords: A vocabulary of Culture and Society.* New York: Oxford University Press.

Wong, M. Y. H. (2021). Democratisation as institutional change: Hong Kong 1992–2015. *Asian Journal of Comparative Politics,* 6(1), 92–106.

Wong, J. M. S., & Rao, N. (2020). Pursuing quality in early childhood education with a government-regulated voucher: Views of parents and service providers in Hong Kong. *Journal of Education Policy,* 37(1), 39–68. DOI: 10.1080/02680939.2020.1764628

Woodhead, M. (1997). Psychology and the cultural construction of children's needs. In: A. James and A. Prout (Eds.), *Constructing and reconstructing childhood.* Falmer Press.

Working Group of 15-year Free Education. (2012). *Full subsidy for early childhood education: Proposal for implementing 15-year free education* (in Chinese). https://www.legco.gov.hk/yr12-13/chinese/panels/ed/papers/ed0319cb4-486-22-c.pdf

Working Group on Review of the Pre-primary Education Voucher. (2010). *Report on review of the Pre-primary Education Voucher Scheme.* https://www.edb.gov.hk/attachment/en/edu-system/preprimary-kindergarten/preprimary-voucher/wgpevs(eng).pdf

World Bank. (2021). *Early Childhood Development.* https://www.worldbank.org/en/topic/earlychildhooddevelopment#1

World Health Organization. (2020). *Improving early childhood development: WHO guideline.* https://www.who.int/publications/i/item/97892400020986.

Young, I. M. (2011). *Responsibility for justice.* New York: Oxford University Press.

Young, S. (1965). *Education policy.* Hong Kong: Government Press.

Yuen, G. (2008). Education reform policy and early childhood teacher education in Hong Kong Before and after the transfer of sovereignty to China in 1997. *Early Years,* 28(1), 23–45.

Yuen, G. (2010). The displaced early childhood education in the postcolonial era of Hong Kong. In N. Yelland (Ed.), *Contemporary perspectives on early childhood education* (pp. 83–99). London: Open University Press.

Yuen, G. (2012). Tinkering with early childhood education and care: The case of early education vouchers in Hong Kong. In E. Llody & H. Penn (Eds.), *Childcare markets local and global: Can they deliver and equitable service?* (pp. 79–95). Bristol: Policy Press.

Yuen, G. (2013). Tinkering with Early childhood education and care: Early education vouchers in Hong Kong. In H. Lloyd & H. Penn (Eds.), *Childcare markets. Can they deliver an equitable service?* (pp. 79–95). Bristol: Policy Press.

Yuen, G. (2015). Markets, choice of kindergarten, mothers' care responsibilities and the voucher scheme in Hong Kong. *Children and Youth Services Review, 48*, 167–176.

Yuen, G. (2018). Masks, masquerades and ironic performances: Getting our(selves) heard. In K. J. Kennedy & J. C. K. Lee (Eds.), *Routledge handbook on schools and schooling and Asia* (pp. 441–449). London; New York: Routledge.

Yuen, G. (2021). Kindergarten education scheme in Hong Kong: Policy measures, rhizomatic connections and early childhood teacher education. *Children & Society, 35*(2), 259–273.

Yuen, G., & Grieshaber, S. (2009). Parents' choice of early childhood education services in Hong Kong: A pilot study about vouchers. *Contemporary Issues in Early Childhood, 10*(3), 263–279.

Yuen, G., & Lam, M. S. (2017). Mothers' experiences of a voucher scheme within the context of Hong Kong's early education: Issues of affordability and justice. *Children and Youth Services Review, 82*, 185–194.

Yuen, G., & Yu, W. B. (2010). *Parents' choice in the use of full-day early childhood education service* (in Chinese). Hong Kong: Education Policy Forum, The Education University of Hong Kong.

Yulindrasar, H., & Ujianti, P. R. (2018). "Trapped in the reform": Kindergarten teachers' experiences of teacher professionalisation in buleleng, Indonesia. *Policy Futures in Education, 16*(1), 66–79. https://doi.org/10.1177/1478210317736206

Zeraatkar, D., Duku, E., Bennett, T., Guhn, M., Forer, B., Brownell, M., & Janus, M. (2020). Socioeconomic gradient in the developmental health of Canadian children with disabilities at school entry: A cross-sectional study. *BMJ Open, 10*(4), e032396.

INDEX

Abecedarian Study 159
accountability: to children development 45, 62; democratic accountability 13; in New Zealand 186; test-based accountability 4
Act on Day Care Facilities (Denmark) 195
advocacy 114, 117, 162, 164, 165, 167, 193–194, 205–207, 209–210, 213
Africa: ECEC in 56–60; Government Reservation Areas (GRAs) 59
Alberta, Canada 42; British Columbia 42; Ontario 148, , 161–163, 166, 204, 205, 213; Quebec 19, 66, 219
American Federation of State, County and Municipal Employees 177
Aotearoa New Zealand: 5, 26, 27, 78, 148, 149, 161, 162, 221; collective advocacy for pay parity 191–193; ECEC in 186–194; Education Review Office (ERO) 45; New Zealand Aid Programme 182; New Zealand Childcare Association 192; for profit-making 187–189; Provincial Education 5; South Auckland 189; State Sector Act 192, 209; teacher for change 189–190
Asia: ECEC in 55
Association of Early Childhood Educators Ontario (AECEO) 162–164
Australia 78, 157; Australian Child Care Benefit 19; Australian daycare centre 25; Cheating at cards 32–34; encounters of commodification 34; individualism and success 35–38

Ball, S. 1, 2, 3, 5, 9, 10, 12, 113
belonging, 32, 33, 36–38
Biden, J. 178, 210
Brazil 22
British Child Care Act 19
Buddhism 51
budgetary constraints 47, 48, 106, 106 22, 127

Cadart, Marie-Laure 96, 146
Canada 42, 43, 80n1; AECEO 162–164; College of Early Childhood Educators (CECE) 162–163; New Brunswickx (Canada) 42; Ontario 26, 42, 80n1, 163–164; Quebec 19, 40, 66, 67; Wartime Day Nurseries Act in Canada 39; *see also* Alberta
capitalism 11, 95; capitalistic thinking 106; capitalist market 93
care, concepts of 79, 148
Center for the Study of Child Care Employment (CSCCE) at Berkeley 161, 171
child-centred pedagogy/practices 51, 113
child development 50–52, 62–64, 69, 166; gaps 34; norms 31, 42; projects 200
children and childhood: well-being 63, 68, 106

Chile 26, 143; Chilean community-based preschools 216; parent/parental participation in 129
China: Chinese refugees 107
citizenship and rights 13, 93, 172
collective organisation 193
Communities of Practice (CoPs) 164, 165, 208
Community Education Centres (Chile) 131, 134
Continuous Professional Learning (CPL) 162
corporate chains/childcare/practices 17, 54, 55, 147, 157, 172, 177; Busy Bees Childcare 5
Covid-19 pandemic 12, 24, 40, 97, 103–104, 161, 163–164, 169, 176, 213
culture/cultural: assimilation 25, 41–43, 42; differences 124; diversity 84, 104, 123; domination 145, 218; group 36; hegemony 10, 22–25, 95; heritage 57, 146; identities 186; norms 41–42; renewal 98, 144, 146; settings 45; stories 186; values 42, 43, 56, 79, 222
curriculum 144: academic curriculum 113, 144, 201; and assessment 159, 211–212; debate 201; documents 42, 43; frameworks 31; implementation 182; planned curriculum 57; pre-packaged curriculum 42; standardised curricula 42; training 50; reformed pedagogical curriculum 201

decision-making processes 45, 47, 141, 149, 160, 183, 184, 187, 217
delinquency: juvenile delinquency 61, 92, 119
demand-side funding 20, 22, 94, 96, 111; supply and demand 21
democracy 8, 27, 68, 117, 142, 144, 145, 212; democratic accountability 8, 13; democratic education 18, 145; democratic politics 4; values and image of teachers 160–162
Denmark 26, 27, 63, 68, 69, 194–203; BUPL 194–207, 211–212; Danish Centre for Research in Early Childhood Education and Care (CeDif) 200–201; Danish Trade Union Confederation 194; developmental projects 200; ECEC curriculum debate 200–201; ECEC in 194–203; Education International (EI) 194; minimum child/staff ratios 202–203; national funded research 201–202; reformed pedagogical curriculum 201; research and developmental activities 199–200; research projects 199–200
development/developmental *see* child development
disparities 18, 108, 170
drug abuse 132, 145

Early Childhood Regulatory Framework (Kôhanga reo) 44
Early Development Instrument. 50
economic\economisation 2: adversity 106; arguments and identity of teachers 158–160; discourse 49, 53, 159; economic crises 3, 92, 99; growth 28, 148, 179; investment 25, 30, 60–62; thinking 83; valuation 3; value 83, 109
educare 38, 132
educational 100–103; centre 102, 104; institution 98, 130; policies 90, 180; responsibilities 93, 143; values 121, 129
emotional: security 128; support 85
empirical research 95; evidence-based policies 95; scientific discourse 91; "scientific" knowledge 60; scientific research 94
employment: legislation 210–211; policies 90
England 3, 5, 6, 40, 156
English language 44, 91
equity 7, 27, 37
ethnocentric universalism 140
Europe 20, 39, 41; European Child Guarantee 20; European Trade Union Committee on Education (ETUCE) 194–195; European Union 20; Systems of Early Education and Professionalisation in Europe (SEEPRO) study 151; Western Europe 39

Facebook *see* social media
family: culture 125, 128; home practices 124; policies 26, 119, 222; practices 126, 139
fascism 97
feminism: educators 135; employment 99, 104; movements 15, 172; organisations 98; rights 145; volunteers 130
financial crisis 11, 12, 202
Finland 19, 26, 68, 85; Child Home Care Allowance 18, 86–88; ECEC in 85–97; Finnish childcare policy discourse 89

Index

Flanders 21, 26, 84, 218
Foucault, M. 12, 47, 49, 53, 90, 107, 142–143
France 21, 97, 118–120, 144; childcare in 118–120; commodification in 20; crèches parentales in 117–118; French Federation of Nursery Companies (FFEC) 119: Paris 123
freedom of association 210–21
Freire, P. 142, 145
Froebel, F. 53
funding 40, 80n1, 118, 192–193, 208–210

gender: essentialism 156; policies 90
genocide 42
gestione sociale (social governance), Italy 96–100, 104, 142, 144, 217
Global Education Reform Movement (GERM) 4
global North 29, 42, 50
global South 18, 40, 50, 53
governmental: decisions 20, 90; funding 42, 169, 177–178, 188; policies 114, 147; regulations 82
Gramsci, A. 22, 24, 25, 27, 95, 214, 215
Gross Domestic Product (GDP) 182

Heckman, J. J. 48, 114, 158
higher education institutions 105
Hinduism 51
Hong Kong: Childcare Centre Subsidy Scheme 109, 111; civil action and advocacy 26; commodification in 217; flat-rate voucher 112; Kindergarten Education Scheme 106; Kindergarten Subsidy Scheme 109; voucher system 19, 105–117
hyperindividualism 28, 43

ideology and hegemony 94–95
immigrant children 80n5, 202
indigenous: belief 51; children 42; curriculum 56; education 56, 57; knowledges 216
Indo-Mauritians 23
Indonesia 25, 50, 51, 52, 78, 179; Centre for Statistics Indonesia 50; Directorate General of Early Childhood 180; ECEC in 47–53; ECE workforce in 179–182; educational reform in 178–179; educators and policymakers 52; Indonesian early childhood education and care 47–53; Ministry of Education (Indonesia) 44, 48, 71; Ministry of Education, Culture, Research and Technology (MoECRT) (Indonesia) 179–180; Ministry of Religious Affairs (MORA) 180; national curriculum 182; national policy guidance 182; state responsibility 47
infant schools 38, 41–43, 53, 54
information asymmetry 81, 82
institutional violence 24
intercultural: confrontations 126; programme 124–126
international contexts 68
international donor agencies 48, 52
International Institute for Capacity Building in Africa (IICBA) 59
International Labour Organisation Policy Guidelines 171, 211
international organisations 38
International Task Force on Teachers (ITFT) 60
International Women's Year 149
interpersonal relationships 100, 102
intervention programmes 92
investment/investors: foreign investors 6; fund 119; marketplace of buyers 7; return on investment (ROI) 32
Ireland: ECEC in 153
Islam 51; Islamic form of early childhood education 58; Muslim children 58; religious discourse 25, 43; values 51
Italy: COVID-19 pandemic challenges 103–104; ECEC in 26, 97–104; educational alliance and professionals and parents 100–103; and gestione sociale 97–99; national Act 103; "Reggio-Emilia approach" 18

Just Childcare(nursery) 6
juvenile delinquency *see* delinquency

Kahuroa, R. 162, 208, 212
Kamenarac, O. 158, 161–162, 208
Kids Foundation (Europe) 6
kindergarten 38, 52, 53–56, 74: Kindergarten Day 77; Kindergarten Education Scheme (Hong Kong) 106; Kindergarten Subsidy Scheme (Hong Kong) 109
Kōhanga reo 43–45

labour market 2, 18, 82, 145, 177
labour movement 172
laissez faire doctrine 107–110
Langford, R. 79, 154, 157

language of choice: child home care allowance 86–90; and individual responsibility 90–94; of parents 84; resistance and refusal 95–97; skills 69, 73
learning 68; goals 8; materials 184
legal parenthood 93
liberal: policies 21; social democratic welfare states 20, 21; social-liberal party 196–197
license-exempt provider 19
local communities 27, 102

Malaguzzi, L, 10, 53
marginalised communities 29, 172
marginalization: lower socio-economic groups 23; low pay 148, 171, 199, 216, 221
marketisation 7, 16, 27, 81; agenda 36; approach 114, 117; competition 105, 113; consolidation 6; economy 25, 78; laws 119; logic 4, 107; malfunctioning 8; market of consumers 7; model 166; operations 81; provision 163; responsiveness 111; sale and leaseback 7; trend 6
Marx, Karl 53
maternal discourses 154–156
Mauritius: ECEC in 23; Mauritian educational system 23; social inequalities in 23
media pressure 74
medical discourse 118
mentor: in Kupang 182–184; mentoring programme 178–186, 183; teacher strategies 184; training workshops 183
micro and macro politics 25
Montessori 18, 53, 54
moral: development 58; education 57; obligations 187–188, 189, 193
Moscow Framework for Action and Cooperation-Harnessing the Wealth of Nations 59

National Association for the Education of Young Children (NAEYC) (U.S) 171; leadership 173; NAEYC Annual Conference 171; national Conference 171
National Policy on Education, in Nigeria 59
National Quality Framework, in Australia 32

Neatherland: commodification in 219; Dutch Childcare Act 19
neoliberalism 1, 105; Anglosphere, origin 5; charge sheet 10; colonialism and 52; defined 2–3; and developmentalism 49–51; discourses 43; ECEC policies 16; education policies 31; global imperialism 48; individual choice and calculation 3; and resistance 115–117; resisting and replacing 10–14; societies 95; values 28
"new public management" 4
New Zealand see Aotearoa New Zealand
Next Generation Fund (Italy) 103
Nigeria 25, 56, 78
non-disclosure agreements 177
non-formal: children learning 130; education body 180; Non-Formal and Informal Education (PAUDNI) 180
non-government organization 80n2, 157, 189
normative policy analysis 81
North America 39, 42, 55
Norway 25, 68, 78; Barnehageopprøret (childcare rebellion) 70–72, 217; kindergarten programmes in 69; uprising 74–77
numeracy: learning activities 54; math instruction 55
Nusa Tenggara Timur 218

obedience 43
Onex Partners 6
Organization for Economic Community Development (OECD) 38, 154; ECEC in 150; OECD International Early Learning Study (IELS) 159

parent child collectives 121
parenting 49, 91, 92, 93, 94
parents 14n1, 18, 26, 29, 63, 83, 84, 91, 92, 93, 94, 97, 100, 113, 120, 122–123, 124, 128, 137, 142, 145; Māori language 43, 44
pedagogical: approach 43, 128, 139; coordinator 100
peer mentoring 183, 184
Perry Preschool Study 159
Petrie, Pat 160
Piagetian theory 60
play: and play-based education 30, 144; playschool 38

policy: alignment and support 44; enactment 113; initiatives 180; makers 21, 82
politics/political 3, 146; actors 25, 32; belief 95; choice 89–90; decisions 95; identity 53; ideologies 21
primary education 52, 105; school teachers 193
privatisation 5, 7, 16, 27, 210–211; business 4; childcare markets 21; donors 180; equity 5, 7, 157; initiatives 20, 103; institutions 180; market 108; organisations 16; ownership 8; private early childhood market 107–110; providers 2, 21; of public utilities 2; sector 180–182; services 5
professional: and cultural knowledge 185; decision-making 181; ethics 189; identity 148; knowledge 185; and marketing discourse 54; and parents 100–103
prophetic pedagogy 10
Protestantism 51
psychological: commitment 102; Psychological Pedagogical Services (PPT) 72
psychosocial: surveillance 60
public: choices 4, 110; discourse 23, 24, 175; funds 40, 119, 172; policies 31, 119; public K-8 system 170; responsibility 25, 82; schools 110, 176; services 2, 4

quality: childcare quality 64–67, 85; ECEC quality 27, 66, 91, 97, 98, 100, 103, 150, 155, 197, 203, 222; programmes 37
Quality Rating and Improvement Systems 176

rebels 74–76, 75
religious: Buddhism 41; and/or philanthropic organisations 39; development 51, 52; discourse 51–53; domain 52; Hinduism 51; on Indonesian early childhood education and care 47–53; Islam 25, 51, 58–60; kindergarten 52; obligation 49; Roman Catholicism 51; sphere 52; teaching 49; traditions 51
residential schools 42, 54
resistance: and refusal 95–97; resistance movement 110–115, 114, 115

Roman Catholicism 51
Rousseau, Jean Jacques 53

salary and wages: disparities 170; in education and care sector 192–193; kindergarten teachers 191–192; low pay 148, 171, 199, 216, 221; paid employment 149; paid labour market 16; pay gap 171; salary scales 173; Worthy Wage Campaign 27, 161, 171, 174, 175, 211; Worthy Wage Day 174–175; Worthy Wagers 178
school readiness EDI 52
shareholders 6
social 139, 145; cohesion 27, 126, 146; commitment 143; cooperatives 99; economy 129; and emotional development 36; events 102; evolutions 119; governance 13; inclusion 104; infrastructure 163; injustice 37; integration 129; justice 38; mobility 113; needs 15n2, 59, 108; network 121; norms 147; palingenesis 98; pedagogy 96; policy 24, 91; project 218–220; provision 47, 50; sociopolitical dimension 133–134; support 146; well-being 104
social media 69, 74; Facebook 72, 73, 75; Twitter 76
solidarity 8
Sri Suwarningsih, Dwi Purwestri 161, 178
subordinate groups 23, 24
subsidised services 177
Sustainable Development Goals 50
Sweden 15, 16, 68, 69, 74

tax avoidance 157
teaching strategies 176
T e Kōhanga Reo ki Rotokawa 45–46
Te Kōhanga Reo National Trust 45
Te Whāriki a te Kōhanga Reo 45
Thatcher, Margaret 3
Tiananmen Incident 109
Tobin, J. 144
trade unions 2, 98
training: workshop 183–184
Tronto, J. 79, 112
Twitter *see* social media

UNICEF 38, 178, 183
Union: Service Employees International Union 177

United Nation's Committee on the Rights of the Child 70
United Nations Organization for Education, Science and Culture 180
United States 3, 26; California Department of Education 19; Child Care Employee Caucus 171; Child Care Employee News 171, 173; Child Care Employee Project 173; ECEC in 169–178; Employee Caucus 172, 173, 206, 207, 208; for families and workforce 169–171; Lanham Act in the United States 39; NAEYC 171–174; New Mexico 78; post Covid 175–178; North Carolina (U.S) 177: state preschool program standards 176; US-based Model Work Standards for Centers and Homes 171; US early educatorled movement 169; worthy wage movement 169–178
unorganised child care employees 177
urban segregation 133

venture capital 177
vocational training 57
voluntary organisations 106, 163
voucher scheme *see* Hong Kong H

wages *see* salary and wages
Whitebook, M. 161, 206
World Bank 42, 48, 49, 61, 179
World Health Organization (WHO) 61
World Trade Organisation (WTO) 119

Yoruba Indigenous approach 56
Yuen, G. 96, 112, 113